THE VEIL OF ISIS

PIERRE
HADOT

THE VEIL OF ISIS

*An Essay on the History of the
Idea of Nature*

Translated by Michael Chase

THE BELKNAP PRESS OF
HARVARD UNIVERSITY PRESS
Cambridge, Massachusetts
London, England
2006

This book was originally published as *Le Voile d'Isis: Essai sur l'histoire de
l'idée de Nature* by Éditions Gallimard, copyright © 2004 by Éditions
Gallimard, Paris

Library of Congress Cataloging-in-Publication Data
Hadot, Pierre.
[Voile d'Isis. English]
The Veil of Isis: an essay on the history of the idea of nature /
Pierre Hadot; translated by Michael Chase.
p. cm.
Includes bibliographical references and index.
ISBN-13: 978-0-674-02316-1
ISBN-10: 0-674-02316-1
1. Philosophy of nature.   I. Title.

BD581.H2813 2006
113.09—dc22   2006044554

Contents

Preface

I have been thinking about this book for more than forty years. Around 1960 I began to be interested in the various meanings assumed by the secret of nature in antiquity and in modern times. In the years that followed I became passionately enthralled by the philosophy of nature, and I wondered if it were possible that a renewal, and no doubt a metamorphosis, of this type of research might take place in the contemporary world. Absorbed by my teaching and by other tasks, however, I was never able to devote myself intensely to this study. Nevertheless, in the perspective of the research I was then carrying out on Plotinus, I wrote for the Eranos meetings of 1968 a paper on the contribution of Neoplatonism to the philosophy of nature in the West, in which I was able to present a few ideas that were dear to me. I concentrated especially on the case of Goethe, a poet and at the same time a scholar, who seemed to me to offer the model of an approach to nature that was both scientific and aesthetic. It was on this occasion that I encountered the image and the text that were the starting point for the writing of this work.

Let me briefly situate this image and this text within their historical context. From July 16, 1799, to March 7, 1804, the German scholar Alexander von Humboldt, together with the botanist Aimé Bonpland, had embarked on an extraordinary journey of scientific exploration in South America, whence he had brought back a considerable mass of geographical and ethnographical observations. The first result of these years of discoveries was a communication to the Institute of France in 1805, which was published in 1807 under the title *Essai sur la géographie des plantes*.[1] A German version of this work was published in Tübingen in 1807, under the title *Ideen zu einer Geographie der Pflanzen*,[2] with a dedication to Goethe, intended to give public recognition to Humboldt's debt to the author of *The Metamorphosis of Plants*. This dedicatory page was adorned with an engraving made after a drawing that the Swedish sculptor Thorvaldsen had conceived to respond to the wishes of the great explorer (Fig. 1).[3] This allegorical engraving, which is quite beautiful in itself, is a measure of how distant we are from the spiritual world in which scholars, artists, and poets still lived at the beginning of the nineteenth century. The allegory was perfectly clear to educated people of this time. It is perfectly obscure for our contemporaries. Who is this nude personage, holding a lyre in his left hand and unveiling with his right hand the statue of a strange goddess? Which goddess is this, with her hands and her fingers spread wide apart, whose chest bears three rows of breasts, and the lower part of whose body is enclosed in a tight sheath, adorned with the figures of various animals? Why is Goethe's book *The Metamorphosis of Plants* placed at the statue's feet?

Goethe himself sketched an initial answer to these questions when he wrote, "A. von Humboldt sent me the translation of his *Essay on the Geography of Plants* with a flattering illustration that implies that Poetry, too, might lift the veil of Nature."[4] However, the contemporary reader understands this explanation scarcely better than the enigma. Why does Goethe recognize Nature in this goddess? Why does this Nature have secrets? Why must she be unveiled? Why can Poetry accomplish this task?

I answered these questions briefly in a lecture given in June 1980 to the Academy of Sciences and Literature of Mainz.[5] The notion of a secret of nature must be understood in the perspective of Heraclitus' aphorism "Nature loves to hide." The statue unveiled by Apollo, the god of poetry, was a representation of the goddess Nature, who had emerged from a fusion between the figure of Artemis of Ephesus and that of Isis, who, according to an ancient inscription reported by Plutarch, said, "No mortal has raised my veil." In that lecture I sketched a brief history of the metaphor of the unveiling of nature. These themes were also the subject of my seminars at the Collège de France during the year 1982–83. During the following years, I continued to work on what I consider to be three aspects of the same phenomenon: the history of the exegesis of the Heraclitean fragment, the evolution of the notion of a secret of nature, and the figure of Isis in iconography and in literature.

This book sets forth the results of that research. It is above all a historical work, which deals especially with the period extending from antiquity to the beginning of the twentieth century and traces the evolution of mankind's attitudes toward nature solely from the perspective of the metaphor of unveiling. I must specify, moreover, that I have not dealt with two problems that are linked to the notion of a secret of nature. The first is of a sociological order, and refers to esotericism: not only does Nature refuse to be unveiled, but he who thinks he has penetrated her secrets refuses to communicate them. The reader who is interested in this theme should read the remarkable and monumental work by William Eamon, *Science and the Secrets of Nature: Books of Secrets in Medieval and Early Modern Culture*. This book studies in great depth the phenomenon represented, on the one hand, by the numerous books of "secrets" that flourished in the Middle Ages and at the beginning of modern times and, on the other, the academies which, in Italy, France, and England, united scholars in the search for the secrets of nature. This historical phenomenon played a major role in the birth of modern science. From this sociological perspective, one can also read the essay by Carlo Ginzburg "High and Low: The Theme of Forbidden Knowledge in the Sixteenth and Seventeenth Centuries."

The second aspect is the psychological and psychoanalytical one implied in the representation of the unveiling of a feminine figure, Isis, who symbolizes nature. Since I lack the necessary medical and psychoanalytical training, I have contented myself with alluding to this question in the chapter devoted to Nietzsche. This problem has been dealt with from a feminist perspective by Carolyn Merchant in *The Death of Nature: Women, Ecology, and the Scientific Revolution.* This work is invaluable because of its vast range of information and its intense reflection of the destiny of Western civilization. I must also mention an essay by Evelyn Fox Keller, "Secrets of God, Nature, and Life."

In this book, I have tried to show that in order to explain the concepts and the images that, down to the present day, have served to define the method and ends of the science of nature, we must turn first and foremost to the ancient Greco-Latin tradition. For instance, in a remarkable study on physico-chemical order, Bertrand de Saint-Sernin cites a text by Pascal in which we find the following statement: "The secrets of Nature are hidden; although she always acts, we do not always discover her effects." He comments on this text as follows: "This passage brings to the fore the religious origin of positivism in the theory of knowledge. Indeed, the allusion to the hidden secrets of knowledge recalls the Book of Job, where God parades the wonders of creation before Job, without unveiling the modes of their fashioning."[6] It is quite true that, up to a point, we can recognize the religious origins of positivism, insofar as it is an attitude that refuses to go beyond the effects known through the observation of experience—a point I will discuss in Chapter 11. Nevertheless, the expression "hidden secrets of nature" comes not from the Bible but from no other source than Greco-Latin philosophy, in which formulas such as *arcana naturae, secreta naturae,* or *aporrhēta tēs phuseōs* are frequently used. This will be the subject of Chapter 3.

Hans Blumenberg, who was a friend of mine, and whose loss I deeply regret, showed in a striking way in his book *Paradigmen zu einer Metaphorologie* how the history of certain metaphors, many of which cannot be adequately translated into propositions and concepts—for instance, the nakedness of truth, nature as writing and as a book, or the world as a clock—enable us to glimpse the evolution of spiritual attitudes and visions of the world throughout the ages. These traditional metaphors are linked intimately with what are called commonplaces in rhetoric. These are formulas, images, and metaphors adopted by philosophers and writers like prefabricated models, which they think they use freely, but which nevertheless have an influence on their thought. They hold sway for centuries over successive generations like a kind of program to be realized, a task to be accomplished, or an attitude to be assumed, even if, throughout the ages, the meaning given to these sentences, images, and metaphors can be profoundly modified. These ideas, images, and symbols can inspire works of art, poems, philosophical discourse, or the practice of life itself. The present study takes its place within the history of these metaphors and commonplaces, whether in the guise of the formula "Nature loves to hide," of the notions of veiling and unveiling, or of the figure of Isis. These metaphors and images have both expressed and influenced mankind's attitude toward nature.

The reader will perhaps be surprised to note that the word "nature" is sometimes written in this book with a small *n*, and sometimes with a capital *N*. I have chosen to write it with a capital letter if the word bears a capital letter in a given text that I cite, or again if it obviously designates an entity that is personified or is transcendent in nature, or even a goddess.

I thank with all my heart those who have helped me write this book through the documents they have supplied, the advice they have given, and the corrections they have suggested. In particular, I thank Eric Vigne for his patience and judicious remarks, and Sylvie Simon for the help she contributed. All my gratitude also goes to Concetta Luna, who assisted me with such amiability and efficacy in all the problems raised by the bibliography and the writing of this work. I have also profited from the valuable help and advice of Monique Alexandre, Véronique Boudon-Millot, Ilsetraut Hadot, Sandra Laugier, Jean-François Balaudé, René Bonnet, Louis Frank, Richard Goulet, Dieter Harlfinger, Philippe Hoffmann, Nuccio Ordine, Alain Segonds, Brian Stock, and Jacques Thuillier. I express my gratitude to them all.

THE VEIL OF ISIS

Prologue at Ephesus

An Enigmatic Saying

Throughout our story, we will recognize three guiding threads woven together: Heraclitus' famous formula "Nature loves to hide" and its fortunes throughout the ages; the notion of a secret of nature; and finally the veiled image of Nature, represented as Artemis/Isis. The story I am about to tell therefore begins symbolically at Ephesus, in Asia Minor, around 500 BCE, on the day when tradition reports that Heraclitus, one of the most ancient thinkers of Greece, deposited the book, probably without a title, in which he had summarized all his knowledge, in the temple of the celebrated Artemis of Ephesus.[1]

The book contained an enigmatic saying, made up of three little Greek words—"phusis kruptesthai philei," which traditionally have been translated by the formula "Nature loves to hide," although in all likelihood this meaning never occurred to Heraclitus—three words that future generations never ceased trying to interpret.[2] They provide us with a glimpse of what may be the beginning of reflection on the mystery of reality, but perhaps also of the end result of a long meditation, come down through the mists of the ages. In this temple at Ephesus there was a statue of Artemis, an idol made of dark wood adorned with various vestments or ornaments hanging from her neck and chest, the lower part of her body encased in a tight sheath. She too was a strange and enigmatic figure, emerging from prehistory (Fig. 2).

Throughout the itinerary on which we are about to embark, we

shall follow the destinies that became linked on that day, and for millennia to come, between these words and this figure of Artemis,
which, as we shall see, became identified with Isis. Step by step we
shall follow the metamorphoses of the theme of the veil and of unveiling, be it the veil of Death, of Isis, of the secrets of Nature, or of
the mystery of Being.

The three Greek words "phusis kruptesthai philei," uttered and
written by Heraclitus, were always heavy with meaning: heavy with
the meaning Heraclitus gave them, and heavy with the meaning future centuries were to believe they discovered in them. For a long
time yet, perhaps even forever, they will maintain their mystery. Like
Nature, they love to hide.

What did Heraclitus himself mean when he uttered or wrote these
words? To speak frankly, this is extremely hard to know, for two reasons. First, Heraclitus' obscurity has been proverbial since antiquity.
Two centuries after him, Aristotle said that no one knew how to
punctuate the Ephesian philosopher's text "because they could not
tell whether a given word belonged to the next clause or to the preceding one."[3] This obscurity was, moreover, one of the features of ancient wisdom, which loved to express itself in the form of enigmas. In
the *Protagoras,* Plato's Seven Sages prove their wisdom by the "brief
and memorable words" they offer as first fruits to Apollo in the temple of Delphi. Such is the style of ancient philosophy, says Plato: "La-
conic brevity."[4] Yet Heraclitus did not limit himself to enigmatic con-
ciseness. By this literary form, he also wanted to provide a glimpse of
what, for him, is the law of all reality: the battle among contraries,
and the perpetual metamorphosis that results from this eternal combat between opposing forces.

There can therefore be no question of relying on the interpretations that the ancients gave of this obscure text, all the more so because, since they are later than Socrates, Plato, and Aristotle, they are
situated in a mental world wholly different from that of the thinker

from Ephesus. Language evolves, thought adopts other channels, and the authors of the time—like modern authors—were not even aware of the mistakes they committed. In order to try to understand, we must rather compare Heraclitus with Heraclitus, or at least with authors not too distant from him in time. As far as Heraclitus himself is concerned, the possibilities for comparison are unfortunately very limited: we now possess only 126 fragments of his work, or a dozen pages at the very most. These fragments appear in the form of short sayings or enigmatic aphorisms which tend to adopt an antithetical structure that thereby reflects the very constitution of reality, in which contraries coincide.

The Veil of Death

1

Heraclitus' Aphorism

"What Is Born Tends to Disappear"

In order to understand Heraclitus' aphorism, we have to try to understand three words. First of all, we can say that this kind of sentence containing the word *philein* (to love) is often found in Heraclitus himself, but also in the tragedians, or again in Herodotus, for instance, "The wind 'loves' [is accustomed] to blow,"[1] or in Democritus, "Thanks to these exercises [the efforts at learning reading and music], respect 'loves' to develop [is habitually developed]."[2] Here, the word "loves" *(philei)* denotes not a feeling but a natural or habitual tendency, or a process that occurs necessarily or frequently.

Yet what is the subject of which it is said that it "has a tendency to hide," or that it "habitually hides?" It is *phusis,* a word that had a wealth of meaning in Heraclitus' time but certainly did not mean nature as a whole or as the principle of phenomena. At the time, it had primarily two meanings. On the one hand, it could mean the constitution or proper nature of each thing, and on the other, a thing's process of realization, genesis, appearance, or growth.

The first meaning is attested in Heraclitus. He declares, for instance, that his own method consists in dividing each thing in accordance with its nature.[3] From the perspective of Heraclitus' doctrine, this may mean to divide each thing while revealing within it the coincidence of contraries that is proper to it. If we understand *phusis* in this sense, we could suppose that "to hide" refers to the difficulty of discovering the proper nature of each thing. In Heraclitus, the words *kruptein* or *kruptesthai* can have the meaning of "to hide from knowledge," for instance, with regard to Apollo at Delphi: "His discourse neither states nor hides, but it *indicates*."[4] The meaning of our aphorism might thus quite possibly be the following: "Nature (in the sense of the proper constitution, proper force, or life of a thing) loves to hide, or not to be apparent." This interpretation, moreover, would allow two nuances: either the nature of things is hard to understand, or else the nature of things demands to be hidden, that is, the sage must hide it.[5]

We can legitimately wonder, however, if we ought not rather understand *phusis* here in the second sense, that of a process; that is, in the sense of the appearance or birth of a thing and of things. This meaning existed in Heraclitus' time, and the best example is found in Empedocles: "There is absolutely no birth [*phusis*] for all mortal things, nor end, in detested death, but there is only mixture and distinction of mixed-up things, and this is what men call *phusis*."[6] Empedocles means that if people believe the word *phusis* designates the process whereby a thing begins to exist, they are wrong: *phusis* is a process of mixture and distinction of preexisting things. However the problem raised by Empedocles should be solved, it is clear that the word *phusis* means the process by which things appear. Heraclitus' aphorism might then mean, "The process of birth and formation tends to hide itself." We would still be within the register of the difficulty of knowledge, and we could compare our aphorism with another aphorism by Heraclitus: "The limits of the soul, as you go on your way, you could not find, even if you explored all paths: so deep is the *logos*."[7] We could deduce from the comparison of the two sayings that *phusis* is identical to *logos*, that is, to the breath that unites contraries.

Nevertheless, it seems we must ultimately interpret *kruptesthai* in a wholly different sense. Either in its active form, *kruptein*, or in its middle form, *kruptesthai*, this verb, like the verb *kaluptein*, can signify "to bury." "Calypso," the famous nymph who detained Odysseus, is "she who hides," that is, the goddess of death.[8] This meaning corresponds to the representation both of the earth that hides the body and of the veil with which the heads of the dead are covered. In Euripides' *Hippolytus,* for instance, Phaedra, horrified by the passion devouring her, asks her nurse to conceal her head. The nurse obeys but adds, "I veil you, but when will death cover my body?"[9] Death thus appears here as a veil, a darkness, or a cloud.[10] This possible meaning of *kruptein, kruptesthai,* can orient us toward another interpretation of the Heraclitean fragment. We have just seen that the word *phusis* could designate birth, while the word *kruptesthai,* for its part, could evoke disappearance or death. We would thus have an opposition between birth and death, appearance and disappearance, and the saying would take on an antithetical turn, in complete agreement with Heraclitus' overall spirit.

Here again, we would have two possible forms of the antithesis. First, we can suppose that *phusis* and *kruptesthai* (with this verb being taken in the middle voice) are to be understood in an active sense. This would give us the following meaning: "What causes birth also tends to cause disappearance." In other words, it is the same force that causes birth and makes things disappear. Yet we can also allow the two words to have a passive sense. As in Aristotle, the word *phusis* could designate the result of the process of formation, and thus the form that appears at the end of the process of formation.[11] Our aphorism would then mean, "That which results from the process of birth tends to disappear" or "The form that appears tends to disappear."

I have now mentioned five possible translations of the enigmatic saying—which shows how difficult it is to understand Heraclitus:

The constitution of each thing tends to hide (i.e., is hard to know).

The constitution of each thing wants to be hidden (i.e., does not want to be revealed).

The origin tends to hide itself (i.e., the origin of things is hard to know).

What causes things to appear tends to make them disappear (i.e., what causes birth tends to cause death).

Form (or appearance) tends to disappear (i.e., what is born wants to die).

The last two translations are probably closest to what Heraclitus meant, since they have the antithetical character that is typical of his thought. Reality is such that within each thing there are two aspects that destroy each other mutually. For instance, death is life and life is death: "Immortals, mortals; mortals, immortals; for the ones live the death of the latter, and others die the life of the former."[12] "Once they are born, they want to live, and thus they have the fate of death, and they leave children behind them so that still more fates of death may be produced."[13] "The name of the bow is life (*biós* = *bíos*), but its work is death."[14]

We find this link, for instance, between birth and death, appearance and disappearance, in a famous passage from Sophocles' *Ajax*, which has sometimes been called "the discourse of dissimulation."[15] Ajax has previously announced his intention to die. Suddenly, at the moment when the chorus has already begun its lament, he declaims a long speech which gives the impression that he has changed his mind. His speech begins:

> Yea, great Time, uncountable,
> makes all things appear [*phuei*] that were not apparent [*adēla*]
> and once they have appeared [*phanenta*], it makes them
>   disappear [*kruptetai*].
> Nothing, therefore, is unexpected,
> but dread Oath and the hardest mind are conquered.
> For I too, once so steadfast, now feel
> my words are become effeminate.[16]

The image of Time the Revealer was to live on in the rich theme of the Truth revealed by Time.[17] The theme of destructive Time is a remarkably fertile commonplace, of which I shall give only the example of a verse by Shakespeare, who addresses Time as follows: "Thou nursest all and murder'st all that are."[18]

Some authors have already pointed out the kinship between this passage from Sophocles and the aphorisms of Heraclitus,[19] particularly the one that mentions *Aiōn* (duration or time): "*Aiōn* is a child playing dice."[20] To make this comparison, they have relied on a text by Lucian that sums up the whole of Heraclitus' philosophy as follows: Everything is mixed together; knowledge, ignorance, large, small, up, and down penetrate one another in the game of Time *(Aiōn)*.[21] In fact, it is extremely hard to know what *Aiōn* means in Heraclitus: the time of life? cosmic time? destiny? In any case, we cannot know whether *Aiōn*, already in Heraclitus' time, had the power of veiling and unveiling attributed to it by Sophocles and Lucian.[22] Be that as it may, it is clear that the image of the game of dice does not appear in Sophocles. It is also unlikely that there is an echo of Heraclitus' fragment 123 in the tragic author, since, in our fragment, it is *phusis*, and not time, that makes things appear and disappear.

Yet in a way that is very interesting for our subject, Sophocles' verses oppose the two verbs *phuei* and *kruptetai*, thereby encouraging us to retain the two interpretations that I proposed, that is, in the active sense, "What causes things to appear tends to make them disappear," "What causes birth tends to cause death," or "What unveils is also what veils," and in the passive sense, "What appears tends to disappear" or "What is born wants to die."[23]

Thus, this aphorism expresses astonishment before the mystery of metamorphosis and of the deep identity of life and death. How is it that things are formed, only to disappear? How comes it that within each being, the process of production is indissolubly a process of destruction, that the very movement of life is the very movement of death, with disappearance seeming to be a necessity inscribed within apparition, or within the very process of the production of things? Marcus Aurelius was to say: "Acquire a method for contemplating how all things are transformed into one another. Observe each thing, and imagine that it is in the process of dissolving, that it is in the midst of transformation, in the process of putrefying and being destroyed."[24] Many poets would echo this view, such as Rilke, who sang, "Want transformation,"[25] or Princess Bibesco, who meditated on death as she looked at a bouquet of violets.[26] Montaigne had expressed this mystery strikingly: "The first day of your birth sets you on the track of dying as well as of living . . . The continuous work of your life is to build death. You are in death when you are in life . . . Throughout life, you are dying."[27]

We might reencounter Heraclitean thought—though there is no question of a direct influence—in certain theories of modern biology. Already Claude Bernard had said: "There are two kinds of seemingly opposite vital phenomena, some of organic renovation, which are as it were hidden, and the others of *organic destruction, which are always manifested by the functioning or wearing out of organs.* It is the latter that are usually characterized as the phenomena of life, such that what we call 'life' is in reality death."[28] This is why we can say both that "life is creation" and that "life is death."

Contemporary biology has considered sex and death, "the two important inventions of evolution," to be connected. François Jacob has clearly shown the close relation between reproduction through sexuality and the necessity of the disappearance of individuals. "Nothing obliged a bacterium," he writes, "to practice sexuality in order to multiply itself. As soon as sexuality is obligatory, each genetic program is formed no longer by the exact copy of a single program but by the matching up of two different ones. The other condition necessary for the very possibility of an evolution is death. Not the death that comes from without, as the consequence of some accident, but the death that comes from within, as a prescribed necessity, right from the egg, through the genetic program."[29] In an article in *Le Monde*, Jean-Claude Ameisen, by emphasizing the anthropomorphic character of expressions such as "cellular suicide" or "programmed death," called attention to the importance of the fact that "at every instant, our cells possess the power to destroy themselves within a few hours."[30]

In conclusion, we might open a parenthesis on a mistake made by Félix Ravaisson. When, in his *Philosophical Testament*, we read, "All nature, says Leonardo da Vinci, aspires to its death," we have the impression that Leonardo da Vinci had rediscovered the cosmic vision of Heraclitus. It is true that the commentary Ravaisson gives should be enough to set us on the right track: "This is true in the same sense as that in which Saint Paul says, 'I wish to be dissolved'— in the sense that every day, all creatures aspire to that sleep that renews its exhausted strength; in sum, it aspires to the final sleep, as the necessary passage to a new life."[31] Such a formulation obviously bears no relation to what Heraclitus meant. What is more serious is that Ravaisson's formula has absolutely nothing to do with the text of Leonardo da Vinci. First, Leonardo never wrote, "All nature aspires to its death," but rather speaks of force "running furiously to its own destruction."[32] In fact, when he mentions the desire for death, Leonardo means to speak not of "all nature" but of the "force" that is necessary, quite prosaically, for firing projectiles. He therefore develops a highly original theory of force, which he defines as "a spiritual capacity, an invisible power, which, by accidental violence, sensible bodies have engendered and implanted within insensible bodies, giving them a semblance of life; and this life is wonderful in its actions, as it violates and modifies the place and form of every created thing, running furiously to its own destruction, and producing in its course effects that are different on each occasion."[33]

We can see that Ravaisson—like many contemporary philosophers when they quote texts—has completely deformed Leonardo da Vinci's meaning. As we come to the close of this parenthesis, let us say: to write the history of thought is sometimes to write the history of a series of misinterpretations.

The Veil of Nature

2

From *Phusis* to Nature

I have said that to write the history of thought is to write the history of misunderstandings. Indeed, when Heraclitus' aphorism was cited for the first time in Greek literature—and we have to wait almost five centuries for this to happen—it was given a completely different meaning from the one that I have proposed. It now meant, "Nature loves to hide."

This interpretation can be explained by two considerations. First, the meaning of the word *phusis* had evolved considerably.[1] Second, the idea of a secret of nature had developed in the meantime, and the aphorism was naturally interpreted in this perspective. Again, the notion of a secret of nature might be evidence for the interpretation of Heraclitus' aphorism that was already being given in the schools, although we have no trace of this interpretation before Philo of Alexandria, around the beginning of the Christian era. It will not be possible to write the detailed history of this interpretation, but I shall concentrate above all on showing how the word *phusis,* which first designated a process of growth, finally came to signify a kind of personified ideal.

Initially, as we already glimpsed with regard to Heraclitus, *phusis* designated either the action expressed by the verb *phuesthai*—to be born, to increase, to grow—or its result. The primitive image evoked by this word seems to me to be that of vegetal growth: it is simultaneously the *shoot* that *grows* and the *shoot* that has finished *growing*.

The fundamental image expressed in this word is thus that of a springing-forth of things, an appearance or manifestation of things that result from this spontaneity. Gradually, however, a power was imagined that produces this manifestation. In this chapter, I propose to study only this unexpected passage from *phusis* as a process to *phusis* personified. I will then provide specifics about the evolution of the notion of nature throughout the various periods of its history as our story proceeds.

FROM RELATIVE TO ABSOLUTE USE

In its first usage, which occurs in the eighth century BCE in the *Odyssey,* the word *phusis* designates the result of growth.[2] In order that he may recognize and use it against the sorceries of Circe, Hermes shows Odysseus the aspect *(phusin)*—black root and white flower— of the "herb of life," which the gods, he says, call *molu.* This "aspect" is the particular, definite form that results from a process of natural development.

In its first uses, the word *phusis* is usually accompanied by a genitive: it is the birth *of* or the aspect *of* something. In other words, the notion is always referred to a general or particular reality. As we have seen, Empedocles spoke of the nature *(phusis) of* things,[3] while for his part, Parmenides spoke of the birth *of* the ether: "You will know the birth [*phusis*] of nature, and of all the signs that are in the ether, and the splendid works of the shining sun, and their origin, and the vagabond works of the round-eyed moon, and their origin [*phusin*]."[4]

In the Hippocratic treatises on medicine, which date from the fifth century BCE, the word often corresponds to the physical constitution proper to a patient, or to what results from his or her birth. This meaning gradually widened, in these same treatises, to include the peculiar characteristics of a being, or its primary and original, and therefore normal, way of being: what it is "by birth," what is congenital to it, or again the way in which an organ is constituted, or finally, the organism that results from growth.[5]

In Plato and Aristotle, *phusis* with the genitive eventually came to mean what we call a thing's "nature," or its essence. Sometimes the word was even emptied of all its contents and reduced to a periphrastic meaning. In Plato, for instance, *phusis apeirou* became equivalent to *apeiron,* "the infinite."[6]

Especially from the fifth century on, in the Sophistic movement, the Hippocratic movement, and then in Plato and Aristotle, we begin to see absolute uses of the word *phusis.* Here, *phusis* is no longer the form *of* something but designates the process of formation or its result, taken in general and in an abstract way. In the sixth century we also find such uses in Heraclitus, among others, but their meaning is not very clear. At the outset of his work, Heraclitus defines his method as a division of each reality *kata* (i.e., according to) *phusin.*[7] It certainly seems that we have to do here either with the process of realization of each reality or else with its result; the method consists in discerning the coincidence of contraries that reside within it. Nor can we be absolutely sure whether in fragment 123, of which I have already spoken, the birth or appearing that is opposed to disappearing is considered in general or else in relation to some determinate thing.

This generalization and abstraction of the word *phusis* was carried out when the need arose to designate the subject of philosophers' research prior to the Sophistic and Socratic movements. For instance, the Hippocratic treatise titled *On Ancient Medicine,* probably written near the end of the fifth century BCE,[8] attacks doctors who let themselves be influenced by these philosophers:

Some doctors and scientists declare that it is not possible to know medicine if one does not know what mankind is . . . and the discourse of these people tends toward philosophy, like Empedocles or others who, with regard to *phusis,* wrote about what man is by going back to the origin, how he was formed in the beginning and from what elements he was coagulated. I, however, consider that all that has been said or written on nature [*peri phuseōs*] by some scholar or doctor is less relevant to the art of medicine than to the art of painting, and I consider that the only source for precise knowledge on nature is medicine. And we can acquire this knowledge when we embrace medicine itself correctly in its totality . . . I mean that *historia* or investigation that consists in knowing what man is, the causes of his formation, and all the rest, with precision.[9]

The continuation of this text shows that one cannot know the nature of mankind without the precise observation of the effects produced on human nature by food and exercise.

The author of the treatise is thus opposed to those who wish to base medicine on a general and global theory of man, replaced within the overall process of "nature" and inspired by what is nowadays called the philosophy of the pre-Socratics. The word "nature," here taken absolutely, designates, as we can see from the context, not the whole of the universe but rather the natural process or the working of things, in general, the relation between cause and effect, or the analysis of causality. Therefore, when the author of the treatise says that Empedocles and others have written *peri phuseōs,* this does not mean "on the subject of universal nature" but signifies rather "on the subject of the overall constitution," understanding "constitution" in both an active and a passive sense, as the process by which particular things are born, grow, and die, and have their own constitution by virtue of this process. This notion of "constitution" is less an object, or a domain of the real, than a methodological program. To study it means to study the genesis of a given particular thing and to seek to examine precisely its causes, or the determinate processes that explain its genesis. Aristotle was to take up this method, modifying the notion of *phusis,* which he refused to identify with a purely material process. Yet he describes it in these terms: "The best method should be, in this field as in others, to see things being born and growing."[10] This was to become one of the methods of approaching the secrets of nature.

However, the author of the treatise *On Ancient Medicine* objects that such an approach is not an art of medicine but an art of painting *(graphikē).* He is probably alluding here to Empedocles, who used the analogy of mixing colors to explain the formation of mortal beings from the four elements.[11] From this perspective, medicine is no longer an art of exactitude but an art of "more or less."

PLATO

In Plato, too, the word *phusis* is used absolutely to designate the subject of the pre-Socratics' research. The Socrates of the *Phaedo* (96a7) admits that at one time in his life he had an extraordinary passion for the kind of knowledge called "investigations on nature," to which he attributes a program wholly analogous to that found in the treatise *On Ancient Medicine:* "to know the causes of each thing, to know why each one comes into existence, why it perishes, and why it exists." Yet Socrates informs us of his disappointment: this "investigation on nature" proposed only a strictly material explanation. If he is sitting at this moment in his prison, it is because of the physical necessity represented by the material constitution of his body. Yet is it not rather because of the moral necessity that forces him to choose what he considers to be the best course of action? That is the real cause, of which mechanical necessity is only the condition.

In book 10 of the *Laws,* we find an allusion to people who have devoted themselves to "investigations on nature." They oppose what is produced by spontaneous growth *(phusei),* for instance, fire, water, earth, and air, to what is produced by art, that is, by intelligent activity (889b2). They are utterly wrong, says Plato, because when they defined spontaneous growth *(phusis)* as the birth that pertains to primary beings (892c2), they considered that this primary birth, or *phusis,* corresponded to the material elements, such as fire, air, water, and earth (891c2). In other words, they considered material causes to be the primary causes of the growth of the universe. Instead, Plato continues, what is most ancient and original is the soul, because it is the movement that moves itself (892–896), and is therefore prior to all other movements; the material elements are merely posterior.[12] For those who have concerned themselves with "investigations on nature," nature is merely a blind, spontaneous process, whereas for Plato, the principle of things is an intelligent force: the soul.

If book 10 of the *Laws* opposes nature to the soul, Plato's dialogue *The Sophist* (265c ff.) explains the soul's primacy over the elements. Plato reproaches philosophers who have carried out "investigations on *phusis*" for thinking that this *phusis*—that is, the process of development that engenders things—produces its effects "by spontaneous causation, and without reflection." They therefore distinguish natural activity, which takes place without the intervention of thought, from artistic and technical activity, which presupposes a program elaborated by an intelligence. Taking up this distinction, Plato opposes his conception of nature to that of his adversaries. For him, *phusis* is precisely an art as well, but one that is divine: "I would suppose that the works said to be of nature are the work of a divine art, and those that men compose with them are the work of a human art."[13]

This representation was fundamentally important in the Western tradition, both philosophical and artistic. Thinkers often returned to the idea that nature's action must be conceived on the model of the production of a work of art.[14] Empedocles had already used metaphors of craft with regard to the demiurgic work of Aphrodite:

painting, assembling by means of pegs, ceramics, and gluing.[15] Plato's *Timaeus* alludes to modeling in wax, ceramics, painting, the processes of smelting and mixing alloys, and construction techniques.[16] Above all, divine art is represented mythically by the figure of the Demiurge, who acts on the world from without. For Aristotle, whom we will soon consider, nature acts like a molder: it raises a solid frame around which it carries out its molding.[17] It also proceeds like a painter, drawing a sketch before applying the colors.[18] In this book we will often encounter this crucial theme of the opposition and subsequent reunification of art and nature, where human art is ultimately a mere special case of the original and fundamental art of nature.[19]

If, moreover, *phusis* is a divine art for Plato, there can never be a genuine science, for two reasons. On the one hand, natural processes are the result of operations that are known only to the gods; on the other, these processes are in perpetual transformation. They belong to the order of events, or of becoming; they are not eternal like the idea of Justice or of Truth.

ARISTOTLE

Aristotle also accepts the existence of an analogy between nature and art, but he adds radical oppositions to it.[20] In the first place, he defines nature as a principle of inner motion inside each thing. Each concrete individual has within it a concrete nature that is proper to its species and is the principle of its natural motion. Not only living beings but also the elements thus have within them a nature or an immanent principle of movement: fire, for instance, wants to reach its natural place, which is up above; water its natural place, which is down below. In living beings, this principle of immanent motion is also a principle of growth. At first, one might think that Aristotle conceives of natural processes on the model of artistic processes. In a work of art, there is first a matter that must be modeled and formed; in a natural process, there is a matter that also needs to be formed. In a work of art, there is in addition a form that is thought by the artist, which he seeks to give to the matter; in a natural process, there is also a form that is imposed upon the matter, and it is the goal toward which the process is directed. In fact, however, differences rapidly appear. In the realization of a work of art, a foreign agent externally introduces form into a matter that is foreign to it; in a natural process, the form shapes a matter that is proper to it immediately and from within. Human art has an external finality: medical treatment has as its goal not medical treatment but health. Nature, by contrast, has an internal finality: the process of nature has no other end than nature itself. It becomes what it wants to become, that is, what it already virtually was. The craftsman reasons as he acts, analyzing the operations that will be needed to make the form that is in his mind appear in the matter. Nature does not reason, and its operation is at one with the work itself.[21] Art is imposed upon matter with violence, whereas nature models matter easily and without effort. Ultimately, shouldn't we say that nature is a more perfect art, since it is inside the thing itself, and is immanent and immediate?

This problem was to dominate the entire history of the notion of Nature. It was formulated clearly in the Renaissance, for instance, by Marsilio Ficino, who wrote: "What is human art? A particular nature operating on matter from without. What is nature? An art that gives form to matter from within."[22]

THE MAXIMS OF NATURE

If nature is an art within things, it is in some sense an innate and instinctive knowledge. Such an idea was sketched as early as the fifth century, for instance, in Epicharmus, who speaks of the chicken's instinct and of Nature as instructing herself. He even phrases his thought as follows: "All that is alive is intelligent." We encounter the same idea in the *Corpus hippocraticum,* where the instinctive inventions of nature are mentioned.[23] The nature in question in these texts is probably not universal nature but individual nature, the proper constitution of animals or of mankind. With Aristotle, a new stage is reached, insofar as he uses phrases that seem to define a certain constant behavior of nature as an art and knowledge within things. The general principle runs as follows: "God and nature do nothing in vain."[24] Nature acts like a wise craftsman or artist, who, as Aristotle says in many passages of his studies on animals, proceeds in a rational way, wastes nothing, knows how to avoid the too-much and the not-enough,[25] knows how to make one organ serve several different ends,[26] compensates for excess with deficiency,[27] tries to carry out what is best according to circumstances, and strives to realize the most complete series of realities.[28] This idea of a method proper to nature was to play a very important role in the scientific representations of all of Western thought. Kant would call these principles "maxims of the faculty of judgment."[29] It was on the model of these maxims that late writers, beginning with the first century CE, understood Heraclitus' aphorism as a description of nature's behavior, which consists in wanting to hide, concealing itself, or wrapping itself up in veils.

THE STOICS

The Stoics, for their part, returned to pre-Socratic positions insofar as they made a material element the principle of the genesis of all things; like Aristotle, however, they located this principle of motion inside each thing, and within the totality of things.[30] Nature's operation is thus completely analogous to that of the art within *phusis.* The Stoics define *phusis* as "an artistic fire that proceeds systematically and methodically to engender all things."[31] The original fire gradually condenses into air, water, and earth, only to be set aflame once again after passing through the contrary phases. The world therefore has two aspects: the world taken in its formative and original aspect, and the world taken in the succession of its various states and its periodic becoming. According to its first aspect, the world is identified with the *phusis* that produces and organizes it, and *phusis* itself is identified with the world's soul, that is, with Zeus, or the supreme god. Before the process has been set in motion, *phusis*, Nature, God, Providence, and divine Reason are identical, and God is alone. Once the cosmic process is deployed, Nature sinks into matter, to form and direct bodies and their interactions from within. As Seneca said, "What is Nature other than God himself and the divine reason that is immanent in the world, as a whole and in all its parts?"[32] At the beginning of his *Natural History*, Pliny the Elder also clearly marks the appearance of this divinized Nature, which was long to reign over the minds of Western man:

> The world, or that whole that people have been pleased to call by another name, "the heavens," whose vault covers the life of the entire universe, must be held to be eternal and immense, a divinity: it has not come into being, nor will it ever end. To scrutinize what is outside it has little importance for man, and escapes the conjectures of the human mind. The world is sacred, eternal, immense, wholly present within all things, or rather it is the All, infinite while it seems finite, determinate in all things while appearing indeterminate, embracing all things within and without in itself, it is both the work of the nature of things, and the nature of things itself.

Here, the word *phusis*, which primitively signified an event, a process, or the realization of a thing, has come to mean the invisible power that realizes this event. We here encounter a phenomenon that historians of religion have carefully analyzed: the passage from the experience of an event to the recognition of a power of force intimately linked to this event.[33]

THE PERSONIFICATION OF NATURE

Identified with Zeus by the Stoics, nature was often conceived, beginning in the first century BCE, as a goddess, who could be invoked with the words of Pliny: "Hail, Nature, Mother of all things."[34] Later on, beginning with the second century of our era, hymns to Nature began to be composed. Mesomedes, a freedman of the emperor Hadrian, wrote one that begins:

> Principle and origin of all things
> Ancient mother of the world,
> Night, darkness and silence.[35]

A bit later, we find this invocation in Marcus Aurelius:

> All is fruit for me of what your seasons produce, O Nature,
> From you, in you, for you are all things.[36]

We might also cite the first verses of an Orphic *Hymn to Nature,* which can also be dated approximately to the second century of our era:

> O Nature, mother goddess of all things, mother of innumerable
> ruses,
> Heavenly ancient fecund divinity, queen
> Who tames all and is never tamed,
> Who governs all and sees all.[37]

A funerary inscription found at Salamis in Cyprus reproaches Nature for having caused the deceased to die young:

> O cruel Nature,
> Why then do you produce, you who destroy so quickly?[38]

Here we encounter the Heraclitean theme of death as linked to birth, which was often taken up by poets throughout the ages. In the poet Claudian, writing at the end of antiquity, it is clearly Mother Nature

(Natura parens) that, as Ovid had hinted, puts an end to the battle among the elements.[39] She laments before Zeus on the misfortunes of mankind.[40] As guardian of the entrance, she is seated in front of the cave of an old man, Aion; she is extremely old, yet her face is beautiful.[41]

As Ernst Robert Curtius has shown, Claudian's goddess Nature was to live on in the Middle Ages, particularly in the poems of Bernard Silvester and Alain de Lille.[42] Throughout this book, we shall see that, under very diverse forms, the personification and the deification of Nature continued to remain very much alive, down to the nineteenth century. One could put together a most interesting collection of hymns to Nature throughout the ages.

3

Secrets of the Gods and
Secrets of Nature

Before the elaboration of the notion of nature, which I have briefly described, it was imagined that only the gods had access to the workings of visible and invisible things, which they hid from mankind. Already in the *Odyssey*, when Hermes teaches Odysseus how to recognize the *phusis* or appearance of the "herb of life," he tells him: "It is not without effort that mortals can uproot it; but the gods can do everything." As Alcmeon of Crotona complained in the sixth or fifth century BCE: "Both in the field of the invisible and in that of mortal things, the gods have immediate knowledge. But we, by our human condition, are reduced to conjectures."[1]

DIVINE SECRETS

This was true not only of theoretical knowledge but also of knowledge concerning the most necessary things in life. In Homer, the gods possess *sophia*, that is, know-how, or skill in the construction of objects that enable man to better his lot, whether boats, musical instruments, or techniques of metalworking.[2] Whereas the gods, because of their knowledge, have an easy life, human beings have a hard life, since they are ignorant. As Hesiod says, thanks to Prometheus, human beings were able to snatch some secrets away from the gods:

The gods have hidden what makes human beings live; otherwise, without effort, it would suffice for you to work one day to harvest enough to live on for a year, without doing anything . . . But Zeus hid it away, on the day when, his soul dark with anger, he was fooled by false-hearted Prometheus. From this day on, he prepared sad cares for men. He hid fire away from them. Yet once again, the brave son of Iapetus[3] then stole it from Zeus for men, in the hollow of a ferula, and he fooled the eye of the lightning-launching god.[4]

For Plato himself, the secret of natural processes is inaccessible to man, who has no technical means for discovering it. Speaking of colors, he declares:

But should someone make an experimental test of these facts, he would display his ignorance of the difference between man's nature and God's: that, whereas God is sufficiently wise and powerful to blend the many into one and to dissolve again the one into many, there exists not now, nor ever will exist hereafter, a human being sufficient for either of these tasks.[5]

This concept was to reappear several times in antiquity, for instance, in Seneca, who, speaking of the various theories that have been imagined concerning comets, declares: "Are they true? Only the gods know, who possess the science of the true."[6] In the passage that follows this, he considers that our ignorance of natural processes is merely a particular case of our ignorance with regard to divine things, and especially to the supreme God.

The idea of "secrets of nature" which I am about to discuss did not, moreover, cause the disappearance of the idea of "divine secrets." We encounter it once again, particularly at the beginning of the seventeenth century, at the height of the mechanistic revolution, when for various reasons philosophers and scholars both hoped to discover the "secrets of nature" by means of the experimental method and admitted the existence of one impenetrable secret: that of the omnipotent will of God.[7]

NATURE'S SECRETS

After the emergence of the philosophical notion of nature, people no longer spoke of divine secrets but rather of the secrets of nature. Gradually, personified Nature herself became the guardian of these secrets. Owing to the personification of nature, the difficulty of knowing nature was considered to be somehow explained by the personal behavior of nature, which seeks to conceal itself and is jealous of its secrets. This was to make possible a new interpretation of Heraclitus' aphorism 123, "Nature loves to hide."

The notion of a secret of nature thus appears at a relatively late date, in the first century BCE, and primarily in Latin writers; yet they in turn had certainly found it in their Greek models, whether Stoic, Epicurean, or Platonist. For instance, Cicero, following the Platonist Antiochus of Ascalon, speaks of "things that have been hidden and enveloped by Nature herself."[8] Lucretius affirms that "jealous Nature has hidden the spectacle of atoms from our view,"[9] and elsewhere that Epicurus "robbed Nature of all the veils that concealed her,"[10] or else that he "has forced the tightly closed gates of Nature."[11] Ovid says that Pythagoras has "discovered by the eyes of the heart what Nature refused to human eyes."[12] With regard to the planets, Pliny the Elder's *Natural History* speaks of the secrets of Nature and of the laws to which she has subjected herself.[13]

The secrets of nature are secrets in various senses. In the case of some of them, they can be said to correspond to the invisible aspects of nature. Some are invisible because they are so distant in space or in time. Others are inaccessible because of their extreme smallness, like Epicurus' atoms, of which Lucretius says that "jealous Nature has hidden the spectacle of atoms from our view,"[14] or else because they are hidden within bodies or the earth. In the words of Cicero:

> All that, Lucullus, remains hidden, veiled and wrapped in thick darkness, so that no gaze of the human mind is potent enough to penetrate the sky or to enter into the earth. We know we have a body, but we know nothing of the exact place occupied by our organs. This is why doctors . . . have carried out dissections, in order to see this emplacement of the organs. As the Empiricist physicians say,[15] however, the organs are no better known, for it may be that if they are uncovered and deprived of their envelopes, they are modified.[16]

The secrets of nature can thus be considered invisible parts which escape observation but which have an influence on visible phenomena. Moreover, forced and violent observation, as Cicero hints, following the Empiricist physicians, risks disturbing the phenomena it wishes to study. This was to be a traditional argument of thinkers hostile to experimentation.[17]

In addition, invisible things can become visible, like comets, which, as Seneca remarks, appear only rarely, and of whose withdrawal we are unaware when they are hidden. However, he continues, these are not the only realities in the universe that escape our sight: "Many other beings remain unknown to us, or, perhaps—a still greater wonder!—they both fill our eyes and escape them. Are they so subtle that the human eye cannot perceive them? Or is their majesty hidden in a retreat too sacred for men, and do they rule their domain from there, that is to say, themselves, inaccessible to all, except to the mind? . . . How many animals are known to us only since today! How many objects of which our century itself has no idea!"[18]

Yet the secrets of nature are also the inexplicable phenomena for which we cannot account. Their "causes" remain hidden, whether because, being material, they remain invisible on account of their smallness, like the atoms of Democritus and Epicurus, or else because they have an existence of an intelligible order, like Plato's Ideas or Aristotle's Forms. Platonists, Epicureans, and Stoics agreed in recognizing that sensible phenomena have causes that are not the effect of divine caprice. Speaking of earthquakes, Seneca declares: "The gods play no part in these accidents, and the convulsions of the sky and the earth are not the effects of their anger. These phenomena have their own causes . . . Ignorance is the cause of our terrors. Therefore, is it not worthwhile to know, in order not to fear? Ah, how much better it is to search for causes! . . . Let us therefore search for what comes from the depths to shake the earth."[19]

Ultimately, whether it has to do with phenomena that are inexplicable or hard to perceive, or again with causes, and in particular with unknown secret forces, the idea of secrets of nature always presupposes an opposition between the visible, what appears, or the phenomenon, and what is hidden beyond that appearance, or the invisible. We encounter this opposition, moreover, from the beginnings of Greek thought. On the one hand, as I have already suggested, the first Greek thinkers insist on the difficulty we experience in knowing the things that are hidden from us *(adēla)*.[20] On the other hand, they consider that the "phenomena" can reveal hidden things to us, according to the saying formulated by Anaxagoras and Democritus and repeated throughout antiquity, particularly among the Epicureans: "What appears makes visible what is hidden" *(opsis adēlōn ta phainomena)*.[21] As Hans Diller has shown, we can recognize here the beginning of a scientific method that proceeds by analogical reasoning.[22] Aristotle, in particular, was always to remain faithful to this method, which consists in concluding from visible effects to an invisible cause and not the reverse. For instance, by means of the study of the concrete behavior of human beings, we can draw conclusions concerning the essence of the human soul.[23]

NATURE AS SECRET

The attentive study of a specific phenomenon may lead to the discovery of another phenomenon, more or less hidden, that determines it.

At least for the Stoics, however, the great secret of nature remained the interaction of all causes in the cosmic process in general, or the organic All, and the determining action of the primary cause, or of Nature the creator, the artist, and the producer of the cosmos: in other words, ultimately, of God himself, with whom they identified Nature. In this regard, Seneca remarked: "What that principle is without which nothing exists we cannot know. We are surprised at our poor knowledge of tiny particles of fire [the comets], whereas the greatest thing in the world—God—is hidden from us."[24]

The great secret of nature is thus Nature herself, that is, the invisible reason or force, of which the visible world is only the external manifestation. It is this invisible nature that "loves to hide," or conceal itself from human view. Nature thus has a twofold aspect: it shows itself to our senses in the rich variety of the spectacle presented to us by the living world and the universe, and, at the same time, it conceals itself behind appearances in its most essential, profound, and effective part.

THE SECRETS OF NATURE IN THE MIDDLE AGES
AND IN MODERN TIMES

This metaphor of the "secrets of nature," appearing in the Hellenistic period, was to dominate research on nature, physics, and the natural sciences for nearly two millennia. In an extremely interesting work, William Eamon has studied the fortunes of this concept in the Middle Ages and the beginning of the modern period.[25] From the fifteenth to the seventeenth centuries, this tradition was perpetuated: titles of works alluding to the secrets or the marvels of nature were extremely numerous. This may have been due to the extraordinary success enjoyed throughout the Middle Ages by a work translated from the Arabic and falsely attributed to Aristotle, the *Secretum Secretorum* (Secret of Secrets). Be that as it may, all kinds of works enti-

Secrets of the Gods and Secrets of Nature ⌒ 35

tled "Secrets of Nature" or "Wonders of Nature" proposed medical, alchemical, or magical recipes.

This literature takes its place in the context of a long tradition that developed as early as antiquity, especially from the second century BCE on, which proposed a science whose goal was to "discover the secrets and wonderful forces of the beings of nature, that is, their *phuseis*, their occult properties and virtues, as well as the relations of sympathy and antipathy that derive from this *phuseis* in the three kingdoms. Men, beasts, plants, and stones (including metals) are henceforth considered mere carriers of mysterious forces, and therefore charged with curing all pains and illnesses and with ensuring wealth, happiness, honors, and magical power for man."[26] This tradition manifested itself in particular in the form of collections of *mirabilia*, òr strange and extraordinary natural phenomena. We know this literature, which seems to go back to Bolos of Mendes (around 200 BCE) above all from extracts or allusions in later authors, such as Pliny the Elder, in whom sympathies and antipathies play a considerable role.

Precisely at the time of the flourishing of science in the seventeenth and eighteenth centuries, as Eamon has shown in the same work, modern science, as the heir in this sense to the occult sciences and magic, was to assign itself precisely the goal of unveiling the secrets of nature. As the objects of philosophical physics but also of the pseudosciences in antiquity and the Middle Ages, they were to become in this way the object of the new physics, mathematics, and mechanics. Francis Bacon, for instance, declared that Nature unveils her secrets only under the torture of experimentation.[27] And Pascal was to say: "The secrets of nature are hidden . . . [T]he experiments that give us intelligence thereof are continually multiplied; and since they are the only principles of physics, the consequences are multiplied proportionally."[28] One could also cite Gassendi, who calls objects that are not directly observable but are linked to certain phenomena that are observable *res natura occultae* (things hidden by nature), thus taking up a formula from Cicero.[29]

It was not until the course of the nineteenth century that this metaphor gradually ceased to be used, while at the same time the concept of a divine builder faded out of scientific discourse. Among philosophers and artists it yielded its place, as we shall see later on, to the notion of the mystery of the world, of being, or of existence.

III

"Nature Loves to Hide"

4

Heraclitus' Aphorism and Allegorical Exegesis

Before I set forth the way both ancients and moderns tried to unveil and discover the secrets of nature, it may be useful to investigate what became of Heraclitus' famous saying in antiquity.

THEOLOGICAL PHYSICS

It took five centuries for a citation of this aphorism by Heraclitus, which is one of the main themes of the present work, to appear explicitly attributed to our author. As I have hinted in the preceding pages, the evolution of the notion of *phusis* and the appearance of the metaphor of the "secrets of nature" led philosophers to believe that Heraclitus' aphorism meant "Nature loves to conceal herself." Since the metaphor of the "secrets of nature" was quite widespread at the time of this reappearance, we might expect that our aphorism would have been cited to illustrate the difficulties man experiences in knowing natural phenomena and in constructing the "physical" part of philosophy. This, however, is not the case. When the saying was quoted by Philo of Alexandria at the beginning of the Christian era, and by Porphyry, by Julian, and by Themistius in the third and fourth centuries, although its subject is the word "nature," it was always applied to the divine or the gods and to discourse on the gods, that is, to theology. Julian the Apostate, for instance, speaks in this context of telestic and mystagogic theology.

This fact can be explained in the following way: whereas the word "theology" evokes for us metaphysical considerations that pertain to the dogmas of a religion or to sacred texts, matters were quite otherwise for the Greeks. "Theology" meant "a discourse on the gods," and the word was first used with regard to that "discourse on the gods" exemplified by the works of poets such as Homer, Hesiod, and Orpheus. These poets used the religious representations and myths handed down by tradition, which sometimes came from the Near East, to tell the story of the genealogy of the gods, and thereby give a primitive explanation of the genesis of things *(phusis)*, by personifying natural phenomena. For instance, the Sky *(Ouranos)* impregnates the Earth *(Gaia)* by means of the rain it sprinkles down.[1]

We ought not, therefore, to be surprised if the words *physiologia,* or "discourse on nature," and *theologia,* or "discourse on the gods," are closely connected, as they are in this text by Plutarch, the Platonist philosopher of the first century CE:

> That, among the ancients, Greeks as well as Barbarians, *physiologia* was a discourse on Nature that was wrapped in myths, or a theology most often disguised by enigmas and hidden meanings, and pertaining to the Mysteries, and that, for the crowd, what is said is more obscure[2] than what is not said, and that what is not said is even more problematic than what is said: this is obvious when we consider the Orphic poems and the Egyptian and Phrygian discourses. Yet it is especially the secret rites of the initiations, and what is carried out symbolically in religious ceremonies, that reveal the thought of the ancients.[3]

Thus, rituals and myths contained a hidden teaching on the subject of nature.

The encounter between this poetic theology—linked, moreover, to pagan cults—and philosophical reflection was a subject of controversy. The mythical representation of the gods was criticized by those who were called the *phusikoi*, who gave a purely material explanation for the birth of the world. Philosophers such as Xenophanes and Anaxagoras openly attacked poetic theology. In the fifth century BCE, with the Sophists, there developed a veritable *Aufklärung*, or century of Enlightenment, when the existence of the gods was questioned on the grounds that it was a mere poetic fiction or social convention. Because of this, philosophers of the Platonic and Stoic traditions gradually developed a kind of doctrine of double truth. On the one hand, poetic and religious traditions were left intact, since they were useful for the people, as forming the basis of the education of children and of the official religion of the city-state. On the other hand, these philosophers considered that the poets of yesteryear had, in an enigmatic or hidden way, taught an entire science of nature beneath the veil of myth, which was none other than the Platonic or Stoic science of nature. Through skillful exegesis, called "allegorical exegesis" (*allēgorein* means to make someone understand something other than what is said), a hidden philosophical meaning was discovered under the letter of the texts. As Émile Bréhier pointed out, the need for this method came to be felt when, as a result of the evolution of thought, traditional forms had to be reconciled with new ideas.[4] This phenomenon had already appeared in the sixth century BCE, in a commentator on Homer, Theagenes of Rhegium, whose work is unfortunately known only through late citations, but who seems to have proposed an allegorical exegesis of the Homeric poems that was physical (the battle of the gods becomes the battle of the elements) and moral, perhaps in reaction against the sharp criticisms formulated against Homeric mythology by Xenophanes. In the fourth century, the famous Derveni papyrus proposed an allegorical explanation of an Orphic poem in an exegesis that seeks to find a hidden teaching of a physical nature in the text being commented upon. Here, the Zeus of the Orphic poem was identified with the air, in a manner reminiscent of Diogenes of Apollonia.[5] Plato's disciple

Xenocrates gave divine names to the elements, and even Aristotle did not disdain to provide an allegorical interpretation of Homer's golden chain to illustrate his theory of the Prime Mover.[6]

Yet it was above all the Stoics who used this method systematically in the theological part of their physics. For example, they interpreted the myth of the birth of Athena emerging from the head of Zeus as a function of their theory according to which the organ of thought is situated in the chest: as Athena was identified with thought, it was said that she was produced from Zeus' chest, since thought is manifested in the voice.[7] Again, Hera's fellation of Zeus, represented in a painting at Samos, reflected for them the way in which matter receives seminal reasons within itself with a view to the organization of the world.[8] The Stoics thus tried to present their physical doctrines, deduced from the principles of their philosophy or inspired by the pre-Socratics, by dressing them up in the mythical garb borrowed from the texts of Homer and Hesiod. Speaking of their exegetical method, Cicero gives a good statement of what was in fact proper to all allegorical exegesis—and this also holds for contemporary methods of the interpretation of texts. He writes: "Chrysippus claims to adapt the fabulous tales of Orpheus, Hesiod, and Homer, in such a way that the ancient poets, who never had the slightest idea of their theories, are transformed into Stoics."[9]

Impressive feats of ingenuity were thus deployed to make it possible to find "modern" doctrines in texts written several centuries previously. The eventual result was the rationalization of religious traditions. As Cotta says to the Stoic Balbus in Cicero's dialogue *On the Nature of the Gods:* "When you give yourself such trouble to account for these fables . . . you thereby admit that reality is quite different from what men believe it to be: what they call gods are natural processes [*rerum naturas*], not figures of the gods."[10]

The Stoics would certainly have accepted this conclusion, replying that the only God is Nature. In their view, the different gods of mythology were merely various representations of the one God, who is Nature. Unlike other philosophers who practiced the allegorical method, the Stoics were not content to identify the gods and goddesses with the physical elements; but they did consider that these various gods were only the successive forms assumed by one and the same force. In this regard I cite the summary by Diogenes Laertius:

> God . . . is the father of all things, both generally and in that part of him that penetrates throughout all things and receives multiple appellations according to his powers. Indeed, he is called *Dia* because all things exist because of [*dia*] him, Zeus, in so far as he is the cause of life, or as he penetrates life thoroughly; Athena because of the extension of his guiding part in the ether; Hera because of his extension in the air; Hephaestus because of his extension in the fire that produces things; Poseidon because of his extension in what is wet; and Demeter because of his extension in the earth.[11]

The Stoics had a dynamic conception of nature. The biological model that inspired them was the seed, which develops in accordance with a predetermined program and constructs an organism. In its expansive phase, the primordial force that contains the original seeds successively adopts the various forms of the elements, which are to constitute the cosmos; then it concentrates once again, so that the cosmos is annihilated and the force remains alone; then it deploys itself again to engender the same cosmos, once again and eternally. To describe this process, allegorical exegesis presented Zeus' action as the transformation of Zeus into Athena, then Hera, and so on. The universe was thus subject to periods, that is, an infinite succession of diastoles and systoles. More precisely, Nature was God in its expansive phase. Seneca says that Nature, the creative and destructive process, comes to an end at the conclusion of each period *(cessante natura)*, when Zeus becomes concentrated within himself.[12] Ultimately, these divine names serve only to give an imaged and personified definition of the phases of the universe, and they enable us to glimpse how Stoic doctrine was already sketched in the most ancient traditions. At the same time, however, the literal meaning of this mythology could remain valid just as it was for the common people, since philosophers knew that it had a hidden philosophical meaning.

We can thus discern, at least in the Stoic tradition, and perhaps in the Platonic tradition as well, a twofold aspect of physics. First of all, there is physics in the proper sense, which applies itself to studying the structure of bodies, the movements, and the causes of natural phenomena. Yet there is also a part of physics that must speak of the gods, since mythical traditions and religion place them in relation to the phenomena of nature. This is a physics that is "theological," uses the method of allegorical exegesis, and is therefore the noblest part of philosophy. With regard to it, Cleanthes and Chrysippus go so far as to speak of mysterial initiation.[13] Moreover, we must distinguish three primary meanings of the word "theology": the word may designate the mythical system implied in ancient theogonies or religious texts; it can also refer to the allegorical exegesis of myths; finally, it may mean the theory of first principles, as presented by Plato, Aristotle, or the Neoplatonists.

For those who cite Heraclitus' aphorism, from the first to the fourth centuries of our era, the Nature that hides was therefore divine Nature, whether it was the Divine in general or the various gods that are present in Nature. For instance, the geographer Strabo certainly seems to allude to this aphorism when, with regard to mysterial ceremonies such as those of Eleusis, he speaks of "the secret and the mystery in which these [mysterial] ceremonies magnify the divine, for they imitate the nature of the divine, which escapes our senses."[14]

It seems to me very likely, although no text attests to it clearly, that the Stoics were the first to establish this relation between Heraclitus' "nature that hides" and the divine that is wrapped up in myths and unveiled by allegory.

PHILO OF ALEXANDRIA

The first explicit citation of Heraclitus' aphorism appears in an author who was rather marginal in the perspective of Greek tradition: Philo the Jew of Alexandria. His work would probably have been completely forgotten if Christian writers had not become interested in him, taking him as a model in their attempt at the recuperation of Greek philosophy and the allegorical exegesis of the Hebraic Bible. His commentaries on the Greek version of the Bible conserve for us a great deal of precious information on Greek philosophy, Platonic or Stoic, which he knew either through the education he had received or else owing to the tradition of Jewish commentators who had preceded him. If Philo used the allegorical method abundantly, it was precisely in order to find allusions to concepts of Greek philosophy in the characters of the Bible or the actions they carry out. For instance, he recognizes the four cardinal virtues of the Stoics in the four rivers of Paradise mentioned in Genesis.[15] Philo, however, did not invent the application of allegorical exegesis to the text of the Bible. He often alludes to his predecessors, whom he calls the *phusikoi*, Jewish commentators on the Bible who established a correspondence between the biblical stories and the phenomena of nature, and who were therefore influenced by Stoic allegorism.[16]

As a matter of fact, the context in which the quotation from Heraclitus appears in Philo is rather obscure. The Greek text is lost, but we still have an Armenian translation of it. Commenting on the biblical verse "The Lord God appeared to Abraham at the oak of Mambre,"[17] Philo is supposed to have written: "The literal sense seems quite clear to me. However, only the tree contains an allegorical meaning, which must be explained by the Chaldaean language, in the word Mambre. According to Heraclitus, the tree is our nature, which loves to conceal itself and to hide."[18]

Obviously, Heraclitus never said that the tree is our nature, and that our nature loves to conceal itself. There has certainly been a mistake in translation in the transition from the Greek to the Armenian. In the Greek, the allusion to Heraclitus was no doubt intended to justify the need for using the allegorical method, along the lines of: "We must explain what is meant by the oak of Mambre, for, according to Heraclitus, 'nature loves to hide.'" In fact, it is the word "Mambre" that will be the subject of an allegorical interpretation, since, says Philo, it means etymologically "that which comes from sight," and hence the act of seeing. We might also consider that the text means that divine nature loves to conceal itself, and that here it is concealed in a human form.

This first text by Philo is interesting because it brings up the name of Heraclitus, but the other mentions of our aphorism are much clearer. Commenting on Genesis 2:6, "A spring rose up from the earth," Philo writes, "Those who are not initiated into allegory and Nature, who loves to hide, compare the river in question to the river of Egypt."[19]

For his part, Philo considers that the spring, in conformity with Stoic doctrine, represents the guiding part of our soul: like a spring, it pours into the five powers of sensation. Those who are unaware of Heraclitus' aphorism search for literalist interpretations: if the Bible speaks of a "spring," then it must mean the birth of a river. By contrast, those who, like Philo, know that "Nature loves to hide" try to discover that "something else" which is meant by the biblical text. In the continuation of his commentary, Philo goes on to develop everything that suggests the theme of springs, for instance, the springs of virtue, or else the source of life, which is none other than God. For Philo, Heraclitus' aphorism is therefore an invitation to derive all kinds of instructive and edifying considerations from the biblical text by searching for analogies that can be drawn between the physical reality designated by the text—for example, in our text, the spring—and spiritual realities that can be conceived as sources in the figurative sense.[20]

Etymology is also revealing. God changed Abram's name to Abraham, and such name changes, says Philo, are symbols of "Nature, who always loves to hide."[21] Philo illustrates his statement by declaring that "Abram" means "Father who rises," while "Abraham" means "Father of sound," and by the use of an erudite argument he concludes that the change from "Abram" to "Abraham" corresponds to the transformation of a person who progresses from the study of nature to the practice of wisdom, or from physics to ethics.

Here I can sense the reader's impatience; he must be saying to himself, with cause: What is this Nature whose unveiling ultimately boils down to the discovery of a hidden meaning of the sacred text? I will answer first of all that Philo's task is not to carry out, like the Stoics, an exegesis of the names of the gods, which refer ultimately to cosmic processes; instead, he wants to give an exegesis of the historical facts or legal prescriptions transmitted by the Bible. It is the true meaning hidden in these formulas that must be discovered, for in all probability, *phusis* in Philo is synonymous with *alētheia;* that is, Nature and Truth are closely connected. Both are symbolized by the same reality, mentioned by the Bible: the well. Speaking of the biblical wells, Philo alludes to an opposition between the surface and the depths of knowledge: "The well is the symbol of knowledge; for the nature of knowledge is not situated at the surface, but it is deep. It does not sprawl in daylight but loves to hide in secret, and it is not found easily, but with a great deal of difficulty."[22]

Although the subject is the nature of knowledge, we can obviously discern an allusion to Heraclitus' aphorism here. Yet we are also in the presence of an interesting encounter, which will be reproduced several times, between Heraclitus' aphorism and an aphorism of Democritus, promoted to the rank of a proverb, according to which, in the testimony of the Christian writer Lactantius, the Truth is hidden in a well: "Democritus attests that the Truth is plunged within a deep well."[23] Democritus, for his part, had simply said, "We know nothing in reality, for the Truth is within a deep abyss."[24]

Philo was quite probably thinking of this Truth hidden in the depths.[25] Already prior to him, Cicero had compared the two sayings in speaking of the philosophers of the New Academy who proposed a purely aporetic philosophy and who, in response to those who protested to them that nothing is certain anymore according to their way of thinking, replied: "What can we do about that? Is it our fault? It is Nature that must be accused, she who, as Democritus says, has completely hidden Truth in an abyss."[26] Heraclitus' Nature, Cicero seems to say, has hidden Democritus' Truth in the abyss. What interests us, however, both in Cicero and in Philo, is that in this perspective there is a kind of identification between Nature and Truth. Both are hidden, and both are very hard to find.

At the end of his *Natural Questions,* Seneca urges us to summon all our strength to devote ourselves to the discovery of this Nature and this Truth: "It is only with great difficulty that we can reach this abyss in which Truth has been deposited. Yet we seek this Truth only on the surface, and with hands that lack vigor."[27]

As a matter of fact, *alētheia* means, as it often does in Greek, not so much "truth" in the sense of agreement between reality and thought as "reality" in an ontological sense. And *phusis* can have the same meaning. Whereas the word *phusis* is often used by Philo to designate either the Nature that produces beings or else the general course of nature, or the nature of a thing, or, finally, in a Stoic sense, the life proper to plants, when it comes to biblical exegesis, Philo understands by the word *phusis* the hidden reality or truth that must be discovered beyond the letter of the text, by means of allegory, a reality or truth that is incorporeal and ultimately divine.[28] For instance, the names of the patriarchs Abraham, Isaac, and Jacob hint at "a reality [*phusis*] that is less apparent and far superior to that of sensible objects," because for Philo, these characters correspond allegorically to the three elements that constitute virtue: innate dispositions, theoretical teaching, and practical exercise. He states this explicitly: "What is said [in the Bible] does not stop at the limits of literal and obvious explanation but seems to hint at a reality [*phusis*] that is much more difficult to know for the multitude, one that is recognized by those who rank the intelligible before the sensible, and who are able to see."[29]

Here we could almost translate *phusis* as "meaning," as opposed to the letter of the text. "Reality" is the true "meaning." We find an analogous shift in Latin, where the word *res,* meaning "thing" or "Reality," can in some contexts mean the true signification of a word.[30] Be that as it may, *phusis* in the perspective of allegorical exegesis corresponds to a conceptual content and an incorporeal reality. By opposing *sōmata,* or bodies, to *pragmata*—and by this term he means incorporeal realities—Philo considers that only "those who are able to consider intelligible realities [*pragmata*] in their separation from bodies and their nakedness" are capable of practicing allegory.[31] We can assume that the reason why "nature" loves to hide, for Philo, is that it is not accessible but is situated in the vast domain of the incorporeal, from psychic realities to divine reality, which mortals have great difficulty understanding.

Philonian allegory is thus quite different from Stoic allegory. Whereas Stoic allegory reveals that myths correspond to corporeal realities—that is, living and animated—it is incorporeal realities that Philonian allegory discovers in the biblical text. Such allegory is therefore Platonic in inspiration, and foreshadows the allegory of the Neoplatonists. Let me add that this movement of thought, which, in the reading of a sacred text, rises from the sensible to the intelligible, is a spiritual exercise that Christians, too, would try to practice as they read the Bible.

5

"Nature Loves to Wrap Herself Up"

Mythical Forms and Corporeal Forms

Heraclitus' aphorism was to be cited again several times, beginning at the end of the third century CE. Plotinus' student Porphyry brings it up to justify the use of myth in Plato's *Timaeus,* and also, in a way that seems paradoxical to us, but is perfectly explicable from Porphyry's perspective, to defend the rites of pagan religion. The Heraclitean saying was also placed in the service of an apology for paganism by the emperor Julian and the philosopher Themistius.

THE MYTHICAL PHYSICS OF PLATO'S *TIMAEUS*
AND THE EPICUREAN CRITICISMS

In the *Timaeus,* Plato had proposed a physics that was "probable," and therefore uncertain, and that involved, in particular, the mythical image of a craftsman-god. Epicurus and the Epicureans were strongly opposed to this use of myth in the science of nature: in their view, it was incompatible both with divine majesty, since it imagined a god who assumed a concern for the fabrication and organization of the world, and with the scientific certainty that the soul had to find peace by means of the study of *physiologia.*

In this regard, Porphyry reports the criticisms that Colotes, the disciple of Epicurus, had directed against the Platonists.[1] He reproached Plato for not having hesitated to present expositions pertaining to physical science in the form of mythical stories. He who sets forth scientific truth, says Colotes, must not have recourse to the artifices of lies. Did not Plato himself criticize the poets' mythical inventions, those fables that provoke the fear of death? And yet is not the myth of Er, which ends the dialogue and narrates the souls' pilgrimages after death, liable to provoke the same kind of terrors? And if it is claimed that myths are imagistic modes of expression, adapted for simple people while providing sages with matter for thought, it will be answered that the common man does not understand them, and sages do not need them. Myths are therefore dangerous and useless. Here we recognize the critique of the use of myths in philosophy which had been inaugurated by Epicurus, and which was just as opposed to Plato's *Timaeus* as it was to the Stoics' allegorical explanations, and, in general, to the idea that the allegorical exegesis of traditional or invented myths can contribute to physical science.[2]

NATURE, BECAUSE SHE IS AN INFERIOR REALITY,
LOVES TO WRAP HERSELF UP

Porphyry's answer to the objections posed by Colotes is extremely interesting: it reveals how Platonists justified the "mythical" physics of the *Timaeus* in the name of a specific idea they had of Nature.

In the first place, Plato never confused philosophy with mythical thought. According to the Platonists, Porphyry affirms, on the one hand, philosophy does not accept *all* myths; and on the other, not *all* philosophy accepts myths. In other words, Porphyry proposes two divisions, one of myths, and the other of philosophy, in order to show that only one part of philosophy, "theological physics"—which I discussed in the preceding chapter—admits of a mythical exposition, and only one category of myths, "fabulous narrations," is compatible with this part of philosophy.

Philosophy does not accept just any kind of myth or fable, where it is understood that myth or fable always represents false discourse.

There are false discourses that were invented merely for the pleasure of the ear, such as comedies or novels, and there are false discourses that may have a certain edifying usefulness.[3] Obviously, philosophy will reject this first kind of fable.

Among myths of the second category, we can distinguish between fables properly so called, such as those of Aesop, and fabulous stories. Fables properly so called do not merely assume an imaginary and mendacious form, but also the story itself is a tissue of lies. They too are therefore excluded from the domain of philosophy. By contrast, fabulous narrations tell something true under the veil of fiction. These are, for instance, the stories Hesiod and Orpheus tell us about the genealogies and actions of the gods, but also the rites of the mysteries, or what are referred to as the Pythagorean symbols. Thus, here Porphyry links together theogonies, religious ceremonies, and the Pythagorean symbols *(akousmata)*. These *akousmata* were archaic taboos that had become incomprehensible, such as "Don't step over a balance," "Don't eat the heart," "Don't sit on a bushel."[4] They had long been the object of allegorical interpretations, which the Neoplatonists adopted as their own. In general, if Porphyry affirms that the entire body of myths he gathers together under the appellation of "fabulous narrations" tells the truth beneath the veil of fiction, it is precisely because they are all susceptible of an allegorical interpretation that is able to discern a truth hidden within myth.

Once again, however, we must make a distinction: some myths tell of indecent things, such as the mutilation of Ouranos by Kronos or the adulteries of Zeus, while others, by contrast, utilize decent fictions. Philosophy can accept only myths in the latter category. In addition, these myths that philosophy can accept are used not by all of philosophy, but only by the lower part of theology, which deals with the gods that have some relation to Nature. For Porphyry, higher theology refers to the Good, the Intellect, and the Soul that has remained in the intelligible world, whereas lower theology relates to the Soul of the world and to Nature:

We must know, however, that philosophers do not accept mythical stories in all their discourses, even if they are permitted, but they have the custom of using them only when they speak of the soul or the powers of the air and the ether or the other gods. When, however, their discourse dares to rise to the highest God, who is the first one above all . . . , the Good, the first cause, or else to the Intellect as well . . . , which contains the original Forms of things . . . , and which was generated and proceeded from the supreme God, they do not touch upon anything mythical at all, but if they try to attribute predicates to these realities that transcend not only speech, but also human thought, they have recourse to analogies and comparisons. Thus Plato, wishing to speak of the Good, did not dare to say what it is, because he knew one thing only: that it is not possible for man to know it as it is. Yet he found that the only thing among visible realities that was the most similar to it was the sun. Thus, it was by using the analogy of the sun that, through his discourse, he opened the way that enabled him to rise toward the incomprehensible.

This is why antiquity did not sculpt any statue for the supreme God, whereas it set them up for the other gods, because the sovereign God and the Intellect generated by him are beyond Nature, as they are above the Soul—that is, where it is forbidden to introduce anything mythical.[5]

When he says that the philosopher must speak of the supreme principle not in a mythical way, but only in an analogical way, Porphyry is in disagreement with his master Plotinus, who did not hesitate to establish a correspondence between the One, the Intellect and the Soul, and the three gods Ouranos, Kronos, and Zeus.[6] According to Porphyry, myth begins only with the Soul:

But when we have to do with the other gods and the Soul . . . , it is neither uselessly nor to flatter the ears that philosophers turn to mythical stories, but because they know that *Nature hates to expose herself uncovered and naked in view of all.*[7] Since she has concealed the knowledge of her being from mankind's coarse senses, by hiding beneath the vestments and envelopes of things, likewise, she has wished that sages should discuss her mysteries only under the veil of mythic narratives.[8]

If we take Proclus' testimony into account, it does seem that Porphyry cited the name of Heraclitus when alluding to our famous aphorism. The spirit of the *Timaeus,* and, moreover, of all Platonism, is expressed here. In his dialogue, Plato declares openly that he will not speak of the "principle" or "principles" of all things, because the mode of discourse he has chosen to use, which is suitable for the world and what is within the world—likely discourse and myth—does not allow the discussion of principles.[9] For Plato, as for Porphyry, reality and divinity are identical. There are, however, two levels of reality and of divinity, which are the subject of two different disciplines: on the one hand, the sphere of the supreme divinity, which is totally incorporeal and is the subject of theology; on the other, that of the lower gods who have relations with bodies, that is, the World Soul and the other gods who are linked to physical phenomena, stars, powers of the air and the ether; all these beings are the subject of "theological physics." In fact, mythical discourse appears in Plato only when souls are the subject of discussion.[10]

All divinities are hard to know, but for different reasons. The supreme divinity is hidden from us, precisely insofar as it is not veiled by sensible or material forms. It blinds us by its excessive light, like the sun. It can be spoken of only by making comparisons and negations, in accordance with the traditional methods of theology. In contrast, the lower divinities are hidden, because the divine souls, in their descent toward matter, take on bodies that are more and more numerous and thick. They are hidden, because they are wrapped in visible forms. To this envelopment in bodies must correspond an envelopment in a certain kind of discourse, that of the mendacious fiction of myth, through which allegorical exegesis allows us to discern a truth content, in the same way sensible forms enable us to glimpse, behind the mendacious character of that which is material, the invisible power that animates them. Heraclitus' aphorism thus changes its meaning completely, compared to the interpretation of it that Philo gave. "Nature loves to hide" then meant: that reality which is incorporeal and ultimately divine, hidden in the letter of Scripture, escapes our knowledge because of its power and its transcendence; yet the veil that covers it can be removed by means of allegorical exegesis. For Porphyry, the aphorism means: that Nature escapes our knowledge because of its weakness. It is constrained to wrap itself up in sensible forms, and for this reason, in order to speak of it, we can only use mythical language, or describe it by means of the statues of the gods, or, again, mimic its activity though religious ceremonies. It is the task of the true philosopher to decipher, by means of the allegorical method, these mysterious symbols that allude to nature. Their meaning, however, must not be revealed to the ignorant masses.

The production of sensible things constitutes Nature's occultation. The domain of Nature is therefore considerably reduced in extent, compared to what it had been in Stoicism. For the Stoics, Nature was identical with God, both as the original seed of all things and as the deployment of this seed. Nature was thus identical to the whole of reality, indissolubly rational and corporeal. For the Neoplatonists, by contrast, Nature is henceforth only the lower part of reality, an incorporeal and invisible power enveloped in corporeal and visible forms.[11] It certainly seems that Porphyry called Nature the totality of powers linked in one way or another to a body—the World Soul, the divine souls of the stars, the souls of demons, human beings, animals, plants, and then the mineral world—whereas Proclus reserved the word for souls lower than the rational soul. A shrinkage of the domain of physics corresponded to this shrinkage of the domain of

Nature. For the Stoics, physics is theology: it has as its object the divine, that is, the universal Reason of the All, and the particular rational principles present within the All, and it uses a single method. For Porphyry, there is a radical difference between the scope of higher theology, the domain of the Ideas or substances separated from bodies, and physical theology, the domain of the forces that animate bodies. This physical theology, however, can be said to be resolutely animist in the proper sense of the term, since here the causes that bring about natural phenomena are the souls of gods, demons, animals, or plants.

This is why we must not confuse the Stoics' allegorical method with that of Porphyry. The Stoics' method consists in demythologizing what they called mythical theology, or the fabulous narrations concerning the gods. By means of allegory, we discover that the gods are natural processes or corporeal forces, and that all mythology is nothing but an imagistic story of the history of cosmic processes, that is, of the transformations of the *pneuma*, or original fiery breath. By contrast, Porphyry reproached the Stoic philosopher Chairemon for interpreting myths as referring entirely to physical realities, and never to incorporeal and living essences.[12] Behind material reality, we discover the incorporeal force or divinity incarnate in a given reality, be it an element or a star. For the Stoics, physical phenomena unfold in a way that is rigorously determined; we cannot change anything about it, but merely consent to it. If, however, with Porphyry, we glimpse souls and occult forces behind sensible phenomena, we may be tempted to conjure them and influence them by means of magic.[13]

Let me add that for Porphyry, Nature wraps herself in corporeal forms—this is precisely what makes her visible to sensible eyes and invisible to the eyes of the soul—and that, in addition, the mythical images that allow us to speak of her also seem to manifest her, while in fact they hide her true essence. It is only by allegorical exegesis, which reveals myth's hidden meanings, that Nature's incorporeal essence can be discovered.

Porphyry thought he could justify Plato's *Timaeus* by showing that Nature must be discussed only in a mythical way. In fact, however, he conceives of myth differently from Plato. For the latter, the *Timaeus* myth is the poetic invention of a philosopher, who imitates the creation of the divine Artisan. For Porphyry, myth is a traditional narrative that tells the story of the gods, and in which we can discover allusions to the divine, invisible, and incorporeal forces that animate Nature. As I shall have occasion to repeat, this supposed apology of Plato is in fact a song of praise for the "Genius of paganism."

6

Calypso, or
"Imagination with the Flowing Veil"

The Neoplatonic movement gave a new meaning to Heraclitus' aphorism. "Nature loves to hide" became "Nature loves to wrap herself up." She hides by wrapping herself up, however, not because of her transcendence but, on the contrary, because of her weakness and inferiority. Nature corresponds to the set of incorporeal powers that animate the sensible world. To be sure, they are divinities or demons, yet they need to wrap themselves in visible forms. This, moreover, as Porphyry remarks, is why the inferior divinities that correspond to invisible powers, animating the vast domain of Nature, need to be represented by statues.[1] They want to preserve their mystery, and to be known and to make their presence felt only in the traditional sculpted forms that they themselves have chosen. Consequently, Nature, since she is a power of inferior rank, is condemned to wrap herself in corporeal forms. Conversely, the human soul can perceive only the envelope of this inferior power, that is, on the one hand, her corporeal and sensible appearance, and on the other, her traditional mythic figure, and it can discover her nature only by discovering, through allegorical exegesis, the meaning of that mythical figure and then recognizing it as an incorporeal power. As I shall have occasion to repeat, however, this revelation is reserved for true philosophers, who alone have the right to see Nature unveiled.

This envelope or veil of Nature is a movement descending toward a corporality that is more and more material. It must be understood from the viewpoint of the place of the World Soul and of individual souls within the Neoplatonic view of the whole of reality. Originally, the World Soul and individual souls belong to the domain of Ideas; they are linked to the Idea of Life. The Ideas are inside the divine Mind and are themselves particular Minds. These Form-Minds exist inside one another; they think themselves and they think the Mind.[2] Neither Neoplatonists in general nor Porphyry himself ever explained in a perfectly clear way why the World Soul and individual souls needed to wrap themselves in bodies. Let us say that owing to the diminution of their intellectual activity, they can no longer produce Form-Minds but are reduced to generating sensible and material forms. In any case, we can say that this tendency toward envelopment is linked to the progressive degradation that characterizes the movement of the procession of beings from the One. In Plotinus, for instance, this degradation is already sketched at the level of what comes immediately after the Supreme Principle, or the One. From the presence of the One there emanates a possibility of existence, or a kind of intelligible matter, which, when it turns back toward the One, becomes the Mind. As it constitutes itself, the Mind commits an act of audacity; it is a conquest of its own being, but also a weakening compared to its original unity. Similarly, the World Soul and individual souls wished to belong to themselves, and to conquer their autonomy. They have become distinct from the Mind, distancing themselves from it, in order to project upon matter the images or reflections of themselves in which bodies consist.

NATURE'S ENVELOPMENTS AND THE IMAGINATION

According to Porphyry, the soul will therefore don a body that corresponds to its psychic dispositions or level of intellectuality.[3] It begins by adding to itself an initial body made up of ether, the most subtle material element. Porphyry also speaks of a "pneumatic" body, that is, one made of *pneuma,* or breath.[4] This initial body corresponds to the first level of the soul's degradation as compared to pure spirituality.[5] The imagination *(phantasia)* is a kind of mirror in which the soul can see its own image, and that of the eternal Forms which it previously contemplated intellectually.[6] The imagination also implies along with itself the birth of space, volume, distance, and the externality of parts with regard to one another, and hence of the soul's envelopment.[7]

Clad in this first body, the soul continues to descend, that is, to add additional envelopes, drawn from astral matter, to its imaginative and luminous body, following the same rhythm as the abasement of its intellectual faculties and its descent through the planets. These various envelopes will become more and more coarse, until they reach the visible, earthly body.

The normal or original life of the soul was incorporeal and spiritual. As the soul dons these various envelopes, however, the purity of its intellectual activity diminishes. It needs images. This, in Porphyry's view, is why these successive envelopments donned by the soul in the course of its descent through the spheres amount to so many deaths:

> When it abandons its perfect incorporeality, it puts on its body of mud not all at once but gradually, becoming imperceptibly poorer, and getting farther and farther away from its simple and absolute purity; it becomes swollen as it receives successive additions to its astral body. Indeed, in each of the spheres situated beneath the sphere of the heavens, it puts on an ethereal envelope, and these envelopes prepare it progressively for its union with this garment of clay, and thus, dying as many deaths as the spheres it traverses, it reaches this state that, on earth, is called life.[8]

By means of an unexpected detour, we encounter here again the ancient meaning of *kruptesthai* (to hide oneself) from Heraclitus' aphorism: to be enveloped or covered up is to die.⁹ Once more, the veil of Nature becomes the veil of death.

Olympiodorus (sixth century CE) writes: "In the order of nature, the soul's first tunic is the imagination. This is why Odysseus needed the plant called *molu,* and therefore Hermes, as well as right reason, to escape Calypso, who was imagination, and who, like a cloud, was an obstacle to the sun of Reason. For imagination is a veil [*kalumma*]: this is why someone has spoken of 'imagination of the flowing veil.'"¹⁰ Calypso—etymologically "she who hides" or "she who veils"—as a figure of death thus becomes a figure of the imagination, and therefore, finally, for the Neoplatonists, a figure of Nature. She is the imagination because imagination is an envelope or a veil. We may note in passing that this text gives us an example of allegorical exegesis applied to physics: Odysseus, as Calypso's prisoner, is the soul wrapped up in the subtle body of the imagination. He needs Hermes, symbolized by the plant *molu*—that is, reason—in order to be delivered.¹¹

In the exposition he devotes to Nature, which loves to wrap itself up, Porphyry situates himself on the level of the fallen soul. The human soul, when it falls to this level, cannot know directly and intuitively either the supreme Divinity—which it can know only by negations or comparisons, which are precisely imaginative—or Nature, because the soul cannot grasp this incorporeal reality without taking a detour through myth: "Nature has concealed the knowledge of her being from mankind's coarse senses by hiding beneath the vestments and envelopes of things; likewise, she has wished that sages should discuss her mysteries only under the veil of mythic narratives."¹² As Robert Klein has shown, this doctrine of the imagination as the soul's body was to have a tremendous influence at the beginning of the Renaissance, through the intermediary of Synesius' *Treatise on Dreams,* particularly on Marsilio Ficino and Giordano Bruno.¹³

NATURE'S MODESTY

The exegesis of myths must remain reserved for an elite, like the mysteries. In this regard, Porphyry tells of what happened to the philosopher Numenius, who allegedly unveiled the mysteries of Eleusis by interpreting them rationally.[14] In a dream he saw the goddesses of Eleusis, Demeter and Kore, or in Latin, Ceres and Proserpina, prostituting themselves, dressed like courtesans, in front of the open door of a house of ill repute. When, in his dream, he asked them the reason for this shameful activity, he heard them reply that because of him, they had been torn violently from the sanctuary of their modesty and delivered over without distinction to all passers-by. This story quite certainly means that in the eyes of the philosophers, the mysteries of Eleusis contained secret teachings on Nature.[15] Thus, only the wise can know the incorporeal forces at work within Nature, and perhaps also know how to master them; yet they must let the masses be content with the literal meaning of myths. The profane believe that statues are visible gods, while the sage knows that they symbolize invisible divine powers.

In his glosses on Macrobius' commentary on *Scipio's Dream*, William of Conches, a Christian philosopher of the twelfth century, thought that Numenius' exegesis was purely physical: the Eleusinian divinities Ceres and Proserpina were merely the earth and the moon, and therefore were no longer goddesses.[16] In fact, Porphyry does not tell us what Numenius' interpretation was, but we can suppose that he considered the Eleusinian divinities to be incorporeal powers rather than material realities.

More interesting is the use of the Numenius story made by an anonymous author of the Middle Ages, from the end of the twelfth or the beginning of the thirteenth century, for it brings us back to the Heraclitean theme of Nature who loves to hide. He tells of the dream of a poet who, he says, had dared to enter the secret chamber of Nature and reveal it to the public. He was walking in a forest, terrorized by the howls of wild beasts, when he saw an isolated house, in which he glimpsed the silhouette of a naked girl, whom he asked for shelter. But the girl answered: "Get away from me, and stop attacking my modesty. Why do you treat me like a whore?" The poet then woke up, having learned that one cannot expose everything to everyone, and that what Nature orders us to hide must be revealed only to a tiny number of people of value.[17] This poem offers a good example of the success still enjoyed in the Middle Ages by Porphyry-Macrobius' theory on Nature's envelopment in forms that hide her. One can speak of Nature only while veiling her, that is, only in mythical form, and the sage will not unveil the meaning of myth to the profane, nor will he tear Nature's clothing and forms away from her. The profane will see only the corporeal and sensible forms of beings, but the sage, for his part, will know, by interpreting the myths, that these forms are the envelopment and manifestation of divine and incorporeal powers, which powers he can see in their nudity, that is, in their state of incorporeality.

Numenius' dream and that of the anonymous poet allow us to glimpse, moreover, a dimension, which we may call psychological, of the tradition we are studying: the idea of a Nature that hides evokes the image of a feminine figure that could be unveiled. This will appear even more clearly when we come to study the metaphor of the veil of Isis.[18]

THE NUDE AND THE VESTMENT

Everyone knows the painting titled *Luncheon on the Grass* [*Le déjeuner sur l'herbe*] (1863), by Édouard Manet (Fig 3). The scene takes place on a riverbank. Two men, whose outfits seem to indicate that they are painters, chat beside a woman who is nude because she has just been bathing, while another woman is still in the water.

The presence of this undressed woman gives the painting a touch of sensuality. To our modern sensibility, nudity corresponds to an exaltation of the body and of carnal presence. If one of our contemporaries were suddenly shown the painting by Titian that is known by the title *Sacred and Profane Love* (1515, Fig. 4) and were asked what the naked woman and the richly dressed woman in this painting signify, respectively, he would certainly say that the richly dressed woman represents Sacred Love. Yet Erwin Panofsky and Edgar Wind have brilliantly shown that the contrary is true.[19] For the painters of the Renaissance, who knew Neoplatonic doctrines thanks to Marsilio Ficino, clothing symbolized the body, whereas nudity symbolized the incorporeal power that is separate from the body and therefore from its clothing. In the Venus who rises naked from the sea in the center of Botticelli's painting *The Birth of Venus,* we can recognize, in conformity with the distinction made by Plato and Plotinus, Celestial Aphrodite, who is detached from the body, and in the fully dressed Venus seen in the center of the same artist's *Spring,* we recognize Vulgar Aphrodite, who corresponds ultimately to Nature wrapped up in sensible forms.[20]

There is a certain analogy of subject matter between Manet's *Luncheon on the Grass* and Titian's *Open-Air Concert* (Fig. 5, previously attributed to Giorgione), which also depicts two naked women, together with musicians. Titian's nude women are nymphs, and they are naked because the artist wants to underline the fact that they are incorporeal, divine powers, superior to the men who surround them. In the fifteenth century, Nature was represented as a naked woman in order to symbolize her simplicity and her transcendent character, but also perhaps to suggest that Nature unveils itself to the person who contemplates it.[21]

NATURAL AND IMAGINATIVE PROCESSES

By establishing an intimate link between the imagination and the lower psychic powers, and therefore Nature, Porphyry was led to believe that the physiological process of imagination is the model that enables us to think of the production of the sensible world by its creator, the Demiurge. Porphyry affirms this explicitly when he tries to demonstrate that the Demiurge creates the world by means of the simple fact of existing. The imagination produces what is visible by simple inner vision, without instruments or mechanical labor. This, says Porphyry, is why we need not be surprised that something incorporeal, and not spatial, should be the cause of this visible universe, for in human beings, imagination produces effects within bodies immediately and by itself: "When a person imagines some indecent act, he is ashamed and blushes. When he conceives the idea of danger, he is seized by terror and turns green. These emotions take place within the body, but their cause is inner vision, which uses neither pulleys nor levers but acts by its mere presence."22

We might say that in a sense, Porphyry here opposes a type of action of a magical kind, "mere presence," to a type of action of a mechanical kind, "pulleys and levers." Plotinus had already established the same opposition to define nature's mode of action: "We must set aside any notion of using levers when speaking of nature's mode of production. What thrusting or levers could be capable of producing variegated colors and figures?"23 Porphyry also used the example of the activity of those powers, inferior to Nature, known as demons, who reproduce the forms of what they imagine on the envelope of vaporous air that is joined to them or available to them.24 They can also produce hallucinations.

These ideas on the role of the imagination had considerable repercussions in the Renaissance and the Romantic period under the influence of the tradition of "natural magic."25 To be brief, throughout this tradition, whether in Montaigne, Paracelsus, Giordano Bruno, Boehme, or German Romantics such as Novalis and Baader, the imagination has a kind of magical power, which it exercises by the mere presence of an image, and which is opposed to mechanical laws.[26] The images it produces have a quasi existence and tend toward existence, whether they are produced by the human imagination or by the imagination of the creator. To imagine is already, in some way, to make things real.

Throughout this tradition, from the Middle Ages down to the Romantic period, it was granted that there is an invisible force in thought and imagination, capable of producing visible effects. As Roger Bacon said in the thirteenth century, following Avicenna, "Nature obeys the thoughts of the soul."[27] I will cite only one example—there are many others[28]—of the survival of these representations in the Romantic period: that of Goethe, in his novel *Elective Affinities,* when he describes a double adultery. In the arms of his wife, Charlotte, Eduard thinks of Odile; in the arms of her husband, Eduard, Charlotte thinks of the captain; and the child born from this union resembles the two absent people.[29]

In Porphyry, the imagination, as the soul's body, as well as the mythic knowledge that is its result, and also the theurgic practices prescribed by the *Chaldaean Oracles,* were intended to deliver this astral body from the increasingly impure envelopes that had been added onto it, which were the manifestation of the soul's abasement and inferiority. For the Neoplatonists, nature, closely linked to the imagination, is therefore the scene of a vast phantasmagoria that seduces and fascinates souls. It is the magic of nature, and the spell cast by the variety of forms and by love, which these forms provoke.[30] In modern times, by contrast, the imagination gradually lost its situation of inferiority, finally to become, especially since Boehme, a creative power that has its origin in God himself.[31]

The intimate link Porphyry established between Nature, myth, and imagination thus opened the way in Western thought for a vast field of reflections, which I will continue to explore in the course of this investigation.

7

The Genius of Paganism

After telling the story of Numenius, who dreamed that he saw the divinities of Eleusis prostituting themselves because he had interpreted the rituals of their mysteries philosophically, Macrobius continues his citation of Porphyry as follows: "This shows to what extent the divinities have always preferred to be known and honored in conformity with the myths that the ancients have told for the people, attributing images and statues to them (whereas they are absolutely alien to such forms), and ages (whereas they are unaware of increase and diminution), and divine clothing and adornments (whereas they have no bodies)."[1]

NATURE, THE GODS, AND TRADITIONAL CULTS

A new element appears in this account: the gods that correspond to the various powers of nature absolutely insist on being honored according to the traditional cult as practiced in the city. This means, on the one hand, that philosophers must speak of nature while conserving the names of the gods traditionally linked to the elements and the powers of nature and, on the other, that to renounce traditional cults, as the Christians do, means prohibiting oneself from knowing Nature. Traditional religion is physics in images, presented to the people in the myths and statues of the gods. It is a mythical physics, revealed by the gods at the origin of mankind, whose meaning only the wise understand, through allegorical interpretation.

At first glance, such an idea may appear completely absurd. What do the religious rites of Hellenism have to do with the knowledge of Nature? How can we conceive that it is the same Nature that wraps herself simultaneously in living forms, the statues of gods, and religious rituals? Upon reflection, however, since the various religions had given the gods human, animal, or vegetal forms, an ancient philosopher could legitimately wonder whether it was not the same incorporeal power that manifests itself in the sensible forms of nature and in statues of the gods. Moreover, modern naturalists have insisted on the ostentatious character of living forms, and on the existence of rites and ceremonies in the animal kingdom. A modern philosopher could thus admit that there is a relation between some kinds of behavior among the beings of nature and religious rites. One could also imagine a continuity between human rites and the rites of nature. All that might be thought conventional, artificial, and arbitrary—rites, myths, fiction, art, poetry, religion—could we not imagine it to be already pre-inscribed in the process of the genesis of natural living forms and their behavior? Thus, human creative imagination would prolong nature's power to create forms.

Let us return, however, to Porphyry. By citing Heraclitus' aphorism "Nature loves to hide," he wanted not only to show that discourse on Nature must be mythical but also to justify—against Christianity, which was beginning to gather strength—traditional polytheism and the whole of ancient civilization, with its temples, statues, tragedies, and poems.

If the incorporeal and divine forces that constitute Nature hide beneath visible forms, they are also hidden in the ceremonies of traditional cults and the mysteries. Porphyry seems, moreover, to have linked the mysterious character of religious ceremonies to the dissimulation proper to demons. Nature hides because the divine and demonic souls that constitute it need corporeality and must therefore first be known in a mythical way. The demons themselves love to hide, and the symbolism of religious ceremonies corresponds to this characteristic of the demons:

> The demons that preside over Nature reveal their gifts to us, waking or sleeping, by means of certain fictive apparitions, by giving obscure oracles, signifying one thing by means of another, causing that which has no form to appear, thanks to similitudes endowed with forms, and other things by means of figures that correspond to them. These procedures fill the sacred ceremonies and mystic dramas in the places of initiation, dramas which act, precisely, on the initiates' soul, by that very aspect of them which is secret and unknowable.[2]

In Iamblichus, the demons appear as the jealous guardians of the secrets of Nature—secrets that are hidden in unspeakable mysteries such as those of Isis or of Abydos, for, he says, the organization of the universe is primordially contained in these mysteries: "That which conserves the universe (I mean the fact that ineffable things remain always hidden and that the ineffable essence of the gods can never fail to have a share of the contrary lot), the terrestrial demons cannot bear to hear that it could happen otherwise or be divulged."[3]

"That which conserves the universe" thus means that the secret of Nature must not be unveiled. That is why, in magic, the demons can be terrorized and made to obey by uttering threats, for instance, threatening to reveal the mysteries of Isis or to unveil the secret of Abydos.[4]

AN APOLOGY FOR PAGANISM AND TOLERANCE:
THEMISTIUS AND SYMMACHUS

Heraclitus' aphorism was thus enlisted in the service of an apology for paganism. This apology was, moreover, ambiguous: on the one hand, it aimed to defend the cult of the gods in its ancestral form, yet on the other hand, it saw in this occultation of the gods in living forms, in myths and rites, a ruse of Nature, avid to flatter mankind's senses beneath beautiful sensible forms and lovely mythical stories. Like Nature itself, the cult of the gods is no doubt part of the universal order, yet in the philosopher's view it has an inferior rank. Even as he submits to the customs of the city, the philosopher prefers to be priest of the supreme God, to whom no statues are raised and about whom no myths are told.[5]

A half-century after Porphyry, the Platonic philosopher and pagan Themistius also cited Heraclitus' aphorism in order to give an apology for paganism. Remarkably, he did so in a speech delivered at Constantinople on January 1, 364, on the occasion of the consulate of an emperor, Jovian, who was a Christian.[6] He therefore takes advantage of the opportunity to make a plea in favor of religious tolerance. He skillfully praises the emperor for respecting the law of God, which confers upon the soul of each individual the privilege of choosing his own path to piety.[7] There is a single goal, says Themistius, but the paths for reaching it are different. Did not Homer say, "Each one sacrificed to a different god"?[8] He continues: "Nature, according to Heraclitus, loves to hide, and, prior to Nature, the Demiurge, Nature's creator, whom we revere and admire above all things, because the knowledge we can have of him is not easy or obvious, nor is it thrown in front of us: we cannot achieve it without difficulty or with one hand."[9]

Here, Themistius brings together two ancient authorities: Heraclitus and Plato. The latter had said that to discover the author and father of the universe is a great feat, and when one has discovered him, it is impossible to divulge him to everyone.[10] Not only do Nature and its inferior gods hide, but the Demiurge himself, who has produced them, does so as well. It is therefore not possible to achieve certainty in the area of religion. All human efforts to honor the divinity have an equal value. This apologetic theme was to be used a few years later, in 384, in the Latin West, when the pagan prefect Symmachus protested against the emperor's decision to have the Altar of Victory removed from the hall of the Roman Senate: "We contemplate the same stars, the Heavens are common to us all, and the same world surrounds us. What matters the path of wisdom by which each person seeks the truth? One cannot reach such a great mystery by a single path."[11] This admirable text, which should be inscribed in letters of gold on churches, synagogues, mosques, and temples at this beginning of the third millennium, which has opened under the somber banner of religious quarrels, was probably also inspired by the memory of Heraclitus' aphorism.

The transcendent divinity wants precisely this variety of religious forms and paths of wisdom. For Themistius, as for Plotinus, it is the multiplicity of particular gods that allows us to glimpse the transcendence of the supreme God.[12] There is thus a certain difference between the apologetics of Themistius and that of Porphyry. For the latter, Nature and its inferior divinities want to be honored in the traditional forms of the myths and ceremonies of Greek and Roman religion, which they have chosen and prescribed to the ancient sages. By contrast, according to Themistius, the superior and inferior divinities do not prefer one path to another, but they agree to be honored by diverse paths.

"TELESTICS": THE EMPEROR JULIAN

Two years previously, in 362, the emperor Julian had also cited Heraclitus' aphorism, but in a wholly different spirit: "For Nature loves to hide, and does not tolerate that the secret of the essence of the gods should be flung in naked terms into impure ears."[13] We see clearly that Heraclitus' aphorism is placed here in the service of pagan apologetics. The end of the phrase I have just cited sheds useful light on the meaning assumed for the emperor by the formula "Nature loves to hide." For Julian, it means that the gods must be spoken of in a mysterious, enigmatic, and symbolic way, so that what the gods really are, their essence, may not be expressed "in naked terms." These naked terms cannot be thrown into impure ears; only the person who has been purified has the right to discover, through allegorical exegesis, the profound meaning of the myths and rites. Here we find once again the lesson of Numenius' dream as told by Porphyry.

Like Porphyry, Julian wonders to which branch of philosophy the narration of myths is appropriate. Unlike Porphyry, however, he clearly affirms that neither physics nor logic nor mathematics, which are as it were the "scientific" parts of philosophy, allows the use of myths. Only ethics and the telestic and mysterial part of theology admit of fabulous narrations, each in its own way.[14]

What does Julian mean when he speaks of the telestic and mysterial part of philosophy? The two adjectives are quite probably synonyms, for, a bit further on in his discourse, while invoking the patronage of Iamblichus, Julian links "telestics" to Orpheus, "who instituted the most sacred initiations," that is, the mysteries of Eleusis.[15] In these mysteries, there were *legomena*, or revelations, and *drōmena*, or rites, ceremonies, and dramatic productions. In fact, the word "telestics" has an imprecise meaning, since in his discourse *On King Helios*, Julian uses this word with regard to a theory on the sun's place in the cosmos, a theory he attributes to the *Chaldaean Oracles*, while adding, "Those who affirm these theories say that they have received them from gods or demons," and therefore by divine revelation.[16] The word can also designate rites or ceremonies, which are either those of traditional religion—this appears clearly in Hierocles of Alexandria, who has undergone the influence of Iamblichus and considers that telestics includes the totality of rites related to local divinities—or else those of Orphic mysteries and poems, or, again, of the *Chaldaean Oracles*.[17] But if we read the continuation of Julian's text, we see that he is speaking of "the ineffable and unknown nature of 'characters,'"[18] that is, of magical signs and symbols, which, because of the affinity they have with the gods, "care for souls and bodies and cause the gods to come";[19] in other words, he is speaking of the appearance of the gods. This means that telestics, as Pierre Boyancé has shown, is closely connected with the utilization of signs and symbols: drawings, letters, and formulas, which were placed outside or inside statues of the gods and which ensured the presence of the gods in these statues.[20] This is why, in Proclus, telestics are closely connected with the art of animating statues.[21]

These concepts were traditional in Platonism. It was considered that the mysteries of Eleusis and, more generally, the ceremonies of the cult and the form of the statues, as well as the decorations and symbols on these statues, had been chosen by sages, in the most distant antiquity, with regard to the cosmos.[22] This Platonic idea first appears in Varro, who affirms that the ancient sages chose the form of the statues of the gods and their attributes so that, when they are contemplated with the eyes of the body, we can see the World Soul and its parts, which are the genuine gods. Then at a later stage, for instance in Plotinus, we find the idea that the sages of yesteryear, wishing to enjoy the presence of the gods, saw, when they contemplated the nature of the All, that the Soul could be present everywhere, and that it was easy for all things to receive it, as long as they fashioned some object which, by means of sympathy, was capable of receiving a part thereof. Here again, the particular gods appear as emanations of the Soul of the All, and statues of the gods ensure the gods' presence, insofar as something in these statues is in sympathy with the Soul of the All.[23] In the text by Porphyry, where mention is made of the occultation of nature according to Heraclitus, the gods and the World Soul are just as closely linked, and traditional religion is physics in images.

These practices and ancestral rites were intended, in the Neoplato-

nists' view, to purify the vehicle of the soul, that is, its various envelopes or bodies, in order to enable the soul's rise toward the gods and
toward God.[24] Julian is careful not to give a clear definition of this
"telestic and mystical theology," but we may suppose that he understands by this expression a procedure that pertains both to the soul
and to the body: the former would consist in an edifying exegesis of
myths and the latter in the practice of traditional as well as theurgic
rites. Thus, on the one hand, the purification of the soul's astral body
and, on the other, the soul's ascent toward the supreme principle
would be ensured. We might think that Julian alludes to this last
point when he writes that what is paradoxical and monstrous in
myths "does not leave us in peace until, under the guidance of the
gods, light appears to initiate, or rather to perfect, our intellect and
also that within us which is superior to the intellect: that little share
of the One-Good which possesses the all undividedly, that pleroma
of the soul which, thanks to the presence of the One-Good—superior, separate from all matter and transcendent—is gathered together
in Him."[25] It certainly seems as though Julian is here thinking of a divine illumination that would lead to a mystical union with the supreme principle.

Telestic theology, according to the late Neoplatonists, therefore includes, first of all, a mythical discourse and religious rites, which are
accessible to the profane and place them in relation, in an inexplicable way, with the divine presence, at least of the lower divinities.[26] For
the philosopher, however, the practice of these formulas and actions,
illuminated by exegesis, enables him to reach the higher divinities.

Porphyry, for his part, thought that only philosophy, that is, spiritual effort, allows us to attain union with the transcendent divine,
without myths or rituals. Julian, following Iamblichus, whose doctrine he explicitly accepts, considers that the human soul is sunk
too deeply in matter to be able to achieve this supreme goal by its
own strength. It needs divine assistance, that is, the revelation of

myths, together with the rites and sacrifices prescribed by the gods. In Iamblichus and his disciples, therefore, as in Julian and later in Proclus, we witness a promotion of myth. It is no longer relegated, as in Porphyry, to the lower part of theology, but it can also be found in its higher part, in order to reach the summits of initiation.[27]

The Neoplatonists wanted to protect traditional religion against the invasion of the Christian religion, for they sincerely believed that the cult of the gods was linked to the action of the World Soul, which preserved the universe. Thus, they came to make Heraclitus' aphorism the slogan for a pagan reaction. Nietzsche said that Christianity was a Platonism for the people.[28] For the Neoplatonists, pagan myths and rituals were also a Platonism for the people, or, even more precisely, a hidden physics.

8

The "Gods of Greece"

Pagan Myths in a Christian World

One might say that the Neoplatonists ensured the survival of paganism in the Christian world for centuries, not as a religion but as a poetic and sacred language that enabled this world to talk about nature. It will perhaps be argued that this language is only a language and that, fundamentally, the gods were no longer anything but metaphors. Yet a metaphor is never innocent. It is the vehicle of an entire set of images, feelings, and inner dispositions, which have an unconscious influence on consciousness.

THE MIDDLE AGES

Thanks to the broad diffusion of Macrobius' commentary on Scipio's dream, which I have discussed in preceding chapters, and which contains the translation of a passage from Porphyry's commentary on Plato's *Republic,* the Porphyrian theme of the link between nature, myth, and, ultimately, poetry, left its mark on Western thought.[1] It is quite astonishing that throughout centuries of Christianity, pagan mythology, to a very large extent, supplied subjects and themes for painting, sculpture, theater, poetry, opera, and even philosophy. I shall not try to rewrite here the remarkable work by Jean Seznec, *The Survival of the Pagan Gods,* but will limit myself to pointing out the influence of the "Porphyrian" passage from Macrobius' commentary.[2] This text had a great deal of success in the Middle Ages, especially in what has been called the twelfth-century Renaissance, which manifested itself particularly in the Platonists of the school of Chartres. These philosophers returned to the scholastic explanation of ancient authors: they interpreted Plato's *Timaeus,* Macrobius' commentary on Scipio's dream, and again Boethius' *Consolation of Philosophy.* Following Macrobius, they accepted that in order to speak of nature, we must use myths, that is, the traditional myths of paganism. They often designate these myths by the term *integumenta* (clothing) or *involucra* (envelopes or veils).[3] The recollection of Macrobius appears, for instance, in the following passage from a commentary on Martianus Capella written toward the middle of the twelfth century by Bernard Silvester: "As Macrobius testifies, mythic envelopment [*integumentum*] is not accepted everywhere in philosophical expositions. Only when the topic of discussion is the soul or the powers that are in the ether and the air does it find its place."[4]

Pagan myths were thus used to describe physical phenomena. Following Plato,[5] William of Conches, a philosopher of the school of Chartres, considered that the story of Phaëthon, the son of the Sun who, since he did not know how to drive his father's chariot, set everything on earth afire and died when struck by his father's lightning, signifies astrological and meteorological phenomena: excessive heat, which destroys everything on earth, finally exhausts itself and brings back a temperate climate.[6] While we are on the subject of William of Conches, I should also mention his interpretation of the myth of Semele, who asked Jupiter to reveal himself to her in all his glorious splendor. Jupiter then appeared with his lightning, and Semele died in the flames, while the child Bacchus (the god of wine), whom she carried within her, was saved. This means that in summer, lightning and thunder fall upon the earth, through the intermediary of the air, and dry everything up, yet they do not prevent vines from growing and producing wine.[7] Obviously, such exegesis can scarcely cause the knowledge of nature to progress a great deal. Yet two observations suggest themselves: on the one hand, pagan mythology continued to be mentioned in Christian writings, and on the other hand, it was interpreted in a physical way, as a teaching that refers to nature.

In addition, Bernard Silvester reserves the word *integumentum* to designate myths intended, as in Plato's *Timaeus*, to explain a natural phenomenon (they reveal a true meaning hidden beneath a fabulous story), as opposed to *allēgoria*, which is proper to the explication of biblical texts (it reveals a new meaning in a veridical historical narration). We find this distinction again in Dante.[8] It corresponds to an opposition between the two books written by God, the Bible and Nature, both of which can be deciphered only if one uses an allegorical exegesis, which, in the case of the Bible, refers to sacred texts and, in the case of Nature, to myths.[9] This Nature, we must recall, was conceived in the Middle Ages as a power subordinate to God but enjoying a certain autonomy.

It is interesting to note that William of Conches had a good understanding of the theory of the double truth implied by the Porphyrian conception of myth. He wrote: "Only the wise must know the secrets of the gods, by means of the exegesis of myths. As far as the profane and the foolish are concerned, they must have no knowledge thereof, for if a profane person [*rusticus*] knew that Ceres is none other than the earth's spiritual power to make harvests grow and to multiply them, and that Bacchus is none other than the earth's natural power to make vines grow, such persons would not be dissuaded from shameful actions for fear of Bacchus or Ceres, whom they think are gods."[10]

THE RENAISSANCE

We also encounter the Porphyrian theory of myth in the Renaissance, for instance, in Politian, who "praised the transmission of philosophical knowledge in the cryptic form of fables and enigmas

. . . so that in this manner the religious mysteries of the Eleusinian goddesses are in no way profaned."[11] An analogous idea appears in Pico della Mirandola, who thought, moreover, that there was a hidden concordance between Christian mysteries and pagan mysteries.[12]

As in the Middle Ages, mythology was poetic physics. In the Middle Ages, however, the gods of mythology were mere names, or metaphors corresponding to material realities. In the Renaissance, by contrast, the gods were instead the names or metaphors of the incorporeal forces animating the universe, and they therefore had a quasi personality. We thus witness a kind of renewal of paganism, but of a Neoplatonic paganism, which, as I have said elsewhere, is in fact a "hierarchic monotheism," in which a single divine power diffuses itself and multiplies in hierarchized lower forms, proceeding as far as Nature—a paganism which therefore could cohabit fairly well with Christianity.[13] This Renaissance of paganism took shape in the first half of the fifteenth century near Sparta, at Mistra, where Gemisthus Pletho, like the emperor Julian, proposed an entire program of Neoplatonic paganism, which took up once again the practices of Neoplatonic theurgy and telestics in particular.[14] In the course of the fifteenth century, for instance, in Marsilio Ficino, the first uncertain steps taken by science were associated with the allegorical exegesis of ancient fables.[15] The gods were now not just poetic symbols but powers that organize the world, which itself is arranged according to a poetic order. In the poets, as Eugenio Garin has rightly remarked, poetry becomes "a hymn to the divine incarnate in nature . . . The transfiguration of the ancient gods into animating forces of the universe gives an unusual 'religious' flavor to songs and to prose."[16]

In the sixteenth century, moreover, we see the appearance of handbooks of mythology that collect moral but also physical allegorical interpretations of pagan myths and the figures of the gods, for example, *The History of the Gods* by Giraldi (1548), *Mythology* by Natale Conti (1551), and Vincenzo Cartari's *Images of the Gods* (1556). Natale

Conti, in particular, who continued to use the word *integumentum* as in the Middle Ages, considers, as Jean Seznec points out, that "since the earliest times, the thinkers of Egypt and then of Greece intentionally hid the great truths of science and philosophy beneath the veil of myths in order to shield them from profanation by the vulgar . . . [T]he task of the mythographer is to rediscover their original content."[17]

At the beginning of the seventeenth century, the idea of teachings on nature as hidden in pagan theologies remained alive and well, even in the theoretician of the new modern science, Francis Bacon, who, in his work entitled *On the Wisdom of the Ancients,* made abundant use of Natale Conti's handbook.[18] In Bacon, besides the moral explanation, we find an allegorical exegesis that makes a physical phenomenon correspond to mythical figures: the fight for sovereignty between Ouranos, Kronos, and Zeus represents the birth of the world; Eros is prime matter, Pan is nature, Proserpina the earth's creative energy, and Proteus matter in the multiplicity of its forms.

The pagan gods also continued to appear in the various arts, for instance, in the ideological program expressed in the statues of the château at Versailles that exalts the Sun King, or in the divertimenti that set mythological scenes in motion and in music, following a tradition that goes back to antiquity. From the sixteenth to the eighteenth centuries, the personification of natural phenomena in the form of gods, goddesses, nymphs, and naiads was to have a powerful influence on the feeling for nature, from Pierre de Ronsard to André Chénier, to speak only of France.

SCHILLER'S "GODS OF GREECE"

Gradually, the movement toward the mechanization of nature, inaugurated in the seventeenth century with the rise of the exact sciences, was intensified. In the perspective of this evolution of the perception of nature, at the end of the eighteenth century, in 1788, one year before the French Revolution, Schiller uttered an admirable lament on the departure of the ancient gods in a poem titled "The Gods of Greece."[19] I hope I will be forgiven for quoting a few verses, giving them a brief commentary, for it is a fundamental testimony on the transformation of the perception of nature at the very beginning of the industrial era.

The first three verses deplore the disappearance from the modern world of the myth of Nature as animated by divine forces. In antiquity "a higher nobility" was lent to Nature by the fact that feelings, and therefore a soul, were attributed to her, whereas since that time all feelings and consciousness have been taken away from her. All was then enveloped in "the magic veil of poetry":

I

> Ye of the age gone by,
> Who ruled the world—a world how lovely then!—
> And guided still the steps of happy men
> In the light leading-strings of careless joy!
> Ah, flourished then your service of delight!
> How different, oh, how different, in the day
> When thy sweet fanes with many a wreath were bright,
> O Venus Amathusia![20]

II

> Then, through a veil of dreams
> Woven by song, truth's youthful beauty glowed,
> And life's redundant and rejoicing streams
> Gave to the soulless, soul[21]—where'er they flowed
> Man gifted nature with divinity
> To lift and link her to the breast of love;

> All things betrayed to the initiate eye
> The track of gods above!

III

> Where lifeless—fixed afar,
> A flaming ball to our dull sense is given,
> Phoebus Apollo, in his golden car,
> In silent glory swept the fields of heaven!
> On yonder hill the Oread was adored,
> In yonder tree the Dryad held her home;
> And from her urn the gentle Naiad poured
> The wavelet's silver foam.[22]

The following verses (IV–XI) give an idyllic description of the pagan cult and the life of ancient man, who lived with the gods. The end of the poem laments the definitive mechanization of nature:

XII

> Art thou, fair world, no more?
> Return, thou virgin-bloom on Nature's face;
> Ah, only on the minstrel's magic shore,
> Can we the footstep of sweet fable trace!
> The meadows mourn for the old hallowing life;
> Vainly we search the earth of gods bereft;
> Where once the warm and living shapes were rife,
> Shadows alone are left!

XIII

> Cold, from the north, has gone
> Over the flowers the blast that killed their May;

And, to enrich the worship of the one,
A universe of gods must pass away!
Mourning, I search on yonder starry steeps,
But thee no more, Selene, there I see![23]
And through the woods I call, and o'er the deeps,
And—Echo answers me!

XIV

Deaf to the joys she gives—
Blind to the pomp of which she is possessed—
Unconscious of the spiritual power that lives
Around, and rules her—by our bliss unblessed—
Dull to the art that colors or creates,
Like the dead timepiece, godless nature creeps
Her plodding round, and, by the leaden weights,
The slavish motion keeps.

XV

To-morrow to receive
New life, she digs her proper grave to-day;
And icy moons with weary sameness weave
From their own light their fullness and decay.
Home to the poet's land the gods are flown,
Light use in them that later world discerns,
Which, the diviner leading-strings outgrown,
On its own axle turns.

As Willy Theiler has shown, in the last lines of stanza XV, Schiller alludes to the myth of Plato's *Statesman* (272e–274a): sometimes the world's helmsman guides the ship of the universe, at other times he abandons the rudder, and the gods of the various parts of the world also abandon the regions of the world that had been confided to their care.[24] Then the world, left to its own resources, directs itself in accordance with its own movement, and, in progressive decadence, it runs an ever greater risk of catastrophe and chaos, until the gods consent to guide it once again.

XVI

> Home! and with them are gone
> The hues they gazed on and the tones they heard;
> Life's beauty and life's melody—alone
> Broods o'er the desolate void, the lifeless word;
> Yet rescued from time's deluge, still they throng
> Unseen the Pindus[25] they were wont to cherish:
> All that which gains immortal life in song,
> To mortal life must perish!

If Nature has lost its divinity, Schiller implies, it is because of Christianity, which has allowed modern science to develop. The sun is henceforth just a fiery globe, and Nature a mere clock.

It is correct to say that Christianity contributed to the development of the mechanistic representation of Nature, and to the desacralization of Nature. As early as the fourth century, not long after Porphyry, the Christian convert Firmicus Maternus had already criticized the mythical vision of the world proposed by the pagans. Why, he asked, invent the myth of Attis, with its tears and lamentations shed over plantations and harvests? They are nothing but vain ceremonies that do not ensure a fruitful harvest. Work in the fields, as is well known to peasants, is the real explanation of nature, and it is also the true sacrifice, accomplished all throughout the year by healthy-minded people. This is the simplicity sought by the divinity, which submits to the law of the seasons to harvest the fruits of the season. Firmicus Maternus makes the sun speak: "What I am is what I appear to be, in all simplicity; I don't want you to imagine about me anything other than what I am."[26] Already for Firmicus, the sun is nothing but a fiery ball. From a Christian creationist perspective, Nature is an object fashioned by an artisan who is distinct from her and transcends her. As God's work, she is no longer divine. There is no longer a divine presence in Nature. This image could only support scientists—Schiller is thinking particularly of Newton—in their research on the fundamentally mechanical character of the phenomena of nature. After the invention of the wheelwork clock at the end of the thirteenth century, the workings of nature were conceived after the model of this measuring instrument. By 1377, Nicholas Oresme in his *Treatise on the Heavens and the World* was representing the motion of the heavens as that of a clock which, after being fashioned by God, continues to move by itself according to the laws of mechanics.[27] The metaphor was to survive for centuries, and this is why Schiller speaks of the dead beat of a pendulum with regard to nature. Schiller's poem contains, moreover, quite hostile allusions to Christianity: a horrible wind from the north, the enrichment of a single god (Jesus) with regard to all the others, a hideous skeleton appearing before a dying man's bed (stanza IX). The first version of the poem, which was even more virulent, caused a veritable scandal.[28] In addition, what Schiller deplores is not just that scientists represent the sun as a ball of fire but that human beings, in their daily lives, have lost the poetic and aesthetic perception of this reality.

I believe that this poem can be explained from the perspective of the deceptive mirage of an idealized Greece, which fascinated German authors from Winckelmann to Schiller, Hölderlin, and Goethe, and remained alive until Stefan George and Walter Otto. Fascinated by Greek art and by the immobile and silent beatitude of the statues, they believed in a world of serenity, festivals, the cult of the body, and the harmony of souls. Klaus Schneider has rightly criticized this representation in his book on the "silent gods."[29]

Schiller's poem ends on a hopeful note: the mythic poetry of nature has gone away, but poetry lives on in the ideal. In any case, Schiller was not the only one to evoke the end of the reign of the gods of Greece over the sensibility of Western man. At the beginning of the nineteenth century, Novalis, in his *Hymns to the Night,* and Hölderlin, in his "Bread and Wine," and then, at the beginning of the twentieth century, Rilke, in his *Sonnets to Orpheus* (I, 24), announced in their turn the departure of the Greek gods. "They have gone back up to the sky, those gods who made life beautiful," and our world has been plunged into darkness.[30] For Hölderlin, Christ is ultimately the last of the gods, he who announces the future return of all the others, and of that "beautiful life" in the midst of Nature which they brought to mankind. In fact, Schiller's allusion to the gods of the *Statesman,* who abandon the rudder only to take it up once again, might also imply the hope for such a return, yet the idea remains unexpressed.

In reality, Hölderlin and much later Rilke are witnesses to a completely different concept, and of a total change in perspective in the representation of the relations between mankind and nature. The link between the feeling for nature and poetic polytheism had begun to collapse, in the mid-eighteenth century, with Rousseau, for whom man could rediscover his unity with nature by dissolving into the All.[31] In the first version of his *Empedocles,* Hölderlin clearly announces the end of this poetic polytheism, the forgetting of the "names of the ancient gods," and the coming of a different approach to nature, which will consist in letting oneself be "seized by the life of the world," in Hölderlin's words, and, freed from the veil of mythology, in sensing, in a new and naive sensation, the presence of nature:

> Thus, dare! your heritage, your acquisition,
> Stories, lessons from the mouths of your fathers,

Laws and customs, names of the ancient Gods,
Forget them with hardiness to raise your eyes
like newborns, on divine nature.[32]

"To be one with all living things, to return, by a radiant self-forgetting, to the All of Nature."[33] These were the terms in which Hölderlin's *Hyperion* expressed his Rousseauist ecstasy. Ultimately, Hölderlin is also a witness to this modification of the perception of nature, which takes place in the time of Goethe and Schelling, and which I will discuss later on. At the beginning of the nineteenth century, the metaphor of the veils and the secrets of Nature never ceases to fade, until it gives way to amazement before an unveiled Nature, which, in Goethe's expression, henceforth became "mysterious in full daylight," in the nudity of her presence. For the polytheistic representation of traditional poetry there was substituted the pantheist feeling of a Nature which, as I shall have occasion to repeat, fills mankind with a sacred shudder.[34]

IV

Unveiling Nature's Secrets

9

Prometheus and Orpheus

Now that I have told the story of the reception throughout the centuries of antiquity of Heraclitus' saying "Nature loves to hide," we can return to the theme of the secrets of nature.

PHYSICS AS UNVEILING THE SECRETS OF NATURE

If one accepts that nature hides and conceals its secrets from us, then one can adopt several attitudes with regard to it. One can simply reject all research relating to nature. This was the attitude of Socrates, taken up in particular by Arcesilas during the period of the Platonic school that some historians call Skeptical. In the words of Cicero, "Socrates was the first to turn philosophy away from the things that have been hidden and wrapped up by nature itself, with which the philosophers previous to him concerned themselves, and to bring it back to the level of human life."[1] This amounted to a refusal to discuss things that, on the one hand, transcend human beings, because they are inaccessible to their investigative powers, and, on the other hand, have no importance for them, since the only thing that must interest them is the conduct of moral and political life. As would be said, for different reasons, by Seneca, Rousseau, and Nietzsche, if nature has hidden certain things, then it had good reasons to hide them.[2] If, for philosophers such as Socrates, Aristo of Chios, and the Academic Arcesilas, no research on nature is possible, this means that for them, unlike for other philosophical schools, there is no

91

"physical" part of philosophy, since physics is precisely the study of nature *(phusis)*.

One might also consider mankind capable of unveiling these secrets of nature. From this perspective, physics becomes the part of philosophy that assigns itself the task of discovering what nature wants to conceal from us. This conception of physical philosophy appears explicitly with Antiochus of Ascalon (the end of the second to the beginning of the first century BCE), a Platonist on whose doctrine Cicero reports in his *Academics.*[3] According to Antiochus, the subject of physics is "nature and secret things."

Several models of investigation were available for ancient philosophers and scientists. The choice between these models was guided by the way relations between men and nature were represented, that is, between nature and human activity; it was also oriented by the way the image of the "secrets of nature" was perceived.

If man feels nature to be an enemy, hostile and jealous, which resists him by hiding its secrets, there will then be opposition between nature and human art, based on human reason and will. Man will seek, through technology, to affirm his power, domination, and rights over nature.

If, on the contrary, people consider themselves a part of nature because art is already present in it, there will no longer be opposition between nature and art; instead, human art, especially in its aesthetic aspect, will be in a sense the prolongation of nature, and then there will no longer be any relation of dominance between nature and mankind. The occultation of nature will be perceived not as a resistance that must be conquered but as a mystery into which human beings can be gradually initiated.

JUDICIAL PROCEDURE

If one situates oneself in a relation of hostile opposition, the model of unveiling will be, one might say, judicial. When a judge is in the presence of a defendant who is hiding a secret, he must try to make him confess it. In antiquity, but also still in the contemporary world, so proud of its progress, a method for accomplishing this is foreseen by the law, or at the least by custom or national interest: torture. As early as the end of the fifth century BCE, the author of the Hippocratic treatise *On Art* was certainly thinking of this judicial model when he declared that one must do violence to Nature to make her reveal what she is hiding from us: "When Nature refuses willingly to hand over the signs [i.e., clinical symptoms], art has found the constraining means by which Nature, violated without damage, can let go of them; then when she is freed, she unveils what must be done to those who are familiar with the art."[4]

To do violence, then, but "without damage," for the doctor's first duty is to do no harm. It has been said of Francis Bacon, the founder of modern experimental science, that he "submits the natural process to juridical categories, in the same way as a civil or penal matter."[5] It is true that Bacon uses the vocabulary of violence, constraint, and even torture as he sketches the program of modern experimental science: "The secrets of nature are better revealed under the torture of experiments than when they follow their natural course."[6] Yet as we can see from the Hippocratic text, this judicial model, as well as the conception of the role of reason it implies, had already existed a millennium before Bacon. Indeed, this judicial model supposes that human reason ultimately has a discretionary power over nature, which would, moreover, be confirmed by biblical revelation, since the God of Genesis speaks these words after the creation of Adam and Eve: "Grow and multiply, and fill the earth, and dominate it. Command the fish of the sea, and the birds of the air, and all the beasts that move upon the earth."[7] This is why Bacon proclaimed at the beginning of the seventeenth century, "Let the human race recover its rights over nature, rights granted to it by divine munificence."[8] This power of reason gives man the authority to proceed in a judicial manner and interrogate nature by every means if, in some way, it refused to talk.

At the end of the eighteenth century, the same judicial metaphor is found in Kant, in the preface to the second edition of the *Critique of Pure Reason*. For him, physics began to make decisive progress from the moment when, with Francis Bacon, Galileo, Torricelli, and Stahl, it understood that it had to "oblige nature to answer its questions." With regard to nature, reason must behave "not like a student, who lets himself be told whatever the teacher wishes, but like an appointed judge, who forces witnesses to answer the questions he asks them."[9] Cuvier's celebrated formula takes up the same metaphor: "The observer listens to Nature, the experimenter submits it to interrogation and forces it to unveil itself."[10] And even when Bacon says that "nature can be commanded only by obeying it," thus appearing to urge scientists to submit to nature, one cannot help thinking, with Eugenio Garin, evoking the comedies of Plautus, that for Bacon, "man is a tricky servant who studies his master's habits in order to be able to do whatever he wants with him."[11]

Here violence becomes ruse, and the Greek word that denotes ruse is precisely *mēkhanē*. For the Greeks, mechanics first appeared as a technique for tricking nature, particularly by producing movements that appear to be contrary to nature, and by obliging nature to do what it cannot do by itself, by means of artificial and fabricated instruments, or "machines"—scales, winches, levers, pulleys, wedges, screws, gears—which can serve, for instance, for the construction of war machines or automata.

After experimentation and mechanics, the third form of violence is magic. Like mechanics, magic aims to produce in nature movements that do not seem natural, and, at least in its ancient form, it appears as a technique of constraint exerted over the invisible powers, gods or demons, that preside over the phenomena of nature.

THE PHYSICS OF CONTEMPLATION:
PROMETHEUS AND ORPHEUS

In opposition to this physics which, utilizing various techniques, artificially modifies the perception of things, there is room for a physics that limits itself to what we might call naive perception, which uses only reasoning, imagination, and artistic discourse or activity to contemplate nature. It was above all this philosophical physics—that of Plato's *Timaeus,* of Aristotle, of the Epicureans and the Stoics, but also that of astronomers such as Ptolemy—which, later on, in modern times and in the Romantic period, was to become the philosophy of nature. Poetry also tried to revive the genesis of the world. Finally, painting too appeared as a means of access to the enigmas of nature.

From this perspective, we could speak with Robert Lenoble of a "physics of contemplation," which would consist of disinterested research, as opposed to a "physics of utilization," which, by technical procedures, aims to tear Nature's secrets away from her, for utilitarian ends.[12]

I shall place the first attitude—the one that wishes to discover the secrets of nature, or the secrets of God, by means of tricks and violence—under the patronage of Prometheus, son of the Titan Iapetos, who, according to Hesiod, stole the secret of fire from the gods in order to improve the life of mankind, and who, according to Aeschylus and Plato, brought man the benefits of technology and civilization.[13] In Francis Bacon, at the dawn of modern science, Prometheus was to appear as the founder of experimental science.[14] Promethean man demands the right of domination over nature, and in the Christian era, the story of Genesis, as we have seen, confirmed him in his certainty of having rights over nature. Whereas Zeus wished to reserve the secret of fire and of the forces of nature for himself, and Prometheus wanted to tear it away from him, the biblical God makes man the "master and possessor of nature."[15] From this perspective, in the fine phrase of Robert Lenoble, "in the seventeenth century, Prometheus becomes God's lieutenant."[16]

I dedicate the other attitude toward nature to Orpheus, like Pierre de Ronsard, who wrote:

> Filled with divine fire that has heated my heart,
> I wish, more than ever, following in Orpheus' steps,
> To discover the secrets of Nature and the Heavens.[17]

When he links Orpheus to the discovery of the secrets of nature, Ronsard was no doubt thinking of the theogonic poems placed under the patronage of Orpheus, which recount the genealogy of the gods and the world, and hence the birth *(phusis)* of things. He may also have wished to allude to the seductive power which, according to legend, singing and playing the lyre give Orpheus over living and nonliving beings. Orpheus thus penetrates the secrets of nature not through violence but through melody, rhythm, and harmony. Whereas the Promethean attitude is inspired by audacity, boundless curiosity, the will to power, and the search for utility, the Orphic attitude, by contrast, is inspired by respect in the face of mystery and disinterestedness. In the words of Rilke, who is also speaking of Orpheus:

> Song, as you teach it, is not covetousness
>   or the quest for something one might finally obtain.
> Song is existence.[18]

As in Seneca, for instance, the Orphic attitude represents the secrets of nature after the model of the mysteries of Eleusis, that is, as the subjects of a progressive revelation.[19] Indeed, it seems that the mysteries of Eleusis were intimately linked to the Orphic tradition.[20] This attitude tries to respect "Nature's modesty," to use Nietzsche's expression.[21]

In the modern period, especially in the seventeenth and eighteenth centuries, we can find these two attitudes in books of emblems, as has been admirably shown by Carlo Ginzburg.[22] Here the Promethean attitude is illustrated, for example, by a man climbing a mountain with the help of Father Time,[23] or else by the motto "Sapere aude," meaning "Dare to know!"[24] which is in praise of the explorer's spirit of adventure and of scientific curiosity. According to Kant, this motto was to be that of the *Aufklärung*, or the Spirit of the Enlightenment.[25] The Orphic attitude, or at least a critical attitude with regard to the Promethean spirit, is expressed in emblems that represent the fall of Icarus with the motto "Altum sapere periculosam," which can be translated very loosely to express all that it implies in the historical and philosophical context as "It is dangerous to aspire to excessively lofty pretensions."[26] Prometheus gnawed by a vulture and Icarus falling into the sea attest to the dangers of audacious curiosity.

By opposing the Promethean to the Orphic attitude, I do not mean to oppose a good and a bad attitude. I simply want, through this recourse to Greek myths, to attract attention to these two orientations that can be manifested in the relations between man and nature—two orientations that are equally essential, do not necessarily exclude each other, and are often found united in the same person. For instance, I consider Plato's *Timaeus* to be a characteristic example of the Orphic attitude, in the first place because Plato represents the world as an object fashioned in an artisanal way, and therefore in a certain sense mechanically—which can lead one to conceive of the world as a machine and God as an engineer—and second, because he proposes a mathematical model of the genesis of natural objects. Moreover, Plato did not in general hesitate to use mechanical models to try to make the movement of the world understandable, as we can glimpse in book 10 of the *Republic* and the cosmic myth of the *Statesman*. The two attitudes I have distinguished thus correspond to our ambiguous relation to nature, and they cannot be separated in too definitive a way.

On the one hand, nature can present itself to us in a hostile aspect, against which we must defend ourselves, and as a set of resources necessary for life, which must be exploited. The moral motive force of the Promethean attitude—which is also that of Aeschylus' *Prometheus*—is the desire to help humanity. In his *Discourse on Method*, Descartes affirms that it was "for the general good of all human beings" that he refused to keep hidden the discoveries he had made in physics.[27] The blind development of technology and industrialization, however, spurred on by the appetite for profit, places our relation to nature, and nature itself, in danger. On the other hand, nature is both a spectacle that fascinates us, even if it terrifies us, and a process that surrounds us. The Orphic attitude, which respects it, seeks to preserve a living perception of nature; at the opposite extreme from the Promethean attitude, however, it often professes a primitivism that is not without danger either.

As I shall have occasion to repeat, the same person can, simultaneously or successively, have several apparently contradictory attitudes with regard to nature. When a scientist is carrying out an experiment, his body perceives the earth, despite the Copernican revolution, as a fixed, immobile base, and he may perhaps take a distracted glance at the sun's "setting." The Orphic attitude and the Promethean attitude may very well succeed each other or coexist or even combine. They nevertheless remain radically and fundamentally opposed.

The Promethean Attitude

Unveiling Secrets through Technology

10

Mechanics and Magic
from Antiquity to the Renaissance

The Promethean attitude, which consists of using technical procedures to tear Nature's "secrets" from her in order to dominate and
exploit her, has had a gigantic influence. It has engendered our modern civilization and the worldwide expansion of science and indus-
try. In the context of this book, I shall obviously not describe this
immense phenomenon, but will merely specify the role that the metaphor of nature's secrets has played in the self-representation of this
attitude throughout the ages.

In antiquity, the Promethean attitude appears in three forms:
mechanics, magic, and the rudiments of the experimental method,
three practices that share the characteristic of seeking to obtain effects alien to what is considered the normal course of nature, effects whose causes elude those who do not operate according to
these techniques. At the end of the Middle Ages and the beginning
of modern times, these three practices approached and profoundly
transformed one another to give birth to experimental science. The
motto of the modern world would thus be "Knowledge is power" but
also "Power"—that is, fabrication by means of experimentation—"is
knowledge."

ANCIENT MECHANICS

The idea of trickery—and, ultimately, of violence—appears in the
word "mechanics," since *mēkhanē* signifies "trick." The introduction

to the *Problemata mechanica,* an anonymous work probably elaborated in the Peripatetic school at the end of the third or the beginning of the second century BCE, is perfectly clear on this point:

> Everything that occurs in conformity with nature, but of whose
> cause we are unaware, provokes astonishment; as does everything
> that, when it occurs in a manner contrary to nature, is produced by
> technique [*tekhnē*] in the interest of mankind.
>
> For in many cases, nature produces effects that are contrary to our
> interests, for nature always acts in the same way, and simply, whereas
> what is useful to us often changes.
>
> Therefore, when an effect contrary to nature must be produced,
> we are at a loss because of the difficulty of producing such an effect;
> and the cooperation of *tekhnē* is required. This is why we call the
> part of *tekhnē* intended to help us in such difficulties "trickery"
> [*mēkhanē*]. For the situation is, as the poet Antiphon says, "Through
> *tekhnē,* we master the things in which we are vanquished by nature."[1]
>
> For so it is when what is lesser masters what is greater, or when
> what is light moves what is heavy, and all the rest of the problems we
> call problems of trickery [*mēkhanika*]. They are not completely iden-
> tical to physical problems [i.e., concerning nature], nor are they fully
> separated from them, but they are common to mathematical re-
> search and to research on physics. For the "how" becomes clear
> through mathematical research, and the "about what" through re-
> search on nature.[2]

Let us keep in mind four fundamental points here. First, mechanics is situated within the perspective of a struggle between man and
nature, well expressed in the quotation from the tragedian Antiphon.
Technology allows us to regain the upper hand over nature. Next, the
goal of mechanics is to serve mankind's practical interests, and therefore to relieve human suffering, but also, it must be admitted, to sat-
isfy the passions, particularly those of kings and the wealthy: hatred,
pride, and the taste for pleasure and luxury. Moreover, mechanics is a

technique that consists in tricking nature, by means of instruments fashioned by human beings: machines of all kinds that enable the production of effects apparently contrary to nature. The notion of "mechanics" is thus situated within the perspective of the opposition between "nature" and "art" [*tekhnē*], with "art" being understood here in the sense of a human technique, as opposed to nature. Finally, mechanics is closely linked to mathematics, which allows one to determine *how* to produce a given effect.

Although mechanics seems to be opposed to nature, it is nevertheless, in the words of Philo of Byzantium in the third century BCE, based on the laws or the *logoi* of nature. In other words, it relies on the "reasons" that are immanent in nature, and ultimately on its mathematical qualities (particularly those of the circle) and physical qualities (weight, force) in order to obtain results that seem to be contrary to the course of nature: lifting enormous weights or hurling projectiles over tremendous distances.[3] From this perspective, the secrets of nature are rather the unsuspected resources that can be gleaned from natural processes. We find this idea once again in Francis Bacon, when he says, "Nature can be commanded only by obeying it."[4]

At the end of antiquity, Simplicius clearly recognized the close connection between physics and mechanics, writing: "Physics is useful to the things of life; it supplies their principles to medicine and mechanics, and it comes to the aid of the other techniques, for each of them needs to study nature and the differences with regard to the underlying matter of each of these techniques."[5] Simplicius no doubt means that, for example, a person who works with a given material, such as metal or wood, must know the physical properties of the material.

Over the course of antiquity, there was genuine technical progress from the time of the first Greek philosophers through the Pythagoreans, particularly the philosopher, scientist, technician, and statesman Archytas of Tarentum, until it reached a culminating point in the

Hellenistic and Roman period. Speaking of Archimedes' mechanical inventions, Plutarch traces this art back to Archytas of Tarentum, as well as to Plato's contemporary Eudoxus, insofar as they constructed instruments that made possible the solution of geometric problems.[6] In any case, the idea of making war machines occurred very early on, but so did the idea of constructing works of art, that is, tunnels, aqueducts, and fortifications, and of using instruments to carry out astronomical and geographical observations. The engineers of antiquity knew how to profit from the properties of steam and compressed air, for instance, in the invention of the suction pump and the pressure pump.[7] They also knew how to build automata, which were used in particular to animate statues of the gods, to the astonishment of the faithful.[8]

It was above all at Alexandria in the Hellenistic period, beginning more precisely with the end of the fourth century BCE, under the influence of those enlightened princes the Ptolemies, that the decisive flourishing of technology and mechanics took place, especially within the framework of the library and the museum of Alexandria. This "Mousaion," dedicated to the Muses and financed by the state, was a very lively center of studies, which gathered together a large number of scholars.[9]

This mechanical knowledge was not merely empirical know-how, but was also the subject of theoretical reflection and of the beginnings of a scientific systematization that took the form of axioms and was the work of great mathematicians. We still possess several treatises on mechanics dating from both the Hellenistic and the Roman periods, for instance, those of Archimedes of Syracuse, Hero of Alexandria, Pappus, and Philo of Byzantium.[10] In his excellent work *Les mécaniciens grecs*, Bertrand Gille, criticizing almost universally widespread clichés that represent the Greeks as incapable of advancing the elaboration of technology, has shown that the Greek mechanics truly gave birth to technology.[11]

It is true that philosophers, above all Platonists, affected to despise mechanics. Plato himself had criticized the mathematician, astronomer, and philosopher Eudoxus, who, instead of restricting himself to abstract reasoning, had used instruments in order to make the solution to geometrical problems comprehensible by sensible intuition.[12] To this distrust of sensation was added, among the Platonists, a disdain for the manual labor implied in the construction of machines. As a good Platonist, Plutarch wants us to believe that Archimedes, inventor of the hydraulic organ and of many war machines that were used effectively against the Romans in the siege of Syracuse, considered only abstract speculations to be serious, and held the invention of machines to be nothing more than the distraction of "geometry amusing itself." It was supposedly Hieron, king of Syracuse, who was interested in mechanics and urged Archimedes to make his art known to the multitude through the invention of various machines.

In contrast, the Stoic Posidonius, evoking, without speaking explicitly of mechanics, all the techniques man has developed for his comfort in the course of the ages, such as architecture, ironwork, metallurgy, the exploitation of iron and copper mines, agriculture—in other words, technologies that, like mechanics, are "interested"—affirms that wise men invented them when the pure morals of the Golden Age began to be corrupted.[13] From this perspective, philosophy and wisdom themselves appear as the motive forces of technical progress and civilization. This conception of the sage as inventor and benefactor of humanity is in complete conformity with the popular image of the Seven Sages. For instance, it was said that Thales of Miletus had either predicted an eclipse or diverted the course of a river. Wisdom was thus conceived as skill or know-how.

The phenomenon that characterizes the evolution of our civilization and has been called the "mechanization of the world" consists primarily in the application of mathematics to the knowledge of the natural phenomena of the world.[14] Yet this close connection between mechanics and mathematics is an inheritance from the mechanics of antiquity, which was based on the physical and mathematical properties of the objects to which it applied by using mathematical formulas that made precise measurements possible. Ancient mechanics "tricked" nature by using the potential supplied by certain geometrical figures, such as the circle, and the inventions of ancient engineers presuppose complex mathematical calculations. They were cognizant only of "figure and motion," to borrow the expression used, for example, by Leibniz to designate what he calls "mechanical reasons."[15]

If we can accept that, in modern times, the mechanistic explanation of the world "by figure and motion" is the heir to the mechanical techniques of antiquity, we must nevertheless not forget that it is also the heir to purely theoretical traditions, which propose precisely a mechanistic explanation of the world, with no involvement of forces or souls that initiate motion: I mean the atomistic theories of Democritus and Epicurus, who also explained phenomena "by figure and motion." The universe, with all its infinite number of worlds, is like an immense game of Lego or Meccano.[16] The chance assembly of these pieces known as atoms—which are dissimilar in form but capable of hooking up with one another—constitutes bodies and worlds. This, to be sure, has to do not with a physics of utilization but with a physics of contemplation, which for Epicurus is intended above all not to explain the world but to appease souls. The Renaissance and modern times, taking up this atomistic hypothesis once again, were to place it in the service of the other tradition, that of the mechanical techniques of the engineers of antiquity, who could not help but agree with it.

ANCIENT MAGIC

Magic has the same finality as mechanics: the goal is to tear nature's secrets from it, that is, to discover the occult processes that enable mankind to act on nature in order to place it in the service of human interests.[17] However, it relies originally on the belief that natural phenomena are brought about by invisible powers—gods or demons— and that it is therefore possible to modify natural phenomena by forcing the god or demon to do what one wants to accomplish. One acts on the god or demon by calling it by its true name, and then by performing certain actions and rituals, using plants or animals that are considered to be in sympathy with the invisible power one wishes to constrain. The god then becomes the servant of the person who carries out the magical practice, for magic claims to be able to dominate this power in order to have it at its disposal to carry out what it desires.

Practiced from the most distant times, magic found its theoreticians at the end of antiquity. In his *Apology,* the speech in which he defends himself against the accusation of having devoted himself to magical practices in order, it was said, to win himself a fine marriage with Prudentilla, Apuleius displays a great knowledge of the details of these practices, yet he provides little philosophical reflection on the principles and foundations of magic.[18] Saint Augustine goes much further when he tries to explain the power that enabled the magicians of Egypt, in the time of Moses, to fabricate serpents.[19] This magical operation consisted of extracting from the hidden bosom of nature the beings contained within it. All the effects of divine creation, he wrote, all the beings or phenomena that might appear over the course of the ages, potentially exist in the texture of the elements: "As females are great with their litter, the world too is great with the causes of the beings that are to be born."[20] Since the Stoics, these hidden causes had been called "seminal reasons." They were seminal because they were the seeds of beings, and reasons because these seeds deploy themselves and develop in a rational, methodical, and programmatic way. They contain, in a state of involution and virtuality, the various organs that will be brought to their full development in the future living being. Nature thus becomes an immense reservoir that contains hidden within it the totality of seminal reasons. Here we see the evolution of the notion of a secret of nature, which assumes an ontological meaning under the influence of the Stoic doctrine of seminal reasons. The secrets of nature are genuine beings, or at least possibilities, that are hidden in the "bosom of nature." It is God, says Saint Augustine, who brings it about that "seeds develop their numbers," that is, the entire program they contain, and that "they cause to appear before our eyes visible forms full of beauty, freeing them of the hidden and invisible veils that cover them."[21] There is thus a natural development of things, intrinsic to nature and willed by God. Yet there can also be external interventions that unleash these forces and their program. The magical operation is just such an external intervention: "To use external causes—which, although they are not natural, are nevertheless used in conformity with nature—so that the things that are contained in a hidden way in the secret bosom of nature may burst free and are, as it were, produced outside, deploying the measures, numbers, and weights that they have received, in secret, from Him 'who has disposed all things with measure, number, and weight': of this, not only evil angels but even evil men are capable."[22]

Here, therefore, the secrets of nature are secret forces hidden in the bosom of nature, and the demons, who, according to Augustine, are the true authors of magical operations, are able to unleash them. In this connection, we should recall that Plato in the *Symposium* (203a1) had already established a relation between demons and magic. This idea of a "secret bosom of nature" is found once again in the High Middle Ages, in Johannes Scotus Eriugena,[23] but also in the Renaissance, in the partisans of "natural magic." In this secret bosom of nature all kinds of virtualities and possibilities, albeit hidden, are present; and they can give birth to forms or effects which then become visible as well.

NATURAL MAGIC IN THE LATE MIDDLE AGES
AND THE RENAISSANCE

From the end of the twelfth century to the sixteenth century, an abundant magical literature developed in the Latin West: to a large extent, this consisted of works translated from the Arabic. In the Middle Ages, especially in its late stages, and the Renaissance, the notion of a "natural magic" gradually came into its own. The idea caught on as soon as it was thought possible to give a natural, almost scientific explanation for the phenomena that had until then been thought to be the work of demons, who were the only ones to know nature's secrets. Natural magic admits that human beings, too, can know the occult virtues of things. The assistance of demons is not necessary for using the secret virtualities hidden in the bosom of nature. For this to be possible, it was necessary to discover the astral influences and occult qualities of animals and plants, as well as the sympathies and antipathies that exist among the beings of nature.

In the Middle Ages this notion was sketched at the beginning of the thirteenth century by William of Auvergne, who brought the practices of natural magic closer to those of medicine. Roger Bacon, in his opuscule *On the Secret Works of Art and Nature* (1260), continued to reserve the name "magic" for demoniacal magic, but he gives us to understand that "experimental science," or "the art that uses nature as an instrument," can produce effects much more extraordinary than those of magic.

Natural magic made its definitive appearance with Marsilio Ficino, who, on this occasion, took up Plotinian ideas while transforming them.[24] Plotinus had already proposed a purely physical explanation for magic. The spells of magic, he said, are no more surprising than the magic of nature, of which music is one of the best illustrations.[25] For the first magician is Love, who attracts beings toward one another. It is this universal sympathy that makes all magic possible. The artificial actions of magic may seem to provoke a change in the course of things, but they are nothing other than the magician's use of natural actions and reactions that take place between the parts of the world. "Even without anybody carrying out a magical practice," says Plotinus, "there are many attractions and enchantments [in the world]."[26] Many natural processes seem to be magical processes because they are carried out at a distance: for instance, musical chords, arranged harmoniously, begin to vibrate when one of them is struck.[27] This immediate and spontaneous magic is simply the magic of love. Gardeners "marry" the vine to the elm: such has been the consecrated expression since antiquity.[28] In so doing, however, they merely promote the natural affinity or love which, in a way, joins the two plants together.[29] To exist in the sensible world means to be condemned to undergo all these reciprocal and distant influences that are exerted among all these parts of the universe; it therefore means being subject to passion. Even the stars, as parts of the universe, undergo affections and passions—unconsciously, moreover.[30] This is how they grant prayers or are "charmed" by magical practices, without realizing it, absorbed as they are in the impassibility of contemplation.[31] Universal interaction is thus, for Plotinus, the magic of nature: "All that is in relation to something else is fascinated by that something, for that with which it is in relation fascinates it and moves it."[32]

In the Renaissance, Marsilio Ficino takes up, following Plotinus, this theme of Love the Magician:

The operation of magic is the attraction of one thing to another by virtue of a natural affinity. Now the parts of this world, like the members of one and the same living being, all depending on the same creator, are connected one to another by the community of a unique nature . . . From their common kinship a common love is born, and from this love a common attraction. But this is true magic

. . . Thus, the magnet attracts iron, amber attracts straw, and sulfur fire. The sun makes many a flower and leaf turn toward it; the moon has the custom of attracting water, Mars the winds, and various herbs also attract various kinds of animals to themselves. Even in human affairs, each one undergoes the attraction of his own pleasure.[33] The works of magic are therefore works of nature,[34] and art is a mere instrument of nature . . . The ancients attributed this art to the demons, for they knew what the kinship of natural things is, what is fitting for each one, and how to reestablish concord between things, should it come to be wanting . . . And all of nature is called "magician" by virtue of this reciprocal love . . . Consequently, no one can doubt that Love is a magician, since all the power of magic resides in Love, and the work of Love is accomplished by fascination, incantation, and spells.[35]

The pejorative nuance that, in Plotinus, accompanied the idea of a magic of nature has completely disappeared in Ficino. Two causes, it seems to me, explain this change in the value of the notion of magic. First, the Neoplatonists after Plotinus, above all Iamblichus and Proclus, developed, under the influence of the *Chaldaean Oracles,* a new conception of magic which, it must be emphasized, corresponds to a rehabilitation of the role of certain sensible things in the service of the spiritual life of the soul.[36] We thus witness the development in late Neoplatonism of a kind of sacramentalism: certain sensible signs, or "symbols," and certain material rites can, in Neoplatonic theurgy, enable the soul's return to its divine origin. In the process, it was admitted that certain material substances possess a divine energy within them, and an effort was made to decipher the code of universal sympathy, to reconstruct the chains that connect all the degrees of reality, down to the lowest one, with the gods. Second, as Eugenio Garin has shown, from the end of the twelfth century we see the development in the Latin West of a growing interest in works of magic, accompanied by obscure desires, inherent in every magical procedure, to increase man's power over his fellow man and over matter.[37]

This trend was amplified in the Renaissance under the influence of Hermeticism, which attributes to mankind a wonderful power over nature.[38] "Magnum miraculum est homo," as the Hermetic work *Asclepius* had said: man is a great wonder.[39] Ficino belongs to this trend of thought. For him, "love," "magic," and "nature" take on a whole new meaning. No doubt Plotinus, like Ficino, could have written, "Nature has been called a 'magician' by virtue of the reciprocal love of things for one another." For him, however, this phrase would have had a negative meaning: it would have meant that the beings of the sensible world are nature's prisoners by virtue of the universal interaction that reigns in the world and the passions that beings experience against their will. For Ficino, by contrast, this phrase takes on a positive meaning: love is the great law of the world, and it explains the attractions that exist among all the parts of the world.[40] If such is the secret of the magic of nature, we can seek to know these laws of universal attraction in order to draw the celestial forces into material objects, and especially into the "figures" and "images" that are in harmony and affinity with a transcendent model.[41] The magic of nature thus founds the possibility of a doctrine and a practice that seek to uncover and utilize all these secret correspondences, naturally and rationally. This magic, in a sense natural, is to nature what agriculture is to the spontaneous productions of the earth: it activates and disciplines natural processes by means of the science of sympathies and affinities.[42]

In the three books of his *De occulta philosophia* (1533), Agrippa von Nettesheim collected and synthesized all the natural magic amassed for centuries in the ancient, Arabic, and medieval traditions. Conceiving of magic as the natural philosophy par excellence, he presented it in the context of a vast cosmic system of the Neoplatonic type, in which the World Soul plays a central part.[43] The possibility of magic was based on the fact that contained within the matter of each thing is an "occult virtue," that hidden power already mentioned by Augustine, which is proper to each thing. The discovery of these occult virtues makes possible the establishment of the series of sympathetic correspondences between things, from planets to metals and stones, by way of living beings, and, by using these sympathies, the achievement of surprising effects. Thanks to magic and, at the same time, to the spiritual ascetics it demands, "it comes to pass that we, who are in nature, can dominate nature."[44]

The profound meaning of the notion of natural magic appears clearly in the summary written by Giambattista della Porta of his own unpublished work entitled "Criptologia": "This book deals with the most profound secrets that are buried in the intimacy of the bosom of nature, for which no natural principles or probable explanations can be found, but which are not, for all that, mere superstition." Della Porta concentrates on uncovering the demoniacal or, by contrast, the natural elements of certain magical recipes. In the two editions of his work *Magia Naturalis* (1558 and 1589), he attempts, in the words of William Eamon, to give "natural explanations of what are thought to be marvelous phenomena."[45] In broad outline, he presents the same universe as his predecessors: a universe endowed with occult qualities, among which attractions and repulsions, correspondences, sympathies, and antipathies are established among all levels of reality.

Like Paracelsus, he thinks that these occult qualities can be discovered by "signatures," willed by God; that is, certain details of the external form of beings, animate or inanimate, which enable us to guess that such-and-such a being will have an influence on such-and-such another. Della Porta conceives of this natural magic as a practical science, able to use nature with a view to mankind's interests. Here, all human activity finds its place: innumerable recipes are proposed, for instance, in the fields of agriculture and metallurgy. In the latter domain, he makes some very interesting observations.

Insofar as it presents itself as a catalogue of observations of the oddities of nature and of recipes for obtaining extraordinary and astonishing results, natural magic is situated in the tradition of that literature, already very much alive in antiquity, of the secrets and wonders of nature, which I discussed earlier.[46] It differs from it, however, by its use of Neoplatonic metaphysics to explain the correspondences and series, the sympathies and antipathies, which manifest themselves in a universe that is both unified and hierarchical.

The tradition of *magia naturalis* remained alive until the time of German Romanticism. In 1765, for instance, a work titled *Magia Naturalis* was published at Tübingen, whose coauthors included, among others, Prokop Divisch, Friedrich Christoph Oetinger, and Gottlob Friedrich Rösler, and in which the phenomena of electricity and magnetism were interpreted from the perspective of natural magic. These speculations had a great influence on the philosophy of nature of the German Romantics, particularly Franz von Baader.[47]

MECHANICS AND MAGIC IN THE MIDDLE AGES
AND THE RENAISSANCE

The kind of mathematical physics known as ancient mechanics continued to be cultivated and even developed in the Middle Ages. The mathematical treatment of mechanical problems appears clearly in the thirteenth century, for instance, in the works attributed to Jordanus Nemerarius, in which one finds, in particular, calculations concerning the raising of weights and the problem of levers. In the fourteenth century, Nicolas Oresme imagined the geometrical representation of the variations in a body's velocity.

Parallel to these applications of a rigorous mathematical method, we also witness, from the thirteenth to the fifteenth centuries, the development of imaginings, aspirations, and hopes, a faith in the future flourishing of technology and mechanics. These imaginings, aspirations, and hopes in fact coincided with those of magic. Roger Bacon, whom I have already mentioned, sketched the program of an "art that uses nature like an instrument," which would be superior to the magic of charlatans.[48] For instance, he imagines ships without oarsmen, flying machines in which a man sits and moves wings analogous to those of a bird, a machine enabling weights to be raised and lowered, a machine capable of dragging a thousand men toward it, another that would allow people to walk on the bottom of the sea, bridges without piers, giant mirrors, apparatuses for seeing distant objects better or provoking optical illusions, and convex mirrors for starting fires.[49] Add to this all the means, such as petroleum, for igniting and maintaining fires, machines for generating terrible noises in the sky, as well as everything that could be realized in the area of magnetism. As far as astronomy was concerned, there would be instruments for establishing a map of the heavens. Finally, one could mention alchemical research, with a view to the fabrication of gold and the prolongation of life.

When we read of all these projects, we might think that Roger Bacon was a true son of Prometheus, who wished to do violence to Nature. Ought we to see in him a precursor to the modern flourishing of technology? In fact, we must resituate these imaginings within the perspective of his Christian vision of history, which is not at all that of a modern person but that of a theologian of the Middle Ages, a Franciscan and professor at Oxford in the thirteenth century, who, moreover, manifests an encyclopedic knowledge. Not only was he a theologian and a philosopher, but also he practiced mathematics, astronomy, and optics. Rather than a "Faustian figure," as Hans Blumenberg would have it, we should speak of him, with Émile Bréhier, as an "enlightened theocrat."[50] Roger Bacon wished to hasten the conversion of the entire world to Christianity, which was threatened by the imminent appearance of the Antichrist. All these mechanical inventions were to be placed in the service of apologetics. To the infidels, they would appear as genuine miracles, which would persuade them of the need to believe. If, they would say, our human mind cannot comprehend the wonders of nature and of mechanical art, must it not submit itself to the divine truths it does not understand?[51] As far as military inventions were concerned, they should serve the defense of Christianity in its struggle, which might be imminent, against the Antichrist.

Once we resituate them in the context of his vision of the world and of history, Roger Bacon's projects for mechanical inventions are therefore seen as very far removed from a modern mentality. It is highly significant, however, that Bacon could have thought that machines might be used as an apologetical argument. This implies that he understood the importance, both for the mind and for the body, that could be assumed by the discovery of the "secrets of nature," that is, the marvelous possibilities in nature which mechanics, in its further development, was to use to produce prodigious effects. The goal was no longer simply to contemplate the world but to transform it and place it in the service of mankind. This attitude is not an isolated phenomenon. René Taton is right to emphasize that, beginning precisely in the thirteenth century, "a new kind of human being appears: the architect or engineer," and that a growing interest then develops in practical and technical activity. For him, the flourishing of the "mechanical" sciences, such as statics, dynamics, hydrostatics, and magnetism, which we can also observe from the beginning of the thirteenth century, cannot be explained without close contact between Scholastics and technicians, who were the heirs to ancient mechanics. Roger Bacon, for instance, was in contact with a practitioner of the mechanical arts, Pierre de Maricourt, who was himself the author of a treatise on magnetism.[52] We thus witness a growing awareness of the powers of technology and its importance for human life.

This movement continued in the fourteenth and fifteenth centuries, and culminated with the engineers of the Renaissance, including Leonardo da Vinci. Leonardo's projects for mechanical inventions are justifiably famous. His life and activity were much more those of an engineer than of an artist.[53] He imagined an airplane, a submarine, and an assault tank; he built automata, such as the mechanical lion used several times in the princely celebrations of the time. We must not, however, exaggerate his role as a precursor of modern science, any more than we should that of Bacon. His notations, which are sometimes brilliant, are always fragmentary, and his contributions to the solution of problems of physics or mechanics is, in the last analysis, fairly meager.[54]

It is extremely interesting to encounter in Leonardo da Vinci a mind that united within itself the Promethean aspiration to use nature in the service of mankind and the attitude, which I've called "Orphic," of respectful and admiring observation of nature. If he thinks of building a flying machine, he begins by attentively observing and drawing the flight of birds in order to understand its mechanical workings.[55]

This curiosity and desire to invent, which come to light from the thirteenth to the fifteenth centuries, could be compared with the Hellenistic spirit that flourished at Alexandria under the reign of the Ptolemies. In both cases there was the same reaction against abstraction, the same beneficial influence of sovereigns who were enlightened, like the Medicis, or sometimes even extremely learned, like Frederick II of Hohenstaufen or Alfonso X of Castille.[56] In any case, the ferment of scientific work and bold imagination that characterized this period during which mechanics and natural magic converge in their aspirations was to offer a propitious terrain for the scientific revolution of the seventeenth century.

11

Experimental Science and the Mechanization of Nature

In a previous chapter I quoted a text written at the end of the fifth century BCE by the author of the Hippocratic treatise *On Art*, which already considered experimentation a kind of violence inflicted on nature to oblige it to reveal what it hides from us: "When Nature refuses willingly to hand over the signs [i.e., clinical symptoms], art has found the constraining means by which Nature, violated without damage, can let go of them; then, when it is freed, she unveils what must be done to those who are familiar with the art."[1] Here, as I also noted, we already see the analogy between the search for nature's secrets and a judicial and even criminal prosecution, which we find again at the beginning of modern times in Francis Bacon.[2]

ANCIENT AND MEDIEVAL EXPERIMENTATION

The continuation of the Hippocratic text shows that the author intends to speak of medical treatments that force the patient's body to present the symptoms that will make it possible to diagnose a specific illness. Quite obviously, we are far from modern experimentation, which is charged with the rigorous verification of a hypothesis, particularly by precise measurements. Nevertheless, rudimentary experimental techniques continued to be put in practice, particularly by Aristotelians, such as Strato of Lampsacus, with regard to weight and the void;[3] by doctors, who carried out vivisections not only on animals but also on human beings (prisoners or convicts sentenced to death);[4] by Ptolemy, author of remarkable experiments in the field of optics;[5] and also by John Philoponus, on the ratio of the weight and speed of freely falling bodies.[6] According to Nelly Tsouyopoulos and Mirko Drazen Grmek, Philoponus, who wrote in the sixth century CE, is "the first author to propose the hypothetico-deductive method for solving the problem of induction."[7]

In the last chapter I spoke of the Franciscan Roger Bacon, who thought that his *scientia experimentalis* would surpass the prodigies of magic. This should not, however, mislead us into turning him into the inventor of science and the experimental method. In his time and work, the word *experimentum* did not designate what modern scientists call an "experiment." Here, *experimentum* is above all opposed to abstract and purely rational knowledge. It was instead an immediate knowledge or lived experience that might be either sensible or spiritual. By means of *experimentum,* we may become "experts," skilled at uncovering and using the secrets of nature and at using nature as an instrument. Roger Bacon's experimental science was, fundamentally, nothing other than natural magic, closely linked to mechanics, and, like natural magic, it aimed particularly at realizing extraordinary effects, intended above all to cause admiration and astonishment, which, from Roger Bacon's viewpoint, would be capable of converting the infidels.

THE LEGACY OF MAGIC AND MECHANICS

Historians agree in considering Francis Bacon the first theoretician of the methods and hopes of experimental science. For him, natural magic, which seeks to operate by using the sympathies and antipathies that exist among things, is ultimately useless.[8] If those who practice it "have produced some work, this work is of the kind appropriate to admiration and the taste for novelty, but not to profit and utility." It may conserve something of natural operations, for instance, in the phenomena of fascination or communication at a distance between minds and bodies. He notes that a genuine natural magic does not yet exist, any more than a genuine metaphysics, from which it might derive, for natural magic presupposes the knowledge of forms.[9] Its task would be to draw up an inventory of all that man has invented and of all that could and should be invented.

To formulate his project of discovering and dominating nature, Bacon, consciously or unconsciously, uses expressions borrowed from the conceptual world of magic or mechanics. Thus, like Augustine describing how magic works, he speaks of what is hidden in the "bosom of nature."[10] He writes, "There is every reason to hope that Nature still keeps hidden in her bosom many secrets of excellent use, which have no kinship or analogy with what has already been invented and completely leave the paths of imagination behind."[11]

Elsewhere he takes up once again the vocabulary of violence traditionally used in both these arts. Bacon wants to show the importance of experimentation for the progress of the sciences. Since antiquity, scholars had contented themselves with collecting observations on natural phenomena. This was how Aristotle had collected his documentation for his *History of Animals*. What counts, however, are not more or less veridical accounts of observations but the experiments one carries out oneself with the help of the mechanical arts: "For as in public life the nature of an individual and the hidden deposition of his mind and his passions are better uncovered when he is disturbed than at any other moment, so the secrets [*occulta*] of nature are better discovered under the torture of the [mechanical] arts than when it proceeds in its natural course."[12] Here, then, we encounter once again the image of unveiling the secrets of nature obtained in a manner analogous to that of a judicial procedure.[13] Nature is a defendant (or a witch?) from whom one extorts confessions.

Nascent science thus shared its hopes and its projects with magic and mechanics: the goal was to produce all kinds of wonderful and useful effects from the virtualities hidden in nature. In the *New Atlantis*, Francis Bacon imagined a kind of Center of Scientific Research, the "House of Solomon," divided into laboratories devoted to different kinds of problems. The father of this House of Solomon defines the enterprise's priorities as follows: "The goal of our Foundation is to know the causes and secret movements of things and to move back the borders of mankind's empire over things, with a view to realizing everything that is possible."[14] This was a collective undertaking. Each researcher has a well-defined task and contributes to the common work. The father then enumerates the various research projects for his interlocutor. For instance, in vast underground grottos, scientists try to produce new artificial metals; elsewhere, thanks to the addition of vitriol, sulfur, steel, copper, lead, nitrate, and other minerals, fountains are created that imitate natural and thermal springs; in vast buildings others struggle to master the meteorological phenomena of rain, snow, and thunder; in the gardens people try to make plants more precocious or late-blooming, to modify the form of fruits, and to produce completely new plants; or again, in parks and enclosures animals are raised on which experiments of all kind are carried out, including the ingestion of poisons, vivisection, sterilization, modification of their form, color, and size, and the creation of new species. Francis Bacon believed in spontaneous generation, and he imagines that snakes, worms, insects, and fish can be born from putrefied matter.[15] Carolyn Merchant is right to compare this program to that of the natural magic of Giambattista della Porta, who also hoped, for instance, to change the colors of flowers, and above all to create worms, snakes, and fish from putrefactions.[16] This enumeration of projects, moreover, evokes the memory of the lists of imaginary inventions proposed by Roger Bacon or even Leonardo da Vinci. Here, for example, we find the optical instruments able to make distant objects seem close or vice versa, and to magnify small objects; we also find flying machines, submarines, and automata. As Merchant rightly emphasizes, Francis Bacon's program is a program for the manipulation of the environment and of nature itself, precisely the one that our current period is trying to realize, in a way that risks bringing about disastrous consequences not just for nature but for mankind.[17]

THE MECHANISTIC REVOLUTION OF THE SEVENTEENTH CENTURY

In a letter addressed in 1644 to one of his innumerable correspondents, Father Mersenne, a confirmed partisan of the mechanistic explanation of phenomena, writes that his time "is the father of a universal movement . . . What do you think of these renewals: Do they not give us the premonition of the end of the world?"[18]

In a remarkable passage Robert Lenoble has described the event, of incalculable importance for the history of mankind and of the earth, known as the mechanistic revolution, which began with Galileo:

The time is coming when, in a few years, Nature will fall from her rank of universal goddess to become—a disgrace that has never yet been known—a machine. This sensational event could well be given a precise date: 1632. This was when Galileo published the *Dialogues on the Two Principal Systems of the World,* and the characters who speak are in the Venice arsenal. That genuine physics could emerge from a discussion among engineers: we can no longer imagine today what was so revolutionary about such a scenario, apparently so anodyne . . . The engineer has conquered the dignity of a scientist, because the art of fabricating has become the prototype of science. This implies a new definition of knowledge, which is no longer contemplation but utilization, and a new attitude of man in the face of Nature: he ceases to look at her as a child looks at his mother, taking her as a model; he wants to conquer her, and become her master and possessor.[19]

Unlike Robert Lenoble, I would not say that "man"—that is, humanity—henceforth has a new attitude with regard to nature. There are several reasons for this. First of all, and generally speaking, we must be very prudent when we wish to define the mentality of an entire period. Also, generally, as I have already said and shall have occasion to repeat,[20] "man"—meaning the same human being—does not have one single attitude toward nature: he can have what one might call a day-to-day perception of it, or an aesthetic perception, or a scientific knowledge. Scientists know perfectly well that the earth revolves around the sun, but they do not think about that when they talk about the sunset. Second, the dominating attitude of modern science is nothing new. This Promethean tendency has long existed among mechanics and magicians; and already in Genesis, God ordered human beings to dominate the earth. What we must say, I think, is that with Francis Bacon, Descartes, Galileo, and Newton, a definitive break, not with the aspirations of magic but with its methods, may have taken place, and these scholars discovered the means of progressing in a decisive and definitive way in this project of dominating nature, limiting themselves to the rigorous analysis of what is measurable and quantifiable in sensible phenomena.

This event—like almost all events—has several concurrent causes. First of all, there is the triumph of the engineers, of which Robert Lenoble speaks. As we have seen, it had been prepared since the end of the Middle Ages and during the Renaissance;[21] it was accelerated by the spectacular nature of the progress in knowledge realized in the fifteenth and sixteenth centuries, thanks to the great discoveries, such as the discovery of America, made by the navigators, and the great inventions, such as printing, made by artisans. The value and dignity of manual labor increased as a result. It is significant that in 1563 an artisan such as Bernard Palissy wrote a book whose title gives a good statement of its program: *Veritable Recipe by Which All the Men of France Shall be Able to Learn How to Multiply Their Treasures: Item Those Who Have Never Had Knowledge of Letters Shall Be Able to Learn a Philosophy Necessary for All Inhabitants of the Earth.*[22] For him, natural philosophy is learned not from books but from contact with nature, and by working with one's hands. At the beginning of the sixteenth century, Juan Luis Vives, in his book on the teaching of sciences (*De Tradendis Disciplinis*, 1531), and Rabelais, in his *Gargantua* (1533), encouraged students to visit the shops of artisans to observe the techniques and procedures of people who are in direct contact with nature.

The progress achieved in the fabrication of instruments helped make possible in particular the construction of the microscope, from the beginning of the sixteenth century, and of the telescope, in the seventeenth and eighteenth centuries. They revolutionized the possibility of observation, but some naturalists refused to use them, as I shall have occasion to repeat, because they feared that such instruments might interfere with the precise view of things.[23]

At the time this infatuation with practical knowledge brought with it a profound and almost generalized contempt for bookish knowledge and arguments from authority. Henceforth, science was to rely not on what people said either with regard to phenomena—Aristotle had collected a great deal of information of this kind in his works on natural history—or still less on what Aristotle or Galen or Ptolemy said, but on what one can experience, either oneself or collectively, and on what one can fabricate or construct. It was the end of the argument from authority. Truth is the daughter of Time, that is, of the collective efforts of mankind.[24]

The goal was no longer to read, explain texts, and borrow one's knowledge from the ancients, but to make one's reason work on the occasion of concrete observations and well-thought-out experiments. At the end of his *Discourse on Method*, Descartes wrote that he hoped that those who use their natural reason in all its purity, that is, whose mind has not been spoiled by scholastics, will be better judges of his opinions than those who believe only in old books.[25]

The mechanistic revolution was thus closely linked to what we might call the democratization of knowledge. Science was no longer the prerogative of a few initiates, as was the case with magic, or of a few privileged people, students or university professors; it was accessible by right to all of mankind. Francis Bacon in his *Novum Organum* and Descartes in the *Discourse on Method* consider that the method they propose is an instrument that enables any mind to accede to scientific knowledge. When we draw a circle by hand, it may be drawn more or less well; this depends on the hand's skill. Drawing a circle, however, no longer depends on the qualities of the hand if we draw it with a compass. The scientific method is a compass that enables all talents to be equalized.[26]

Moreover, as Francis Bacon had already glimpsed in the *New Atlantis*, scientific discoveries are the product not of isolated work but of collaboration among scientists. Thus, in the seventeenth century we witness the flourishing of academies of science, in which the work of various scientists was presented and discussed.

With Galileo, a radical change was introduced into the definition of mechanics. Whereas throughout antiquity and in the Middle Ages, mechanics was the science of artificial objects, that is, objects fabricated by human beings to force nature to act in mankind's service and in a way that was "against nature"—although it was well known that the laws of nature had to be used with a view to this goal[27]—henceforth, with Galileo, physics and mechanics began to be definitively identified. On the one hand, mechanics consists in the application of the laws of nature, and, on the other, in order to study nature, Galilean physics made use of the calculations and mathematical notions that ancient mechanics used to build artificial objects. The scientist therefore operated like an engineer, who had to reconstruct the gears and functions of the machine known as nature.

This process is clearly stated by Descartes in a chapter of his *Principles of Philosophy* titled "How Can We Achieve Knowledge of the Figures, Size, and Movements of Insensible Bodies?" Descartes answers this question as follows. First, he recognizes that the smallest parts of bodies are insensible, that is, they cannot be perceived by means of the senses. The only clear and distinct ideas we can have of material realities are the notions of shape, size, and movement. But the rules concerning these notions are those of geometry and mechanics. All the knowledge human beings can have of nature can be derived only from these rules. In this research, says Descartes,

the example of several bodies composed by the artifice of men has been a great help to me; for I do not recognize any difference between the machines made by artisans and the various bodies that nature alone composes, except that the effects of machines depend only on the arrangement of certain tubes or springs or other instruments which, since they must have some proportion with the hands of those who make them, are always so large that their figures and movements can be seen, whereas the tubes or strings that cause the effects of natural bodies are ordinarily too small to be perceived by our senses. It is, moreover, certain that all the rules of mechanics belong to physics, so that everything that is artificial is likewise natural. For instance, when a watch marks the time by means of the wheels of which it consists, this is no less natural for it than it is for a tree to produce fruit. This is why, just as a watchmaker, seeing a watch he has not made, can ordinarily judge, from whichever of its parts he considers, what are all the others that he does not see; so, by considering the effects and sensible parts of natural bodies, I have tried to come to know what those of their parts that are insensible must be.[28]

Descartes and the mechanists thus reject the traditional distinction between the procedures of human art and natural processes. In the article "Nature" in his *Philosophical Dictionary,* Voltaire gave a good summary of this situation: "My poor child, do you want me to tell you the truth? I've been given a name that does not suit me: for I am called *nature,* yet I am all art."

Henceforth the machine, rather than the living organism, is the model that serves to conceive and explain nature, and from this perspective God appears as the builder of the world's machine, who is external to it: the great engineer, architect, or watchmaker. Such expressions appear frequently in the seventeenth and eighteenth centuries.[29] Then there are Voltaire's well-known lines:

> The universe embarrasses me, and I cannot imagine
> that such a clock should exist without a clockmaker.[30]

It is true that in antiquity, authors both pagan and Christian—Lucretius, Calcidius, and Lactantius, for instance—had spoken of nature as a *machine.*[31] Yet it is also true that by using this metaphor, these authors only wished to allude to the beautiful organization of nature. In Christian writers such as Lactantius, however, this metaphor could open the door to a mechanistic conception of the universe. When, in 1377, the comparison of nature to a clock occurs in Nicolas Oresme, the specifically mechanistic perspective becomes clearer.[32] In 1599, at the end of the dedicatory epistle that precedes his translation of Pseudo-Aristotle's *Mechanical Questions,* Monantheuil declares that the universe is God's instrument, insofar as it is the biggest, most powerful, and most structured of all machines, and because it is the system *(complexio)* of all bodies.[33] This metaphor was to assume its full importance and significance in Mersenne and Descartes.

Given the very close relationships that, since antiquity, had linked mathematics and mechanics, this image of nature as a mechanism had as its fundamental consequence the appearance, thanks to Kepler, Galileo, Descartes, Huygens, and Newton, of a mathematical physics, which restricted itself to the quantifiable and measurable data of phenomena and aimed to formulate the laws that regulate them in the form of equations. For Galileo, for instance, the world is a book written in a language that cannot be understood unless we know its characters, which are none other than mathematical figures.[34] Beginning with this decisive turn toward the mathematization of nature, the way was open for the possibility of the evolution of science toward modern physics.

SECRETS OF NATURE

The scientific revolution did not put an end to the use of the metaphor of the secrets of nature; scholars continued to have recourse to it. For instance, in his *Life of Descartes,* written at the end of the seventeenth century, Adrien Baillet says with regard to Father Mersenne, "Never was a mortal more curious than he to penetrate all the secrets of nature and to bring all the sciences and all the arts to perfection."[35] Pascal, for instance, writes, "The secrets of nature are hidden; although it always acts, one does not always discover its effects."[36] Without using the word "secret," Molière, in *The Imaginary Invalid* of 1672, has Beraldus say:

> The workings of our machine are mysteries so far,
> in which men see not a whit:
> . . . nature has placed before our eyes
> veils too thick for us to know one bit.

Paradoxically, it was at the beginning of the seventeenth century, at the time of the scientific revolution currently under discussion, a time when nature was losing its value as active subject and ceasing to be imagined as a goddess, that it appears depicted on the frontispiece of a great many scientific handbooks in the form of Isis unveiling herself.[37]

The secrets of nature, however, are no longer the occult and invisible qualities, hidden forces, and unsuspected possibilities that lie beyond appearances and that nature conceals from us. Thanks to the microscope and the telescope, mankind was first able to see unknown material entities. The secrets of nature were finally uncovered, and man became the "master of God's works," in the words of Kepler.[38] One of the pioneers of research carried out with the help of the microscope, Anton van Leeuwenhoek, published his observations in a book titled *Arcana Naturae Detecta*.[39] These "secrets of nature unveiled" are, for instance, the realities he describes in his work: animalcules, now called "infusoria" or else blood corpuscles, bacteria, or spermatozoa. All these discoveries raised entirely new problems for biology. The secrets of nature also included the uneven terrain of the moon, the stars of the Milky Way, the satellite of Jupiter that Galileo discovered with the help of a telescope, and sunspots.

The secrets of nature were the mechanisms and the hidden workings behind appearances, mechanisms one hoped to discover by means of instruments that developed the power of the senses, but also, and above all, thanks to experimentation and mathematical calculations, which made possible the formulation of the equations that govern the motions of matter, and hence the reproduction of the effects caused by the machines that made up the great machine of the world.[40]

THE CHRISTIAN INSPIRATION OF MECHANISM

The Christian character of this mechanistic revolution of the seventeenth century cannot be overemphasized. In the first place, the project of dominating nature which characterizes it, and which, moreover, was not, as we have seen, alien to pagan antiquity, echoes God's exhortation to Adam and Eve: "Subjugate the earth." We have seen how Francis Bacon considered that the mission of science consisted in giving man the rights over nature that God had conceded to him. Through original sin, man had lost both his state of innocence and his power over nature. Of these two losses, religion could repair the first and science the second.[41] Opposing it to the speculative philosophy taught in the schools, Descartes proposed a practical philosophy which, aware of the force and the actions of fire and the other elements, as well as of the other bodies that surround us, would render us, as it were, "masters and possessors of nature." He considered that it was his duty to make his physics known for the general good of mankind.[42]

The image of the world as a machine corresponded perfectly to the Christian idea of a creative God, absolutely transcendent over his work. Moreover, a biblical text, "He arranged all things with measure, number, and weight," even seemed to invite scientists to retain only the mathematical elements as essential.[43] Saint Augustine had cited this biblical text in support of the cosmological conception of Plato, who, he said, "presents God as utilizing numbers to fashion the earth."[44] Here, Augustine was echoing Plutarch's affirmation, "According to Plato, God never ceases doing geometry."[45] In the seventeenth and eighteenth centuries, God was also conceived as a geometer[46] and a mathematician;[47] and especially in the seventeenth century, scientists such as Bacon, Mersenne, Descartes, and Pascal had the impression of a profound harmony between their mechanistic vision of the world and their religious faith.

Nevertheless, I cannot share the optimism of Robert Lenoble, who contrasts the eighteenth century, during which there reigned a feeling of guilt caused by the opposition of religion and science, and the seventeenth century, which offers "that ever so rare example" of "human growth occurring in peace and agreement with God."[48] According to him, the seventeenth century rediscovered the emotional equilibrium of the thirteenth century, "when science and religion walked hand in hand." To realize the falsity of this description, it suffices to recall Galileo's condemnation by the Inquisition and the uncertainty, if not anguish, that it henceforth caused to weigh on scientific research. Descartes, for example, insisted heavily on the hypothetical nature of his theories and hesitated to publish his *Treatise on the World*.[49] Let us say instead that scientists of the seventeenth century may have been encouraged in their scientific activities by their Christian faith, but they were not encouraged at all by the ecclesiastical authorities, who claimed to represent religion.

DIVINE SECRETS

These scientists found a way to escape condemnation by means of the theological doctrine of the absolute liberty of divine omnipotence, which the late Middle Ages had developed to exalt God's transcendence, and which continued to be widely accepted. To understand the importance this theological doctrine had at the time, we must return to the text by Descartes cited earlier.[50] Mechanistic explanation consisted in trying to define how specific parts of the world machine worked, to explain in this way how they appear to us the way they do, but without our being able to know whether they actually work in the way that has been reconstructed. Mechanistic explanation is thus hypothetical. It hypothesizes a certain function, defined, if possible, by a mathematical ratio, to explain the phenomenon we have before our eyes. It is possible, however, that the workings may in fact be different, and that another hypothesis may be conceivable. Descartes puts things quite clearly: just as a clockmaker can make two clocks that look the same but have a different mechanism, so God can create different worlds that are apparently identical, but which he makes function with a different mechanism: "God has an infinity of means, by each of which he may have brought it about that all the things in this world appear as they now appear, without it being possible for the human mind to know which of all these means he has chosen to use in making them."[51]

Descartes therefore claims only to describe an ideal and possible world of phenomena. Even if phenomena in fact occur in accordance with a different process, it would nevertheless remain true that they could be reproduced according to the mechanism that had been defined, which, as Descartes observes, could be useful in medicine and the other arts.[52] What matters is not the knowledge of what actually causes a given effect—for this we cannot know—but the possibility of reproducing such an effect.

Let us note in passing that we can recognize here two methodological principles inherited from antiquity, which I will have occasion to discuss later: on the one hand, the possibility of proposing a plurality of explanations for the same phenomenon, and on the other, the necessity of choosing in every case an explanation that is in conformity with phenomena, or of "saving the phenomena," if we may so translate the Greek formula *sōzein ta phainomena*.[53]

Let us return, however, to our theological principle. It appears in the Latin text of the *Principles of Philosophy*, where Descartes claims that ultimately, on the subject of the mechanistic explanations he has proposed, one can have only a "moral certainty," that is, "a certainty that suffices for the conduct of life, but which remains uncertain, if it is considered from the viewpoint of divine omnipotence."[54]

As Richard Goulet points out, this doctrine of divine omnipotence was implied throughout Jewish and Christian beliefs, as Galen the physician in the second century and Porphyry in the fourth century of our era were well aware.[55] Against the creationist doctrine of Moses, Galen affirms that there are things that are impossible by nature, which God does not undertake to do.[56] As far as Porphyry is concerned, the Christian dogma of the Resurrection, or the idea of God annihilating the world he had created, implied in his view the complete arbitrariness of divine omnipotence: "It will be replied: 'God can do everything.' But this is not true. God cannot do everything. He cannot bring it about that Homer was not a poet, that Ilion was not destroyed, or that two and two make one hundred instead of four."[57]

According to theological voluntarism, by contrast, if two plus two are four, it is because God so willed it. There is no intelligible necessity to impose itself on God's absolute power: "The mathematical truths that you call eternal have been established by God and depend entirely on him, as do all other creatures. Indeed, to say that these truths are independent of God is to speak of him as a Jupiter or a Saturn, and to subject him to the Styx and the Fates."[58]

God has established these truths "as a king establishes laws in his kingdom," as Descartes wrote on April 15, 1630, to Father Mersenne. This doctrine of complete divine freedom had two consequences. First of all, it is possible that phenomena, or that which appears to us, may be produced by processes different from those we can reconstruct mathematically and according to the laws of mechanics. We must renounce the idea of an absolutely certain science that knows genuine causes. The result is that we can observe and measure natural phenomena, but we cannot truly understand their causes. Seventeenth-century scientists found a sufficient motive for renouncing worries about the finalities and essence of phenomena in theological reasons; it was enough for them to determine how these phenomena occur according to the laws of mechanics. This is perhaps what Father Mersenne meant when he wrote, "We see only the bark and the surface of nature without being able to enter into it."[59]

In addition—and here we return to the theme of the fear of the Inquisition—seventeenth-century scientists found in this doctrine of theological voluntarism a way to escape the fulminations of the ecclesiastical magisterium. By affirming that "God has an infinity of means, by each of which he may have brought it about that all the things in this world appear as they now appear, without it being possible for the human mind to know which of all these means he has chosen to use in making them," Descartes hints not that he is not affirming that things actually happen as he has tried to demonstrate but that he can only propose a likely rational explanation.[60] This is what Galileo had refused to admit. As Eduard Jan Dijksterhuis rightly notes, Cardinal Bellarmino had indeed advised Galileo to content himself with affirming that apparent motions are better explained mathematically if the earth's revolution around the sun is accepted, and that this was therefore a mere hypothesis, and thus to admit that it could not be affirmed with absolute certainty that things really do occur in that way.[61]

The idea of the complete freedom of the creative will also bring us back to the ancient doctrine of the divine secret. Seneca had said: "Are these hypotheses true? Only the gods know, they who possess the knowledge of the truth. For us, it is possible only to investigate these domains and to make progress in these hidden things, with the help of conjectures, no doubt deprived of the certainty of discovering, but not bereft of all hope."[62]

Yet the night of the secret concealed by the free and omnipotent Christian God is still more impenetrable. For the God of the Stoics was himself Reason: he was rational necessity, choosing the best of worlds and repeating it endlessly, by means of the eternal return, whereas the "omnipotent" God is the creator, entirely free, of any world he might choose among infinite and indifferent possibilities, a world in which rational necessity is itself God's free creation. Rational necessity thus depends on a choice that is ultimately quite arbitrary.[63]

THE "RETIRED ENGINEER"

The harmony—which was, moreover, quite fragile—between religion and science was to be short-lived, for the religious justification of mechanism, of which I have just spoken, bore its own negation within it and was soon to lose all meaning. First of all, the mechanism of phenomena could very well be studied while putting God in parentheses. Ultimately, in the system of mechanism, the role of God was limited simply to giving the initial shove that set in motion the constitutive process of the world machine and its functioning. This is why Pascal reproached Descartes: "I cannot forgive Descartes; throughout his philosophy, he would have liked to do without God, but he could not prevent himself from making him give an initial flick to set the world in motion; after this, he had no more need for God."[64]

It has also been said that in Newton's system, God is in the situation of a "retired engineer," who no longer has any reason to intervene.[65] God thus gradually became a useless hypothesis. Laplace is said to have replied to Napoleon, who asked him the role of God in his *System of the World*, "Sire, I did not need this hypothesis."[66]

There was also the seed of self-destruction in the doctrine of theological voluntarism that was closely connected to the mechanistic approach to nature. The intention had been to exalt divine transcendence by affirming the absolute freedom of God's will. Yet as Leibniz remarked in his controversy with Clarke on the subject of Newton's physics, there is an absolute equivalence between the system of absolute will, accepted by the mechanists, and the Epicurean system of absolute chance: "Will without reason would be the Epicureans' chance."[67]

Ultimately, on both sides, there is complete irrationality, since the world's appearance has no rational justification, either in voluntarist absolutism or in the uncaused deviations of Epicurean atoms. On neither side could any rational decision be made between possibilities that are completely indifferent, in the case either of Epicurean atoms or of Newton's absolute space. Beginning with the end of the eighteenth century, and especially in the nineteenth century, mechanistic science, which did without the consideration of causes and ends and stuck to the phenomena, was totally indifferent to the problem of the existence or nonexistence of God and the way he may have created the world.

"THE DEATH OF NATURE"

The extraordinarily complex phenomenon of the mechanistic revolution, which I have described all too briefly, has been the subject of many studies. Some of them have spoken, with regard to this phenomenon, of a "death of nature." This is, for instance, the title of a highly interesting book by Carolyn Merchant.[68]

It is a striking expression, but ultimately rather imprecise. It might simply mean the disappearance of the image that philosophers and scientists had of nature before the mechanistic revolution. This is indeed what happened, and the philosophers of the seventeenth century were aware of it. Until then, nature had been represented as an active subject, whether it was God himself or a power subordinate to God and acting as his instrument. In his *Treatise on the World,* Descartes expressly rejects this representation: "By Nature, I do not by any means understand here some Goddess or any other kind of imaginary power, but . . . I use this word to signify Matter itself."[69] In fact, for Descartes, the word "Nature" can designate either divine action upon Matter, or Matter itself, or the totality of laws established by God within Matter. Robert Boyle devoted a treatise to the notion of nature in 1686. He absolutely rejects the idea of a Nature conceived as a personality. Instead of saying, "Nature does this or that," it is better, according to him, to say, "Such-and-such a thing was done according to nature, that is, according to the system of laws established by God."[70]

We may wonder, however, whether the transformation of the idea of nature in the mind of a tiny group of philosophers and scientists was really able to provoke a radical transformation of man's attitude with regard to nature or a "death of nature." It was not until the beginning of the nineteenth century, from the time when production began to be industrialized and the flourishing of technology became universal, that man's relation to nature was gradually modified in depth. In the eighteenth century, some philosophers had a premonition of this evolution and proposed a different approach to nature.[71] Yet in the seventeenth and eighteenth centuries, in the artistic works often commissioned by scientists themselves, nature continued to be personalized. Paradoxically, as we shall soon see, it was precisely in the frontispieces of scientific handbooks that nature appeared personified in the form of the goddess Isis.[72] In addition, Isis/Nature became the subject of a veritable cult in the revolutionary and Romantic periods.

12

Criticism of the Promethean Attitude

In the Middle Ages and in modern times, mechanics, magicians, and scientists tried to tear from nature what they called its secrets. Yet there were powerful currents of thought that sought to restrain what was considered inordinate audacity precisely insofar as it was Promethean, since it sought to do violence to nature by artificial means.

VAIN CURIOSITY

Already in antiquity, and precisely in the story of Prometheus, who, having stolen the secret of fire from the gods, was delivered over to eternal torture, and in that of Icarus, who, flying artificially like a bird, wished to rise up as far as the sun but fell into the sea, there appeared in mythic form the presentiment of the danger represented by audacity, or hubris, for whoever sought to know the divine secrets. As I have already said, in the emblem books of the sixteenth and seventeenth centuries, these two figures symbolized the dangers of curiosity or the pretension to dominate nature.[1]

First of all, I must mention the philosophical tradition that was opposed to vain curiosity, which distracts the soul from caring about its moral life.[2] As we have seen, this was already Socrates' position, which consisted in the complete rejection of research on nature.[3] Other philosophers, while they recognized the importance of physical research, were afraid of seeing man absorb himself in it. Seneca, although he wrote a work dealing with "natural questions," thought that wishing to know more than one needs is a form of intemperance.[4] In this regard he may have been influenced by Demetrius the Cynic, from whom he quotes remarks that tend in exactly the same direction. There are many questions concerning nature, said Demetrius, which it is both impossible and useless to resolve: "Truth is hidden in the depths of the abyss, hidden in darkness."[5] Nature, however, is not jealous of its secrets, for it has placed all that leads us to happiness and moral progress within our view, and quite close to us. This must be enough for us.

As far as the Epicureans are concerned, physical research interested them only insofar as it produced peace of mind by freeing man from fear of the gods and of death. Epicurus wrote: "If we were not troubled by our apprehensions concerning celestial phenomena and death, fearing lest it be something for us because of our ignorance of the limits of pain and pleasures, we would have no need of the study of nature."[6]

The idea of God as creator, as we glimpse it in the *Timaeus,* could lead people scrupulously to respect the divine secret of the fabrication of the universe and to renounce putting forth hypotheses concerning the production of natural phenomena. Philo of Alexandria, the Jewish Platonist, speaks of the "limits of knowledge," and advises human beings to know themselves instead of imagining that they know the origin of the world.[7] We cannot be so proud as to pierce this divine secret, like those so-called sages who not only boast that they know what each being is but, out of bravado, add the knowledge of causes "as if they had been present at creation . . . as if they had been the Creator's advisers in its fabrication."[8] It is much better to seek to know ourselves. A few centuries later, Augustine condemns curiosity as the "concupiscence of the eyes" and as a need to have new experiences, even if painful.[9] We succumb to curiosity by attending spectacles and practicing magic, but also by seeking to know works of nature that are beyond our grasp, and by asking God for miracles.

For Jews and Christians, as we have seen, God's words to Adam, as recounted in the Genesis story, conferred on him a right of domination over the earth and the right to make use of inferior creatures, and had therefore, at the end of the Middle Ages, in the Renaissance, and in modern times, urged man, especially once he had observed the progress of science owing to the application of the scientific method, to seek to discover the secrets of nature and devote himself to scientific research.[10] Scientists of the seventeenth century, however, were forced to recognize a limit to this undertaking: the need to stop, after the study of phenomena, before the impenetrable secret of the divine will, which chose this world from among all possible worlds.

THE CRITIQUE OF TECHNIQUES THAT FORCE NATURE

In the second place, doubts had been raised since antiquity about the legitimacy of any technique that forces nature. In his *Memorabilia*, Xenophon recounts that Socrates doubted that research on nature was disinterested, and he suspected that those who sought to know divine things believed that once they knew "through what necessities each thing comes into being," they could, when they wished, produce wind, rain, the seasons, and whatever such things they might need.[11] Thus, already in this period, we can foresee science's Promethean ambitions.

We have seen Cicero mention the scruples of Empiricist doctors, who were afraid that, when uncovered by dissection, "organs, deprived of their envelopes[,] might be modified."[12] Entrails look different in a living being and a dead body; already altered by emotions, they are changed even more as a result of death.[13] This view of the Empiricist doctors is also reported by Celsus, the Latin encyclopedist who wrote in the first century of our era. For them, vivisection, carried out on criminals by the Dogmatic doctors Herophilus and Erasistratus in the Hellenistic period, was an act of cruelty: "An art charged with watching over mankind's health has inflicted upon someone not merely death but the most atrocious death." This death was, moreover, useless, "for what is sought at the cost of so much violence cannot be known."[14]

In addition to these methodological and moral doubts, there were also fears that could be called ecological. Magicians and experimenters sought to tear the veil away from Nature. Yet if Nature hides herself, does she not have her reasons? Does she not want to protect us in this way from the dangers that await us lest, once we have dominated and mastered her, we may be threatened by our own technical progress?

These fears bore in particular on the exploitation of mines and the digging of subterranean galleries. From the perspective of human decadence after the Golden Age, Ovid had seen in these techniques a characteristic of the complete immorality of people of the Age of Iron: "Mankind was no longer content to ask the fruitful earth for harvests and the food she owed, but he penetrated as far as her entrails; he tore from her what she had hidden, . . . the treasures that aggravate our evils. Soon pernicious iron and gold, more pernicious than iron, came forth to the light of day. Following them, came war."[15]

Seneca repeats the same theme. Instead of contemplating the immensity of the universe, we dig up the earth to extract what is hidden within it, that is, what is harmful, instead of being content with the good things it offers us: "God the father has placed within our reach whatever would be good for us. He did not wait for us to carry out our investigations, but gave to us spontaneously, burying harmful things as deep as possible. We can complain only about ourselves. We have uncovered what will cause our downfall against the will of Nature, who had hidden it from us."[16] Unlike Posidonius, whom he criticizes sharply, Seneca considers technical progress, at any rate—not the progress of knowledge—a danger to moral life, since its motive force is the love of luxury and pleasure.[17]

In the second half of the first century CE, Pliny the Elder, in his *Natural History*, was to take up the same grievances.[18] He worries about the moral consequences of technical progress, which leads to luxury and finally to the decadence of morals, instead of being content with the satisfaction of mankind's essential needs.[19] Mining research has cupidity as its motive force when its object is gold and silver and hatred when its goal is iron. This is all the more unacceptable because the earth offers us, on its surface, all that is necessary for our life and health: "How innocent and happy our life would be, nay, how refined it would be, if we only lusted for what is on the earth's surface; that is, what is right at our feet." Apart from these moralizing considerations, we also see in Pliny the emergence of fears concerning the danger that mankind's undertakings cause nature to incur. He worries about the consequences that mines excavated within the earth will have on the mountains.[20] Here the image of the earth's maternity steps in. For Pliny, earthquakes seem to be a manifestation of the "indignation of this sacred mother," for we are penetrating inside her entrails to tear from her the objects of our lust. The anonymous author of the poem "Etna" also deplores that human beings, instead of giving themselves over to disinterested scientific research, which should be their primary concern, prefer to torture the earth to tear her treasures from her.[21]

PRIMITIVISM

All this corresponds to a tendency that has been called primitivism, which was inspired by the myth of the Golden Age, that is, the image of an ideal primitive life.[22] Here, the perfection of the human race was situated at the origin of time, and technical progress was a sign of decadence. The Golden Age was the age of Kronos, as evoked by Hesiod in *Works and Days*.[23] People then lived like gods under the reign of Dike, or Justice, their hearts free from care. There was no private property. The earth was fruitful and could feed human beings, who had no need to work. For Empedocles, the first men, under the reign of Aphrodite, knew no war and were vegetarians.[24] We find this theme of the Golden Age among the Romans as well. Ovid praises this ideal time in his *Metamorphoses*.[25] With neither repression nor laws, good faith and virtue were the norm. There were no judges, no navigation, commerce, war, or weapons. The earth produced fruits and harvests without being cultivated. After such a good start, however, the human race degenerated. The golden race was succeeded by the races of silver, bronze, and iron. This last race, which corresponds to mankind's present state, is so bad that Justice, Good Faith, and Virtue have fled and risen back up to Olympus. Civilization now begins to flourish: boats are built, seas are crisscrossed, fields are delimited by surveying. Mines are dug to tear from the earth what she has hidden, and weapons can henceforth be constructed. This theory of degeneracy is linked to that of the world's growing old, which was accepted both by an Epicurean such as Lucretius, who speaks of the earth as "exhausted and tired of generating,"[26] and by a Stoic such as Seneca,[27] who foresees the final cataclysm, which would, moreover, be followed by a new world period in which the same ages of humanity would be reproduced.

Following Posidonius, Seneca evokes a Golden Age when kingship was exercised by sages, and when people lived very simply, without technology or luxury.[28] Gradually, however, degeneracy insinuated itself among mankind. Kingship was transformed into tyranny. Wise men such as the Seven Sages, of whom Solon, for instance, was a member, then had to invent laws. The decline of morals also had the result that mankind was no longer able to be content with primitive simplicity. According to Posidonius, it was once again the sages who sought to remedy this evil by inventing the various technologies. On this last point, Seneca no longer agrees with Posidonius. If, as is said, Democritus invented the vault and the keystone, it was not because he was a sage but because he was a man; for the sage must concern himself only with morality and the disinterested knowledge of nature. In addition, as Seneca remarks, Posidonius had to admit that although the sages invented new techniques, they did not practice them, but confided them to humble craftsmen. Finally, he gives an idyllic description of the Golden Age. Nature, like a mother, protected mankind. There was no private property, but everything was fraternally shared. The earth was more fertile. People slept under the stars, and thus contemplated the nocturnal sky and the movements of the stars. Nevertheless, these first men were not sages, for it was their ignorance that accounted for their innocence.

In fact, this primitivism and praise of the simple life was common to almost all the other philosophical schools. The Cynics and Epicureans in particular agreed to reject the superfluous, luxury, and wealth. Diogenes the Cynic threw away his cup after seeing a child drink from his hands, declaring that "the life accorded to mankind by the gods is easy, but this ease escapes their notice, for they seek honey cakes, perfumes, and other such refinements."[29] For Diogenes, Zeus was right to punish Prometheus for discovering fire, for fire was the origin of man's effeminacy and taste for luxury.[30] As far as Epicurus is concerned, he accepted only necessary and natural desires, which implies a rejection of civilization's refinements.

The most remarkable text from antiquity on primitivism is found in a Hermetic work that is hard to date (perhaps after the fourth century CE), and whose title is *Kore Kosmou* (a term designating Isis as the "pupil of the world's eye" or the "virgin of the world").[31] Mōmos, that is, criticism personified, reproaches Hermes for having given human bodies to the souls created by God, thus producing rash and arrogant beings who will be able, in their audacity, to see "nature's beautiful mysteries."[32] They will explore all that is hidden: "Men will tear out the roots of plants, and will examine the qualities of juices. They will scrutinize the nature of stones, and they will open down the middle not only those living beings that have no reason; nay, they will dissect their fellow men, in their desire to examine how they have been formed."[33] They will venture onto the sea by constructing boats; they will reach the ends of the earth and will rise up to the stars. For Mōmos there is only one way to humiliate man in his arrogance and limitless audacity: that is, to fill him with worries and cares. Men will be devoured by the thirst to realize their projects, and when they fail, they will be tormented by grief and sadness. Here we think of Hyginus' fable, quoted by Heidegger in *Being and Time*, which tells that it was Care that modeled the clay of which mankind is made.[34] This is probably an allusion to Prometheus, commonly considered in antiquity to be the creator of mankind, for "Prometheus" means "the foreseer" but also "worried." In any case, we are in the presence here of a deep psychological truth, for it is Promethean desire and projects, and in particular technical projects, that generate worry.

MODERN FEARS: ROUSSEAU AND GOETHE

These protests continued down through the centuries and increased as the sciences and technology developed. I shall consider only a few examples. In 1530, Agrippa von Nettesheim, though a fervent partisan of natural magic, gave a virulent critique of the artifices of civilization and the manipulations carried out against nature in the various scientific and artisanal activities, for instance, the search for precious metals in mines or the enslavement of animals in agriculture.[35]

In the eighteenth century, we note the emergence of doubts about the evolution of scientific knowledge. In the first place, there was the discouraged attitude of Diderot, who by no means rejected what he called experimental philosophy but did not believe that the scientists' efforts to build this new Tower of Babel might someday achieve their goal: "When we come to compare the infinite multitude of the phenomena of nature with the limits of our understanding and weakness of our organs, can we ever expect anything else from the slowness of our labors, their long and frequent interruptions, and the rarity of creative geniuses, than a few broken and separated pieces of the great chain that links all things together?"[36]

In Jean-Jacques Rousseau we find a remarkable echo of ancient worries and criticisms, particularly those expressed by Ovid, Seneca, and Pliny. In his discourse of 1750, he peremptorily answered "no" to the question proposed by the Academy of Dijon: "Did the restoration of sciences and arts contribute to the purification of morals?" Quite to the contrary, science and art have corrupted them, for mankind has refused to listen to nature's warnings:

> The thick veil with which she [i.e., eternal wisdom] has covered all her operations seemed sufficiently to warn us that she did not intend us for vain investigations. Yet have we been able to profit from a single one of her lessons, or is there one that we have neglected with impunity? O peoples, know therefore that Nature has wished to preserve us from science, as a mother snatches a dangerous weapon from the arms of her child; that all the secrets she hides from you are so many evils from which she protects you; and that the difficulty you experience in learning is not the least of her blessings.[37]

Nevertheless, Rousseau does not believe that we can return to the Golden Age of a state of nature, for the first human beings lived in a kind of unconsciousness and apathy, without communication among them. In addition, for him, the Golden Age could never have existed, since "the stupid men of the initial times were unable to profit from it," and it "has escaped the attention of the enlightened men of later times."[38] We cannot go back and suppress the progress of the sciences and the arts, even if it has led to the softening of morals, depravation, and hypocrisy. Yet we must be aware of the evil caused by unveiling the secrets of nature. It is therefore by perfecting "art" that we will be able to "repair the damage that art, once it had begun, did to nature."[39]

Rousseau thus saw in the idea of the secrets of nature a warning that Nature gave mankind about the dangers represented for him by sciences, technology, and civilization. Yet he accepted that Nature should allow herself to be unveiled by experimental science and the advances of civilization, albeit at man's risk and peril. In his *Anthropology*, Kant gave a good summary of Rousseau's thought on this point:

> With regard to the hypochondriacal [i.e., dark-colored] portrait that Rousseau sketches of the human race taking the risk of leaving the state of nature: we must not see in this advice to return to it and to take the path into the forests once more. This is not his genuine opinion, but he wished to express the difficulty for our race of reaching its destination by following the route of a continuous approach. Such an opinion is not to be considered a castle in Spain: the experience of ancient and modern times must embarrass every individual who reflects and make the progress of our race doubtful . . . Rousseau did not think that man should return to the state of nature, but rather that he should take a retrospective glance at it from the level he has reached today.[40]

Rousseau may also have been influenced by the Epicurean description given by Lucretius in his poem on the evolution of mankind. On the one hand, Lucretius here describes the first human beings as completely bereft of astonishment, and seemingly completely ignorant of the common good.[41] On the other hand, he distinguishes two periods in the development of culture.[42] In the first stage, it was through need and necessity, and not through the desire for knowledge, that people were constrained to discover the things that were indispensable for life, that is, natural and necessary things. In a second phase, the desires that were not necessary led to the invention of technologies such as navigation, weaving, and metallurgy, intended to produce things which, if they are desired in an immoderate way, generate luxury and war: "The human race works ceaselessly and in vain, and consumes itself in vain cares. For man does not know where possession must stop, and what is the limit true pleasure can reach."[43]

For Rousseau, the arts are born from mankind's passions, from ambition, avarice, and vain curiosity. In Lucretius, as in Rousseau, reason must therefore learn to moderate desires and "repair the damage that art, once it had begun, did to nature." Happiness consists not in exaggerated well-being but in a life that is simple and close to nature. Ultimately, Rousseau doubts that mankind can reach the truth: "Are we therefore born to die, tied to the edge of the well where truth has retired?"[44]

A few years later Goethe would criticize experimental science from a wholly different perspective. He fits into another tradition, that of the Empiricist doctors mentioned by Cicero who rejected dissection because it disturbed the phenomena it was intended to observe. For him, everything that is artificial is incapable of unveiling Nature, for the excellent reason that Nature, paradoxically, is "mysterious in broad daylight," and that, as I shall have occasion to repeat, her real veil consists in having no veil; in other words, she hides because we do not know how to see her, although she is right before our eyes:

> You instruments, you mock me, I can see,
> With wheel and pulley, cylinder and cords:
> I faced the gate, you were to be the key,
> But cannot lift the bolts, however shrewd your wards.
> Mysterious in broad daylight, never

Will Nature be defrauded of her veil.
What to your spirit she reveal not, that you fail
to torture out of her with screw or lever.[45]

Goethe thus contradicts Francis Bacon, who sought to force Nature to talk under the torture of experimentation. For Goethe, rather than talk, "Nature keeps silent under torture." However, as the Gospels advise, she replies frankly to questions she is asked forthrightly. "Her answer to an honest question is: Yes! Yes! No! No! All the rest comes from the evil One."[46]

When assisted by mechanical means, observation disturbs the "healthy" vision of natural phenomena: "Microscope and telescope are only good for confusing healthy reason."[47] Furthermore, "man in himself, insofar as he uses healthy reason, is the greatest and most exact instrument that can exist. And precisely the greatest disorder of the new physics consists in the fact that men have been separated from experiences and have wished to recognize Nature only in what is shown by artificial instruments, and even to delimit and prescribe the effects she can carry out."[48]

For Goethe, the only real way to discover the secrets of nature is through perception and the aesthetic description of perception. Only nature—that is, mankind's senses, understood as free from all intermediaries—can see nature. Even observation, which disturbs the phenomenon and immobilizes it, prevents us from seeing living reality. In this regard, Goethe wrote a delightful poem on the dragonfly:

> The changeful dragonfly
> Flutters around the fountain;
> Long it delights my view.

It is now dark, now light; now red, now blue. Yet when it stops, and one seizes it in one's hand, one no longer sees anything but a funereal blue: "This is what is in store for you, O you who dissect your plea-sure."[49]

In the twentieth century, scientists and philosophers expressed the same fears with regard to the mechanization of nature. Some have spoken of the "disenchantment of the world" or the "death of nature." I cannot enter into the details of the abundant literature that has been devoted to this problem, though Georges Duhamel, Aldous Huxley, Rainer Maria Rilke, and many others should be cited. Two lectures on this theme delivered November 17 and 18, 1953, are particularly significant, the first by Martin Heidegger and the second by the physicist Werner Heisenberg. Heidegger insists forcefully in his lecture on what I have called the Promethean character of contemporary technology.[50] In his view, this is a violent approach aimed at obtaining nature's unveiling: "The unveiling that rules over modern technology is a provocation [herausfordern] by which nature is summoned to hand over an energy which, as such, can be extracted and accumulated."[51] Catherine Chevalley gives an excellent summary of Heidegger's position with regard to this phenomenon: "The contemporary period is one in which man perceives everything in the form of a device and an exploitable supply, including himself, and simultaneously loses his own being."[52] For Heidegger, mankind must return to Greek poiēsis, which is also a form of unveiling, or making-something-come-to-light.[53] Thus, for contemporary man, art could be a means for rediscovering his authentic relation to being and to himself. In his lecture titled "The Image of Nature in Contemporary Physics," Heisenberg denounces the same danger: "We live in a world so completely transformed by man that we everywhere encounter structures of which he is the author: the use of instruments in daily life, the preparation of food by machines, the transformation of the countryside . . . , so that man no longer encounters anything but himself."[54] Unlike Heidegger, he does not think that it is technology in itself that constitutes the danger; it is rather the fact that mankind has not yet been able to adapt itself to its new conditions of life.

Fifty years later, we must indeed admit that mankind, far from having mastered this situation, finds itself, on the contrary, faced with still more serious dangers. Technology is engendering a way of life and ways of thinking that have as their consequence the ever-increasing mechanization of human beings themselves. It is impossible, however, to stop the implacable progress of this kind of civilization. In the process, mankind risks losing its soul as well as its body.

VI

The Orphic Attitude

Unveiling Secrets through Discourse, Poetry, and Art

13

Physics as a Conjectural Science

I have distinguished two methods of unveiling the secrets of nature: one I called Promethean and one I called Orphic. In Part V I sketched the history of the former method, which extends from the beginnings of Greek mechanics to the mechanistic revolution of the seventeenth century and opened the way for the technological and industrialized world in which we live.

The time has now come to describe the other method, which seeks to discover the secrets of nature while confining itself to perception, without the help of instruments, and using the resources of philosophical and poetic discourse or those of the pictorial arts. From Plato's *Timaeus* to Paul Claudel's *Art poétique,* but also to Roger Caillois's *Esthétique généralisée,* we will now discover another tradition, whose method of approaching nature differs radically from the Promethean tradition.

At certain moments, however, the two traditions meet and complete each other. Already sketched in Plato's *Timaeus,* this reciprocal influence becomes more specific in the research on nature of a Stoic such as Seneca, appears clearly in the engineers and artists of the Renaissance such as Leonardo da Vinci and Albrecht Dürer, and continues to live on down to the present day, whether in the mathematical vision of nature or again in the definition of "maxims" or fundamental laws of nature's behavior and action.

PLATO'S *TIMAEUS*

The *Timaeus* is the archetypal model of what I have called the Orphic attitude. The birth of the world and all natural processes are divine secrets. Human beings, by contrast, can understand only what they can produce by their own art. They therefore have no technical means for discovering the secrets of the construction carried out by the gods. Plato writes: "If one wished to test this by checking it against experience, one would ignore the difference between the human and the divine condition; for only a god knows well how different elements can be mixed together into a Whole, in order to dissociate them later, and he is also the only one capable of this. Yet no man is capable of doing either one at present, and no doubt he will never be so in the future."[1]

The only means accessible to mankind is discourse. From this perspective, when it comes to the secret of the fashioning of the world, we should try to imitate the generation of the universe—that is, by a divine being—through the generation of discourse; in other words, we should try to rediscover the genetic movement of things in the motion of discourse. This is why the *Timaeus* is presented as a *poiēsis*, that is, as both a discourse and a poem, or an artistic game that imitates the artistic game of that poet of the universe, the divinity.[2] Thus, Plato believes that the god World is born in his discourse ("this god who once was truly born one day, and who has just been born in our discourse").[3]

We here encounter for the first time a theme that will play a vital role in our story: that of the work of art, the discourse or poem, as a means of knowing Nature. Such knowledge, in the words of Paul Claudel, is nothing other than "being born together," for the artist espouses Nature's creative movement, and the event of the birth of a work of art is ultimately a mere moment in the event of the birth of Nature.[4]

Nevertheless, says Plato, this discourse belongs to the literary genre of "likely myth."[5] As Francis MacDonald Cornford has remarked, Plato seems to be alluding here to the fact that his dialogue takes its place in the series of great theogonic poems of the pre-Socratics, alongside Hesiod, Xenophanes, and Parmenides, who had used the word "likely" or even "lies" with regard to their work.[6] Plato speaks with irony of his own effort, but this irony does nothing to diminish the importance he gives to this game that consists in forging a likely myth. In any case, Plato insists on the approximate and merely likely character of all that can be said about the overall process of the generation of the universe:

> If, then, on several points and many questions—the gods and the generation of the universe—it is impossible for us to propose explanations that are completely coherent within themselves in every point and perfectly exact, don't be surprised! But if we come upon some that do not yield to any others in likeliness, we must be satisfied with this, remembering that I who now speak, and you who are my judges, are mere human beings, so that if we are presented with a likely myth in these matters, it is not fitting to seek further.[7]

As far as particular natural processes are concerned, Plato also insists on the fact that all he claims to risk is an explanation that is merely likely. While discussing metals, he makes the following remark: "And likewise for all the other bodies of the same kind, it is not very difficult to speak about them when we pursue the genre of 'likely fables.' When, as a kind of respite, and abandoning discourse that pertains to eternal beings, we examine a likely one concerning the birth of things, and thereby obtain pleasure without remorse, we introduce a moderate and reasonable pleasure into our lives."[8] The *Timaeus* is thus a story that lays claim to mere likelihood. This is why, from the perspective of Aristotle's *Poetics,* it is of the order of poetry rather than that of history, for it tells not what really happened—only a god could do that—but what could or should have happened.[9]

Plato thus describes an ideal genesis, and, for instance, when it comes to determining which triangles are involved in the constitution of the elements, he thinks that to answer this question, we must inquire which are the most beautiful scalene triangles. He notes, moreover, that he will consider anyone who can discover more beautiful ones not an enemy but a friend, thus indicating both the limits of his hypotheses and his disinterested search for the truth.

The goal of this likely discourse is to supply a model in the modern sense of the term, that is, a possible schema that enables us to consider the genesis of the world. Descartes adopted the same procedure, for other reasons—namely, out of fear of the Inquisition—when, in his *Discourse on Method*,[10] he presented his *Treatise on the World* as "a fable feigned for pleasure, bereft of any claim to historicity," in the words of Étienne Gilson, commenting on the following text by Descartes: "I resolved . . . to speak only of what would happen in a new [world], if God now created somewhere in the space of the imagination enough matter to compose it . . . After that, I showed how most of the matter of this chaos should, as a result of these laws, be disposed and arranged in a certain way that would make it similar to our heavens."[11]

In the *Timaeus,* as Jürgen Mittelstrass pointed out, Plato does not try to give an exact account of the world such as it is.[12] Instead, he aims to show how the world would appear to us if it were fashioned rationally, that is, in the image of the model constituted by the Ideas.

At the beginning of this chapter I spoke of the meeting points between the two methods of approaching nature. Plato's *Timaeus* provides us with the first example, for this comparison between Plato and Descartes allows us to glimpse, despite the almost insurmountable distance between their methods, an analogous procedure. Like "idealist" explanations, mechanistic explanations claim mere likelihood and are only hypothetical. They hypothesize a certain mode of functioning, defined, if possible, by a mathematical ratio, to explain the effect that appears before our eyes. As we have seen, however, they accept that in reality, beneath the same appearance, the mode of functioning can be different, and another hypothesis may be possible.[13]

In his description, Plato begins, like the geometers, from indemonstrable axioms, in particular the principle of causality and the distinction between "being" and "becoming," as Proclus points out.[14] He then uses mythical elements such as the Demiurge, the Nursemaid, the Mixing Bowl, and mathematical elements, for instance, the triangles intended to explain the composition of the elements.[15] As Luc Brisson and F. Walter Meyerstein have shown, the *Timaeus* thus appears as the model of future scientific theories, even contemporary ones, particularly because it has its starting point in axioms that are indemonstrable in themselves but are capable of helping to construct a reasonable and likely representation of the universe; that is, ultimately, to "invent" it.[16]

There is another point of contact between the two methods: the idea that mathematical models can account for phenomena. Plato's geometer God, as we have seen, became the eternal geometer of the Enlightenment.[17] The structure of reality was thus mathematical. What had been an unverifiable hypothesis in Plato, however, was to become rigorous calculation among the mechanists.

THE CONJECTURAL NATURE OF PHYSICS

In antiquity, physics was a discourse and not—with very rare exceptions, to which I have alluded—an experimental practice.[18] It was a discourse, but a conjectural discourse. The conjectural nature of physics, in its totality or at least in its details, seems indeed to have been recognized not only by the Platonists but also by all the philosophical schools of antiquity. As far as Aristotle and his school are concerned, Simplicius (sixth century CE), the commentator on the *Physics*, notes that by defining what characterizes a rigorous demonstration and by affirming that it must start from principles that are obvious in themselves, Aristotle implicitly suggested that physics is only conjectural in nature, since it does not fulfill these criteria. In this context, Simplicius cites Theophrastus, Aristotle's disciple, who said that we must not despise physics because of this but must begin with it, since it is best adapted to our human nature and our capacities.[19] It is hard to say whether, in this passage, we should attribute the affirmation of the conjectural nature of natural research to Theophrastus, but this is quite possible, since Proclus tells us that Theophrastus sought to explain the origin of thunder, wind, storms, rain, snow, and hail in a likely way.[20] It was especially in this kind of question that all the schools renounced dogmatism and accepted the possibility of a plurality of explanations.

In his *Lucullus*, Cicero insists on the conjectural character of research on nature, detailing all the questions that confront philosophers with regard to the things that are invisible and inaccessible to us: the earth's location, the inhabitants and mountains of the moon, the existence of human beings at the poles, the earth's rotation on its axis, the dimensions of the sun, the existence and nature of the soul, atoms and the void, the plurality of worlds, and the origin of the images in dreams. "The sage," he says, "will fear to judge in a rash way, and he will think he has done well if, in these kinds of matters, he discovers something likely."[21] He rightly emphasizes that opinions may vary on these problems within each philosophical school.

In the *Natural Questions* of the Stoic Seneca, we find the same attitude with regard to terrestrial and celestial phenomena. For him there is no orthodox Stoic doctrine concerning physical problems; instead he chooses the explanation that seems to him most likely. Strabo, also of Stoic tendencies, insists on the state of concealment in which the causes of physical phenomena lie hidden *(epikrupsis tōn aitiōn).*[22] Marcus Aurelius also alludes to this attitude: "Things are, in a way, hidden by such a veil, that some philosophers—no small number of them, and not the least, either—have thought that they cannot be grasped; and moreover, the Stoics themselves have considered them hard to grasp."[23]

A work falsely attributed to Galen, but which may be contemporary with him, defined science as a solid, firm knowledge, free of error, and based on reason, and concludes that it cannot be found in philosophy, especially when it discourses upon nature, or in medicine, which is a mere art.[24]

Obviously, the Neoplatonists were faithful to the Platonic tradition that considers nature a derivative, inferior reality, sensible and therefore difficult to know. Proclus repeats several times that *phusiologia,* or the study of *phusis,* is an *eikotologia,* or likely discourse.[25] Whether in the domain of terrestrial bodies, which are subject to becoming, or of celestial bodies, we must be content with what is approximate, for we reside very far away and very low within the universe. This approximate character of the knowledge of nature appears clearly in the astronomical hypotheses that result in identical conclusions from different hypotheses. Some claim to "save the appearances (or the phenomena)" *(sōzein ta phainomena)* by means of the theory of eccentrics; others affirm the same thing by means of epicycles, and still others, finally, by means of spheres that rotate in opposite directions.[26]

MULTIPLE EXPLANATIONS OF A SINGLE PHENOMENON

Epicurus, who obviously held fast to the fundamental principles of his physics—atoms and the void, since they enabled him to forgo the hypothesis of divine creation—was happy to admit that throughout an entire section of physics, it is possible to propose different explanations for the same phenomenon, for instance, solstices or eclipses; multiple explanations, then, each of which must agree with appearances.[27] Lucretius, as a faithful disciple of Epicurus, set forth this principle with maximum clarity:

> To determine with certainty which of these explanations is true in our world is difficult. What I am setting forth, however, is what might be true and could exist in the totality of all worlds, among the different worlds each one of which has been produced differently. As far as the stars' motion is concerned, by proposing several explanations, I strive to set forth the causes that might exist in the totality of all the worlds. In our world as elsewhere, however, there must necessarily be one single cause that makes the stars move. Yet to teach what this cause is, is not possible for one who advances only one step at a time.[28]

It is interesting to note in Lucretius that this theory of multiple explanations involves the Epicurean idea of the plurality of worlds. The proposed explanations are hypotheses that correspond to different types of the formation of worlds. This procedure is similar to that of Descartes, who claimed "to speak only of what would happen in a new [world]."

This theory of multiple explanations also corresponds to another aspect of the ancient conception of physics, which I will discuss later on. Physics is conceived as a spiritual exercise, which, particularly among the Epicureans, was intended to ensure peace of mind by suppressing fear of the gods and of death. To propose multiple explanations, all of which are likely, because they can all account for the phenomena that can be observed, is therefore to help the soul remain in serenity.

"SAVING THE PHENOMENA"

Another point of contact between the two approaches to nature, the methodological principle of ancient astronomers, *sōzein ta phai-*

nomena (save the phenomena)—that is, to propose explanations that enable us to account for what appears to us—continued to be accepted by the first mechanistic physicists, but its meaning changed completely. Simplicius attributes it to Plato, but in fact, as Jürgen Mittelstrass has shown, this principle goes back to the astronomer Eudoxus.[29] In any case, in order to understand its meaning, we must recall that for the ancients, the stars were divine and were moved by divine intelligences. Their movements had to be perfect, regular, and therefore circular. Upon observation, however, the stars' motions appear irregular, and therefore irrational. Speaking of the motion of planets like Venus and Mars, Pliny the Elder saw "secrets of nature" in them.[30] To explain this discord between sensible appearances and what was considered to be the truth concerning the divine stars, it was necessary to imagine a geometrical model that could show how regular circular movements could appear irregular to a human observer. Thanks to these hypotheses, it was thus possible to "save the phenomena" (or the appearances), that is, to reconcile theoretical postulates and sensible evidence. More and more refined systems of circular movements were invented by supposing that the earth was impassible at the center of the universe, or, on the contrary, like Heraclides of Pontus, that the earth was in motion and the sun immobile. Astronomers willingly accepted the possibility of multiple hypotheses, each of which could, in its way, "save the phenomena," without the possibility of determining what really occurs in the heavens.[31] In the words of Simplicius, "to disagree on these hypotheses cannot give rise to reproaches, for what we propose is to know what must be laid down as hypotheses in order for phenomena to be saved. It is therefore not surprising if some have sought to save the phenomena by means of certain hypotheses and others by means of other hypotheses."[32]

The same conception was stated in the sixteenth century by the Lutheran theologian Osiander in his prologue to Copernicus's *De*

Revolutionibus, with regard to the latter's heliocentric hypothesis: "It is not necessary that these hypotheses be true; what is more, it is not necessary that they be probable, but it is enough for them to propose a calculus that agrees with observations [that is, the phenomena] . . . Let no one expect anything certain from astronomy, as far as hypotheses are concerned, for it can propose no such thing."[33]

The principle of "saving the phenomena" thus still seems to be alive. It is true, however, that Osiander, like Cardinal Bellarmino, whom I mentioned earlier with regard to Galileo,[34] was a theologian who sought to minimize the importance of Copernicus's theses, for fear of entering into conflict with the Christian faith, which upheld geocentrism. Yet his attitude provoked a genuine scandal, not only among Copernicus's friends such as Tiedemann Giese, but also with Kepler and Giordano Bruno, because they held Copernicus's hypothesis to be fundamentally true.[35] At the beginning of the seventeenth century, the principle of "saving the phenomena" changed its meaning completely. For Kepler and Galileo, the "phenomena" are no longer just celestial phenomena; they are the phenomena of nature.[36] The difference between the status of celestial objects and the status of earthly objects was abolished. The stars were no longer divine beings. Astronomy and physics met. Henceforth, the goal would be to seek to explain physical phenomena, whether celestial or terrestrial, not by possible mathematic models that might have equivalent probability, but by mathematical models that are empirically verifiable, and that observation and experience are able to confirm. Science wants to be exact; this is why the word "hypothesis" would henceforth be tinged with suspicion. Kepler wanted to establish an "astronomy without hypotheses,"[37] and Newton wrote the famous saying, "I have not yet been able to deduce the reason for these properties of weight from the phenomena, and *hypotheses non fingo,* I do not imagine hypotheses."[38] Newton here understands the word "hypothesis" in the sense of an unverifiable construction: where experimentation is not yet possible for the moment, we must reject arbitrary speculations. He prefers to use the word "theory" to designate the model that experimentation is supposed to verify.

This ideal of a verifiable experimental science is still, in principle, that of modern science, although the gigantic progress of science has led scientists to correct an over-simplistic realism. Clearly, however, this progress in observation and experimentation can always put in question what had been taken for granted. In this perspective, the truth is only the correction of an error, or, what amounts to the same thing, it is the daughter of Time.

14

Truth as the Daughter of Time

Faithful to the tradition of Plato's *Timaeus,* Seneca was quite aware of the conjectural nature of knowledge. "Is what I and others have said about comets true?" he asked. "Only the gods know, they who possess the knowledge of the truth. For us, it is possible only to investigate these domains and to make progress in these hidden things, with the help of conjectures, no doubt deprived of the certainty of discovering, but not bereft of all hope."[1] However, he also glimpsed the possibility of a progress of science and a slow and difficult discovery of the secrets of Nature: "If we were to combine all our efforts, we would be able only with the greatest difficulty to reach the abyss in which the Truth has been placed."[2]

THE HOPES OF RESEARCH

If there is any hope of progress, it is, first of all, because Nature does not hide her secrets with too much intransigence. In a treatise in which he tries to cure the curious of their passion, Plutarch advises them to orient their curiosity toward research on nature: sunrise and sunset, for instance, or the phases of the moon. Nor can he prevent himself from remarking, "These are the secrets of Nature, yet she is by no means unhappy that they are stolen from her."[3]

For some Stoic philosophers, God and Nature reveal their secrets voluntarily. Thus, according to Aratus, who wrote his poem on astronomy in the third century BCE: "Zeus has not yet accorded the knowledge of everything to us mortals. There are still many things of which Zeus, if he so wills, will also inform us."[4]

As Philo of Alexandria affirms, if "nature loves to hide," as Heraclitus would have it, Nature also has within her at the same time a tendency to manifest herself, just as the truth has within it a force that demands to be brought to light.[5] This is why, says Philo, the inventions of false prophets are quickly unveiled. "When the time comes, Nature, thanks to her invisible powers, unveils the beauty that characterizes her." Moreover, it is not her works and productions that Nature hides.[6] On the contrary, she lets us see the stars and the sky in order to inspire within us a passion for philosophy, and provides us with earthly things for our use and our pleasure. We can assume that Philo, who always cites Heraclitus' aphorism with enthusiasm, considers that what Nature hides are the causes of these phenomena— phenomena that she is pleased to set before our eyes. It is precisely because Nature appears before our eyes in a magnificent and marvelous way that we wonder what founds this apparition.

THE IDEA OF THE PROGRESS OF SCIENTIFIC KNOWLEDGE IN ANTIQUITY

The idea of a progressive unveiling of what man does not know had appeared as early as the fifth century BCE[7] in Xenophanes, who wrote:

> Not since the beginning have the gods
> unveiled all things to mortals, but, by seeking,
> with time they discover what is better.[8]

Thinkers of the fifth century, whether Sophists or tragic authors, often returned to the same theme: human civilization makes progress by means of inventions and discoveries. As Jacques Jouanna has noted, texts from this period do not agree on the causes of this transformation of the human condition.[9] We must admit that progress appears sometimes as a gift of the gods and sometimes as the fruit of human effort. Aeschylus in the *Prometheus* and Euripides in the *Suppliants* attribute the rise from bestiality to humanity to the intervention of a god, which does not imply that such progress will continue into the future.[10] By contrast, other authors affirmed that man makes progress in his knowledge by means of his research, experiences, and efforts. This was the case for Sophocles in his *Antigone*, when he recognized man as the most prodigious and terrifying phenomenon on earth: by his audacity, he has dominated all other beings, the seas by navigation, the earth by agriculture, animals by hunting; words and thought, he has taught himself everything.[11] Progress is thus considered above all technical progress, which, according to Manilius or Lucretius, for instance, is due to the need and necessity that constrain man progressively to discover the secrets of nature.[12] Yet other thinkers, such as Aristotle or Seneca, envisage progress only from the perspective of disinterested knowledge. For Aristotle, the flourishing of disinterested science—that is, for him, of philosophy—was possible only "because almost all the necessities of life and the things important for mankind's well-being had been satisfied."[13]

PROGRESS AS PROGRESSIVE REVELATION

Seneca contributed in an important way to the formation of the idea of scientific progress in our Western philosophy. Yet we have seen how hostile he was to the idea of technical progress.[14] For him, the only true progress is progress in knowledge and in moral life.

In his *Natural Questions*, written in the first century of our era, he deals with various specific problems and discusses comets in particular. After enumerating the different hypotheses on this subject, he raises the question of their truth. And as we saw at the beginning of this chapter, he admits the conjectural character of the research that man is able to carry out in this field. However, in this quest for knowledge, we are not bereft of all hope, if we apply ourselves enthusiastically. First of all, many things hidden by nature eventually appear. This is precisely the case with comets. Rejecting Panaetius' theory, according to which a comet is merely a phenomenon that looks like a star, Seneca affirms that a comet is a regular star, but one that appears only rarely. It is the course of the universe's motion that reveals it to us.

This idea can be explained within the overall perspective of Stoic physics. The Stoic universe develops within a finite period, which is always eternally repeated in an identical way. However, this period is delimited by a movement of diastole that provokes the expansion of the universe, which, in successive phases, reaches a point of maximal complexity until, in a movement of systole, the world returns to its initial point. New phenomena thus appear in the course of a cosmic period; they are new in the sense that they reveal hidden virtualities. This concept of hidden virtualities corresponds rather well to the notion of "seminal reasons," that is, hidden seeds that develop in a methodical and rational way, according to a definite program, in order to give life to organisms.[15]

For Seneca, we know only a minute part of the entire world, yet some things will be revealed only in the future, and we must therefore resign ourselves to abandoning these discoveries to the generations that will come after us: "How many animals has our century been the first to know, how many objects have not even come to the knowledge of our century! Many things that are completely unknown to us will be known only to the coming generation. Many discoveries are reserved for future centuries, when all memories of us will be extinguished."[16]

Nature is thus not given once and for all but is a process that unfolds in time and is revealed to man only gradually and partially. This process follows definite stages, and new phenomena can appear that had never manifested themselves before. On this subject, the Christian writer Lactantius reports a controversy between Academics and Stoics.[17] The former made fun of the Stoics, who affirmed that everything was made for mankind. Did God, they asked, also make for mankind all the things in the sea and on the earth that are hostile to mankind and bring him every kind of evil? The Stoics replied that there are still many things whose usefulness has not yet appeared but will be discovered in the course of time, just as need and experience have already led us to discover many things that were unknown to the centuries that preceded us.

For Seneca, this progressive revelation evokes the revelation, likewise progressive, accomplished in the Eleusinian mysteries. In a grandiose image, the world now appears as an immense Eleusis and humanity as a neophyte who gradually traverses the degrees of initiation:

> Some mysteries are not revealed all at once. Eleusis reserves new objects to display to those who return to visit it. Likewise, Nature does not reveal all her mysteries at the same time. We think we are initiated, and yet we are still merely waiting in the vestibule of the Temple. These arcana are not revealed indiscriminately to all human beings. They are far away, closed up in the innermost sanctuary. Our century will see only a part of these mysteries, and the following century will see another one.[18]

The true mysteries are ultimately not those of the little sanctuary of Eleusis but the mysteries of Nature itself, into which all of mankind is gradually initiated, and which are revealed in the immensity of the cosmos. This was, moreover, a traditional metaphor in Stoicism. Cleanthes and Chrysippus had already compared the study of physics to the rites of Eleusinian initiation.[19] This metaphor implies that as in the mysteries, where initiates achieve perfect contemplation of the object of initiation, mankind, at the end of the cosmic period, achieves a global vision of the whole of reality. Yet I do not think that Seneca envisaged this consequence; instead, he was thinking of a progressive initiation, without particularly imagining a final illumination.

The scientist in the temple of the world must therefore behave like a believer in the temple of a god.[20] In fact, this attitude of religious reverence consists, for Seneca, in the exercise of scientific objectivity: not to affirm something when one does not know it, or not to deform the truth when one does know something. It is interesting to note that for the Stoic philosophers, from the perspective of knowledge of the cosmos, the seriousness of research takes on a sacred value.

PROGRESS AS THE COLLECTIVE RESEARCH
OF SUCCESSIVE GENERATIONS

Scientific progress, however, is not linked only to the cosmic process that makes new objects appear to people who passively discover the divine work; it also consists in an intense effort at research and reflection to unveil the secrets of nature.[21] Ever since antiquity, people have been aware of the importance of the efforts of successive generations for the progress of studies. This was an argument that dogmatic Platonists, such as Antiochus of Ascalon, as reported by Cicero, proposed in opposition to probabilist Platonists: "If, in the presence of completely new objects, the first philosophers, who were like newborns, had hesitations, can we believe that nothing has been illuminated, after such considerable efforts carried out for so many centuries, by such great minds?"[22]

The appeal to research resounds from one end to the other of Seneca's *Natural Questions,* and the presentiment of future success manifests itself. Yet it takes time, a very long time, to make progress, especially in the field of celestial phenomena such as comets, which appear only seldom. Astronomy, says Seneca, emerged scarcely fifteen hundred years ago, and many peoples are still unaware of it today. It is only very recently, according to Seneca, that the "motions of the five planets" have been discovered.

Progress is a slow, collective work of man. Knowledge advances only gradually. This, moreover, is what inspires tolerance but also gratitude toward the ancients:

> All was still new for those who made their first effort . . . But if we find something, nevertheless, it is to the ancients that we must attribute what we have received. Greatness of soul was required to dissipate the darkness in which nature is enclosed, so as not to be content with looking at it from outside but to plunge into the secrets of the gods. He who has contributed the most to discoveries is he who has thought them possible. We must therefore listen to our predecessors with indulgence. Nothing is perfect right from the beginning.[23]

Pliny the Elder said the same thing: if we modify the opinions of our predecessors, it is because of them that we can do so, precisely because it is they who have traced the path.[24] Nor must we imagine that we are superior to them. The truth is no one's property.[25] Our turn will come. We will be criticized, we who think we possess the truth: *"There will come a time when our ignorance of such obvious facts will amaze posterity."*[26]

I have italicized this text by Seneca, on which our contemporaries would do well to meditate. They might be inspired by his modesty, particularly certain scientists who find various scientific errors of the ancients "absurd." In two thousand years, who knows if scientific certitudes that seem indisputable to us today will not be treated as "absurd"? And yet scientific certitudes, reinforced by medical successes, are only partial, and therefore relative, visions of reality. Even the doctors of antiquity, with all their ideas that seem false to us, succeeded in curing the sick, thanks to remedies chosen by the animal instinct that persists in mankind, but also thanks to surgical techniques elaborated as a result of precise and repeated observations or experiments, which, unfortunately, as is also the case for contemporary scientists, were not capable of embracing the totality of the complex aspects of reality, or, as the ancients would have said, all the "secrets of nature."

In Seneca, then, we find the firm hope that the efforts of future generations will cause science to progress.[27] The ancients have left us not definitive discoveries but paths for research. An immense task awaits future generations, yet this task is not reserved for a few human beings but is incumbent on all of mankind. One human life cannot suffice: "The world would be a puny thing indeed if it gave the whole of humanity nothing to search for."[28] The history of mankind therefore appears as a long initiation, which is transmitted by successive generations.

SENECA AND THE MODERN DEVELOPMENT
OF THE IDEA OF PROGRESS

These passages from the *Natural Questions* were to play a crucial role in the development of the modern idea of progress. It began as early as the thirteenth century, with that extraordinary personage we have already encountered, Roger Bacon, the Franciscan from Oxford. Seneca would probably have been horrified by Bacon's imaginary technical inventions, which I have discussed.[29] Nevertheless, Bacon takes up Seneca's very words from the *Natural Questions* to express his faith in progress: "The day will come when time and lengthy research will reveal in broad daylight all these things that are hidden for the moment."[30]

At the end of the sixteenth century, Louis le Roy, amazed by recent great discoveries, also took up Seneca's words to express his hope for the progress of knowledge: "All God's mysteries and the secrets of nature cannot be discovered at the same time. How many things have been known and discovered in our period!"[31]

We encounter this hope for discoveries once again at the dawn of modern science, for instance, when Francis Bacon, hoping that Nature still keeps secrets of great utility hidden in her bosom, repeats, following Seneca: "These secrets have not yet been discovered; and no doubt one day they too will come to light, throughout the multiple circuits and windings of the coming centuries, as previous inventions have done."[32]

We have seen that Seneca felt both gratitude and indulgence toward his predecessors, who had the merit of harboring the hope of unveiling the secrets of nature but still lacked experience. The moderns are more enlightened because they profit from the efforts and teachings of the ancients. This is affirmed by Roger Bacon: "The youngest are the most perspicacious."[33] Here he is citing not Seneca but, as Édouard Jeauneau has shown, the ancient grammarian Priscian.[34]

From this perspective, however, a reversal was about to occur. If the "young" knew better than the "old," might not the old be the moderns? Giordano Bruno did not hesitate to make this affirmation: "We [i.e., we who are present at this moment] are older and more advanced in age than our predecessors."[35] To be a modern, if we consider the history of mankind to be like that of a human being who learns and instructs himself, is to be old; and to be an ancient is to be young. The ancients were young by virtue of their inexperience, but also by virtue of the freshness of their intuitions. The moderns are old because they have profited from the groping and the experience of the ancients. The moderns, however, having inherited the work of successive generations, must not let themselves be impressed by the so-called authority of the so-called ancients, who were in fact only young beginners.[36]

Michelet takes up this idea in an admirable passage from his *Journal,* so that he, too, can rehabilitate the ancients:

One could, moreover, maintain that we are the elders. Who is older, Virgil or Homer? In the latter, one senses a sap of eternal youth; in Virgil, on the contrary, the world is old and melancholy.

New ideas constantly come to rejuvenate the world; each day it is more powerful, more complex, and more varied. Yet antiquity is simpler, and it contains ideas in a concentrated state, or the state of an elixir.[37]

At the end of the sixteenth century, the dawn of the modern age, this conception led Francis Bacon to urge his contemporaries to free themselves from respect for the authority of the ancients:

> What has prevented men from making progress in the sciences, and has kept them as under the effect of a spell, is again the respect for antiquity, and the authority of those who have been considered masters in philosophy, and finally consensus . . . As far as antiquity is concerned, the opinion that men form of it is quite superficial, and is scarcely in agreement with the word itself; for it is the world's old age that must be considered true antiquity, and these features are to be attributed to our time, and not to the younger age of the world that belonged to the ancients. For the age that is most ancient and advanced with regard to us was with regard to the world itself the newest and most precocious.[38]

This, Bacon continues, is why we must expect a great deal from our time, insofar as it has been enriched by an infinity of experiences and observations.

Like Seneca, Bacon can invoke all the recent discoveries that have enriched man's knowledge, all the more legitimately in that, as he himself says, "through voyages and distant navigations (which have been multiplied in our time), numerous things in nature have been revealed and discovered which may spread a new light for philosophy." He continues: "As far as authorities are concerned, it takes a great deal of cowardice to attribute infinite credit to them and deny its rights to the authority of authorities, and the author of all authorities: I mean Time. For it is rightly said, 'Truth the daughter of Time,' and not of authority."[39] It is therefore not surprising that the illustrator of the first edition of Francis Bacon's *New Atlantis* represented Father Time on the frontispiece, scythe in hand, dragging a naked young woman, who represents Truth, from a cave.[40]

This critique of the argument from authority was to have a great deal of resonance in modern times, for instance, in Pascal's "Fragment d'un traité du vide," where he argues that the ancients did not hesitate to criticize their predecessors, so why should we not do so ourselves? Profiting from their discoveries, we must have the ambition of making new ones in order to bequeath them to posterity. This is how science makes progress: "The secrets of Nature are hidden. Although she always acts, we do not always discover her effects. Time reveals them from era to era, and although she is always equal to herself, she is not always equally well known."[41]

TRUTH, DAUGHTER OF TIME

The role of Time in human progress was already recognized in antiquity.[42] The author of the treatise *On Ancient Medicine* presents the discovery of medicine as the result of man's long and laborious research. The dimension of time appears clearly in this Hippocratic treatise, for it insists that a great deal of time was required to achieve current results, and that there will be many more discoveries in this field in the future.[43]

We encounter the same theme in Aristotle and in Plato. In the *Nicomachean Ethics,* Aristotle urges his audience and his readers themselves to complete the sketch he has given of the idea of the good.[44] This exhortation may seem to be banal, but as Franz Dirlmeier points out, we can recognize here a reflection on the role played by time in human progress.[45] Some people achieve an initial sketch; others, in the course of time, will fill in the sketch, as is the case with painters. For time, says Aristotle, is an inventor, and it discovers the truth bit by bit. It is time that makes progress in technologies possible, each person filling in the lacunae from which they originally suffered. Plato had already alluded to the importance of time in the evolution of human institutions.[46] Above all, he had shown in the *Laws* how the precision, exactness, and rectification of legislation can come about only with time, when other legislators come after one another to refine and correct initial outlines.[47]

In Lucretius it is also time that slowly makes possible the progress of the sciences, technology, and civilization: "Navigation, agriculture, fortifications, laws, weapons, roads, clothing, and all other such advantages, and also the delights of life, all without exception, it is simultaneously need but also the experience of the tireless spirit progressing step by step that have taught them bit by bit. Thus, each of these things time brings to light, and reasoning raises it to the shores of light."[48]

We have just seen that Francis Bacon uses the expression "Truth, the daughter of Time." Yet he gives this formula a different meaning from the one it traditionally had. For the wisdom of the nations, it meant that with time, there is nothing hidden that will not be uncovered. Alternatively, in the words of Sophocles, "time, which sees all, hears all, and unveils all,"[49] ends up, in the long run, by revealing the best-hidden secrets, and also misdeeds:

> Vast time, impossible to measure,
> causes the appearance [*phuei*] of things that were not apparent
> [*adēla*],
> as it hides what has shone in the light.[50]

The same idea may be found in several Greek authors.[51] It takes on a moral meaning in Seneca: in order to master anger, one must not react right away but must give oneself time, for time unveils the truth.[52]

The proverbial formula "Veritas filia temporis" did not appear until rather late, in an unknown Latin poet: Aulus Gellius cites it to illustrate the idea that people would commit fewer misdeeds if they feared that they would be disclosed.[53] In this case, the truth under discussion is a determinate truth that is unveiled: the enigma is solved, and there is no longer anything to search for.

Yet this formula can also have the meaning given to it by Francis Bacon. Here it denotes the progressive unveiling of Truth by Time, and the slow discovery of the secrets of Nature, thanks to the efforts of mankind. From this perspective, the Truth will be based not on the authority of the ancients but on the long quest of generations. We have seen that the idea was already present in Xenophanes, and Plato, and in Aristotle, who spoke of Time "the inventor."

This theme was still alive in modern times. For instance, in 1719, on the title page of his book *Epistolae ad Societatem Regiam Anglicam* (Letters to the English Royal Society), Anton van Leeuwenhoek, when he informed the world of his first scientific discoveries obtained by means of the microscope, had represented a man climbing a steep slope, helped by Father Time, scythe in hand, with the motto "Dum audes ardua vinces" (with audacity, you will conquer arduous difficulties).[54]

THE PROGRESS OF SCIENCE AS THE WORK OF ALL OF MANKIND AND INFINITE TASK

As we have seen, Seneca thought that progress is the work of all of mankind: the discovery of Nature can be realized only by the contribution of successive generations, past and future.[55] From this perspective, Pascal compared the history of mankind to that of a single human being "who always persists and learns continuously."[56]

It is difficult, however, to define exactly all that this metaphor implies. Is mankind itself a kind of knowing subject, a super-subject, or a kind of collective Spirit, possessing a perception of the whole of reality? In this case, should we see in "cyberculture" the first symptoms of its appearance? Jean-Marc Mandosio evoked the apostles of this cyberculture who rejoice to see autonomy and individual reflection finally disappear "in favor of a 'collective intelligence' explicitly presented as an avatar of the 'eternal divinity,' with 'virtual worlds' instead of the 'angelic or celestial world.'"[57] This problem is no doubt too serious to be invoked in a few lines, but I feel I must point it out to the reader.

Goethe also thought that Nature could be discovered only by the whole of mankind, because all human observations cannot help but be biased and partial, and they grasp only one aspect of phenomena. Yet since there is no perception proper to all of mankind, and mankind is ultimately a merely fictitious subject, Nature will always continue to hide from human beings: "Nature is so unfathomable, because no single man could conceive it, although mankind in its totality could do so. Since this precious mankind never fully exists at the same time, however, then Nature has an easy time hiding from our eyes . . . It is only men in their totality who know Nature, and it is only men in their totality who live what is human."[58]

This means that a complete knowledge of Nature, accompanied by an absolute certitude, will never be accessible to man. In a sense, it is not Truth that is the daughter of Time but infinite research. Was this already Pascal's idea when he said that mankind "is only produced for infinity?"[59] It is not likely that he was thinking of an infinite progress of human knowledge, for, as a good Christian, he foresaw an end to the world and to man. He used this expression to signify the grandeur of mankind as opposed to animals, as we can see in the context of his affirmation, and he was no doubt influenced, once again, by a text from Seneca: "It is natural for mankind to extend its thought as far as infinity. The human soul, a great and generous thing, gives itself no other limits than those it has in common with God."[60]

In any case, Kepler, in his dedicatory letter to the emperor Rudolph II at the beginning of *The Optical Part of Astronomy,* already evoked the idea of endless research in 1604: "Inexhaustible is the treasure of the secrets of nature; it offers indescribable wealth, and he who discovers something in this area does nothing other than open up for others the path toward new research."[61]

G. E. Lessing praised this infinite research in a famous text that deserves to be cited in its entirety:

> A man's value resides not in the truth he possesses or claims to possess but in the sincere effort he furnishes to attain it. For the only forces that increase human perfectibility are increased not by possession but by the search for truth. If God, holding all of truth in his right hand and stretching forth in his left only the ever ardent desire for the truth, were to say, "Choose!" at the risk of making a mistake forever and for eternity, I would bow humbly toward his left hand and say, "Father, give me this hand; for absolute truth belongs only to you."[62]

Can we speak of infinite progress in man's research? It is obviously impossible for us to foresee the future of the world and of mankind, and to say whether the latter is destined for eternal research. Lessing, for his part, saw it being pursued in the hereafter: he thought that human beings would carry on their research after their death, in the course of the migration of souls. In any case, what we can ask of future generations is that they know how to receive the inheritance of the past, without fearing to go against it, and to be ready in their turn to bequeath their discoveries to their successors, without pretending to possess a definitive, absolute truth, but, on the contrary, accepting being perpetually called into question. We must concede, however, that sometimes those who speak of progress in knowledge do not really accept such challenges, especially if these concern their own discoveries. Already in Lucretius we have the impression that the history of thought stops with Epicurus, who has solved all problems and who, moreover, once elementary needs have been satisfied, has fixed a limit to mankind's further desires. This is why I do not believe that there is in Lucretius the Promethean spirit discerned by Robert Lenoble.[63]

Recently, Pierre-Gilles de Gennes recalled the need for this perpetual reexamination: "Some philosophers imagine researchers as people who establish a truth. Many of us cannot see ourselves as fitting into this scheme. Today's researchers never claim to construct an ultimate truth. We only fashion, with much hesitation and clumsiness, an approximate description of nature."[64]

François Jacob gives us a glimpse of scientific progress as he ends his book *La logique du vivant* with the questions: "Tomorrow, what new dissection will dismantle our objects, only to put them back together in a new space? What new Russian doll will emerge from it?"[65] In the perspective of the metaphor of the secrets of nature, one might say that to open up one of these secrets means to be confronted with a new secret, which merely hides another one, and so on.

15

The Study of Nature as a Spiritual Exercise

In the *Timaeus,* Plato speaks of his research as an exercise that provides pleasure and relaxation precisely because it proposes nothing but probability and conjecture: "And likewise for all the other bodies of the same kind, it is not very difficult to speak about them when we pursue the literary genre of 'likely fables.' When, as a kind of respite, and abandoning discourse that pertains to eternal beings, we examine a likely one concerning the birth of things, and thereby obtain pleasure without remorse, we introduce a moderate and reasonable pleasure into our lives. And that is precisely what we are heading toward."[1]

THE PLEASURE OF KNOWING

Research is a diversion, and it brings pleasure because it is akin to the game that consists of solving puzzles. With regard to the dialogue of the *Timaeus,* this effort to solve the enigma of the universe takes place within the framework of a religious celebration. At the beginning of the dialogue, Socrates recalls that the day of its occurrence is a festival day in which a sacrifice is offered to the goddess Athena, and he is delighted that the theme of the dialogue is perfectly appropriate to the sacrifice offered on that day. The theme is praise of the city of Athens and the story of its origins, but it is a story placed within a story of the origin of mankind, which in turn is set within a story of the origin of the world. It will ultimately be a cosmogony, or "Genesis" in the biblical sense, in accordance with the model of the cosmogonies of the pre-Socratics, which were themselves influenced by the model of the cosmogonic poems of the Near East, such as the famous *Enuma Elish,* which, moreover, were also linked to religious ceremonies.[2] In this regard, it is interesting to recall that Johan Huizinga has also shown how the playing out of the cosmogonic mystery could be a part of sacrifice in the Brahmanic religion.[3] We would thus be in the presence here of behavior that goes back to an extremely distant origin. In general, play, celebration, and the search for divine secrets could be intimately linked. For Plato, at any rate, human play responds to divine play. One thinks of the famous text from the *Laws* which affirms that man was made as an object of amusement for the divinity, and that being such an object of amusement really constitutes what is best in him.[4] Mankind must therefore offer the gods the finest amusements, which would be the songs and dances of religious festivals, but also the mythic hymn that recounts the birth of the world. Similarly, in the *Phaedrus,* Socrates says, "By composing a discourse that was not entirely lacking in persuasive force, we have, while amusing ourselves in an appropriate and pious way, offered up a mythic hymn . . . to Love."[5]

For Plato, however, physics is not only a discourse but also a practice. The point is not merely to compose a mythic hymn but, as the *Timaeus* says explicitly, to live the excellent life which the gods propose to human beings, in the present and the future.[6] This life consists of contemplating the universe, thinking of the All, and harmonizing oneself with its movements. Here, the contemplative way of life is recommended, together with the effort to free oneself from individual passions, in order to turn toward the rational study of the world. It is rational, insofar as reason seeks to discover axioms that are indemonstrable in themselves, but capable of founding the construction of a likely representation of the universe.

CONTEMPLATION OF NATURE AND GREATNESS OF SOUL

Faithful in this to the spirit of Platonism, Aristotle strongly affirms that the contemplation of Nature will provide "inexpressible pleasures" to whoever knows how to contemplate, that is, to replace each being within the general plan of Nature.[7] A few centuries later, Cicero echoed him. In the *Lucullus*, he starts by insisting on the conjectural character of research on nature.[8] He rightly emphasizes that in each philosophical school, opinions might diverge on these problems. These hesitations and contradictions are not, Cicero continues, a reason for abandoning physical research:

> I do not think, however, that we must renounce these questions of the physicists. The observation and contemplation of nature are a kind of natural food for souls and minds; we stand up straight, we seem to rise up, and we look at human affairs from on high; when we think of the things on high and the celestial things, we despise the things down here below as small and puny. The search for things that are simultaneously the highest and the most hidden brings with it pleasure. And if we find something that seems to us to be true, our mind is filled with a noble pleasure.[9]

Cicero, like Aristotle, thus speaks of pleasure. Yet the pleasure in question is a pleasure of the mind, completely disinterested: "It is science all by itself that makes us rejoice, even if it brings unpleasant things."[10] He continues: "We need only ask ourselves how much we are moved by the motion of the stars and the contemplation of celestial things, the efforts to know all *that nature veils in darkness* . . . One of the most noble activities is the observation and study of celestial things, as well as that of things *that nature keeps hidden and far from our eyes.*"[11]

Perhaps recalling the festival of the *Timaeus*,[12] and perhaps also Diogenes the Cynic, who had said that a good man celebrates a festival every day, Philo of Alexandria and Plutarch considered the phi-

losopher's life a "spiritual festival," contemplating, in the temple constituted by the world, those mysteries that are the works of Nature,
that is, the beauties of the heavens and the earth.[13] Seneca, for his
part, makes the following fine comparison: the soul wishes to take a
deep breath before the spectacle of nature like a worker who, tired of
the darkness of the workshop, rests his eyes in the open light.[14]

Since Plato, the fruit of the contemplation of nature and its study
had been called "greatness of soul." For him, the soul that never
ceases contemplating the totality of time and being could not contain within it any pettiness or baseness; it looked down upon human
affairs from above and did not fear death.[15] The echo of this idea resounds throughout the history of ancient physics. We have just seen
Cicero extol the benefits of studying the secrets of nature by saying
that we seem to raise ourselves up and consider things down here below as small and petty. For Seneca, this study, because it lets us see
the things up above, frees us from all base thoughts and brings with
it greatness of soul.[16] It answers the soul's aspirations to free itself
from the prison of the body and to take flight amid the vast spaces of
the heavens and the earth. A millennium after the *Timaeus*, in the
preface he wrote for his commentary on Aristotle's *Physics*, the Neoplatonist Simplicius gives a very long exposition on the theme of the
usefulness of physics for ethics, showing how all the moral virtues
are developed through the observation of natural phenomena, and
also how concentrating on physical research diverts us from the pleasures of the body and delivers us from the fear of death, how physics
brings greatness and elevation of the soul and enables us to look
down on human affairs from above.[17]

THE STUDY OF NATURE AS AN ETHICS OF OBJECTIVITY

Yet the study of nature also requires objectivity and disinterestedness. It was Aristotle's great merit that he clearly defined the ethics
implied in scientific knowledge.[18] Just as ethics consists in not choos-

ing any other end than virtue, and in wanting to be a good person without seeking any particular interest, so science demands that we not choose any end other than knowledge, and that we seek knowledge for itself, without any other utilitarian consideration. It is this principle that defines the physics of contemplation I am discussing, which refuses to profit from the discovery of the secrets of nature. Seneca admits that the study of earthquakes may have its practical utility, yet he clarifies his meaning as follows: "You ask me what profit will we derive from this study. The greatest one of all: knowledge of Nature. For the finest thing about research on such a subject—although it could have a great deal of usefulness in the future—is the fact that by its very sublimity it captivates mankind and is practiced not for the sake of the profit we might derive from it but because of the wonder we admire."[19]

By defining science as he did, Aristotle posited objective knowledge itself as a value, thereby creating the ethics of objectivity on which Jacques Monod has written some remarkable passages. On this subject, moreover, I would note, as I said in another work, that it is always the ethical choice of a value that founds a specific type of knowledge.[20] This is precisely the view of Monod: "To place the postulate of objectivity as the condition of true knowledge constitutes an ethical choice, and not a judgment of knowledge, since, according to the postulate itself, there could be no 'true' knowledge prior to this arbitral choice."[21]

For Monod, such a choice posits an ideal that transcends the individual. In any case, in this perspective, scientific research is a "spiritual exercise"[22] to the highest degree, because, in Monod's words, it presupposes an "ascetics of the mind," or an effort at transcending oneself and mastering the passions. He adds that "the *Discourse on Method* proposes a normative epistemology, but it must also, and above all, be read as a moral meditation, or an ascetics of the mind."[23]

In a perspective wholly different from the attitudes of violence and respect I have qualified as Promethean and Orphic, we might discern, from one end to another of the history of science, both ancient and modern, a tension between two ethical orientations: on the one hand, an ethics of objective and disinterested research, of which we have just seen the continuity from Aristotle to Jacques Monod, and on the other, an ethics of useful research placed in the service of mankind, having as its objective either the moral perfection of the individual himself—in which case study becomes a "spiritual exercise"—or else the transformation of the conditions of human life.

THE STUDY OF NATURE IN THE SERVICE OF MANKIND

In the practice of disinterested research, as I have just shown in discussing Jacques Monod, the two orientations are not opposed: by choosing the *askēsis* of objectivity, the scientist transforms herself or himself morally, and transcends his or her individuality. Yet this surpassing is not sought or willed for its own sake. It is scientific research that is an end in itself; elevation of consciousness and pleasure in knowing come along as an extra. In antiquity, according to Aristotelian and Platonic tradition, we achieve, by means of objective and disinterested knowledge, a divine state and a kind of immortality,[24] which the astronomer Ptolemy describes in poetic and mythological terms: "I know that I am mortal and last only for a day. Yet when I accompany the tight ranks of stars in their circular course, my feet no longer touch the ground, and I go to Zeus himself to eat my fill of ambrosia, like the gods."[25]

Among the Epicureans and the Stoics, things were entirely different. They indeed claim disinterested objectivity; nevertheless, their respective physics were placed in the service of a way of life: a life of pleasure unmixed with pain for Epicurus; a life of rational coherence for Chrysippus. Ultimately, their physics were intended to justify moral attitudes. For Epicurus, human beings are anguished because they are afraid of the gods and of death. The theory of atoms teaches them that the gods are not concerned with the world, because the universe is eternal, and the bodies that compose it are born and perish by the continuous movements of atoms in the void. By also teaching them that the soul dies together with the body and that in this way death is nothing for us, it will free them from worry. For the Stoic Chrysippus, by contrast, the study of nature will reveal that the rationality of human action is based on the rationality of Nature, and that mankind itself is a part of Nature. The entire universe, and each part of the universe, tend toward coherence with itself. The Stoic will achieve peace of mind by placing himself in a disposition of consent to the will of the Reason that directs the universe, while the Epicurean will also achieve peace of mind by thinking of the infinity of worlds in the infinite void, without having to fear either the whims of the divinity or the onslaught of death, which is nothing for us. The physical theories proposed in the schools were thus intended to deliver man from the anguish he feels in the face of the enigma of the universe. In this perspective, disinterested, thorough research on the secrets of nature and on the workings of various natural phenomena might appear to be a useless luxury, for Nature has hidden nothing of what can constitute our happiness.[26]

Yet the science of nature can also be useful from the perspective of a transformation of the material conditions of human life. Prometheus was traditionally considered the benefactor of humanity. We have seen that the Greeks and Romans had developed a quite remarkable theory and practice of mechanics, and we have also seen how ancient mechanics, which aimed at placing nature in the service of mankind, inspired modern science.

In fact, we must admit that in all periods, and since antiquity, the "service of mankind" has been in danger of meaning the service of individual or collective egoisms. Modern science is more and more in danger of being closely linked to industrial technology, the demands of corporations, and the will to power and profit. By the will of states themselves, scientific research must orient itself as a function of the usefulness it can have for technical and commercial progress. Basic and disinterested research becomes more and more precarious. This is why we must be grateful to scientists like Jacques Monod for bearing witness, despite these pressures from the state and from society, in favor of the absolute value of the ethics of objectivity, and of an ideal of disinterested knowledge that has no other goal than itself.

16

Nature's Behavior

Thrifty, Joyful, or Spendthrift?

"Jacques Monod wanted to be logical, even purely logical," writes
François Jacob:

> Yet it was not enough for him to be purely logical: nature had to be
> so as well. It had to work according to strict rules, and once it had
> found the "solution" to some "problem," it had to stick to it hence-
> forth, and use it thoroughly, each time and in every situation, in ev-
> ery living being. Ultimately, for Jacques, natural selection had
> sculpted each organism, each cell, and each molecule, down to the
> smallest detail, until one reached a perfection that could no longer
> be distinguished from what others recognized as a sign of the divine
> will. Jacques attributed Cartesianism and elegance to nature; hence
> his taste for unique solutions. For my part, I did not think the world
> was quite so strict or so rational. What amazed me was neither its el-
> egance nor its perfection but rather its state: the fact that it is as it is
> and not otherwise. I saw nature as a rather nice girl who was gener-
> ous but a bit sloppy, a bit muddleheaded, working at one thing at a
> time, and doing her best with what she found handy.[1]

This text by Jacob shows that in the twentieth century, and no doubt
in the twenty-first, it can still happen that scientists, when they want
to speak to the wider public about their research, use the metaphor
of personified Nature, which has its own character, habits, or behavior that is specific to it. From the perspective of ways of unveiling the

190

secrets of nature, which we are considering, this type of thinking should help us define nature's mode or method of action.

NATURE AS THRIFTY

As we have glimpsed with regard to the evolution of the notion of *phusis*,[2] this kind of description of nature's behavior already existed in antiquity, particularly in the Hippocratic corpus and in Aristotle. Aristotle thought that nature acts in a rational manner, or more precisely that everything happens *as if* nature acted in a rational, reflective way. As he puts it, "One would say that nature foresees what might happen."[3]

In the Aristotelian perspective, the fundamental principle that makes possible the explanation of the phenomena of nature, especially those of living nature, is that nature always acts with a view to an end, and therefore never accepts the incomplete, the infinite, or the indeterminate, either in the organisms it produces or in the series of beings it causes to appear. The characteristic of living beings is to be full and complete. Consequently, Nature does nothing in vain. On the one hand, she does nothing useless; on the other hand, if she does something, she has a reason for doing so.[4] This principle is often used to justify the presence or absence of a faculty or an organ. Nature, one could say, is a good housekeeper who saves as much as she can. She knows how to avoid what is too much and too little, too soon and too late. She makes a single organ serve various different ends: for instance, the tongue serves both for taste, which is necessary for existence, and for elocution, which is useful for a better existence. Again, the mouth serves to absorb food but also to breathe. "Like a prudent man," says Aristotle, Nature gives organs only to those who are able to use them; she utilizes the possibilities that present themselves to the maximum extent; "like a good housekeeper," she does not throw away anything that might have some usefulness; she knows how to take advantage of leftovers "to make bones, tendons, hair, and hooves," and how to compensate for an excess with a deficit, or vice versa, since she cannot distribute the excess to several points at the same time. For instance, during nursing, menstruation does not take place, and there is normally no conception. If there is conception, the milk dries up, for nature is not wealthy enough to be able to ensure the two functions.

These Aristotelian formulas had great success in the Middle Ages and the Renaissance. In the seventeenth century, however, Robert Boyle, after enumerating several such propositions, usefully recalled that these were only metaphors, of the same kind as an expression such as, "The law forbids doing this or that."[5] Nature is not an active subject, any more than the law is. Boyle is right; but could we not say that this kind of proposition, in the case of nature or of the law, allows us to glimpse a norm that regulates natural processes or human actions?

Ultimately, the Aristotelian formulas can all be reduced to the principle of economy, which expresses the ideal of perfectly rational action that sets means and ends in precise proportion. This principle of economy was to have a crucial influence on the philosophical and scientific notions of nature's action down to the twentieth century. In the seventeenth and eighteenth centuries, it was even introduced into mechanical physics, becoming specified and modified in the form of the principle of least action, according to which in nature, optimal action takes place with a minimum of expenditure. Fermat, Leibniz, Maupertuis, and, in the nineteenth century, W. R. Hamilton, proposed various formulations of this principle.[6] Maupertuis formulates it as follows: "When a change occurs in Nature, the quantity of action used for this change is always the smallest possible."[7] Maupertuis's expositions gave rise to a controversy in which the participants were Voltaire, who attacked them virulently, and Euler, who defended them with vigor. Maupertuis had emphasized the metaphysical implications of this principle: the Creator always uses his power in the wisest and therefore the most economical way. Yet this obviously meant leaving the door open to a fundamental objection: Whether the responsible agent is God or Nature, why should we admit that their power is limited and that they are condemned to parsimony?

The principle of economy also has as its consequence the principle of continuity: neither too much (and therefore without useless reduplications) nor too little (and therefore without missing links).[8] Nature thus rises, with no interruption in its continuity, from inanimate beings to animals by way of plants, but in such a continuous way that it is extremely hard to define the border that separates the various groups, and it may happen that one does not know to what group a given being belongs.[9] Leibniz formulated this principle of continuity as follows: "Nothing occurs all at once, and it is one of my greatest and best-verified maxims that nature never makes a leap: what I called the *law of continuity,* when I spoke of it in my first *News from the Republic of Letters,* and the usefulness of this law is very considerable in physics."[10]

Plato had already emphasized the need for the existence of intermediaries between different terms.[11] This principle of continuity and plenitude, with the idea of the "chain of being" that is linked to it, played a highly important role in the history of philosophy and biology, as was shown by Arthur O. Lovejoy.[12]

From the Aristotelian perspective, a certain number of functions are necessary for the life of each species: nutrition, locomotion, reproduction, defense, respiration, and so on. In order to ensure these functions, each species has the right to a determinate quantity of means. Nature varies in the distribution of these means to each species, but in such a way that the sum always remains the same. If she suppresses or diminishes the means to realize a given function, she is obliged to donate or increase others. This principle of compensation could also be called a principle of equilibrium, or else a principle of totality, in the sense that each species must have the totality of the means indispensable to the exercise of vital functions, and must produce organisms that are sufficient unto themselves. The animals to which nature has not given horns, says Aristotle, "have all received from it another means of defense, for instance, speed among horses, and bodily size among camels. What nature takes away with regard to teeth, it contributes to horns, and the nourishment that would be intended for these teeth is used for the growth of horns."[13]

It is interesting to observe that Plotinus takes up this idea when he notes that once an animal no longer has the means to survive, then nails, claws, and razor-sharp teeth make their appearance as compensation.[14] In Plotinus, however, this compensation is already located at the level of the Idea of each species. The ideal Forms, or prototypes, of the various species undergo a degradation with regard to the ideal Form or the perfect Prototype of the Living Being, since they are particularized, and the result of this degradation is that a given deficiency must be compensated, so that the sum of the excesses and deficiencies may balance out.

This principle of compensation, postulated by Aristotle, is the result of the conflict, already recognized by Plato in the *Timaeus*, between nature's tendency to realize the best end possible, and the material necessity that faces it as an obstacle.[15] Economy, moreover, is the sign of a certain weakness and poverty, brought about by the resistance of matter. Nature therefore seeks to realize what is best as a function of the circumstances. If several possibilities are open to her, she chooses the best, insofar as it is possible.

The principle of compensation was still alive and well at the beginning of the nineteenth century. Speaking of the zoological philosophy of Geoffroy Saint-Hilaire, Goethe says that Nature has set herself a definite budget: she considers herself free to spend the various components as she pleases, but she cannot change the total sum. If she has spent too much on the one side, she is obliged to save on the other.[16] What could be more Aristotelian? This concept corresponds, moreover, to the idea of the balance of organs as discussed by Saint-Hilaire from the perspective of a unique level of structure common to all animals.[17]

This perspective of a unique level of structure was already envisaged in the eighteenth century by Buffon, Maupertuis, Robinet, and Bonnet.[18] An original prototype would thus be the model for all products of nature, and would authorize us to think, as is done, for instance, by Jean-Baptiste Robinet, that there exists a complete continuity among all the realms of nature: "A rock, an oak, a horse, an ape, and a man are graduated variations on the prototype that began to be realized with the fewest elements possible."[19] According to this perspective of numerous variations on a single theme, the principle of economy is maintained insofar as nature remains faithful to a fundamental model. We could say that once Nature has found a recipe or a model that succeeds, she sticks with it. Contemporary biology sometimes allows itself considerations of this kind. For instance, François Jacob writes: "Beyond the diversity of forms and the variety of performances, all organisms use the same materials to carry out similar reactions. We must therefore admit that once the recipe that turns out to be the best is found, nature has stuck to it in the course of evolution."[20] We also find analogous concepts in astronomers such as Michel Cassé, who writes: "Nature seems to have given herself a few models that she reproduces ceaselessly and everywhere; or a few intemporal rules that she introduces into her universal praxis. She constantly repeats herself until certain goals have been achieved."[21]

All these principles, which are so many variations on the Aristotelian principle of economy, amount, it seems to me, to postulating a priori that there is a rational order or legality in nature. As Wittgenstein wrote in his *Notebooks:* "This is the great problem around which everything I write turns: is there a priori an order in the world, and if so, of what does it consist?"[22] More specifically, speaking this time of all the formulations of the principle of economy, he notes: "All propositions, like the proposition of sufficient reason, of the continuity of nature, of the least expenditure in nature, and so on: all such propositions are a priori intuitions of the possible formation of propositions of science."[23] Or again: "One had a premonition that there must be a 'law of least action' before even knowing the formula. (Here, as always, a priori certainty reveals itself as something purely logical.)"[24] All these principles, as Kant affirms, "say not what happens but how we must judge."[25] They state a logical necessity.

NATURE AS PLAYFUL

Yet could we not say that Aristotle's thrifty good housekeeper becomes a bit playful or fanciful if, as we have just seen, she allows herself multiple variations on the theme she has chosen? This is what Diderot implied: "Nature seems to have taken pleasure in varying the same mechanism in an infinity of different ways. She does not abandon one kind of production until she has multiplied its individuals in every conceivable aspect . . . She is a woman who loves to disguise herself, and whose different disguises, allowing now one part and now another to escape, give some hope to those who follow her assiduously that one day they shall know her entire person."[26]

This idea appears as far back as antiquity. Seneca speaks of Nature as putting all her pride in producing diversity ("ipsa uarietate se iactat").[27] Although the Stoics, even more than Aristotle, were convinced that Nature, which they identified with universal Reason, did nothing in vain, they were still forced to admit that her products appear to occur without reason. Nature did not always aim at usefulness, for instance, when she produced the peacock's extravagant tail. According to Chrysippus, the reason Nature created this appendage, which is a superfluous luxury, is that she loves beauty and takes pleasure in the variety of colors.[28] The great naturalist of antiquity Pliny the Elder goes even further: he does not hesitate to speak of Nature's gaiety or playfulness.[29] In her playful *(lasciuia)* mood, she amuses herself by imagining all kinds of variations *(uarie ludens)* on a theme that pleases her: the forms of animals' horns, or the spirals of seashells. She indulges in a variety of games, such as painting the colors of flowers.[30] Sometimes she takes pleasure in arranging spectacles for herself, such as fights between animals.[31] Although she is always ready to play, Nature seems unpredictable. She sometimes proceeds by trial and error, amusing herself by making several test versions: when she wanted to make the lily, she made bindweed first.[32] She thus no longer appears as a thrifty good housekeeper but as an inventive artist who loves beauty, who is happy in her fruitfulness, and who is trying to realize all that she imagines. Although she is still a beginner, she gradually makes progress, and can even produce masterpieces. As we discover this playful Nature of the Stoics, we may wonder whether she is not ultimately related to Aion the child, who Heraclitus said likes to play dice,[33] a game which, in Nietzsche, would become the terrible game of Dionysus.[34]

In any case, this metaphor of playful Nature had an important role, beginning with the eighteenth century, in the rise of the idea of evolutionism.[35] When, in 1768, Jean-Baptiste Robinet titled one of his books *Philosophical View of the Natural Gradation of the Forms of Being, or Nature's Trial Attempts as She Learns to Create Mankind,* he was clearly alluding to Pliny's Nature, who, as she plays, learns how to make a lily by fashioning bindweed first. At the beginning of the nineteenth century, Goethe too saw in the appearance of more and more complex natural forms the result of a game on Nature's part, linked both to random chance and to the fantasy of imagination. When Nature invents a form, she plays with this form, and as she plays with it, she produces the diversity of life.[36] She strives to develop the most diverse variations on the theme she has invented. When she sits down at her gaming table, she plays for double or nothing: "Mineral, Animal, Vegetable, all that, obtained by a favorable throw of the dice, is constantly put in play again, and who knows whether mankind itself is not, once again, a throw of the dice that prepares an even higher end?"[37]

Risk, trial and error, and research: such is Nature's method: "The skeletons of many marine animals show us that Nature was thinking about a higher genus of terrestrial animals when she conceived them. What Nature must leave behind for the moment, she takes up later on, under more favorable circumstances."[38]

NATURE THE SPENDTHRIFT

The idea of a game leads to that of freedom, whim, and prodigality, that is, ultimately, to the destruction of the Aristotelian concept of Nature as a good and thrifty housekeeper. In Nietzsche, nature's prodigal exuberance becomes a central theme:

> In Nature, there reigns not a situation of distress but, on the contrary, of profusion, prodigality, even to the point of absurdity.
>
> Do you wish to live in conformity with nature? O noble Stoics, what fraudulent words! Imagine a being that is like Nature is, prodigal without measure, indifferent without measure, without intentions nor consideration, without pity nor justice, simultaneously fruitful and sterile and uncertain!
>
> Nature, such as she is, with all the grandiose character of this prodigality and this indifference that revolt us, but which are nevertheless noble.[39]

In Nietzsche, this concept of nature produces both mankind's terror and his happiness: terror, because he feels himself to be the plaything of the blind cruelty of nature, and happiness, Dionysian happiness, since, through the play of art, he plunges once again into the great game of the world by accepting its cruelty and arbitrariness.[40]

Bergson, while praising William James and his "pluralism," opposes to the intelligence that wants "nature to have arranged itself so as to demand from us only the smallest possible sum of work" the data of experience that reveal to us an exuberant reality: "Whereas our intelligence, with its economical habits, represents effects as being in strict proportion to their causes, nature, which is prodigal, places in the cause much more than is required to produce the effect. Whereas our motto is *Just what is necessary,* nature's is *More than is necessary,* too much of this, too much of that, too much of everything."[41]

Nature, as Bergson conceives it, is prodigal but also an artist. As Pliny and Seneca had said, she "seems to create with love, for pleasure, the varieties of vegetable and animal species," and each of her products "has the absolute value of a great work of art." She "appears as an immense efflorescence of unpredictable novelty."[42] Indeed, one must note that at least in the area of living organisms, it is not only the principle of economy that regulates their formation. They are not machines that can be reduced to the mechanisms that are indispensable for their working, but are masterpieces, which display luxuriant colors, an extraordinary wealth of strange and unexpected forms, in an almost wanton wastefulness.[43] Yet however beautiful they may be, these works of art, in Bergson's view, impede the movement of the vital impulse, which demands to continue its ascent toward specifically human moral progress.

It is interesting to note that there are basically two ways of picturing nature's behavior metaphorically. The text by François Jacob which I cited at the beginning of this chapter shows us that scientists who accept fundamentally the same scientific theories can conceive the workings of nature in completely different ways. One could say, as Bergson implies, that those who picture Nature as thrifty tend to think that natural processes are rigorously logical, because a perfectly rational adaptation of means to end could be found in her, whereas those who imagine her as joyful, prodigal, and exuberant tend, by contrast, to conceive natural processes as spontaneous, immediate, and even unpredictable. The interest of this second kind of description of nature's behavior is less scientific than philosophical. As we can see from the example of Nietzsche or Bergson, it is mankind's existential and ethical relation to nature and to existence that is at stake here.

1. Apollo unveiling a statue of Isis/Artemis, symbol of nature. Engraving by
Bertel Thorvaldsen for the dedication page to Goethe, in Alexander von
Humboldt, *Ideen zu einer Geographie der Pflanzen* (1807).

2. Statue of Artemis of Ephesus (Roman copy). National
Museum, Naples, no. 665. Photograph © Alinari-Viollet.

3. Édouard Manet, *Le déjeuner sur l'herbe* (Luncheon on the grass, 1863).
Musée d'Orsay, Paris. Photograph: Erich Lessing/Art Resource, New York.

4. Titian, *Sacred and Profane Love* (1515). Galleria Borghese, Rome.

5. Titian, *Le concert champêtre* (Pastoral concert, c. 1510–1511). Musée du Louvre, Paris. Photograph: Scala/Art Resource, New York.

6. Raphael, *Philosophy* (1508). Stanza della Segnatura, Vatican. Supporting the throne are two figures of Artemis representing Nature. Photograph © Anderson-Viollet.

7. Niccolò Tribolo, *Nature* (1529). Château de Fontainebleau, France. Photograph: Lagiewski, Réunion des Musées Nationaux/Art Resource, New York.

8. Statue of Isis/Artemis representing Nature. Frontispiece to Athanasius Kircher, *Mundus subterraneus*, vol. 2 (Amsterdam, 1664). By permission of Houghton Library, Harvard University.

9. Science unveiling Nature. Frontispiece to Gerhard Blasius, *Anatome animalium* (Amsterdam, 1681).

10. Isis unveiled. Frontispiece to Anton van Leeuwenhoek, *Anatomia seu interiora rerum* (Leyden, 1687). Courtesy of the Francis A. Countway Library of Medicine, Boston.

11. Peter Paul Rubens and Jan Brueghel the Elder, *Nature Adorned by the Graces* (1620). By permission of the Glasgow City Council (Museums).

12. William Hogarth, *Boys Peeping at Nature* (1730–1731).

D. Johann Andreas Segners
Einleitung
in die
Natur = Lehre.

QVA LICET.

Neuman fecit Göttingae.

Mit Kupfern.
Zweyte Auflage.

Göttingen,
Verlegts Abram Vandenhoecks seel. Wittwe 1754.

13. The sciences examining the footprints of Isis/Nature. Title page
to Andreas von Segner, *Einleitung in die Natur-Lehre,* 2nd ed.
(Göttingen, 1754).

14. Philosophy unveiling Nature. Frontispiece to François Peyrard, *De la nature et de ses lois* (Paris, 1793). By permission of Houghton Library, Harvard University.

LUCRÈCE,

DE

LA NATURE DES CHOSES,

TRADUIT

Par LA GRANGE.

TOME PREMIER.

À PARIS,

Chez BLEUET père, Libraire, pont S. Michel.

L'an troisième de la République.

Le génie d'Epicure découvre la Nature que
le fanatisme et l'erreur tenoient enveloppées.

LUCRÈCE

15. The genius of Epicurus unveiling Nature. Frontispiece to Lucretius, *De la nature des choses (On the Nature of Things),* translation by La Grange (Paris, 1795). Bibliothèque de la Sorbonne, Paris.

16. Louis-Ernest Barrias, *La Nature se dévoilant devant la Science* (Nature unveiling herself before Science, 1899). Musée d'Orsay, Paris. Photograph © RMN-Lagiewski.

17. *Genius Unveiling a Bust of Nature,* in *Weimars Jubelfest am 3.
September 1825* (Weimar, 1825). Frankfurter Goethemuseum, Frankfurt am
Main.

18. Engraving by Heinrich Füssli. Title page to Erasmus Darwin, *The Temple of Nature, or The Origin of Society, a Poem* (Edinburgh, 1809).

17

The Poetic Model

Since earliest antiquity, the poet has been thought to be the true interpreter of nature, who knew its secrets precisely insofar as it was imagined that nature acts like a poet, and that what nature produces is a poem. I have said that the *Timaeus* was a kind of poem, or an artistic game that imitates the artistic game of the poet of the universe known as the divinity.[1] If the god that is the World can be reborn in Plato's discourse, it is because the universe is a kind of poem composed by God. We find this idea in Philo of Alexandria, who presents the works of nature as God's poem.[2] The Stoics, as well as Plotinus, also speak of a poem of the Universe. Yet for them, this poem is a drama in which beings are characters who have received their role from the Poet of the Universe, that is, for the Stoics from Nature and for Plotinus from the World Soul.[3] It was not until Augustine, probably under the influence of Neoplatonism, that the picture of a poem, or more precisely a song, of the Universe was set in relation to the numerical and harmonic structure of the world. He speaks of the progression of centuries as a great song, the work of an ineffable musician: "Velut magnum carmen cuiusdam ineffabilis modulatoris";[4] the flow of time is thus set in relation to the rhythm of song. For his part, the Neoplatonist Proclus speaks of Apollo as the great Poet of the Universe.[5] The image is found once again, for instance, in Bonaventure in the Middle Ages.[6] From the metaphor of the poem we pass very easily to that of a book.[7] This metaphor of the book of the world was to reappear very often from the Renaissance down to modern times.

NATURE'S HIEROGLYPHIC LANGUAGE

Combined with the theme of Nature as a poem we find, beginning with the seventeenth century, the theme of the language of Nature, a language which functions not by means of words or discourse but by means of signs and symbols, represented by the forms of various beings.[8] Nature composes not just a poem but a coded poem. The codes of Nature's language are presented as "signatures" or hieroglyphs. The term "signature" appears in the seventeenth century in Paracelsus and della Porta.[9] In the first instance, these are signs, characteristics, and appearances which reveal the properties of plants, particularly medicinal ones, thanks to the analogy of the external parts of these plants with the external form of the parts of the human body. Soon, however, the term took on deeper meanings. For Jacob Boehme, who wrote a book titled *De signatura rerum,* all of Nature is the language of God, and each particular being is, in a sense, a word of this language, a word that presents itself in the form of a sign or a figure corresponding to what God expresses in Nature.[10]

The idea of a hieroglyph, that is, a sign or a symbol representing an essence, is to be found, for instance, in Thomas Browne's work *Religio medici.*[11] Following the Christian tradition, he distinguishes two divine books, the Bible and the world. For him, however, the world was written not by God but by his servant Nature. Christians, he says, especially attentive to the Bible, have paid little attention to the book written by Nature, and it was the pagans who were able to read it best, by linking the sacred letters together, whereas the Christians have neglected these "hieroglyphs." For J. G. Hamann as well, this time in the eighteenth century, Nature is "a book, a letter, a fable

..., a Hebrew word that is written with simple letters, to which the understanding must add points [diacritical marks]."[12]

For Kant, living forms, understood as symbols or as significant sketches, are the ciphers of nature's "coded language." These beautiful forms, he continues, are not necessary to the internal ends of natural beings. They thus seem to be made for the human eye. Thanks to them, in a way, Nature "speaks to us symbolically."[13]

For Goethe as well, Nature reveals herself by symbols or forms that are a kind of hieroglyphics. In his book titled *The Metamorphosis of Plants*, he speaks of the hieroglyph of the goddess which one must know how to recognize and decipher in the phenomenon of the metamorphosis of plants.[14]

The metamorphosis of forms is the sacred writing of the goddess, that is, of Isis/Nature, whom I shall soon discuss. Nature's language is not a discourse in which the words are separate from one another. What natural phenomena reveal to us are not the maxims or formulas of Nature but configurations, sketches, or emblems, which require only to be perceived: "I would like to lose the habit of discourse and express myself only like Nature the artist in eloquent designs. This fig tree, this little snake, this cocoon, . . . all these are 'signatures,' heavy with meaning."[15] Here, we might think we hear an echo of Nature's prosopopoeia in Plotinus: "I keep silent, and I am not accustomed to speak."[16] But Plotinus' Nature contents herself with contemplating the eternal Forms, and, says Plotinus, the lines of bodies are born from her glance, whereas Goethe's Nature invents the forms in which she manifests herself.

Natural forms are also conceived as coded writing in Novalis. Here I must cite the entire beginning of *Disciples at Saïs*:

> Diverse are the paths of men. Who follows and compares them, witnesses the birth of strange figures, which seem to belong to that great coded writing we find everywhere: on wings and eggshells, in clouds,

snow, crystals, and rock formations; in freezing waters, in the internal and external forms of mountains, plants, animals, human beings; in the celestial luminaries, on buffed or polished disks of resin or glass; in filings round a magnet, and in the strange circumstances of chance. In all these things, we sense the key of that wondrous script and its grammar, but this premonition refuses to fix itself in definite forms and seems not to want to become the key to anything higher.[17]

Two voices then sound forth, two kinds of oracles, which state the attitude we must have with regard to the hieroglyphs of nature. The first one says: the mistake lies in seeking to understand. The language of nature, one might say, is pure expression; it speaks for the sake of speaking, and words are its very being and its joy. The other one says: true writing is a harmonic chord in the symphony of the universe. We could say that the two voices affirm basically the same thing: hieroglyphs must not be understood discursively, but must be perceived, like a sketched form or a melody.

A poem, and a poem composed in coded writing: such is Nature for Schelling, too: "What we call Nature is a poem whose wondrous and mysterious writing remains indecipherable for us. Yet if we could solve the enigma, we would discover therein the Odyssey of the Spirit, which, as the victim of a remarkable illusion, flees from itself as it seeks itself, for it only appears through the World like meaning through words."[18] There is obviously an idealistic background here, which probably also existed in Novalis. Nature is already the Spirit, which is still unconscious of itself. The coded script of living forms is already the language of the Spirit.

Nature, as Franz von Baader said, "is an audacious poem, whose meaning, always the same, manifests itself in appearances that are constantly new." He too invites mankind to decipher the "divine hieroglyph" and to "divine, sense, and have a premonition, in Nature, of the great ideal of God."[19]

This metaphor of hieroglyphs and signatures is thus a variation on the theme of the secrets of Nature. In fact, the philosophers who used this metaphor did not all conceive the decipherment of this coded script in the same way. Some, such as Boehme, Schelling, Novalis, and Baader, thought that Nature allows us to know something of the "ideal of God," whereas others, such as Goethe, thought instead, as I shall have occasion to repeat, that this writing is an enigma: we cannot go beyond it, or decipher it, terrified as we are by the seriousness and silence of Nature.[20]

THE UNIVERSE AS POEM

If the Universe is a poem, the poet can unveil its meaning and its secret by composing a poem in his turn, which in some sense will be the Universe. For according to a concept that is archaic but has remained alive throughout the ages, the artist has the power of recreating that which he sings. The poet's word is creative. Émile Benveniste has shown clearly how the verb *krainō*, among others, has quite a strong meaning. It means to execute, to accomplish, to cause to come into existence. He interprets the following verses from the *Homeric Hymn to Hermes* in this sense: "Hermes raises his voice while playing harmoniously on the cithara, whose pleasant song accompanies him, promoting to existence *(krainōn)* the immortal gods and the dark Earth, saying what they were at the beginning, and what was the lot of each one." As Benveniste comments: "The poet causes things to exist, and things are born in his song."[21] Here, not only does the poet give existence to what he sings, but also, since what he sings is the universe, it is to the universe itself that he gives existence by recreating it in the magical space of the song. "Gesang ist Dasein," as Rilke was to say: "Song is existence."[22] In Plato's *Timaeus*, the underlying idea, already implicit in the pre-Socratic cosmogonic songs, is that a literary work is a microcosm that somehow imitates the gigantic poem of the universe.[23]

We find the oldest testimony to this concept in the *Iliad*. Here, the poet describes the making of Achilles' shield as a work of art, which is being forged by the god Hephaistos.[24] There is a kind of mirror game, going back and forth between the bronze image of Achilles' shield and the poem's sonorous image: the latter reflects the birth of the shield, whose plastic image in turn reflects the past and present of the universe. In this sonorous world the poem simultaneously brings into existence Hephaistos' work of art and the entire universe that this work of art represents, and the beauty of divine and human things, of which the work of art is itself the description. The divine things are therefore represented, no doubt in superposed strips: on the one hand, the earth, the sky and the sea, the sun and the moon, the celestial constellations, and, on the other hand, human things. We see two cities: in one, peace reigns, weddings are celebrated, and justice is rendered; in the other, we witness a wartime ambush, but also work in the fields, a harvest, grape picking, a flock being attacked by lions, as well as dances of young men and women. The rim of the shield represents the limit of the universe, or the river Ocean. The poet celebrates the skill of the god who is fashioning this representation of the universe and of all that lives in the universe, but he himself, as it were, recreates the work of art made by means of metals and fire by forging himself, in the time of words, his own work of art. Thus, in the words of Alain, "The world is once again created, as it is, as it was, and as it shall be."[25] The poetic word enables that living reality that was fixed and immobilized in the work of art to be set in motion once again, and replaced within time.

We find the same idea in Virgil's sixth Eclogue, in which the song of Silenus, Dionysus' companion, appears as powerful and moving as that of Orpheus.[26] He tells of the genesis of the universe: the appearance of the four elements, the sky, the sun, plants, animals, human beings; the Golden Age, Prometheus' benefits to humanity; then a series of unhappy stories, those of Hylas, Pasiphaë, Atalanta, and the metamorphosis of the Heliades, the sisters of Phaëthon. Here, however, what might seem to be a simple description is in fact presented as a kind of creation: "He wraps Phaëthon's sisters," says Virgil, "in the moss of a bitter bark, and he makes them surge forth from the soil, like slender alders."[27] Silenus thus appears not to sing the event that occurred but to bring it about by singing it. For Virgil, Silenus has not only described the universe but also made it present: in a sense, he has recreated it. As Godo Lieberg has shown, Virgil assimilates Silenus to Orpheus, whose song has an active power over nature.[28]

Ovid's *Metamorphoses* also presents itself as a microcosm, or a universe recreated in the poem. The work actually begins with the origins of the world; then comes the story of the succession of the four ages (the Golden, Silver, Bronze, and Iron ages), and the poem ends in the fifteenth book with a vision of the peace brought to the world by Augustus. Between the origins and the present, the history of metamorphoses depicts the chain of causes and effects, or of the world's events.

We find the same situation in Lucretius' poem *On Nature*. It is a "reduced cosmos," because, in the perspective of Epicurean physics, as Pierre Boyancé points out, there is an analogy between the elements and the letters of the alphabet.[29] Just as the elements, as they organize themselves, produce all the beings in the world, so the letters of the alphabet, as they organize themselves, form the poem and the world that it makes present.[30] This time, however, the poet knows the universe's mode of production, or the way in which it was constituted.

The pre-Socratics had already sought to recreate the production of the universe in their treatises. We may wonder whether the treatise *On Ancient Medicine*, which I discussed at the beginning of this book,[31] was not alluding to this claim when, in an enigmatic passage, it said that the speculations of philosophers of nature such as Empedocles belonged rather to the domain of *graphikē,* where *graphikē* is either the art of writing letters or the art of painting. The treatise probably meant that philosophers of nature seek to reconstruct the universe with a small number of elements analogous to letters or colors.[32] The philosophy treatise, whether written in prose or in verse, then appears as a kind of a microcosm, whose genesis and structure reproduce those of the universe.

Plato's *Timaeus* is situated within this pre-Socratic tradition, as appears clearly at the beginning of the *Critias,* the dialogue which is supposed to be the continuation of the *Timaeus.* Here, Plato invokes the God who is the world, as he summarizes the preceding dialogue: "This God [that is, the world] who once was truly born, and who has just been born once more in our discourse." For Plato, the discourse of the *Timaeus* is thus a new birth of the Cosmos: it is the Universe as a Poem, since, by its structure, it imitates the genesis and structure of the Cosmos.[33] The philosopher's role is to mimic in the *poiēsis* of discourse, insofar as is possible, the *poiēsis* of the Universe. Such an act is a poetic offering, or the Poet's celebration of the Universe. This tradition was perpetuated in Neoplatonism.[34]

It might also be interesting to recall that in Plato's time, reduced models of the world existed in the form of armillary spheres, and these objects, as Luc Brisson has pointed out, served as models, for instance, for the description of the fabrication of the World Soul in the *Timaeus.*[35] Just as Homer describes the shield of Achilles, fashioned by the god Hephaistos—that is, he proposes a reduced model of the world, and thus somehow recreates the world itself—in the same way Plato describes the fabrication of the armillary sphere, a reduced model of the world, and thus describes the fabrication of the world. Similar mechanical models are to be found in book 10 of the *Republic* (616c) and in the *Statesman* (270a).

In the Renaissance, the idea of the Universe as Poem remained very much alive, but it often assumed a form that could be called

Pythagorean, inspired by the Neoplatonic tradition. I mean by this that poets claimed to compose poems which, by their numerical relations—their number of songs, stanzas, or verses—reproduce the numbers and measures of the universe.[36]

It was above all at the end of the eighteenth and the beginning of the nineteenth centuries that the nostalgia for a Universe as Poem was most intense. People dreamed of a new Lucretius. André Chénier's poem "Hermes" was an attempt to write a new *On Nature*. Yet the poet's effort to remain faithful to Newton's scientific teachings acted to the detriment of his poetical inspiration. It does, however, contain some fine passages, such as the flight of the poet, a star among the stars, who plunges ecstatically into the infinite. Goethe, who also dreamed of being a new Lucretius, was never able to realize the vast cosmic poem he wanted to write with Schelling.[37] Yet the poems that constitute the group titled *Gott und Welt* (God and the World) are, one might say, fragments or sketches for this project.

In the nineteenth century, more precisely in 1848, one finds the idea of the Universe as Poem once again in Edgar Allan Poe's "Eureka." It describes the great pulsation and eternal return of the universe, the play of the forces of dilation and contraction, of diastole and systole, in a prose poem whose very beauty, Poe declares, is the guarantee of its truth. The universe is thus identified with a work of art, and the work of art with the universe.[38]

Another modern witness to the persistence of this idea is Paul Claudel, who placed at the head of his *Art poétique* the famous phrase by Saint Augustine, "Velut magnum carmen cuiusdam ineffabilis modulatoris." This *Art poétique* was in fact intended to be a poetical art of the universe, or a philosophy of Nature that reveals the secret correspondences that link things together in time. From these few remarks, we should retain the idea that knowledge is being-born-together, or the simultaneous growth of beings within the unity of *phusis,* in the sense of growth and birth: "Truly, blue knows [i.e., is born together with] the color orange, truly the hand knows its shadow on the wall; really and truly, the angle of a triangle knows the other two in the same sense that Isaac knew Rebecca. All that is . . . designates that without which it could not have been."[39]

18

Aesthetic Perception and the Genesis of Forms

I have so far distinguished between a Promethean attitude and an Orphic attitude toward the problem of understanding the "secrets of nature." Prolonging this distinction, but this time renouncing the use of mythic terms, we might oppose two different procedures in the approach to nature. The first one would use the methods of science and technology, the second the methods of what I would call aesthetic perception, insofar as art could be considered a mode of understanding nature.

THE THREE MODES OF APPROACHING REALITY

Ultimately, however, there would be three modes of relation to nature that would have to be distinguished and defined in our human experience. First, there would be what we might call the world of daily perception, regulated by habits and also by the orientation of our interests. We look only at what is useful for us. We usually ignore the stars, and if we are city dwellers, we consider the sea and the countryside only as opportunities for rest and relaxation, or, if we are sailors or farmers, as means of earning a living.[1] To this world of daily perception is opposed the world of scientific knowledge, in which, for instance, the earth revolves around the sun. The Copernican revolution transformed the theoretical discourse of scientists and philosophers, but in fact it changed nothing in their lived experience. Edmund Husserl, and following him Maurice Merleau-Ponty, have shown convincingly how, for our lived experience, there is no Copernican revolution.[2] In our lived experience, it is the earth that we feel to be immobile, so human beings apply this experience psychologically to the ground everywhere.

The world of habitual perception is opposed, however, not only by the world of scientific knowledge but also by the world of aesthetic perception. Bergson spoke of "contemplating the universe with the eyes of an artist."[3] This means no longer perceiving things from a utilitarian point of view, by selecting only what concerns our action upon things, and thereby becoming incapable of seeing things as they appear in their reality and unity. "Why do we divide the world?" asks Cézanne. "Is it our egotism that is reflected? We want everything for our own use."[4] On the contrary, says Bergson, when artists look at a thing, "they see it for itself, and no longer for them." That is, "they no longer perceive simply with a view to action; they perceive in order to perceive—for nothing, just for the pleasure."[5] Bergson concludes that philosophy, too, ought to lead to a complete change in our way of perceiving the world.

Moreover, by privileging aesthetic perception as a model for philosophical perception, Bergson takes his place within a millennium-old tradition. Since antiquity, people had been aware of the degradation of perception brought about by habit and interest. In order to rediscover pure perception, which is aesthetic perception, we must, says Lucretius, look at the world as if we were seeing it for the first time:

> First of all, contemplate the clear, pure color of the sky, and all it contains within it: the stars wandering everywhere, the moon, the sun and its light with its incomparable brilliance: if all these objects appeared to mortals today for the first time, if they appeared before their eyes suddenly and unexpectedly, what could one cite that would

be more marvelous than this totality, and whose existence man's imagination would less have dared to conceive? Nothing, in my opinion, so prodigious as this spectacle. Look, then: we are so tired and bored by this sight, that no one deigns any longer to raise their eyes to the luminous regions.[6]

Seneca echoes his words: "For my part, I am accustomed to take a great deal of time to contemplate wisdom; I look at it with the same stupefaction with which, at other times, I look at the world, that world that it often occurs to me to contemplate as if I were seeing it for the first time."[7]

To see things for the first time is to rid one's glance of all that hides from it the nudity of nature, freed from all the utilitarian representations with which we cover it; it is to perceive in a naive and disinterested way, an attitude that is far from being simple, since we must tear ourselves away from our habits and our egotism. Seneca rightly points out that we are astonished only by things that are rare, and that we ignore sublime spectacles if we see them every day.[8]

It was in the eighteenth century that people became aware of the necessity of opposing increasing mechanization by an aesthetic approach to nature. In his book titled *Kosmos*, the great scientist and explorer Alexander von Humboldt mentions the fear people sensed in his time of the danger with which the development of scientific knowledge was threatening the free pleasure we experience in the face of nature.[9] As early as 1750, Alexander Baumgarten in his *Aesthetica* affirmed that in addition to a "logical truth" there was also room for an "aesthetic truth," opposing, for instance, an eclipse observed by astronomers and mathematicians to an eclipse observed in an emotive way by a shepherd talking about it to his beloved.[10] In his *Critique of the Faculty of Judgment* (1790), Kant gives an excellent definition of the difference between the two methods of approaching nature, the scientific and the aesthetic. In order to perceive the ocean as sublime, we must not look at it from the perspective of geography or meteorology, but "we must seek to see the ocean as poets do, exclusively according to what is shown to the eye when it is contemplated, either at rest, like a bright mirror of water, limited only by the sky, or else when it is agitated, like an abyss threatening to swallow everything up."[11] This aspect, emotive and therefore subjective, of aesthetic perception is very important: we speak of pleasure and wonder in the face of beauty, but also of terror in the face of the sublime. This is a reflection not only of emotions linked to our daily interests but also of disinterested emotions brought about by the contemplation of nature.

This disinterested character of emotion is extremely important. Kant held that "to take an immediate interest in the beauty of nature . . . is always the sign of a soul that is good."[12] By "immediate interest," Kant means the fact of finding one's pleasure in the pure existence of natural beauty, and of having an interest only in beauty, without any egoistic consideration: "He who, in solitude (and without the intention of wishing to communicate his observations to others) contemplates the beautiful form of a wildflower, a bird, an insect, etc., in order to admire them and love them . . . takes an immediate interest in the beauty of nature."[13] There is thus a deep connection between the aesthetic and the ethical approach: the former is ruled by interest in the beautiful and the latter by interest in the good. Alexander Baumgarten, moreover, recommended exercises to whoever wished to acquire aesthetic training, or an "askēsis," in order to set the powers of the mind in harmony with those of feeling.[14]

Schopenhauer was also situated in this tradition when he described the disinterested contemplation that occurs when the individual frees himself from the principle of reason, from his desires and interests, and annihilates himself in order to lose himself in the object, becoming a "pure subject" and freeing himself from time; for—to adopt, with Schopenhauer, the language of Spinoza—the mind becomes eternal insofar as it perceives things *sub specie aeternitatis,* "from the perspective of eternity."[15]

For Goethe, this aesthetic perception enables us to accede to the experience of nature. In *Wilhelm Meister,* for instance, the book's hero is staying on the shores of Lake Como in the company of a priest who helps him discover the magic of art:

> Nature had not given our old friend the eye of a painter. Since he had thus far tasted sensible beauty only in human form, he suddenly discovered that, thanks to a friend of the same sensitivity, but trained to wholly other enjoyments, and a wholly other kind of activities, it was the world that was now revealing itself to him . . . He identified himself intimately with his new friend, and, impressionable as he was, he learned to see the world with the eyes of an artist, and while nature unfolded the *mystery in broad daylight*[16] of its beauty, he felt himself irresistibly attracted toward art, which is its most worthy exegete.[17]

For Goethe, art is indeed the best interpreter of nature.[18] Unlike science, art does not discover hidden laws, equations, or structures behind phenomena; on the contrary, it learns to see phenomena, or appearance, what is in broad daylight, what is under our very noses, and which we do not know how to see.[19] It teaches us that what is most mysterious, what is most secret, is precisely that which is in broad daylight, or the visible: more precisely, the movement by which nature makes itself visible. Goethe dreams of a contact with nature that would abandon language in order to be nothing but the perception or the creation of forms. Human art would thus communicate in silence with the spontaneous art of nature: "To have before one, all day long, the magnificence of the world, and to feel capable of making it suddenly revealed by this gift [painting]. What joy, to be able to come closer to the inexpressible by means of line and color!"[20]

GENERALIZED AESTHETICS

In a little book titled *Generalized Aesthetics,* published forty years ago, Roger Caillois had sketched what was both a theory of modern art, especially of *art brut,* and a philosophy of nature.[21] Here he affirmed, essentially, that nature and nature alone is the creator of beauty and art, with the same natural structures producing decoration, that is, works of art, and the power to appreciate this decoration, that is, aesthetic pleasure. In his view, art merely obeys the organic law of nature, which is an art that is immanent in forms: "The forms that are dependent on life were not created by anyone. They seem to be their own sculptor to themselves . . . The author blends with the work."[22] Natural creations are artistic, and artistic creations are natural: "Art constitutes a particular case of nature, that which occurs when the aesthetic procedure goes through the supplementary procedure of drawing and execution."[23]

From this essay, which gives us a great deal to think about, I will retain only a single teaching: it is good for human beings always to remember that they themselves are natural beings, and that nature, in its diverse manifestations, often sketches out procedures that seem to us to be artistic in the proper sense of the term, and that there is therefore a deep commonality between nature and art. Nature's spontaneous art manifests itself, for instance, in the "painting" of butterfly wings or the ostentatious luxury—which can be truly explained only by the need to maintain life—of flowers or the plumage of birds, which give us the impression, obviously from an anthropomorphic perspective, of wanting to be seen in daylight.[24] Schopenhauer had insisted on the importance of this anthropomorphic way of looking at things, which, he remarks, "is close to madness," but which allows us to sense the intimate link between art and nature. Alluding to the perfumes and colors of flowers, he says, "It is curious to see how insistently the vegetable world, in particular, solicits us, and, so to speak, constrains us to contemplate it."[25] And he adds, "Only a very intimate and very deep contemplation of nature can suggest or confirm this idea." He is pleased to find it in Augustine, who said that plants, since they cannot know, seem to want to be known.[26]

According to the formula of Eugen Fink, summarizing Nietzsche's thought, "human art is itself a cosmic event."[27] Such was indeed Nietzsche's great intuition, as early as his first work, *The Birth of Tragedy,* where he speaks of nature's aesthetic instincts: he remained faithful to this concept throughout his life.[28] The world is art through and through.[29] It is a work of art that engenders itself; for in Nietzsche's view, all creation of forms is art.[30] Nature sculpts an entire universe of forms; she spreads forth an extraordinary variety of colors and unfolds a whole gamut of sounds within space. Human art is an integral part of this universe of appearance, and, as Nietzsche often repeats, it is this appearance that must be "adored."

In the chapter of his *Theory of Modern Art* titled "Diverse Paths in the Study of Nature," Paul Klee writes: "The dialogue with nature remains the condition *sine qua non* for the artist. The artist is a human being; he is himself nature, and a piece of nature within the area of nature . . . a creature on earth and a creature in the universe: a creature on one star among other stars."[31] We find this theme in Paul Claudel: "Our works and their means do not differ from those of nature."[32]

If one thinks that there is a relation between the production of forms by Nature and the production of forms by the human imagination, one might say that to invent myths is to prolong the fundamental gesture of Nature, who produces her forms. Is this a freakish idea? In any case, Paul Valéry had entertained it, if only for a moment: "When I dream and invent without return, am I not . . . nature? . . . Does not nature, in its way, do the same thing in its games, when it gives generously, transforms, causes damage, forgets, and rediscovers so many chances and figures of life in the midst of the rainbows and atoms in which all that is possible and inconceivable is alive, thrives, and entangles itself?"[33] At the end of a book in which he pointed out the extraordinary play of living forms, Adolph Portmann made the following remark: "We sometimes feel ill at ease with regard to these creatures that resemble the phantasmagoria of our dreams or the products of our imagination. This feeling must be taken seriously, not as a scientific intuition but rather as the sign that the unknown is in us and around us. Wasn't artistic creation, more attentive than previously to the works of these secret forms, inspired by the astonishing animal diversity, in which it saw a kind of brotherhood?"[34]

In this view, the Neoplatonic idea according to which nature is mythical could thus rediscover a very deep meaning.[35] For the human brain, which is a piece of nature, to invent myths or forms is simply to carry out the fundamental gesture of Nature as she invents forms.[36]

THE GENESIS OF FORMS

If art is nature, and if nature is art, artists and philosophers will, through aesthetic experience, be able to know nature, that is, become aware of all the dimensions of the world of perception, but in two different ways.

First of all, the attentive observation of natural forms will enable them to glimpse the method according to which nature seems to work, that is, the great laws of the appearance of forms. Yet this familiarity with nature may also lead them to a wholly different experience: that of the existential presence of nature as a creative source. Immersed within Nature's creative impulse, they will have the impression of identifying themselves with her. They will then transcend the search for the secrets of nature, to achieve amazement before the world's beauty.

In their first approach, they will thus seek to know the very procedures of nature. The more experience the artist acquires, the more he has the impression of deepening his familiarity with nature. Hokusai's fine declaration, reported by Rilke, is well known: "At the age of seventy-three, I more or less understood the form and the true nature of birds, fish, and plants."[37] "Understanding the form" ultimately means being able to reproduce the very act by which nature creates this form. Plotinus had already said that the arts do not imitate directly what is seen, but go back to the rational principles, or *logoi*, of which the visible effect of natural processes is the result. This is the same as to say that the artist, as it were, embraces the process of the generation of forms and operates like it.[38] As Goethe said, "I presume that the Greek artists proceeded in accordance with the laws of Nature herself, which laws I am now pursuing."[39]

"The point is not to imitate Nature, but to work like her," as Picasso was to say. This remark was cited by Pierre Ryckmans to illustrate the pictorial theories of the Chinese painter Shitao, which he summarizes as follows: "The painter's activity is not to imitate the various data of Creation but to reproduce the very act by which nature creates," which proves that the creative experience of Far Eastern artists brought them, too, to think that they were proceeding according to the secret laws of nature.[40]

It is also this creative process that attracts the painter's attention according to Paul Klee: "Naturizing nature matters more to him than naturized nature." For it is "in the bosom of nature, in the primordial dregs of creation where the keys to all things lie buried," that he seeks to establish his sojourn as an artist.[41] From this perspective, Klee takes the liberty of creating abstract forms that are, in his view, the prolongation by man of nature's action.

When Goethe says that art is the best exegete of nature, he means to suggest precisely that aesthetic experience allows us to glimpse specific laws that might explain the entire variety of natural living forms. Likewise, Roger Caillois, in his *Generalized Aesthetics*, notes that there is only a small number of what he calls the "natural orderings," that is, schemata that generate forms.[42] He too thus tries to identify the geometrical figures chosen by nature—the spiral, for instance—and to let us glimpse "the immense canvas that determines the form of crystals, shells, leaves, and corollas."[43]

Nevertheless, when we say that art prolongs nature, or proceeds according to nature's method, we must add a correction. Up until now, at any rate, human art has never been able to reproduce nature's spontaneity in all its specificity. There is a lovely passage in Kant on the interest we take in the beauty of nature as nature, which vanishes immediately if we realize that what we have before us is an imitation, however perfect it may be.[44] The creations of human art, especially in the area of technology, may reach a very high level of perfection and give the impression of transcending nature; and yet nothing can surpass the beauty of a living being. As Goethe said: "What a delicious and magnificent thing a living being is! How well adapted it is to its condition, and how true; how it *is!*"[45] "How it is!" What characterizes nature is precisely this existential presence, absolutely inimitable, which imposes itself upon us. This is nature's unexplorable secret.

POLARITY AND ASCENT

Goethe sought to discover the Form-types of Nature, which he calls the originary phenomena *(Urphänomene)*, for instance, the originary plant. He explained these Form-types by fundamental laws that preside in a general way over natural movements, particularly the two forces of polarity *(Polarität)* and intensification or ascension *(Steigerung)*, which we see at work, for example, in the growth of a plant.[46] Indeed, the double movement of spirality and verticality that characterizes it corresponds to the fundamental rhythm of nature that is the opposition between *Polarität* and *Steigerung,* or between "splitting into two" and "ennobling" or "intensification." "That which appears," says Goethe, "must separate itself in order to appear. The separated parts seek each other out once again and may find one another and reunite . . . This reunification may be carried out in a transcendent mode, insofar as that which has been separated is initially ennobled [*sich steigert*], and by the linkage between ennobled parts it produces a third, which is new, superior, and unexpected."[47] By division and the opposition of contraries, nature is able to bring about the appearance of a superior form of existence that reconciles and transcends them. The archetype-plant, which, by means of the opposition of vertical and spiral, and of the male and female principles, causes the successive appearance of the "unexpected" of flowers and the "unexpected" of fruits, thus rediscovering in a transcendent form its original androgyny, is the paradigmatic model of the great law of nature that regulates all natural and human processes. In his poem "The Metamorphosis of Plants," dedicated to his wife, Christiane Vulpius, Goethe describes this rise of the plant toward transcendent unity, and then, broadening the symbol, he applies this model to all life and all love:

Each plant henceforth announces eternal laws to you; each flower speaks to you in a more distinct language. But if you here decipher the goddess's hieroglyph,[48] you will then recognize it everywhere, even if its outline has changed: in the caterpillar slowly crawling, in the butterfly that flutters alarmed, in the human being who, as he molds himself, changes his characteristic form. One also thinks of how, from the germ of an initial meeting, sweet habit gradually develops within us, of how friendship flourishes powerfully in our breast; finally, of how Love caused the birth of flowers and fruits . . .

As if to its finest fruit, sacred Love aspires to an identity of feeling, and an identity in the vision of things, so that the couple, in harmonious contemplation and perfect union, may rise up to the higher world.[49]

This universal law also applies to artistic creation, and it applies to what Goethe did in composing his literary works. Their structure is determined by what he considers the two motors of natural growth: polarity and intensification.[50]

The artist Philipp Otto Runge, inspired by the Goethean idea of the archetype-plant, amused himself by painting flowers, which he called "geometric bluebell," "lily of light," and "amaryllis formosissima," trying to grasp the secret of the genesis of living forms in their generative schemata.[51]

SPIRAL AND SERPENTINE LINE

Goethe, who was highly visual, "saw" the fundamental law of natural phenomena in the two forces of polarity and intensification, which, in his view, engender, for example, the plant's double movement of verticality and spirality. He "saw" it, because this law appeared to him in the emblem of the spiral—for him, the fundamental tendency of vegetation—or of the caduceus.[52]

Pascal may have thought of another "habitual" movement of nature when he wrote: "Nature acts by progress, *itus et reditus* [going and returning]. It passes by and returns, then goes further, then twice as little, then more than ever, etc. The flux of the sea takes place in this way, and the sun seems to advance in this way."[53]

Like the spiral, this movement of ebb and flow evokes undulation. Since the Renaissance, painters have been attentive to this movement, which is simultaneously a phenomenon of nature and an element of the arts of painting and sculpture. They called this movement the "serpentine line," which can be observed in flames, in waves, in some bodily postures, and obviously in the motion of serpents. Michelangelo seems to have been the first to direct the attention of painters to the importance this type of line can have for expressing grace and life.[54] As far as Leonardo da Vinci is concerned, here is the advice he gives to painters: "Observe with the greatest care the contours of each body, and the mode of their serpentine movement. These serpentine movements must be studied separately, to investigate whether their curves participate in an arc-shaped convexity or an angle-shaped concavity."[55]

As Erwin Panofsky remarked, "The contortions and foreshortenings of mannerist figures could not be explained if they had no recourse to the imagination of the person contemplating them."[56] The spectator is thus obliged to circle the statue, to obtain a view of it that is always new but always incomplete. In the eighteenth century, in his *Analysis of Beauty,* Hogarth becomes the theoretician of the use of the serpentine line, which he considered the most beautiful of all lines, or the line of grace.[57] According to Hogarth, the serpentine line moves not in a two-dimensional but in a three-dimensional space. He represents it as rising in a spiral around a cone. This flexuous line is found later on in the *Jugendstil.*[58]

It is therefore not surprising that Goethe, author of an essay on the tendency toward spirals in vegetation,[59] was highly attentive to this theory of Hogarth's, and thought he detected a general law of nature in it: "The living being, when it reaches its completed form, likes to curve itself, as we are accustomed to seeing in horns, claws, and teeth; if it curves and turns at the same time in a serpentine motion, the result is grace and beauty."[60] From this point, says Goethe, Hogarth was led to seek the line of beauty in its simplest form. The ancients utilized such lines to represent horns of plenty, which entwined harmoniously with the arms of goddesses.[61]

Félix Ravaisson's reflections on the method of teaching drawing sought to attach themselves to this tradition.[62] For Ravaisson, the artist was to fix his attention above all on serpentine motion, as the movement that generates form, instead of giving priority to the lines that enclose things within their contours: "The secret of the art of drawing would thus consist in discovering within each particular object the particular way in which there travels throughout its extent, like a central wave that unfolds into superficial waves, a certain flexuous line that is like its generative axis."[63] Some passages of Ravaisson's *Philosophical Testament*, written from 1896 to 1900, rely on this methodology of the art of drawing to go still further. They strive to discover what he calls "the method and law of nature," which would ultimately be, as it were, the secret of nature. Ravaisson thinks he can recognize this fundamental law in the heartbeat, or movement proper to the heart, the elevation and lowering, diastole and systole, that is, ultimately, undulation:

> One expression [of the heartbeat] is found in the vibrations that are attributed to light; another, more obvious one, in the undulations of waves; another in the gait of animals, but especially of the serpent, who, having limbs only potentially, transports himself by movements—alternating and therefore sinuous—of its entire body; movements that are still perceptible, albeit half hidden, in the human gait, which is the only one capable of every kind of grace. From movement, the law extends to forms. Every form, said Michelangelo, is serpentine, and serpentine motion differs according to conformations and instincts. Observe, says Leonardo da Vinci, the serpentine motion of all things.
>
> (As if he thought that in each manner of serpentine motion or of undulating the proper character of each being was revealed; each being would thus be a particular expression of the general method of nature.)
>
> Thus, then, the immense poem of creation is developed. Thus Na-

ture progresses in her highest parts, which the other ones imitate, in an unfolding of fecund undulations.[64]

This undulating motion or serpentine line is the line of grace because it is the expression of abandonment, which is a graceful movement. "The agitated wave that falls, as if abandoning itself, is a movement of grace,"[65] and this movement of abandonment reveals the nature of the creative principle.

Bergson, praising Ravaisson, was to take up this theme, which corresponds quite well to his own thought: "Thus, for whoever contemplates the universe with the eyes of an artist, it is grace that is read through beauty, and goodness that shines beneath grace. Each thing, in the movement that its form registers, manifests the infinite generosity of a principle that gives itself. Not incorrectly is the same name used to name the charm we see in movement and the act of liberality that is characteristic of divine goodness: the two meanings of the word *grace* were but one for M. Ravaisson."[66]

We thus see how the serpentine line could become a kind of symbol of the laws and methods of nature. Serpentine line or the pairing of polarity and intensification: we thus have two examples of the search, within the context of pictorial experience, for a procedure, method, or fundamental movement of nature that would enable us to understand and embrace, in a way, the generation of forms.

COSMIC ECSTASY

From the perspective of aesthetic perception, I have said that beyond the attention accorded to the generation of forms, the artist, in his effort to embrace the creative impulse of nature, comes to identify himself with nature. Paul Klee speaks of both "terrestrial rootedness" and "cosmic participation."[67]

The painter may paint in a state in which he feels his deep unity with the earth and the universe. Here, the point is no longer to discover a secret of the world's fashioning but to undergo an experience of identification with the creative movement of forms, or with *phusis* in the original sense of the word; to abandon oneself to the "torrent of the world," according to Cézanne's expression.[68]

Such experiences are perhaps not very frequent in a pictorial context. They appear at specific periods in the West, for instance, in the Romantic period or at the end of the nineteenth century, or, by contrast, in a traditional way in the East. In remarks on the painting of Chinese and Japanese painters, we find numerous testimonies on this subject.[69] For instance, one might cite Chang Yen-yuan (ca. 847): "By concentrating our spirit, and letting our thought frolic toward the infinite, we subtly penetrate the mysteries of Nature. Things and I are both forgotten. We leave the body and reject knowledge . . . Is this not to have attained the mysterious Principle? This is what is called the Tao of painting."[70] Su Che (eleventh century) speaks of an artist who, while painting a stalk of bamboo, loses consciousness of himself and abandons his own body. He himself becomes bamboo.[71]

In the *Remarks on Painting by the Monk Bitter-Pumpkin*, Shitao declares: "Fifty years ago, there had not yet been a being-born-together[72] of my Ego with the Mountains and the Rivers; not that they were of negligible value, but I merely let them exist by themselves. But now the Mountains and the Rivers charge me to speak for them; they are born in me and I in them. I have ceaselessly sought extraordinary peaks, I have made sketches of them, Mountains and Rivers have met with my spirit and their imprint was metamorphosed, so that finally they are reduced to me."[73] In this regard, Ryckmans cites a saying of Chuang Tzu: "My birth is in solidarity with that of the universe; I am but one with the infinity of beings."[74]

In the West, we might find a comparable and analogous experience in some Romantics. Carl Gustav Carus, author of *Nine Letters on Landscape Painting,* pleads for a "mystical" painting: not mystical in the religious sense (for instance, "Rosicrucian") of the term, which would imply a determinate belief, but a mysticism of cosmic unity, or "a mysticism that is as eternal as Nature herself, because she is but nature, *mysterious nature in plain daylight,*[75] because she wants nothing other than intimacy with the elements and with God and she must, through this very fact, remain comprehensible to all times and all peoples."[76] In Goethe's *Werther,* the hero, who is a painter, describes his state of mind, which could be qualified as mystical, in one of his letters, saying, "I could not draw a line, and yet never was I a greater painter." He continues:

> When the vapors from the valley rise before me, and the sun hurls its fire straight down upon the impenetrable vault of my dark forest, and only a few scattered rays slip to the bottom of the sanctuary; when, lying on the ground in the high grass, near a stream, I discover a thousand unknown tiny plants in the thickness of the grass; when my heart senses close at hand the existence of that tiny world that swarms among the grass; of that innumerable world of tiny worms and midges of every forms; when I sense the presence of the Almighty who created us in his image, and the breath of the All-loving, who carries us along and holds us up, floating on a sea of eternal delights, . . . then I sigh and cry within myself: "Ah! If only you could express what you feel! If only you could exhale and fix upon paper this life that flows in you with such abundant heat!"[77]

Here we see the artist incapable of completing a picture because emotion, which precisely should invite him to paint, is too strong. In that very moment, however, he feels that he has never been a greater painter. The Romantic painter Philipp Otto Runge recalled this text in one of his letters, in which the ecstatic aspect appears even more intensely:

When the sky above me seethes with innumerable stars, when the wind whistles in the immense space, when the waves break roaring in the vast night, when the ether reddens above the forest and the sun illuminates the world, vapors rise in the valley and I throw myself in the grass among the shining drops of dew, each leaf, each blade of grass overflows with life, the earth lives and stirs all around me, everything resonates together in a single concord; then my soul cries with joy and soars in all directions in the incommensurable space around me; there is no more up or down, no time, no beginning or end, I hear and sense the living breath of God, who holds and supports the world and in whom all things live and move.[78]

At the end of the nineteenth century, perhaps under the influence of the discovery of the painting of the Far East, some artists also alluded to this kind of sensation, tinged with a certain mystical experience. Vincent van Gogh, for instance, in a letter to his brother Theo, alludes explicitly to the Japanese painters:

If one studies the Japanese painters, then one sees a man indisputably wise, philosophical, and intelligent, who spends his time doing what? Studying the distance from the earth to the moon? No. Studying Bismarck's politics? No, he studies a single blade of grass. Yet this blade of grass leads him to draw all plants, then the seasons, the great aspects of landscapes, finally animals, then the human figure . . . Let us see: is it not almost a real religion that we are taught by these oh-so-simple Japanese, who live within nature as if they themselves were flowers?[79]

When van Gogh uses the term "religion," he certainly seems to be thinking not of a religious practice but of an emotion of a mystical order, or a feeling of communion with nature, as in the letter that follows the one just cited: "I have a terrible need for religion—therefore I go at night to paint the stars." We could, moreover, compare these remarks by van Gogh to what Cézanne said to Joaquim Gasquet: "Art, I believe, places us in that state of grace in which universal emotion is translated as it were religiously, but very naturally to us. As in colors, we must find overall harmony everywhere."[80] Above all, "if my canvas is saturated with this vague cosmic religion, which moves me and makes me better, it will touch others at a point of their sensibility of which they may be unaware."[81] Alluding to a painting by Tintoretto, Cézanne speaks of that "cosmic obsession that devours us." He writes: "For my part, I want to lose myself in nature, and grow again with her, like her . . . In a patch of green, my entire brain will flow with the sap-like tide of the tree . . . The immensity and torrent of the world, in a tiny inch of water."[82]

VII

The Veil of Isis

19

Artemis and Isis

We now come to the third theme of this book. After having seen how the traditional interpretation of Heraclitus' aphorism, which was our starting point, was intimately linked to the idea of a secret of nature, we will now see the Nature who hides her secrets personified with the features of Isis, identified with Artemis or, in Latin culture, with Diana of Ephesus.[1]

ARTEMIS OF EPHESUS

In the history of European art, Nature was represented in different ways, and these diverse models coexisted through the ages. In the fifteenth century, for instance, Nature appears in the guise of a naked woman, making milk flow over the world from her breast.[2] This motif reappears in the French revolutionary festivals in honor of the goddess Nature.[3] Nature's nudity was justified three centuries later, precisely at the time of the Revolution, in H. F. Gravelot and C. N. Cochin's handbook of iconography, in these terms: "Nature is designated by a naked woman, whose attitude expresses the simplicity of her essence."[4] At the beginning of the seventeenth century, another type made its appearance: a naked women, her breasts swollen with milk, but this time accompanied by a vulture; it is attested to particularly in Cesare Ripa's handbook of iconology.[5] This vulture leads us to suppose that there was a tendency to imagine Nature in an Egyp-

233

tian context, for in Horapollo's *Hieroglyphica* the vulture is placed in relation with nature. According to this work from the end of antiquity, translated in the Renaissance, the vulture symbolizes nature, for all the individuals of this species are of the female sex, and they engender without having need of a male. The vulture can therefore represent nature's fecundity and maternity.[6] The motif of the vulture, this time associated with another type of representation of Nature, that of Isis/Artemis, was taken up once again in the seventeenth century, for instance, in the frontispiece of Blasius's book on the anatomy of animals.[7]

The beginning of the sixteenth century marks the appearance of the type of allegory that interests us in the overall perspective of the present work. This time, Nature was represented in conformity with the ancient model of Artemis of Ephesus, in the form of a feminine figure whose head bears a crown and a veil, whose chest features numerous breasts, and whose lower body is enclosed in a tight sheath on which one can see representations of various animals. Several ancient statues give us a good idea of this traditional representation of Artemis of Ephesus. It was according to this type that, in 1508, Raphael painted Nature, the object of the study of physics, on the two supports of the throne of Philosophy, in a fresco of the Stanza della Segnatura in the Vatican (Fig. 6). We can assume that this motif was already known at the end of the preceding century, perhaps under the influence of the fashion for the grotesque, which had been launched by the discovery of certain ancient paintings, particularly those of Nero's famous Domus Aurea, whose fantastic decorations included the Artemis of Ephesus.[8] The same model reappears in the statue of the goddess Nature sculpted by Niccolò Tribolo in 1529, at Fontainebleau, and in which we see various animals nursing at Nature's breasts (Fig. 7).

This was the period in which emblem books began to appear, that is, collections of drawings symbolizing an idea or notion, accompanied by a brief formula or short saying—what the ancients called an enthymeme. Artemis of Ephesus, as an allegory of Nature, found her place among them, for instance, in Sambucus's *Emblemata* (1564), to illustrate the difference between physics and metaphysics.[9]

This identification of Nature with Artemis of Ephesus could base itself on some texts from antiquity, such as the following from Saint Jerome: "The Ephesians honor Diana, not the famous huntress, but Diana of the many breasts whom the Greeks call *polymaston*, so as to make people believe by this image that she nourishes all animals and all living beings."[10] In this regard, I should also mention a magical Greco-Egyptian intaglio in which we see the goddess "surrounded by astral symbols and the hieroglyphic sign '*nh*, which seems to express a wish translated into Greek in a text that should probably be spelled correctly as *phusis panti biōi*, 'productive force for all creatures,' a formula perfectly adapted to the Ephesian goddess and still close to those Anatolian 'Mistresses of Nature and Life' whom she supplanted."[11]

According to some modern scholars, what the ancients took to be breasts might in fact, like the rest of the goddess's attributes, be the sculpted reproduction of the clothes and decorations with which the goddess's statue was adorned. The statue would have been made of wood and covered with adornments. It was the custom in Asia Minor, and even in Greece, to dress goddesses; in fact, this was an essential part of daily worship.[12] On this hypothesis, the form of the statues corresponds to the sculpted representation of the adornments that covered the wooden statue. What had been assumed to be breasts would thus be jewels, or chains with pendants.[13] Alternatively, they could be the testicles of bulls offered to the goddess on the occasion of the sacrifices that took place in her honor.[14] It would thus be a mistaken interpretation—once again, a creative misunderstanding—that led people to see a personification of Nature in Artemis of the many breasts.

ISIS

Since the end of antiquity there had been a tendency to identify Ephesian Artemis with Egyptian Isis in order to personify Nature.[15] For instance, Macrobius describes the statue of Isis as follows: "Isis is the earth or nature that is under the sun.[16] This is why the goddess's entire body bristles with a multitude of breasts placed close to one another [as in the case of Artemis of Ephesus], because all things are nourished by earth or by nature."[17] In arithmology, that is, the discipline of Pythagorean origin that established a correspondence between numbers and metaphysical entities and the divinities that symbolized these entities, the Dyad was identified with Isis, Artemis, and Nature.[18]

In the sixteenth century, Vincenzo Cartari, in his handbook of iconography titled *Images of the Gods*, published in 1556, cites this text by Macrobius to prove that the ancients liked to represent Nature with the features of Isis/Artemis.[19] He specifies that a statue of this kind was found at Rome, and that he himself has seen an analogous figure on a medal of the emperor Hadrian. He might also have recalled, so far as the identification of Isis with Nature is concerned, how Isis presents herself in the *Metamorphoses* of Apuleius: "I come to you, Lucius, . . . I, mother of all of nature, mistress of all the elements."[20]

From the sixteenth to the nineteenth centuries there was perfect awareness of this confusion between the two goddesses.[21] Claude Ménétrier, for instance, points it out in his book entitled *Symbolica Dianae Ephesiae Statua*, published in 1657, where, like Cartari, he relies on the text by Macrobius to justify it. Here he itemizes the statue's various features, that is, the deer, lions, and bees that were characteristic of Ephesian Artemis: "The hierophants of Ephesus," he says, "hid beneath these symbols the causes of the nature of things."[22] In 1735, Romeyn de Hooghe, in his *Hieroglyphica*, also speaks of this representation of Isis/Artemis as of a woman with multiple breasts, bearing a tower on her head, and wearing a veil.[23] We find her once again in 1664 on the frontispiece of the second volume of the *Mundus Subterraneus* by the Jesuit Athanasius Kircher, and again in 1713, in an illustration in Shaftesbury's *Characteristics* (Fig. 8).[24]

THE VEIL OF ISIS

Owing to its identification with Artemis, the statue of Isis thus represented a woman wearing a veil.[25] The veil of Nature, without any explicit allusion to Isis, appears in the work of Edmund Spenser.[26] The poet affirms that no one knows her face, and that no creature could uncover it, for it is hidden by a veil that covers it. Some say that the veil is intended to conceal the terrifying nature of her appearance, for she has the look of a lion. Human eyes could not bear the sight of her. Others say that it is because she is so beautiful and splendid, more so than the sun, that she can only be seen in the reflection of a mirror.

In the seventeenth century, Athanasius Kircher, in his *Œdipus Ægyptiacus,* which deals with Egyptian enigmas, interprets the veil of Isis as a symbol of the secrets of Nature.[27] This is perhaps the first symptom of the fashion, both iconographical and literary, which was to inspire the entire modern and Romantic period, and which has been dubbed Egyptomania.

Be that as it may, in the eighteenth century, the iconographical theme of the veil of Isis was linked explicitly to that of the secrets of Nature. I think it was in the *Iconology* of Jean-Baptiste Boudard, published in 1759, that the emblem representing Nature was defined for the first time: "Nature, being the assemblage and the perpetuation of all created beings, is represented by a young woman whose lower part is enclosed in a sheath that is adorned with different kinds of terrestrial animals, and on her arms, which are outstretched, are different kinds of birds. She has several breasts, filled with milk. Her head, covered with a veil, signifies, according to the opinion of the Egyptians, that the most perfect secrets of Nature are reserved for the Creator."[28] As Honoré Lacombe de Prézel remarked in his *Iconological Dictionary* of 1779, this theme can assume several forms: "The Egyptians represented her [Nature] by the image of a woman covered by a veil, an expression that is simple yet sublime. Sometimes this veil does not cover her entirely but lets us glimpse a part of her breast, to indicate to us that what we know best of the operations of Nature are the things concerning needs of primary necessity. The rest of the body and the head are veiled, a living emblem of our ignorance of the how and why of these operations."[29]

THE THEME OF UNVEILING

Although the secrets of Nature, in the words of Jean-Baptiste Boudard, are reserved for the Creator, with the rise of science and the improvement of scientific instruments, people of the seventeenth and eighteenth centuries considered that the human mind could penetrate the secrets of Nature and therefore raise the veil of Isis.

We can distinguish several types of representations of the unveiling of Isis. First of all, some of them feature the unveiling of a *statue* of Isis/Artemis. This is the case, for instance, with the engraving by Thorvaldsen that adorned the dedication to Goethe of the German translation of Alexander von Humboldt's *Essai sur la géographie des plantes*.[30] Here, however, it is Apollo, god of poetry, who unveils the statue of Nature, at whose foot lies Goethe's book *The Metamorphosis of Plants* (Fig. 1). Goethe himself commented on this drawing by saying that it suggests that poetry might indeed raise Nature's veil.[31] The same holds true of the engraving by Hogarth and Füssli, which I will soon discuss. The strange character of the representation of Nature is thereby accentuated. Other artists, however, broke free of this fixed representation and dared to represent a living young woman bearing several breasts on her chest. This is the case with the other drawings we shall study.

Elsewhere, in some engravings, an allegorical personage takes the veil away from Isis, whereas in others it is rather respect in the presence of the mystery that is stressed. The representation of unveiling seems to appear for the first time in the frontispiece of Blasius' work *Anatome Animalium* (1681, Fig. 9).[32] Here we see Science, represented in the form of a young woman with a flame above her head, symbol of the desire for knowledge,[33] a magnifying glass, and a scalpel in her hands, unveiling a woman who has four breasts on her chest. Nature also bears the symbols of the seven planets on her chest. On her right arm, which bears a scepter, perches a vulture, a reminder of the first types of images of Nature, discussed earlier. Other animals are gathered around her, and at her feet we see two putti, the symbols of scientific labor: one of them is dissecting an animal; the other examines entrails while looking at Nature with admiration.

Anton van Leeuwenhoek played a very important role in the history of biology, thanks to the use of the microscope, which he did not invent but considerably perfected. He announced his discoveries, particularly that of protozoa, in letters to the Academies of London and Paris. He collected these letters in numerous works, one of which was entitled *Arcana Naturae Detecta,* "The Secrets of Nature Unveiled."[34] Almost all Leeuwenhoek's frontispieces represent the unveiling of Isis/Nature by Philosophy or the Science of Nature. Of these many engravings I will mention only the one placed at the beginning of his book *Anatomia seu Interiora Rerum,* published in 1687 (Fig. 10).[35] Here, Isis/Artemis seems to be unveiling herself as she holds her veil in her left hand, but an old man, who might perhaps represent Father Time, is also pulling her veil aside.[36] Nature's chest bears five breasts. In her inclined right hand she holds a cornucopia, from which emerge, among other things, flowers, a toad, a snake, and a butterfly. To the right of Isis, we see a female personage who quite probably represents Philosophy or the Science of Nature. Under her left arm she holds a book, on whose cover a sphinx is depicted; here, the sphinx symbolizes the perspicacity that unveils the secrets of nature. Philosophy points out with a wand to another female personage, probably Scientific Research, the objects that have come forth from the cornucopia and which she must study. Research is looking into a microscope and drawing what she sees. Like Hermes, she has wings on the sides of her head. Hermes symbolized intellectual ingenuity or the interpretation of secrets.[37] In the foreground are seated a man and a woman, who seem to be supplying Scientific Research with animals and flowers. The totality of the engraving thus gives an allegorical representation of Scientific Research, armed with a microscope, discovering the secrets of nature.

In other representations, by contrast, there is only a fleeting allusion to unveiling, and the respectful attitude predominates instead. It is perhaps in this sense that we must understand the picture by Rubens, painted before 1648, in which the three Graces are adorning the statue of Nature, designated as Cybele, but in conformity with the traditional representation of Isis (Fig. 11). In 1730–31 it was putti, representing the arts, who surrounded the statue of Isis in Hogarth's engraving, *Boys Peeping at Nature* (Fig. 12). In fact, the statue is here wrapped in a kind of skirt, and while a faun tries to raise it, a girl, recognizable by her chignon, tries to stop him.[38] Another child is drawing the face of Isis, while a final child is drawing a figure using a compass, without looking at the goddess. Two texts appear in the drawing, one by Virgil, "Antiquam inquirite matrem" (Seek your ancient mother),[39] Apollo's advice to Aeneas, who desires to find a homeland, and the other by Horace, severely shortened: "Necesse est indiciis monstrare abdita rerum [. . .] dabiturque licentia sumpta pudenter."[40] This text, which in Horace relates to the problem of neologisms, seems completely diverted from its meaning when Hogarth introduces it into his engraving. Quite probably Hogarth applied it to the secrets of nature: "It is necessary to show that which is hidden by new revelations . . . and we will have the freedom, if we take this freedom with modesty." Hogarth may thus have wanted to suggest that the artistic discovery of the secrets of nature should be practiced with reserve and modesty. If we consider the engraving in itself, this is the interpretation that can be given. If, however, we take into account that it is, as it were, an advertising flyer recommending the series of engravings titled *The Harlot's Progress*, we must seek another explanation. Given the scabrous subject matter of this series of engravings, we might think that Hogarth wants to suggest that we must not be afraid to represent nature and reality, as long as we do so with decency.[41]

We encounter the theme of respect once again in the frontispiece that Johann Andreas Segner placed at the beginning of the second edition of his *Introduction to the Theory of Nature* (1754, Fig. 13). Here we see Isis, advancing in profile, crowned and carrying the *sistrum*, dressed in a robe covered with the figures of animals and plants and half-veiled by a wide mantle, near a ruined monument on whose pedestal we see Greek letters and a geometrical figure. Three putti are observing the goddess, one near the monument, with his finger to his lips, another measuring with his compass the tracks of her steps, another, finally, holding the lower fringe of her mantle in his hand. At the bottom of the medallion we read the motto "Qua licet," meaning "Insofar as it is permitted," which conveys the same recommendation of respect as the one in Hogarth's engraving. The scene suggests that we may unveil Nature only insofar as is permitted and that ultimately it is not Nature herself we may know but only, by measuring them mathematically, her footsteps, that is, phenomena, which are merely the results of her actions. Kant was to devote to this image a famous note in his *Critique of the Faculty of Judgment*, which I will discuss later on. The motif had already been sketched in the seventeenth century, in emblem 42 of the alchemical work *Atalanta Fugiens* by Michael Maier (1618), where we see a philosopher-alchemist studying by the light of a lantern the footsteps of a veiled young woman who advances rapidly in the night.

Many engravings represented the unveiling of Nature as the triumph of the philosophy of the Enlightenment over the forces of obscurantism. This was one of the favorite themes of the French Revolution, and it had already been sketched in the frontispiece of Delisle de Sales's work *The Philosophy of Nature,* published in London in 1777: "This pre-revolutionary Nature," writes René Pomeau, "offers her chest, which is moreover less richly endowed than Tribolo's, not to a child but to a robust philosopher, an impetuous champion who overturns Despotism, armed with a dagger, and Superstition, with its horned brow."[42] We find an analogous motif in the frontispiece to the book by François Peyrard *On Nature and Her Laws,* (1793), where we see an old man, representing Philosophy, denuding Isis/Nature and crushing under his feet masks that symbolize hypocrisy and lies (Fig. 14). From this perspective, Nature and Truth become quite close to each other, as in antiquity. One could also mention the translation of Lucretius' work by Lagrange. The engraving, opposite the title, alludes to a passage from Lucretius which says that Epicurus' genius has unveiled Nature, "which had been wrapped in fanaticism and error." Nature appears in the form of Isis/Artemis, and the genius of Epicurus is represented by a female personage who, as she draws aside the veil, knocks over the figures of Fanaticism and Error (Fig. 15).[43]

The iconographical theme of unveiling remained alive throughout the nineteenth century. For instance, at the end of the century, in 1899, the sculptor Louis-Ernest Barrias created two polychrome statues, titled *Nature Unveiling Herself before Science,* for the faculties of medicine of Paris and Bordeaux (Fig. 16). Here the motif of multiple breasts has disappeared, but the woman who raises her veil wears a scarab at her waist, which could be understood as an allusion to Isis.

In general, this theme of the unveiling of Isis played a crucial role in the illustration of scientific books in the seventeenth and eighteenth centuries. Yet it was also a very important literary and philosophical theme at the end of the eighteenth century and the beginning of the nineteenth, which bespeaks a significant transformation of the attitudes of philosophers and poets toward nature.

VIII

From the Secret of Nature
to the Mystery of Existence

Terror and Wonder

20

Isis Has No Veils

In 1814, when the archduke Karl August returned from a trip to England, there was a celebration at Weimar to mark his homecoming. Goethe had the town's drawing school decorated with eight paintings that were intended to symbolize the various arts and the protection Karl August accorded to them.[1] Among these symbolic figures executed in the style of emblems was one that represented *Genius Unveiling a Bust of Nature,* with Nature represented in her traditional aspect as Isis/Artemis (Fig. 17). In the distant background, behind the figure, a landscape could be seen, which contrasted strongly with the somewhat artificial atmosphere created by this statue of Nature unveiled. Goethe used these same pictures to decorate his own house for the jubilee of Karl August on September 3, 1825, and for his own jubilee, or more precisely for the anniversary of his entry into the service of the archduke, on November 7 of the same year.

"GENIUS UNVEILING A BUST OF NATURE"

It is very interesting to observe how the same emblem is susceptible of contradictory interpretations. Contemporaries, referring to the notion current at the end of the seventeenth century and during the eighteenth century, interpreted the gesture of Genius unveiling Nature as an allusion to Goethe's scientific activity. On the occasion of Goethe's jubilee, the poet Gerhardt, commenting on this emblem in verse, praised the alliance of poetry and science in Goethe: "Not content with sounding the golden lyre, the poet penetrates within Nature, and dares to raise the magic veil of Isis."[2] The illustration that Alexander von Humboldt had placed at the beginning of his 1808 *Essay on the Geography of Plants* had already alluded to this traditional representation of the unveiling of Isis. Ultimately, however, for Goethe, as we shall see throughout this chapter, Isis had no veil.

In fact, Goethe himself, when he imagined this emblem, was thinking of something quite different from the traditional cliché of Science unveiling Nature. In the first place, in the group of pictures painted to honor Karl August and intended to represent the various arts, this emblem was symbolic of sculpture. The brochure published at Weimar in 1825, which was anonymous, but probably inspired by Goethe, gives the following description of it: "A young boy, kneeling in a modest attitude, unveils the bust of Nature, which is represented symbolically. This bust of white marble alludes immediately to sculpture, as the most perfect representation of creation's most perfect product."[3] Here, the bust of Isis/Artemis symbolizes both sculpture, the art which "represents" Nature perfectly, and Nature herself, who sculpts forms.

It was Goethe himself, however, who revealed the true meaning he attributed to this figure. He composed a series of poems, related to each of the eight pictures I have mentioned, and collected under the title *Die Kunst* (Art).[4] Around March 1826, he devoted three quatrains to "Genius Unveiling a Bust of Nature," which reveal his genuine attitude with regard to the notion of a secret of nature and the metaphor of the veil of Isis. Not long afterward, he took up one of these quatrains in another collection of poetry, titled *Gentle Epigrams*, in a context that gives a fairly good idea of the meaning these figures and quatrains had for him. I first quote the three quatrains:

> Respect the mystery;
> Let not your eyes give way to lust.

Nature the Sphinx, a monstrous thing,
Will terrify you with her innumerable breasts.

Seek no secret initiation
beneath the veil; leave alone what is fixed.
If you want to live, poor fool,
Look only behind you, toward empty space.

If you succeed in making your intuition
First penetrate within,
Then return toward the outside,
Then you will be instructed in the best way.[5]

The second quatrain is reproduced in book 6 of the *Zahme Xenien*, following two stanzas, the first one of which criticizes Newton's theory of colors, while the second is directed against Symbolist historians of myths, such as Georg Friedrich Creuzer:[6]

If you, despised suitors
Do not silence your out-of-tune lyre,
Then I give up completely.
Isis shows herself without a veil,
But mankind has cataracts.

Symbols explained by history:[7]
He who grants them importance is quite mad.
He endlessly carries out sterile research
And lets the world's wealth escape.

Seek no secret initiation
beneath the veil; leave alone what is fixed.
If you want to live, poor fool,
Look only behind you, toward empty space.[8]

The first stanza just quoted may seem somewhat obscure. The suitors would appear to be the scientists who would like to unveil Isis by means of experimentation, like Newton; but they are despised, because they are unable to see, as is suggested by the following lines about Isis, who has no veils. In part 1 of *Faust,* Goethe had vehemently criticized experimentation, artificial observation, and the pretension of tearing her veil away from Nature: "Mysterious in broad daylight, Nature does not let herself be robbed of her veil, and what she does not wish to reveal to your mind, you could not constrain her to do with levers and screws."[9]

Goethe particularly reproached Newton for carrying out experiments on light, for instance, by passing it through a prism, experiments which, in his view, profoundly disturbed the true luminous phenomenon. In one of the subsequent stanzas, he declares, still against Newton: "To divide the unity of eternal light we must consider senseless." In general, he criticized experiments for trying to discover, by violent and mechanical means, something hidden behind phenomena, or behind the appearance of things.

Yet the group of brief poems from the *Gentle Epigrams* now under discussion was also aimed at other adversaries. In one manuscript, the poem "Seek No Secret Initiation" bears the note "To the Symbolist,"[10] and the poem that precedes it begins with the words: "Historical symbols." This is an allusion to the Symbolists of the school of Georg Friedrich Creuzer, against whom Goethe leveled a reproach analogous to the one he leveled against the experimenters. In the words of Mephistopheles in a paralipomenon to part 2 of *Faust,* with regard to the death of Euphorion:

> Others think that it [the story of Euphorion] must not be understood in a coarse and immediate way. There is something hidden behind it. One might easily guess the presence of mysteries, and per-

haps of mystifications as well: something Hindu or Egyptian, and he who holds them tight and blends everything together well, who takes pleasure in moving etymologically in every which way, that is the man we need. We too say this, and our deepest desire is to be faithful disciples of the new Symbolism.[11]

"There is something hidden behind it." This is the mistaken belief of both experimenters and Symbolists. The former practice a hermeneutics of nature that seeks to discover what lies hidden behind phenomena, while the latter also propose a hermeneutics, this time of myth, which tries to uncover the hidden meaning of mythic images, by discovering a historical background, whether Hindu or Egyptian, behind the myths.

We ought not to be surprised by this unexpected parallel between experimenting scientists and interpreters of mythology. We recall that for Porphyry, Nature wraps herself up in natural forms as well as in myths. Symbolists and experimenters allow what is most important to escape: the "free space" for the Genius who unveils the statue of Isis, or the "wealth of the world" for whoever tries to explain myths and symbols historically. They think the form is veiled, and they must find something else behind the veil. Yet the reason they seek something behind what they think is a veil is that they do not understand that everything is right before their eyes, and that the natural or mythical form they see has its reason within itself, and that we ought not to try to understand by means of anything other than itself; the veil is over their eyes, not over the eyes of Isis. To see Isis, all we have to do is look. She reveals herself without veils; she consists entirely in the splendor of her appearance.

Let us now reread the quatrains devoted to the image of "Genius Unveiling a Bust of Nature." They need to be explained by each other. For instance, the first quatrain warns the young child who is unveiling the statue of Isis that he is going to be frightened by her monstrous appearance. The second one, taking up the threat of death that hangs over a sacrilegious unveiling, urges the child, if he wants to live, to turn toward what is behind him, in other words, according to the drawing that accompanies the poem, toward the landscape of mountains and trees that appears in the background of the picture. We thus have here a critique of the traditional interpretation of the unveiling of the statue of Artemis/Isis. Nature is alive and moving, not an immobile statue. The so-called search for the secrets of nature by experimentation reaches not living nature, but something fixed. As Mephistopheles tells the student, the experimenter, wishing to understand living beings, chases the spiritual bond out of them, and leaves only pieces behind.[12] When he turns around, the child will see Nature no longer in her "fixed" form, but alive, as Nature in the process of becoming. We must not seek Nature anywhere other than where she is; we must not look for something dead beyond visible appearances.

"If you want to live, poor fool." Ancient Isis had said, "No mortal has raised my *peplos*." He who raises the goddess's veil therefore risks death. In Goethe's view, however, the death in question is, as it were, a spiritual one. By representing Nature as being hidden by a veil, one risks being hypnotized by what is supposed to be hidden beneath the veil, and above all, one risks petrifying oneself, and no longer perceiving the process of becoming and living Nature. "To respect the mystery" means contenting ourselves with seeing Nature as she is, without forcing her by experimentation, which attacks Nature's normal mode of functioning, and forces her to transform herself into states that are artificial and contrary to nature. For Goethe, the only valid instrument capable of enabling us to know nature are mankind's senses: perception guided by reason, and above all the aesthetic perception of nature. For him, as we have seen, art is the best interpreter of nature.[13]

GOETHE'S SCIENTIFIC METHOD

The idea of a secret of nature and the image of the veil of Isis presuppose the distinction between external appearance and a reality situated behind this appearance.[14] This is why Goethe rejected the opposition between internal and external, as expressed in the following verses by the Swiss poet Albrecht von Haller:

> Within Nature
> no created mind can penetrate.
> Happy is he to whom she shows
> only her external envelope.[15]

For Goethe, to admit that Nature refuses to unveil herself means either to resign oneself to ignorance, or, by contrast, to authorize the experimenter's violence. He radically contradicts Haller's affirmations:

> Nature gives all with generosity and benevolence.
> She has no pit
> or shell.
> She is all at once.[16]

This generosity and benevolence are the precise opposite of the attitude of a Nature who refuses to let herself be seen, and who "loves to hide." This corresponds precisely to the representation of a veilless Isis. There is no opposition between the phenomenon and that which is hidden in the phenomenon.

Why, then, in the last quatrain of the poem "Genius Unveiling a Bust of Nature," do we find an opposition between the internal and the external?

> If you succeed in making your intuition [*Anschauen*]
> First penetrate within,

Then return toward the outside,
Then you will be instructed in the best way.

How can it be possible to go within, and then return to the outside? If Goethe expresses himself in this way, it is because he is thinking, not of the movement of experimental knowledge, which starts out from external phenomena to discover a kind of internal mechanism that explains phenomena, but of the movement of intuitive thought that embraces the movement of genesis and growth, *phusis* in the Greek sense, or the formative impulse, *nisus formativus*,[17] which goes precisely from the internal to the external. Form is not *Gestalt*, an immobile configuration, but *Bildung*, formation or growth. Goethe himself tells us that what he loved in Kant's *Critique of the Faculty of Judgment* was the analogy that appears in it between the life of art and the life of nature, "their own way of acting from the inside to the outside."[18] There is something Bergsonian in this theory of nature's living intuition, "which can be reached if we ourselves remain mobile and supple."[19] Goethe's scientific method consists in an attentive perception of the movement of formation.[20] It is above all a morphology. We must pay attention to each particular form, and observe it for a long time. Then we must try to perceive these forms in their connection with other forms, thereby disclosing a sequence or series in which they take their place genetically, in order to see forms in their metamorphosis, see them being born from one another, and above all—this is what counts most for Goethe—to discover the simple and fundamental form, or *Urform*, from which the series of transformations develops. This is how we will discover that the formation of plants is in fact a metamorphosis of the leaf; that the formation of the bones of the skull is a metamorphosis of the vertebrae; that the formation of colors is a metamorphosis of light as it enters into relation with darkness through the intermediary of an opaque medium. Goethe calls the phenomenon at the origin of the process of metamorphosis the *Urphänomen*, or originary phenomenon, because there is nothing beyond it in the phenomena that appear to us, and, at the same time, by starting from it we can return to shed light on the most banal instances of day-to-day experience.[21] Using this method, Goethe hoped to discover an ideal prototype, for example, the originary plant from which all possible plants might be constructed.[22] The sensible perception of nature is thus transfigured into an intellectual perception that discovers the primordial phenomenon we perceive in the sensible phenomenon. As Goethe says in the preface to the *Theory of Colors*, to look at the world attentively is already to construct a theory.[23] "The blue of the sky reveals to us the fundamental law of chromatics. It is useless to seek behind phenomena, for they themselves are the theory."[24]

"MYSTERY IN BROAD DAYLIGHT"

Isis is thus without veils, and there is no secret of Nature in the proper sense of the term. Goethe, however, does use with regard to nature the German word *Geheimnis*, meaning "secret," but he adds to it the adjective *offenbares* or *öffentliches*. We could translate this as "secret in broad daylight," or "manifest secret"; but it is better to translate the word *Geheimnis* as "mystery" rather than as "secret," for it can have both of these meanings in German. On the one hand, the notion of "secret" presupposes the presence of something hidden which can be discovered and unveiled, but which then ceases to be a secret, and this is precisely what Goethe rejects. On the other hand, "mystery" makes us think of something that always remains mysterious, even if it is revealed. The expression chosen by Goethe alludes to a passage from Paul's Letter to the Romans (16:24), where he speaks of a "revealed mystery"—in Martin Luther's German, "das Geheimnis, das nun offenbart ist," or in Greek, *mustēriou phanērōthentos*. What Goethe retained from this expression was not its religious content, but precisely the contrast between visibility and mystery.

This theme of a "mystery in broad daylight" recurs in the most diverse ways in the poet's work. For instance, as early as 1777, in the poem "Winter Journey in the Harz," with regard to a mountain:

> O mountain of unexplored bosom,
> Mysterious in broad daylight,
> Above the astonished world.[25]

As we have just seen, however, it is above all with regard to Nature in general that Goethe, especially in his old age, liked to use this expression. For instance, rejecting the opposition between an inside and outside of nature, he writes:

> Nothing is within, nothing without,
> What is inside is also outside.
> Seize, then, with no delay,
> The sacred mystery in broad daylight.[26]

This notion applies perfectly to originary phenomena. We can say that they are "in broad daylight," because they are open to everyone's eyes; they appear precisely as phenomena: leaves, vertebrae, the play of light and darkness.

Yet we can also say that they are a "mystery." First of all, we usually fail to perceive their meaning, despite their obviousness. Only the person who knows how to see, and who expands sense perception by means of intuition, recognizes in these phenomena the *Urphänomene* or originary phenomena, that let us glimpse the fundamental laws of universal metamorphosis. In his diary for the year 1790, Goethe mentions the observation he made, in the dunes of the Lido near Venice, of a sheep's skull.[27] This observation confirmed his theory regarding the formation of the bone of the skull from the bones of the vertebrae, but above all it reminded him once again, as he emphasizes, that "Nature has no mystery [*Geheimnis*] that she does not place somewhere fully naked before the eyes of the attentive observer." And yet, we must learn how to look: "What is most difficult of all? That which seems to be easiest: To see with your eyes what is right before your eyes!"[28]

Beyond this initial consideration, however, the originary phenomena are above all a mystery because they constitute an impassable barrier to human knowledge. They can help to explain all kinds of phenomena, yet they themselves cannot be explained:

> The supreme point that a person can achieve is astonishment. When an originary phenomenon gives rise to this astonishment in him, he must consider himself satisfied: nothing greater can be conceded to him, and he must not further seek something else behind the phenomenon. Here is the limit. In general, however, the sight of an originary phenomenon is not enough for people; they need more. They are like children who, after looking in a mirror, immediately turn it around to see what is behind it.[29]

Here, the notion of an originary phenomenon merges with that of a symbol, insofar as symbols "show" something ineffable. For example—although this is only an initial stage—magnetism is an originary phenomenon, to which it is sufficient to allude in order to explain all kinds of phenomena; this is why it can serve as a "symbol" for all sorts of other things, for which we no longer have to seek words to express them.[30] Yet Goethe goes further. Alluding to what Kant calls the aesthetic Idea,[31] Goethe affirms that the symbol (and therefore the originary phenomenon), insofar as it is a form and an image, lets us understand a multitude of meanings, but itself remains ultimately inexpressible.[32] It is "the revelation, alive and immediate, of the unexplorable."[33]

Goethe conceived of symbols and originary phenomena as emblems, hieroglyphs, or the silent language of nature. With regard to the forms of the shells of which, he says, are sacred objects to him, he writes: "According to my own way of searching, knowing, and enjoying, I always stick with symbols." In a conversation with Falk, he says: "I would like to lose the habit of speaking, and express myself, like Nature the artist, in eloquent designs."[34]

We might discern a tendency in Goethe to renounce causal explanations—the cause hidden behind the effect—and discourse that unfolds in formulas and maxims, in order to privilege, by contrast, the immediate perception of the meaning that may be assumed by a concrete individual figure, form, design, emblem, or hieroglyph— such as a spiral or a leaf—which in fact represents a universal law: "This fig tree, this little snake, this cocoon . . . , all these things are signatures, heavy with meaning. Yes, he who could decipher their meaning exactly, would soon be able to do without all writing and all words. Yes, the more I think about it, the more it seems to me that there is something useless, idle, and even fatuous, I might say, in human discourse, so that we are terrified by Nature's silent seriousness, and by her silence."[35] Symbols are not the vehicle of conceptual content, but they allow something to shine through that is beyond all expression, and that can be grasped only by intuition.

Goethe always assumes a solemn tone when he speaks of originary phenomena as of an impassable limit: "Let him who explores nature leave the originary phenomena in their eternal rest and their eternal splendor."[36] Moreover, Goethe considers that only a genius is able to discover and contemplate the originary phenomena.[37] We must therefore respect and venerate these phenomena, which allow us to glimpse an inconceivable, unexplorable, unfathomable transcendence, never directly accessible to human knowledge, but of which we can have a premonition by means of reflections and symbols.[38] Thus Faust, at the beginning of part 2 of *Faust,* is forced to turn his back to the sun that blinds him, but he looks in ecstasy at the waterfall, where he sees the light of the day-star reflected in a rainbow:

"In the colored reflections we have life."[39] In *Pandora,* Prometheus praises Eos (the dawn), who gently accustoms our feeble eyes to the light so that the shafts launched by the sun do not blind man, who is meant to see things that are illuminated, but not light itself.[40] And in his *Maxims and Reflections,* Goethe compares his approach as a scientist to that of a man who, having risen early, waits impatiently for the dawn at daybreak, and for sunrise at dawn, but is blinded when the latter appears.[41]

Obviously, when Goethe declares that Isis has no veils, we must understand this critique of the traditional metaphor in a metaphorical sense. For Goethe, in fact, the veil does not hide anything. It is not opaque, but transparent and luminous, "woven," as is said in the poem "Dedication," "from the morning mist and the light of the sun."[42] It does not hide, but reveals, diffusing a transcendent light. Paradoxically, we could say that if Isis is without veils, it is because she is entirely form, that is, entirely veil; she is inseparable from her veils and her forms.

Form is a veil, veil is form, for Nature is the genesis of forms. The notion of form is essential here. Goethe reproached his old friend Friedrich Heinrich Jacobi for proposing a formless God in his book *On Divine Things and Their Revelation,* and claiming that Nature conceals God. In his *Tag- und Jahreshefte* (1811), he states that this book contradicts the way of seeing the world that is innate and deeply imprinted within him: to see God in Nature and Nature in God.[43] In the letter he wrote to Jacobi, expressing his disagreement, he presents himself ironically as a worshipper of Artemis of Ephesus.[44] He thereby alludes to a passage from the Acts of the Apostles, which narrates the uprising of the people of Ephesus against Saint Paul, stirred up by the tradesmen who feared that his preaching might put an end to the trade in the little silver temples they fashioned: "I am one of those Ephesian goldsmiths, who has devoted his whole life to contemplating, admiring, and venerating the wonderful

temple of the goddess and to imitating her forms, full of mysteries, and who cannot feel a favorable impression when some apostle
wants to impose some other god, and, what is worse, a god without
form." The poem "Great Is the Diana of the Ephesians" is an echo of
this opposition to Jacobi. Goethe rejects a formless God, not because
he attributes to him a particular form, but because for him, God is
inseparable from Nature; that is, he is inseparable from the forms,
both visible and mysterious, that God/Nature constantly engenders.
Nature reveals herself in the metamorphoses of her multiple forms.
As Diderot had said, in the playful tones of a man of the eighteenth
century: "It is obvious that Nature was not able to maintain so much
resemblance in her parts and effect so much variety in forms, without often making sensible in one organized being what she has hidden in another. She is a woman who loves to dress up, and whose
various disguises, allowing now one part, now another to escape, give
some hope to those who follow her assiduously that they may one
day come to know her entire person."[45]

Goethe took up this image, in a mystical tone, in the *Divan:*

> You may hide beneath a thousand forms.
> And yet, Oh beloved! I recognize you right away.
> You can cover yourself with magic veils, all-present One!
> I recognize you right away.[46]

Here the beloved is both Suleika—that is, Marianne of Willemer—
God, and Nature. In Goethe's mind, the phrase "You may hide beneath a thousand forms" in fact means "You can take on a thousand
forms, but they reveal you instead of hiding you."

Perhaps now we can better understand in what sense the Nature
that appears in originary phenomena is a "mystery in broad daylight." On the one hand, in these originary phenomena, which explain other phenomena, Nature appears clearly to perception, or to
the senses that are illuminated by intuition. On the other hand, these

phenomena are a limit that cannot be exceeded: one cannot go beyond them and submit them to an explanation. Yet, in this absence of reasons why, we sense a mystery, which Goethe called "the unexplorable."

Here we have, it seems to me, a sketch of a radical transformation of the notion of a secret of nature. Traditionally, it was admitted that there existed hidden forces or secret mechanisms that first magic, then science, were able gradually to discover, and whose secret or mystery progressively disappeared. This time, there is no secret to discover; nothing is hidden, and we see everything, but what we see is crowned in mystery, and ineffably shows the ineffable and unexplorable. Here we see the first glimmers of the dawn of a new relation to nature. The basic feeling will no longer be curiosity, the desire to know, or to solve a problem, but admiration, veneration, and perhaps anguish as well, in the face of the unfathomable mystery of existence.

21

The Sacred Shudder

In conformity with mythological schemes of the classical period, the traditional and conventional iconographic theme of the unveiling of Isis, which appears in scientific books in the seventeenth and eighteenth centuries, did not imply any metaphysical affirmation with regard to nature. Isis simply represented natural phenomena, and her unveiling symbolized the progress of a science dominated by a mechanistic conception of nature. At the end of the eighteenth century, however, the motif of Isis/Nature was to invade literature and philosophy and bring about a radical change in attitude with regard to nature, under the influence of various factors, in particular Freemasonry.

THE EVOLUTION OF THE ATTITUDE TOWARD NATURE

First of all, we must examine Robert Lenoble's idea that the mechanization of the world brought about "delayed-action anguish."[1] He meant by this that the mechanistic revolution had brought about, within the collective imagination, a kind of separation of man from Mother Nature, and hence his maturity, and that such transformations are always accompanied by a feeling of anguish. Yet this was a "delayed-action" anguish because this crisis, which should have occurred in the seventeenth century, did not begin to manifest itself until the eighteenth. Only gradually did people become aware of the upheaval that the mechanistic and then the industrial revolutions were to bring about in the human condition. Gradually the need was felt for a renewed contact with nature.

Be that as it may, one of the first symptoms of the evolution to which I am alluding was the appearance of an aesthetic approach to nature, which allows us to know nature in a different way from the scientific approach. As we have seen, around 1750, Baumgarten laid claim, in the face of the *veritas logica* of the mechanized sciences, to a *veritas aesthetica,* which could be found in the artistic vision of nature.[2] We glimpsed this aesthetic approach in Goethe, but we could find it as easily in Rousseau, Kant, Schiller, Schelling, and German Romanticism.

Aesthetic perception always contains an emotional element of pleasure, admiration, enthusiasm, or terror. To recognize a proper value for the aesthetic approach to nature necessarily also means introducing an emotional, sentimental, and irrational element into the relation between mankind and nature. This evolution is already sketched in Rousseau, in whom we can clearly observe how feeling and emotion in the presence of the All are substituted for the search for the secrets of nature. The way Rousseau describes his experience of nature brought about a transformation of sensibility throughout his epoch:

> Soon, from the surface of the earth, I raised my ideas to all the beings of nature, the universal system of things; and the universal being that embraces all things. Then, my mind lost in this immensity, I did not think, I did not reason, I did not philosophize: with a kind of voluptuous pleasure, I felt myself overwhelmed by the weight of this universe . . . I loved to lose myself in space in my imagination; my heart, enclosed within the limits of beings, did not have enough room; I was suffocating within the universe, and would have wished to launch myself forth into the infinite. I think that *if I had unveiled*

all the mysteries of nature, I would have felt myself to be in a situation less delicious than this stunning ecstasy to which my mind abandoned itself without restraint, and which, in the agitation of my transports, sometimes made me cry out: Oh great Being! Oh great Being! without being able to say or think anything more.[3]

I feel ecstasies, inexpressible raptures, when I melt, so to speak, into the system of beings, and when I identify myself with the whole of nature.

[The contemplator] knows and feels nothing, except in the all.[4]

Here we clearly see curiosity with regard to the secrets of nature superseded by an emotional experience that invades one's entire being and consists in feeling oneself to be part of the All. This lived experience was one of the essential components of the phenomenon we are studying. In 1777, F. L. Stolberg already spoke in this regard of the need for an emotional disposition he called "fullness of the heart" ("Fülle des Herzens").[5] This does not, moreover, exclude the existence of clear and rational procedures. The two attitudes coexist, for instance, in Goethe. Kant himself did not hesitate to speak of the "sacred shudder" we must feel in the presence of Nature, and of the "ever-renewed admiration and veneration" we feel when viewing the starry sky. We might say that from Schelling to Heidegger by way of Nietzsche, this experience, accompanied by anguish or terror, pleasure or astonishment, was to become an integral part of certain trends in philosophy.

THE ISIS OF PLUTARCH AND PROCLUS

So far I have not yet discussed two ancient texts concerning Isis, one by Plutarch and the other by Proclus. Plutarch's treatise *Isis and Osiris* is devoted to an allegorical and philosophical interpretation of

Egyptian mythology. For him, there really was a philosophy of the Egyptians, which was hidden in myths and stories that allow the truth only to be glimpsed, as is suggested, he says, by the sphinxes placed at the entrances of sanctuaries, symbolizing an enigmatic wisdom. For instance, we can glimpse this "enigmatic wisdom," he claims, in the inscription on the statue of Neith, the divinity honored at Saïs, who was assimilated to the Greek Athena and to Isis: "At Saïs, the seated statue of Athena, whom they identified with Isis, bears this inscription: 'I am all that has been, that is, and that shall be; no mortal has yet raised my veil [*peplos*].'"[6]

A few centuries later, we find the text of this inscription once again in Proclus, commenting on Plato, *Timaeus*, 21e. This time he situates the inscription within the sanctuary of the goddess and gives it a more developed form: "That which is, that which shall be, that which was, I am that. No one has raised my tunic [*khitōn*]. The fruit I have engendered is the sun [Horus]."[7]

As was noted by John Gwyn Griffiths in his commentary on Plutarch's treatise *Isis and Osiris*, the phrase "I am that which is, that which has been, and that which shall be" is a claim of universal power, usually reserved for Atum and Re, and it recalls the words of Seth to Horus: "I am Yesterday, I am Today, I am Tomorrow, which is not yet."[8] Potentially and virtually, Isis is all things. The allusion in Proclus to Horus and to the tunic that has not been raised indicates that Isis is being presented as a virgin mother. In Plutarch's view, Isis is the feminine aspect of nature, for the Logos leads her to receive all forms and all figures.[9] Plutarch may have been thinking of the idea of a secret of nature when he spoke of the veil of Isis; yet this does not appear explicitly.

This impossibility of raising the *peplos* of Isis, and the fact that she engendered the sun all by herself, allude to the goddess's virginal character. We must note, however, that the converse motif also existed in antiquity, but it was the goddess herself who raised her tunic. Françoise Dunand has recalled the existence of Greco-Egyptian terra cottas in which we see the goddess, wearing the Isiac crown, raising her dress with both hands.[10] This gesture of Baubo, which I shall discuss later on, is also that of the women at festivals of Bubastis, in honor of the goddess Bastet (whom Herodotus identifies with Artemis).[11] Dunand concludes from this that this representation of Isis is of Isis Bubastis, the goddess of fecundity. Moreover, a magical papyrus alludes to the *peplos* of Isis. In order to know whether a love charm has had an effect, the following prayer must be recited: "Isis, pure virgin, give me a sign that may let me know the accomplishment, uncover your sacred *peplos*."[12]

Iconography does not seem to have taken very seriously the warning given by the goddess in Plutarch and in Proclus: "No mortal has yet raised my veil." For the Isis of the seventeenth century and the beginning of the eighteenth was in fact nothing other than Nature as subject to the will of mankind; however only her mechanical and mathematical aspects were discovered. Yet we can discern an allusion to this threat in the frontispiece to the *Physics* of Segner, which I have mentioned, as well as in the engraving by Heinrich Füssli at the beginning of Erasmus Darwin's poem *The Temple of Nature, or The Origin of Society* (Fig. 18).[13] In the engraving a kneeling woman makes gestures of terror while another woman, no doubt a priestess, unveils a statue of Isis/Artemis before her. This image, moreover, corresponds only partially to the poem's content, for, as Irwin Primer has shown, Darwin wished to oppose the religion of terror, which is that of human beings left in ignorance, to the love and confidence that enlightened philosophers feel for nature.[14]

In any case, the warning Isis gives to those who would seek to unveil her was taken very seriously by philosophers and poets at the end of the eighteenth century. The figure of Isis was to undergo a radical change in meaning: henceforth amazement, astonishment, and even anguish in the face of Isis/Nature was to be one of the favorite themes of certain literary works.

THE MASONIC ISIS

One of the prime causes of this evolution does indeed seem to have been the new meaning that Freemasonry was to give to the figure of Isis.[15] The powerful intellectual and social movement of Freemasonry, which flourished at the beginning of the eighteenth century, aimed both to spread the ideals of Enlightenment philosophy and to proclaim itself the heir to the mystery traditions of antiquity, particularly Egyptian traditions. Thus, in Masonic mythology, the figure gradually came to have a role of prime importance.[16] In the last decade of the eighteenth century, the vogue for Egyptian mysteries, or "Egyptomania," was to gain considerable popularity. As Jan Assmann has admirably shown, it was especially in the milieu surrounding the Viennese lodge "Zur wahren Eintracht" (True Harmony) that a new interpretation of Isis/Nature was to develop.[17] In 1787, Karl Leonhard Reinhold, who became affiliated with this lodge in 1783, wrote a treatise on the Hebrew mysteries in which, taking up speculations developed at the end of the seventeenth and the beginning of the eighteenth centuries by John Spencer and William Warburton, he sought to show that the God of the philosophers—and of the Freemasons— was already well known to the Egyptians, and that Moses had borrowed the content of his revelation from Egyptian wisdom, although he concealed it in the rites and ceremonies of the Hebrew religion.[18] From this perspective, Reinhold assimilates the self-description of Isis/Nature of which Plutarch speaks, "I am all that has been, that is, and that shall be," to that of Yahweh on Sinai, "I am who I am." This was a forced interpretation, since Isis says that she is all that exists, whereas Yahweh, by contrast, entrenches himself in his selfhood, or his ego.[19] Whether the affirmation is of being or the self, however, there is above all the refusal to speak the name, for when Isis proclaims that she is all that exists, it becomes apparent that the being of divinity, as Assmann notes, "is too universal to be designated by a name."[20]

We can see the considerable transformation that takes place in the representation of Nature. Through her assimilation to Yahweh, she becomes an anonymous divinity. Isis refuses to speak her name and to be unveiled. She hides herself not by concealing the cause of any specific natural phenomenon but by herself becoming the absolute mystery or enigma that cannot be penetrated, the divinity who is nameless, whether she is being or beyond being.

Assmann was right to place this new meaning of Isis/Nature in relation with the Spinozist movement that characterized the German pre-Romantic period.[21] In particular, he brings up the motto "Hen kai pan," which Lessing had engraved in 1780 on the walls of the cottage of J. W. L. Gleim's garden at Halberstadt. As Friedrich Heinrich Jacobi showed when, in 1785, he published the letters on Spinoza he had written to Moses Mendelssohn, the phrase "One and All" was in fact a declaration of faith in favor of Spinoza's famous "deus sive natura."[22] Spinoza had spoken of "that eternal and infinite Being whom we call God or Nature." We are thus in the presence of an identification between God and Nature, the One and the All, and God and the cosmos. From this perspective, Isis/Nature becomes a cosmic god, object of a cosmotheism.[23] Identified with Yahweh, Isis/Nature was surrounded with the same aura of mystery as he, and she was meant to inspire terror, veneration, and respect. As in the mysteries of Eleusis, she may be contemplated only at the end of a lengthy initiation.[24] Then, as Aristotle said with regard to Eleusis, all learning [mathein] ceases, and there is henceforth only an experience [pathein], which, in the case of Isis/Nature assimilated to Yahweh, can only be an experience of the ineffable.[25]

At the end of the eighteenth century, Isis thus assumes multiple meanings. She represents Nature, the object of science, but also Nature conceived as the mother of all beings, and finally Nature as infinite, divinized, ineffable, and anonymous, or universal Being. She is also identified with Truth, which is conceived as the ultimate, and perhaps inaccessible, object of the efforts of human knowledge.

It was probably under the emphasis of these Masonic representations that Isis/Nature was the object of a cult during the French Revolution. In the decorations of revolutionary festivals, particularly as staged by the painter David, intended to educate the people, Nature appears with the features of Isis, as the mother of all beings.[26] It is to this same Masonic influence that we must attribute the presence of a statue of Isis/Artemis in the gardens of Potsdam, at the time of Friedrich-Wilhelm II, king of Prussia.[27]

THE ISIS OF GERMAN PRE-ROMANTICISM AND ROMANTICISM

The transformation of the approach to nature that took place at the end of the eighteenth century appears clearly in Kant.[28] Here we witness the encounter of two opposing attitudes. On the one hand, in the *Critique of Pure Reason* (1781), we find the mechanistic, judicial, and violent one: reason, as Francis Bacon would have it, should behave toward nature "not like a student, who lets himself be told whatever the teacher wishes, but like an appointed judge, who forces witnesses to answer the questions he asks them."[29] On the other hand, in the *Critique of the Faculty of Judgment* (1790), we find the aesthetic approach, filled with veneration, respect, and fear, which is expressed in Kant's commentary on the illustration placed by the physicist Segner at the beginning of his treatise on physics.[30] Kant writes:

Perhaps no one has said anything more sublime, or expressed a thought more sublimely, than in that inscription on the temple of Isis (Mother Nature): "I am all that is, all that was, and all that shall be, and no mortal has lifted my veil." Segner utilized this idea in an illustration full of meaning that he placed at the beginning of his *Physics,* in order to fill his disciple, whom he was already on the verge of introducing into this temple, with a sacred shudder [*Schauer*], which is to dispose the spirit to solemn attention.[31]

In fact, I think that these two attitudes seem reconcilable to Kant, and probably to Segner as well. For in the illustration in Segner's book, as we have seen with regard to the iconography of Isis/Nature,[32] one of the children is measuring her steps, which seems to mean that by using a mechanistic and mathematical method, man can comprehend only Nature's footprints—that is, her most external effects—but not Nature herself. Yet as is implied by the motto "Qua licet," this research can take place only within allowed limits. Indeed, another child puts his finger to his lips, signifying that we can only be silent in the face of the ineffable, for Nature herself, unlike her footsteps, is an unknowable mystery. In the face of this unfathomable and inaccessible Nature, we can only feel a sacred shudder.

The veiled and terrifying image of Isis reappears in Schiller's poem titled "The Veiled Statue at Saïs," written in 1795.[33] The poem depicts a young man with an avid desire to know the Truth, who penetrates within the temple of Saïs and learns that it is precisely Truth that is hidden beneath the goddess's veil. The hierophant warns him away, for no mortal has the right to raise it: "This veil, no doubt light to the hand, is terribly heavy for your conscience." Yet the imprudent youth returns to the temple at night. He is seized by terror, and an inner voice tries to hold him back, but he raises the veil and falls senseless: "For all time, the serenity had gone from his life. A deep melancholy carried him off to an early grave . . . Woe to whoever approaches the

Truth by the paths of guilt." This poem inspired some hostility, particularly on the part of Johann Gottfried von Herder, who could not accept that the desire to see the truth was a fault.[34]

First of all, we can interpret this poem from the perspective of the pessimism, which we could call Idealist, that is expressed in other works by Schiller. Here, as Schiller says explicitly, Isis represents Truth, as in some allegorical representations from the eighteenth century.[35] More precisely, this Truth may be the Truth on the subject of nature, but it is also Truth on the subject of the concrete situation of mankind. In either case, Schiller implies that this Truth is so hideous that one can no longer live after having known it. From the same perspective, "The Words of Illusion," written in 1799, speaks of Right, Happiness, and Truth. It is an illusion to think that Right will triumph, for it must fight an eternal combat; an illusion to think that a noble-hearted being can achieve Happiness, for it is only a stranger on this earth; an illusion to think that the Truth will appear to earthly understanding. "No mortal hand may raise her veil," writes Schiller. "We can only make conjectures and suppositions."[36]

In Schiller's poem "Kassandra" (1802), Cassandra wonders, during the celebration in honor of Achilles' wedding to Polyxena, daughter of Priam:

> Is it wise to raise the veil
> Where terror, threatening, dwells?
> Life is naught but error,
> And knowledge is but death.[37]

We might think that we already hear Nietzsche, whom I will discuss in the next chapter. Life is celebration, joy, appearance, and illusion; Death is Truth, which consists in knowing, like Cassandra, that all this joy will be destroyed. Only illusion, art, and poetry enable us to live. Here on earth, we can achieve neither Truth nor Happiness, which are as it were forbidden fruit, to the point that for man, Truth is terrifying and dangerous. Schiller's pessimism is quite certainly the price he paid for his idealism: Truth, Nature, Beauty, and the Good are not of this world, or rather they are to be found only in the inner world, that is, ultimately, in moral conscience:

> Therefore, noble soul, tear yourself away from illusion
> and maintain your heavenly faith,
> What no ear has perceived, what eyes have not seen,
> The Beautiful, the True—still exists!
> It is not outside, where fools seek it,
> It is within you: you bring it forth eternally![38]

And again:

> It is in the sacred silence of the spaces of the heart
> that you must flee, far from life's harassing pursuit.
> Freedom exists only in the kingdom of dreams
> And the Good flourishes only in the poet's song.[39]

In "The Veiled Statue at Saïs," however, the veiled statue may also symbolize Nature herself: the Masonic Isis that Schiller knew through Reinhold's work. He too, paraphrasing K. L. Reinhold, had written an essay titled "Moses' Mission," which accepted the identification of Isis and Yahweh.[40] When Schiller writes, "Woe to whoever approaches the Truth by the paths of guilt," we can assume that the guilt consists in failing to assume the requisite disposition of respect toward the goddess, in failing to wait for initiation, in failing to feel the "sacred shudder" of which Kant spoke, in not staying within the allowed limits, and in unveiling by means of violence. If this is the case, then the spirit of this poem would not be so far from that of "The Gods of Greece," which I have discussed.[41] To brutally tear away her secrets from Nature, or her veil from Isis, to seek the truth at any cost and by every means, especially by technology and the mechanization of nature, is to risk killing poetry and the Ideal, and creating a disenchanted world.

It was certainly in opposition to Schiller's poem that Schlegel called upon his contemporaries to confront the danger and surmount their terror: "It is time to tear the veil off Isis and reveal what is secret. He who cannot bear the vision of the goddess, let him flee or perish."[42] In his essay "The Disciples at Saïs," Novalis echoes Schlegel: "If it is true that no mortal can lift the veil, as is indicated by the inscription I see down there, then we will just have to try to become immortal. Whoever gives up trying to raise the veil is no true disciple of Saïs."[43] This allusion to immortality—that is, ultimately, to the power of the spirit[44]—allows us to glimpse how the theme of the veil of Isis was interpreted in the Romantic period within the perspective of an Idealist philosophy. To unveil Isis was to realize that Nature is nothing other than Spirit unaware of itself, that the Non-Ego known as Nature is ultimately identical to the Ego, and that Nature is the genesis of the Spirit. Despite the profound differences that exist between the various Romantic philosophies, whether of Fichte, Schelling, Hegel, or even of Novalis, the same basic tendency, from different perspectives, to identify Nature and Spirit remains constant.

Novalis's study "The Disciples at Saïs" remained unfinished. In the material Novalis had collected with a view to writing it, he expressed the meaning that the German Romantics gave to the unveiling of Isis in a striking way: "One of them succeeded—he raised the veil of the goddess of Saïs. Yet what did he see? He saw—wonder of wonders!—himself."[45] For Novalis, the exploration of inner life will enable us to descend to the sources of nature. It is by returning to ourselves that we can understand nature, and nature is, in a way, a mirror of the spirit. This idea can be found throughout Romantic philosophy.[46] Later on, Bergson would become the heir to this tradition: for him, it is by seizing the genesis of nature in "duration" that the spirit becomes aware of the fact that it itself has sought to realize itself through nature's becoming, and that there is consequently an identity between inner life and universal life.

This theme was particularly dear to Schelling. At the same time that he rediscovers, in his definition of nature, the ancient meaning of *phusis,* that is, of productivity and spontaneous blossoming, he conceives of mankind "as the conscious becoming of natural productivity."[47] I have already mentioned this crucial text: "What we call nature is a poem whose marvelous and mysterious writing remains undecipherable for us. Yet if we could solve this enigma, we would discover therein the Odyssey of the Spirit, which, the victim of a remarkable illusion, flees itself even as it seeks itself, for it only appears through the World like meaning through words."[48]

For Hegel as well, the unveiling of Isis was the spirit's return to itself. For him, however, this process was situated within historical becoming. The formula of Saïs, "No man has lifted my veil," means that Nature is a reality that differs from itself, that it is something other than its immediate appearance, and that it has an inner part that is hidden.[49] Moreover, he criticizes Goethe, who had refused to distinguish an inside and an outside of Nature.[50] For Hegel, however, the occultation of Nature is particular to the Egyptian historical moment. She unveils herself—that is, suppresses herself—in Greek thought, which puts an end to the "enigma." It is not without significance that the Egyptian Sphinx is killed by the Greek Oedipus. The Sphinx dies when mankind is defined in Greek thought, and man defines himself by discovering that the inside of nature is none other than himself,[51] which is to say, that which we think is other than we, nature, is nothing other than what we are, that is, the Spirit.

Let me add another suggestion by Novalis to these Romantic variations on the theme of Isis. It is found in the story of Hyacinth and Rosebud, told by one of the disciples of Saïs. Hyacinth abandons his fiancée, Rosebud, to travel to a distant land in search of the Veiled

Virgin, Mother of All Things. After a long journey, he arrives at her temple, but when he raises the veil of the "celestial Virgin," it is Rosebud who leaps into his arms. The image of Sophie, Novalis's young fiancée who died prematurely, and to whom he dedicated a religious cult throughout his life, comes to coincide with that of Isis, or infinite Nature perceived as the Eternal Feminine. This time, it is love that appears as the best initiation into Isis/Nature. A passage from "The Disciples at Saïs" can help us interpret this new perspective. One of the disciples, the "young man with sparkling eyes," expresses Novalis's deepest thought when he presents the knowledge of nature as absolutely inseparable from an emotional element, or a "sweet anguish," of which only poets are capable:

> What heart would not leap for joy, when the most secret life of Nature fills it with all its fullness, and when this powerful feeling, for which language has no other name than love and pleasure, dilates within it . . . [S]huddering with a sweet anguish, it plunges into the dark and delightful bosom of Nature; it feels its miserable personality being fused, submerged in waves of pleasure, and . . . all that subsists is a center of incommensurable, genesic force, a whirlpool where everything is swallowed up into the vast ocean?[52]

No one can understand Nature "unless a profound and multiple kinship with all bodies impels him to mix himself by emotion with all natural beings, to melt into them, as it were, through feeling."[53] The unveiling of Isis thus appears as a cosmic ecstasy, accompanied by veneration and respect:

> He who possesses a true and practiced feeling of nature enjoys Nature as he studies her . . . When he is near her [Nature], he feels as if he were in the arms of a chaste fiancée, and to her alone he confides, in the sweet hours of intimacy, the thoughts on which he has tarried.

How happy he is, this son, this favorite of Nature, whom she permits to contemplate her, in her duality, as a power of fecundation and childbirth, and in her unity, as an infinite and eternal hymen. The life of that man will be a profusion of delights and an uninterrupted sequence of pleasures, and his religion can be called a true and authentic naturalism.[54]

If Novalis and Schlegel had opposed Schiller, the poet Clemens Brentano attacked them in turn in a quatrain, making cruel fun of the ecstasies, terrors, and metaphysical speculations of the first Romantics:

> It is enough for your hair to stand on end with fear
> For you to call that pure knowledge!
> And if you call that "raising the veil of Isis,"
> What you raise without modesty is only your apron.[55]

In Brentano's view, the Romantics content themselves with emotions instead of reflection and research. Shudders and fright take the place of thought for them. And if they identify Nature with the ego, this is only a pretext for them to unveil their moods and to pour forth their effusions and confessions. Brentano may also have had in view the exhibitionism that can be discerned in Schlegel's "Lucinda."[56]

The veil of Isis was interpreted in a wholly different way by P. S. Ballanche in 1830. For him, Isis always remains veiled. The Egyptian priests, he says, never remove the veil that covers the statue, and they have never seen her without veils. For him, this means that the knowledge of truth is not the result of a gesture of revealing a readymade reality, that is, a teaching received passively; instead, man must find the truth, actively, by himself and in himself: "The Egyptian priests therefore teach nothing, for they believe that all is within mankind; all they do is remove the obstacles." The truth is in mankind's heart.[57]

THE FEELING OF THE SUBLIME AND THE SACRED SHUDDER

Another factor in the transformation of the relation of philosophers and poets to nature was the quite particular attention that the eighteenth century devoted to the feeling of the sublime.[58] It was above all in England that this aesthetic notion was the subject of research, which culminated in particular in Edmund Burke's work *A Philosophical Enquiry into the Origin of Our Ideas of the Sublime and Beautiful*, published in 1756.[59] For Burke, the sublime terrifies us by the impression of danger or infinity, but this feeling of fright is transformed into delight once we have the impression that we are safe.[60]

Kant speaks of the "astonishment, which borders on terror, that seizes the spectator at the sight of mountains rising to the sky, or of deep gorges through which water rages."[61] For him, the sublime is felt only if we place ourselves in the presence of bare reality, through a purely aesthetic vision, which does not involve any finalistic considerations: "When one calls the sight of the starry sky sublime, we must . . . look at it simply as one sees it: as a vast vault that includes everything . . . ; we must succeed in seeing the ocean alone, as poets do, but according to what its appearance shows."[62]

Without any appearance of the word "sublime," we glimpse the presence of this feeling in the famous phrase that appears at the end of the *Critique of Pure Reason*: "Two things fill the soul with ever-renewed and ever-growing admiration and veneration, the more frequently and constantly reflection applies itself to them: the starry sky above me and the moral law within me." In this famous text, I think I perceive a structure analogous to that of a passage from Seneca in which he also associates the moral conscience—that of the sage— with the spectacle of the world: "I look upon wisdom with the same stupefaction with which, at other times, I look at the world, this world that I often contemplate as if I were seeing it for the first time."[63]

It is from this perspective of the sublime that Kant, as we have seen, understands the inscription at Saïs, and that, in a famous note to his *Critique of the Faculty of Judgment,* he sets in relation to the illustration Segner uses at the beginning of his treatise on physics, and which, says Kant, lets us understand that we can approach nature only with a "sacred shudder."[64] Already in 1779 the image of Isis veiled, chosen by the Egyptians to represent Nature, was, for Honoré Lacombe de Prézel, author of the *Iconological Dictionary,* a "simple, yet divine expression."[65]

It was also in the perspective of the sublime that the Isis of Saïs, that is, the mystery of Nature, was perceived by Schiller: "All that is wrapped up and full of mystery contributes to fright, and therefore is susceptible to sublimity. Of this kind is the inscription that could be read at Saïs in Egypt, on the temple of Isis: 'I am all that has been, that is, and all that shall be; no mortal has yet raised my veil.'"[66]

We can also find in Schopenhauer a reflection on the feeling of the sublime which has the merit of recognizing the twofold aspect of this feeling. On the one hand, the contemplation of infinity crushes us, whether it is the duration of the world or the nighttime vision of the immensity of the universe: we then feel that our individuality is no more than "a drop in the ocean."[67] On the other hand, we realize that all these worlds exist only in our representation; that is, they are modifications of the eternal subject of knowledge, that pure subject with which we become merged when we forget our individuality. We then feel that "we are one with the world, and that consequently its infinity lifts us up, far from crushing us . . . There is a delight here that transcends our own individuality; it is the feeling of the sublime."[68]

The theme of the sublime and the shudder was also dear to Goethe. In *Wilhelm Meister's Travels,* he describes the attentive perception of a starry sky: "The most transparent night shone and shimmered with all its stars, enveloping the spectator, who had the impression of contemplating, for the first time, the immense vault of the sky in all its splendor." If the spectator has the impression of seeing "for the first time," says Goethe, it is because he is usually incapable of seeing, blinded as he is by the worries of his heart and the cares of daily life. Goethe describes the emotion that seizes the spectator as he perceives the existence of the world in its naked reality: "Filled with amazement and astonishment, he closed his eyes. The prodigious immensity [*das Ungeheure*] ceases to be sublime, and transcends our capacity of experience, and threatens to annihilate us. 'What am I in the face of the all?' he asks himself within. 'How can I subsist before it, in the midst of it?'"[69]

We have seen that, for Goethe, the knowledge of nature culminates in the discovery of originary phenomena, which explain other phenomena and have no explanation themselves.[70] Once he reaches these originary phenomena, a person need only contemplate, admire, and be astonished, but this astonishment can go as far as terror and anguish:

> We are terrified by the silent gravity of Nature, and by her silence.[71]
>
> The immediate apperception of originary phenomena plunges us into a kind of anguish.
>
> Faced by originary phenomena, when, once unveiled, they appear to our senses, we feel a kind of fear, which may go as far as anguish.[72]

Nature then appears to us as an *Ungeheures,* an ambiguous term that designates as much what is prodigious as what is monstrous.[73] We recall the quatrain from the poem "Genius Unveiling a Bust of Nature":

> Respect the mystery,
> Let not your eyes give in to lust.
> Nature the Sphinx, a monstrous thing [*Ungeheures*],
> Will terrify you with her innumerable breasts.[74]

Finally, for Goethe in his old age, this anguish was not a depressing feeling. Quite the contrary: for one who is capable of bearing it, it is the most elevated state man can attain. At the moment when, to evoke the figure of Helen, Faust is about to venture forth into solitude, out of space and time, there where there is no path, in the terrifying kingdom of the Mothers, who preside over the formation and the transformation of things, he cries out:

> It is not in torpor that I seek my salvation.
> The shudder [*Schaudern*] is the best part of man.
> However dearly the world makes him pay for this feeling,
> It is with emotion that man feels, deep within, the terrifying
> [*das Ungeheure*].[75]

To specify the precise relation that may exist between the myth of the Mothers and the Goethean doctrine of nature would take us too far afield, into a lengthy study.[76] What is essential for us is that the four lines I have just quoted remind us of what Goethe says elsewhere, about the anguish that seizes man in the presence of originary phenomena. Above all, they reveal to us Goethe's concept of the human condition. To be fully human means having the courage to become aware of what is terrible, unfathomable, and enigmatic in the world and in existence, and not to refuse the shudder and the anguish that seize human beings in the face of mystery. Such an attitude presupposes tearing oneself away completely from daily habits, and a complete change of scenery. It is this change of scenery that makes us see things as though we were seeing them for the first time, and which produces as much admiration as terror. This change of scenery does not, moreover, correspond to a loss of contact with the real. On the contrary, it means to become aware of reality and the mystery of existence that is hidden from us by the habits of daily life.

I must add that in Goethe, this feeling of anguish can be provoked by the presence of what is existent, real, and experienced. This, it seems to me, is what is suggested by a passage from *Elective Affinities*, in which Goethe speaks of a series of *tableaux vivants:* "The attitudes were so right, the colors so harmoniously distributed, the lighting so cleverly arranged, that one truly thought oneself to be in another world, except for the fact that the presence of the real, substituted for appearance, produced a kind of impression of anguish."[77]

In addition to this experience of anguish in the face of originary phenomena, we sometimes observe an ambiguous feeling with regard to Nature in Goethe. This is already noticeable in *Werther*. The hero of the novel recounts how the inebriating spectacle of universal life had been transformed for him into a terrifying vision of the universal metamorphosis of things, of that force, of "that devouring monster [*Ungeheuer*] . . . that is hidden within all of nature."[78] We find the same ambiguity in his review of Johann Georg Sulzer's book *The Fine Arts*. To Sulzer, who affirms that everything in nature conspires to provide us with pleasant sensations, Goethe replies:

> Does that which produces unpleasant sensations in us not belong to the plane of Nature as much as that which is most pleasant in her?
>
> Are furious storms, floods, rains of fire, subterranean lava, and death in all the elements not witnesses to the eternal life of nature and are just as true as the sun rising magnificently over opulent vineyards and aromatic orange orchards?
>
> What we see of nature is strength that devours strength: nothing remains present, everything passes, a thousand seeds are crushed, at every instant a thousand seeds are born, . . . beautiful and ugly, good and bad, all existing beside one another with the same rights.[79]

At the same time, the philosopher Carl Gustav Carus wrote, "Every genuine study of nature cannot but lead man to the threshold of higher mysteries, and fill him with a horror that is all the more sacred."[80]

Nevertheless, this feeling of terror in the face of nature is not new.

We cannot write its history here, but we can briefly recall that in antiquity, people spoke of this emotion quite particularly with regard to initiation into the mysteries of Eleusis, which were linked to the vegetation goddesses Demeter and Kore. Concerning them, Plutarch speaks of "shudders," "trembling," "sweat," and "fright."[81] Lucretius, confronted by the vision of nature as Epicurus revealed it, felt, as in a mysteric revelation, both "sacred shudder and divine pleasure."[82] Seneca experienced a feeling of stupor in the face of the world he was contemplating, as if he were seeing it for the first time.[83] It seems to me that this attitude toward nature disappeared at the end of antiquity and in the Middle Ages, perhaps under the influence of Christianity. It reappears at the Renaissance. As we have seen, Spenser, in his poem *The Faerie Queene*, where Nature appears personified, hints that if this Nature is veiled, it is either in order to frighten mortals by her terrifying aspect or else so as not to blind them by her splendor.[84] From the seventeenth century, everyone knows the famous remark by Pascal, a cry which seems to me, moreover, to be quite isolated in its time, but in which Robert Lenoble wished to see the first cry of modern anguish: "The eternal silence of these infinite spaces frightens me."[85] We could also find this first cry of modern anguish in the monologue that Pascal places in the mouth of a man deprived of the light of revelation: "When I look at the whole mute universe, and at man without enlightenment, left to his own resources without knowing who put him there, what he came to do, what will happen to him when he dies, incapable of any knowledge, I become frightened, like a man who has been carried asleep to some awful desert island, and who wakes up without knowing where he is, and without any means of getting out of there."[86]

It seems to me, however, that before the second half of the eighteenth century, never did the expression either of the feeling of anguish or of the feeling of wonder at nature display such intensity as the one that then began to come to light. Under the influence of the

Masonic Isis and the Romantic Isis, and of the cosmotheism they helped to develop, the relation with nature became much more affective, more emotional, and, above all, ambivalent, made up of terror and wonder, anguish and pleasure. The unveiling of the statue of Isis tended more and more to lose its meaning of discovering the secrets of nature and gave way to stupefaction in the face of mystery.

22

Nature as Sphinx

Nietzsche alluded several times, directly or indirectly, to Heraclitus' aphorism "Nature loves to hide." For instance, he claims that "the dithyrambic dramaturge"—that is, Wagner—has seen Nature naked, or again that thanks to him, "Nature, wanting to conceal herself, reveals the essence of her contradictions."[1] Yet the most important allusion to this theme is found at the end of the preface to the second edition (1886) of *The Gay Science*—it was, moreover, to be repeated, except for one phrase, in the epilogue of *Nietzsche contra Wagner* (Christmas 1888). Here, Nietzsche mentions an art which—unlike that of Wagner, whom he had once adored—and unlike the Romantic art of the North, would have no heavy pretensions to the sublime, but would be an "art for artists only." It would be an art that would be "ironic," "light," and "fleeting," more precisely an art full of gaiety, a luminous art, an art of the South.[2]

THE WILL TO TRUTH AND THE ADORATION OF APPEARANCES

It is in this context that Nietzsche evokes both Heraclitus' saying and the statue of Isis:

> And as far as our future is concerned: we shall scarcely be found following the footsteps of those young Egyptians who, at night, make

temples unsafe, embrace statues, and seek to unveil, discover, and expose to broad daylight absolutely everything that there are good reasons to keep hidden. No, this bad taste, this will to truth, to "truth at all costs," this adolescent madness in the love of truth—we've had enough of it: for that, we are too experienced, too serious, too joyous, too weather-beaten, too profound. We no longer believe that the truth is still the truth, if its veils are taken away from it—we've lived too long to believe that. For us today it is a question of decency, that one doesn't want to see everything in its nudity, doesn't want to get involved in everything, or to understand everything, or "know" everything.[3] "Is it true that the good Lord is everywhere?" a little girl asked her mother. "I find that indecent!" A hint to philosophers! We should have more respect for the modesty with which Nature hides behind enigmas and colorful uncertainties. Perhaps Truth is a woman who has reasons for not wanting to let her reasons be seen? Perhaps her name, if we were to speak Greek, is Baubo?—Oh, those Greeks! They knew about *living*: for this, it is necessary to stop courageously at the surface, at the drapery, at the skin, to worship appearances, to believe in forms, sounds, and words, and the entire Olympus of appearances! Those Greeks were superficial—*out of profundity!* . . . Isn't it precisely in this sense that we are Greeks? Worshippers of forms, sounds, and words? And precisely in this sense—artists?[4]

The broad outlines of this passage are fairly clear: Nietzsche opposes the will to truth at all costs to the will to stay at the surface, or the world of appearances: that is, ultimately, art, the world of forms, sounds, and words. What is the meaning of this opposition? To understand it, we must recall that for Nietzsche, knowledge is normally in the service of life, so that our representations are a function of our vital needs. They are errors that are useful for the preservation of the species. "We have set up for ourselves a world in which we can live—

by accepting bodies, lines, surfaces, causes and effects, movement and rest, form and content: without these articles of faith, no man today could bear to live! Yet this is still not the same thing as to prove them. Life is not an argument: among the preconditions of life, there might very well be error."[5]

We thus forge illusions that correspond to our perspectives as living beings. These representations engendered by the necessities of life, these vital errors, are opposed by what Jean Granier calls Originary Truth: that is, the vision or knowledge of the world "as it is," a knowledge that wants to be free of all anthropomorphism, or an inhuman knowledge.[6] For the core of reality is a blind game of destruction and creation, gratuitous and eternal. For Nietzsche, to will the truth at all costs, to wish for knowledge for its own sake, and to renounce vital illusions would be to risk destroying humanity. Man could not survive. He cannot do without the vital illusion, and the entire world of myths and values without which he cannot live. The pure Truth is the negation of Life. The will to truth is fundamentally a will to death.[7]

In Nietzsche's view, however, the will to truth and the worship of appearances are both radically opposed and deeply interdependent, as is shown in the draft Nietzsche wrote of the preface to *The Gay Science*, by certain phrases he eliminated when he published the final version:

This gaiety is hiding something, this will for what is superficial betrays a knowledge, a science of depth, this depth exhales its breath, a cold breath that makes one shudder . . . Let me finally admit it: we men of depth need our gaiety too much not to make it suspect . . . No, there is something pessimistic in us that gives itself away even in our gaiety, we know how to give that appearance—for we love appearance; nay, we worship it—but because with regard to "being" itself, we have our own suspicions . . . Oh, if you could fully understand why it is precisely we that need art, an art that is mocking, divine, and serene.[8]

This draft thus reveals that the will to gaiety and superficiality emanates from a knowledge, or what Nietzsche calls a knowledge of depth, a knowledge of what the core of things is really like; that is, ultimately, a will to truth that is the basis for pessimism. The "men of depth" are pessimists.

Nietzsche thus accepts, in the face of the "will to the truth at all costs,"[9] another will to truth, which he calls "the knowledge of depth." Yet how can we distinguish them? In paragraph 370 of *The Gay Science*, titled "What Is Romanticism?" Nietzsche opposes precisely Romantic pessimism—that of Schopenhauer and Wagner, in which he believed in his youth—to Dionysian pessimism, to which his inner development has led him. Romantic pessimism is the symptom of an impoverishment of life. The core of things appears as suffering, pain, contradiction, and this knowledge provokes disgust with life. Such pessimism then leads, "by means of art and knowledge," to the negation of the will to live, and to a sad renunciation, which would be "rest, calm, a sea of oil, deliverance from the self, or else drunkenness, convulsion, numbness, and madness." This is the attitude that inspires Romantic art. Nietzsche now feels nothing but revulsion for this "country-fair racket."[10] The will to truth at all costs is thus a morbid tendency of hostility to life, an attitude against nature. Dionysian pessimism, Nietzsche's pessimism, by contrast, is an overabundance of life. The core of things is just as terrible, but from this horror, appearance is born, a wonderful world of forms and sounds, the art of nature and the art of mankind. This is the game of Dionysus: to create and to destroy even the most sacred things. Yet whereas Romantic pessimism says "No" to the world, Nietzsche's Dionysian pessimism says "Yes" to the world, in all its splendor and horror, with audacity, lucidity, and enthusiasm.

Whereas the published preface gives the impression that gaiety and the worship of appearance are born from the refusal of knowledge, or a refusal of the will to Truth, the draft reveals that this gaiety is, on the contrary, the consequence of knowledge and a will to Truth, but both of them are Dionysian: they have engendered suspicion with regard to being, and hence pessimism. In the words of the *Posthumous Fragments:* "It seems that we are gay because we are monstrously sad. We are serious, we know the abyss. This is why we defend ourselves against all that is serious."[11]

For Nietzsche, art does not mean the fine arts but refers to the entire activity of creation and production linked to life and nature, as has been shown by Jean Granier, who writes, "Nature is the artist *par excellence.*"[12] Human art has a cosmic meaning; it is one of the forms of the game of nature: "It is a force of nature."[13] It is the entire world of forms, illusions, and representations linked to the vital needs, all that Nietzsche calls "the Olympus of appearances," but also all that is on the surface, as opposed to depth: skin, or the drapery of a veil. This worship of appearances and this gaiety are thus indissolubly connected to the terrifying knowledge of Truth, whose cold breath gives us the shivers: "He who has looked deeply into the world senses how much wisdom there is in mankind's remaining superficial. It is his instinct for preservation that teaches him to be hasty, light, and false."[14]

Already in *The Birth of Tragedy,* Nietzsche recognized the existence among the Greeks of this profound relation between knowledge of Truth and worship of appearance: "The Greek knew and experienced the terrors and horrors of existence; in order simply to live, he had to interpose between this world and himself that shining dream-creation, the Olympian world."[15] This creation of the gods is an artistic creation: it corresponds, says Nietzsche, to the instinct that creates art. Truth and the illusion that enables us to live are inseparable.

THE VEIL OF ISIS AND NATURE AS SPHINX

In the preface to *The Gay Science,* the reflections on the will to Truth and the worship of appearance are placed in the perspective of the unveiling of the statue of the Isis of Saïs. Nietzsche refuses to imitate "those young Egyptians who seek to unveil what there are good reasons to keep hidden."

He may be recalling the triumphant declarations of Schlegel, "He who cannot bear the vision of the goddess, let him flee or perish," and of Novalis, "He who refuses to raise the goddess's veil is no true disciple." For Novalis and other Romantics, to unveil Isis was, as we have seen, to rediscover one's own self.[16] Nietzsche is probably alluding to this when he speaks of the "austere men" who claim to "contemplate reality without veils." It is true that these "austere men" appear, according to the description Nietzsche gives of them, to be less Romantics than realists and objectivists, who claim to liberate themselves from all passion in the search for truth. Nevertheless, he writes with regard to them: "So reality stands unveiled before you alone, and perhaps you yourselves are the best part thereof—O beloved images of Saïs! Yet are you not, in your most unveiled state, highly passionate and dark beings . . . and always too similar to a love-smitten artist?"[17] The exclamation "O beloved images of Saïs!" is obviously ironic. It evokes what the "austere men" are thinking of when they affirm that by unveiling Nature, they unveil their own selves.

In the preface to *The Gay Science,* however, Nietzsche seems above all to be thinking of Schiller's poem "The Veiled Statue at Saïs," which I discussed in a previous chapter: a poem that features a young man consumed by the desire to unveil the statue of Isis because the hierophant told him that the Truth was hiding behind the goddess's veil. He penetrates into the temple at night and decides to tear away the veil, only to die of sorrow, without saying a word about his vision.[18] With regard to this reminiscence of Schiller in Nietzsche, Charles Andler cites the end of Schiller's "Kassandra," "Only error is life. And knowledge is death," which could indeed sum up Nietzsche's thinking.[19] Yet Schiller's pessimism is a Romantic pessimism that takes refuge in the Ideal and the renunciation of life.

In any case, Nietzsche resolutely subscribes to the attitude of all those who, like Rousseau and Goethe, have refused to tear the veil away from Isis: "We should have more respect for the modesty with which Nature hides behind enigmas and colorful uncertainties."

In this last line we recognize an echo of Heraclitus' aphorism, of which I have spoken throughout this book, but also an attitude that is completely analogous to that of Goethe when he recommends respect for the mystery and advises the Genius not to unveil the statue of Isis.[20] In other words, says Goethe, the statue of Nature as Sphinx, a terrifying and "monstrous thing," that Sphinx to which the "enigmas" Nietzsche speaks of certainly allude:

> Respect the mystery,
> Let not your eyes give in to lust.
> Nature the Sphinx, a monstrous thing,
> Will terrify you with her innumerable breasts.[21]

This image of Nature as Sphinx in Goethe's poem no doubt led Nietzsche to represent Nature metaphorically, no longer, as the tradition we have been examining would have it, with the features of Isis but rather with those of the Sphinx. This terrifying figure appears in a rather unexpected context very early in one of Nietzsche's youthful works, "The State among the Greeks" (1872), written while he was still under the influence of Schopenhauer. His point is to explain the sense of shame the Greeks felt with regard to work and to slavery: "In this feeling of shame there is hidden the unconscious knowledge that the genuine goal of existence demands these previous conditions [that is, labor and above all slavery], but that in this demand there resides all there is of horror and animal ferocity in Nature the Sphinx,[22] who nevertheless offers forth so beautifully her young girl's body,[23] thus glorifying free civilized and artistic life."[24] And, Nietzsche continues, "culture, which is above all an authentic need for art, rests on a terrifying foundation." In *The Birth of Tragedy*, he also identifies nature and the Sphinx when discussing Oedipus: "The same man who solves the riddle of nature, that Sphinx with a twofold essence, will also break nature's most sacred laws."[25] In this regard, it is not a matter of indifference that Nietzsche here speaks of the secrets of nature and of the violence against nature implied by their unveiling: "How could one force Nature to give up her secrets, unless by resisting her victoriously, that is, by doing what is against nature in an act that is contrary to nature?"[26] In any case, the Sphinx's twofold aspect, a ferocious beast with the bust of a girl, symbolizes the twofold aspect of Nature: beauty and ferocity, giving rise to wonder and horror within us. Thus, civilization in its twin aspects—atrocious (that of slavery) and radiant (that of artistic creation)—reflects the duplicity of the Sphinx, of Nature, and of the Being that is simultaneously the terrifying and destructive abyss of the Truth and the illusory and seductive appearance of Life.

Let us now return to the preface of *The Gay Science*. The refusal expressed there to unveil what is hidden leads to the resolute decision to stick to that which veils, that which is not hidden, appearance and epidermis, according to the model of the Greeks: "Oh, those Greeks! They knew all about *living*: something for which it is necessary to stop courageously at the surface, at drapery, at skin, to adore appearance, to believe in forms, sounds, and words, in the entire Olympus of appearance! Those Greeks were superficial—out of profundity!"[27]

The Greeks were superficial out of profundity, says Nietzsche. Yet profundity, as I have said, is precisely the vision of the world as it is. The Greeks knew the truth: they knew the terrors and horrors of existence. Yet it was precisely for this reason that they knew how to live. To know how to live means knowing how to construct or create for oneself a universe in which one can live, a universe of forms, sounds, and illusions as well, and dreams, and myths. "To create, for us, is to veil the truth of nature."[28] We thus glimpse the meaning that must be given to this formula: to respect Nature's modesty is in fact to know that she must, we might say, remain artistically veiled: "We no longer believe that the truth remains the truth if its veils are removed—we have lived too much to believe in that."

This respect for the modesty of Nature was already expressed implicitly in this passage from *The Birth of Tragedy* which opposed the artist, that is, the person who adores appearance, to the theoretician, who seeks the truth at all costs: "Whenever the truth is unveiled, the artist will always cling with rapt gaze to what still remains a veil even after such an unveiling; but the theoretician enjoys and finds satisfaction in the discarded veil, and finds the highest object of his pleasure in the process of an ever-happy unveiling that succeeds through his own efforts."[29]

One could say that the Orphic attitude is clearly opposed here to the Promethean attitude. In any case, Nietzsche always remained faithful to his fundamental intuition: truth is inseparable from its veils; appearances, forms, and vital illusion are inseparable from the truth. "The truth is truth only through the non-truth that veils it."[30] From the perspective of the metaphor of Nature as Sphinx, not to unveil Nature is to let the young girl's bosom, a symbol of beauty and art, hide the ferocious, terrifying beast, the symbol of Truth.

THE "MODESTY" OF TRUTH AND BAUBO

By identifying Truth with veiled Isis, Nietzsche is faithful to the pre-Romantic and Romantic problematic, for example, that of Schiller. In this problematic, however, veiled Isis was also Nature. This is why

Nietzsche moves without difficulty from Truth to Nature and from Nature to Truth, all the more easily in that the image of the veil makes him think of the aphorism of Heraclitus, "Nature loves to hide." Nietzsche writes: "We should have more respect for the *modesty* with which Nature hides behind enigmas and colorful uncertainties. Perhaps Truth is a woman who has reasons [*Gründe*] for not wanting to let her reasons [*Gründe*] be seen? Perhaps her name, if we were to speak Greek, is Baubo?"[31] Truth and Nature represent the terrifying ground of reality, which, in the will to knowledge at any cost, one would like to separate from its veil, that is, from the world of appearance, form, and art.

The expressions used here to speak of the modesty of Truth are problematic and cannot be understood, I believe, unless we become aware of all the irony they contain. First of all, the "enigmas" and "colorful uncertainties" of Nature are presented as veils by means of which she protects her modesty, but they also give the impression of being means of seduction. This makes one think of a posthumous poem that relates to Truth: "Truth is a woman. Nothing more. Clever in her modesty . . . You have to force her, that prudish Nature!"[32] As always in Nietzsche the formulas and images are ambiguous.[33] Should Truth's modesty be respected or should it be forced? As I have said, the knowledge of depth reconciles extremes: to have the heroic courage to unveil the truth of the world as it is, as a power of death and a power of creation, and, at the same time, respect the modesty of Truth, veiling it by art and beauty, since vital illusion and the veils of appearance are inseparable from truth.

Yet why does Nietzsche say that Nature is a woman who might have good reasons [*Gründe*] not to let her reasons [*Gründe*] be seen, whereas, in the context of modesty, we would have expected to find, instead of the second *Gründe*, a word designating the female sexual organs? To eliminate this paradox, Marc B. de Launay proposes the following translation: "Isn't truth a woman who has good reasons to

294 of THE VEIL OF ISIS

hide behind, in order not to let her behind be seen?"[34] Yet several objections can be raised against this translation. The translation of *Gründe* by "behind" runs into two obstacles: First, *Gründe* is plural, whereas "behind" is singular. In addition, to give the German word *Gründe* the physiological or anatomical meaning of the French *fondement* is, it seems to me, impossible, all the more so in that it would not be an exhibition of the female sexual organs. I think, for my part, that by means of this repetition, Nietzsche wanted to renounce the metaphor ironically, after he had merely sketched it. The Truth can be compared to a woman, but nevertheless we must not forget that it is the Truth. Nietzsche certainly wanted to surprise the reader, who was expecting a word with sexual connotations, and instead finds only a repetition of the word "reasons." For in the classical representation of the Truth, what is most essential, most intimate, and most profound are its reasons, or the rational principles which, in theory, are supposed to give it its validity. But the will to truth at all costs wants to account for everything, and seeks out the deepest reasons. Playing with the word *Grund* once more, Nietzsche denounces the danger of this attitude in a posthumous poem: "One goes to his last resting place [*zugrunde*] if one always goes to the ultimate reasons [*Gründen*]."[35] This is another way of denouncing the inhuman and dangerous character of the will to truth at all costs. Just as Rousseau, from a different perspective, declared that nature "wished to preserve us from science, as a mother snatches a dangerous weapon from the hands of her child,"[36] so Truth, according to Nietzsche, has good reasons to conceal her ultimate reasons, or her essence, since knowing them is dangerous for mankind. We must therefore respect her "modesty," that is, as the Greeks did, "stop courageously at the surface, . . . believe in forms, sounds, and words, and in the entire Olympus of appearance," or the aesthetic aspect of nature.

From the perspective of the metaphor of the statue of Isis, the

Truth must thus remain veiled, and not be separated from the veil of illusion, error, and beauty that enables us not to perish when we discover it, like the young man in the temple of Saïs. Yet why, then, does Nietzsche add, "Perhaps her name, if we were to speak Greek, is Baubo?" What was he thinking of when he invoked this name? In Greek literature, Baubo appears in two different contexts.

First of all, she is a female mythological figure, linked to the mysteries of Eleusis, and therefore to the story of Demeter and Kore.[37] According to an Orphic poem, Demeter, in tears after the abduction of her daughter and searching everywhere for her, was received at Eleusis into a human home and burst out laughing when Baubo "hoisted up her *peplos* and displayed her genitals."[38] This was the very gesture, as we have seen, also made by Isis Bubastis.[39] It is rather surprising that Nietzsche, speaking of the modesty of Nature and of Truth, designates Truth by the name of a woman famous for her immodest gesture.[40]

Baubo was also a terrifying nocturnal demon, identified with the Gorgon. Nietzsche may have known this figure, for his friend Erwin Rohde had discussed her in his book *Psyche*.[41] Baubo's terrifying aspect might accord perfectly with Nietzsche's idea of the Truth. Yet this figure has no relation with its immediate context, that is, with the problem of veiling and unveiling.

Finally, one may wonder if, rather than thinking of the Baubo of Greek tradition, Nietzsche was not recalling the Baubo evoked by Goethe in his *Walpurgisnacht:* "Old Baubo comes alone, riding on a sow."[42] Several times, when Nietzsche speaks of the Truth, he says that she is an old woman. In this context we can cite Nietzsche's poem "In the South," which is part of the collection of poems titled *Songs of Prince Outlaw,* which Nietzsche placed precisely at the end of *The Gay Science*.[43] The prince imagines that he is flying like a bird of the North toward the South, that is, that he is escaping from the fog of Romanticism to reach the light and heat of the Mediterranean world. He confides the following secret: "I hesitate to admit it, but in the North I loved a little woman, old enough to make you shudder—the name of this old woman was Truth." By evoking this love for the old lady Truth, Nietzsche alludes to his initial enthusiasm for the will to truth at all costs, following Schopenhauer and Wagner. We also encounter this old woman in the aphorisms of *The Gay Science:* "Humanity! Was there ever a more hideous old woman among all old women? (unless it was 'Truth': a question for philosophers)."[44] If the Truth is a woman, she is, for Nietzsche, a "hideous" old woman, "old enough to make you shudder." "Truth is ugly: we have art so that the truth may not kill us."[45]

From this metaphorical perspective, if the Truth has good reasons not to let her "reasons" be seen, it is because she is a horrible and frightening old sorceress who must be kept hidden under the veil of appearance and art. To respect Truth's modesty means above all to respect the "measure" that allows the will to truth to coexist with the will to appearance, which thus enables us to grasp and to perceive that truth and lies, death and life, horror and beauty are indissoluble.[46] According to the image to which Nietzsche held fast all his life, the world is nothing other than the eternal game of Dionysus, who pitilessly and ceaselessly creates and destroys a universe of forms and appearances.[47]

With regard to the figure of Baubo, we must admit that, more than any other author, Nietzsche made rather frequent allusions to the sexual aspect implied in the metaphor of the veil of Isis. The psychological causes and consequences of these representations would have to be analyzed; as I said in the preface, however, since I am neither a psychiatrist nor a psychoanalyst, I do not feel qualified to undertake such an interpretation, and important studies on this subject already exist. I shall limit myself to pointing out a few possible signposts in this research. Knowledge has traditionally been assimilated to the unveiling of the feminine body and to sexual possession.[48] In *Being and Nothingness,* Jean-Paul Sartre described these representations, that is, these metaphors, under the name of "the Actaeon complex." For him, vision is delectation, and to see is to deflower: "One tears away Nature's veils, and unveils her (cf. Schiller's 'Veil of Saïs')[49]: all research always includes the idea of a nudity that one brings to light by setting aside the obstacles that cover it, as Actaeon separates the branches to get a better view of Diana at her bath.[50] Knowledge, moreover, is a hunt: Bacon calls it the hunt of Pan. The scholar is the hunter who catches a pale nudity and violates it with his glance."[51]

As we have seen, Diderot and Goethe likened the metamorphoses of Nature to the successive disguises of a woman.[52] Montesquieu, for his part, compared Nature (and Truth as well, for that matter) to a girl who, after having long refused, surrenders herself unexpectedly in an instant.[53]

DIONYSIAN ECSTASY

One could say that Nietzsche, if he had wanted to translate Heraclitus' aphorism, would have used formulas such as Nature (or Truth) loves to veil herself, loves to lie, loves illusion, loves to create works of art. The knowledge of depth consists in having the courage to admit that the Truth is completely inhuman, and that Life demands error, or illusion: that veil that must not be torn away from Truth, that young girl's bosom that conceals the animal ferocity of the Sphinx.

Nietzsche thus takes his place—but with astonishing originality that renews all its meaning—in the movement of ideas, which, beginning with the mid-eighteenth century, recognized, in reaction against an exclusively scientific approach, the value and legitimacy of an aesthetic approach to nature. Here, human art appears as a means to knowledge of nature, since nature itself is artistic creation:

"To what depth does art penetrate the intimacy of the world? And are there, outside of the artist, other artistic forms?" This question was, as is well known, my *point de départ:* and I answered "Yes" to the second question; and to the first, "The world itself is entirely art." The absolute will to knowledge, truth, and wisdom appeared to me, in this world of appearance, as an outrage to the fundamental metaphysical will, as contrary to nature; and rightly, [the] point of wisdom turns against the sage. The unnatural character of wisdom is revealed in its hostility to art: to want to know, precisely where appearance constitutes salvation—what a reversal, what an instinct for nothingness![54]

And also: "The world as a work of art engendering itself!"[55]

Above all, Nietzsche takes up, while renewing it totally, the vision, simultaneously tragic and enthusiastic, of the mystery of being that was sketched in Goethe and Schelling.[56] In his youth, on the occasion of a class on Heraclitus, Nietzsche already seems to allude to his own feeling of existence when he writes: "Eternal becoming initially has a terrifying and worrisome aspect. The strongest sensation to which it can be compared is that felt by someone who, lost at sea or during an earthquake, sees everything moving around him. A stupefying strength was needed to transform this effect into its contrary, into an impression of sublimity and delighted astonishment."[57]

Somewhat later, in the spring of 1888, this feeling of terror and pleasure, which he now calls "Dionysian," is transfigured into an enthusiastic consent to reality: "An ecstatic yes said to the total character of life, always like unto itself in the midst of what changes, equally powerful, equally blessed: the great pantheistic sym-pathy in joy and in pain, which approves and sanctifies even the most terrible and problematic properties of life, starting out from an eternal will to procreation, to fecundity, to eternity: a unitary feeling of the necessity of creating and destroying."[58]

The knowledge of depth implies a transcendence of individuality. This is what Nietzsche affirms when speaking of Goethe: "Such a spirit stands tall in the midst of the universe with a joyous and confident fatalism, with the deep conviction that only the individual is condemned, but that all will be saved and reconciled in the Totality—he no longer says no. Yet such a faith is the highest of all possible faiths: I have baptized it with the name of Dionysus."[59] And "to go beyond myself and yourself. To feel in a cosmic way," to see things from the perspective of eternity (*sub specie aeternitatis*—perhaps we return here to the position of Schopenhauer's absolute spectator), that eternity which is, for Nietzsche, the eternal return.[60] Man must therefore abandon his partial and partisan viewpoint in order to raise himself up to a cosmic perspective, or to the viewpoint of universal nature, in order to be able to say "an ecstatic yes" to nature in its totality, in the indissoluble union of truth and appearance. This is Dionysian ecstasy.

23

From the Secret of Nature to
the Mystery of Being

Beginning with the end of the eighteenth century, not only did the quest for the secrets of nature, as we have seen, give way to an affective experience of anguish or wonder in the face of the ineffable,[1] but also, throughout the philosophical tradition that extends from the Romantic period to the present day, the very notion of a secret of nature was to be replaced by that of the mystery of being or existence.

SCHELLING: THE MYSTERY OF EXISTENCE AND ANGUISH

We can already observe this change in perspective in the third version (probably dating from 1815) of Schelling's *Ages of the World,* an ambitious work that the philosopher, after several attempts at writing, finally resigned himself to leaving unpublished.[2] Here he takes up his doctrine of the three divine powers, present in various forms in his other works, and he tries to analyze the phases of God's becoming, that is, ultimately, of the emergence of reality. Describing the movement of systole and diastole, Schelling recognizes in it the "initial pulsation of the beginning of that alternating movement that animates all visible nature," which we can observe, for instance, in the life of a plant, whose entire activity consists of giving birth to a seed, to commence the production of a seed from it once again.[3] The movement of being and the movement of life are thus intimately linked. Yet in order for being to posit itself, appear, and reveal itself, it

must first of all be enclosed within itself, so that there may be a subject, that is, a basis or foundation *(Grund)*, for such revelation. Revelation presupposes an initial moment in which being denies itself, re-
tracts, or contracts its essence. It certainly seems as though Schelling
is the heir to Boehme here, for whom the first principle of deity is
fire, wrath, anger, and fury, and the first moment of nature is a contraction that is "terrible, bitter, burning and cold, jealous and angry."[4]
As Schelling writes, "Development presupposes envelopment."[5]

One passage from *The Ages of the World* must particularly capture
our attention. It clearly reveals the transformation of the notion of a
secret of nature, which becomes a moment in the self-positing of being and the fundamental mystery of existence: "This tendency to *enclose being* is acknowledged by the expressions of everyday speech,
especially when we say that *nature evades our glance and conceals
from us her mysteries.* It is only when constrained by a higher force
that she would cause all that becomes to emerge from its hiding
place."[6]

Here we move from nature that hides to being that encloses itself.
This original negation, says Schelling, is "the nurturing mother of
the entire visible universe,"[7] and we can subsequently observe its effects in all the phenomena of envelopment, in space and in bodies. If
it has been said that nature hides, it is because "nature is attached by
its roots to the blind, obscure, and inexpressible side of God."[8] All expansion constitutes a victory over this resistance, or this will to en-
closure. In other words, for Schelling, the secret of nature represents
not a problem that science might solve but the original mystery of
Being, its impenetrable and unexplorable character. In this perspective, "Nature loves to hide" means that "Being is originally in a state
of contraction and non-deployment." Moreover, the notion of Nature in Schelling has an ambiguous character, since, as in the statement just cited, it can designate "physical" nature, but it often refers
to what Vladimir Jankélévitch calls "theosophical Nature, in which

Schelling recognizes the occult divinity of God."[9] In any case, we may say with Jankélévitch, "Here, Nature is nothing other than the *Grund* [foundation] or the hidden mystery of existence."[10]

In his *Aphorisms on the Philosophy of Nature* (1806), Schelling had evoked the anguish that seizes us in the presence of existence, when we separate it from all the familiar forms that conceal it from us. "To whoever might consider it, disregarding its species and form, simple being-there (what is simply called *existence*), if one considers it purely, should appear like a miracle and fill the soul with astonishment. Just as it is undeniably by this pure 'being-there' that, in the most ancient forebodings, souls were seized by fright and a kind of *sacred terror.*"[11]

For Schelling, it is the very genesis of being that explains this impenetrable and terrifying character of existence. It is rooted in the first moment of being, which Schelling calls the foundation *(Grund)*: an original opacity, or a refusal to appear and unveil itself, an opacity and refusal that must be transcended. As Jan Assmann has demonstrated, in the eighteenth century, the inscription from Saïs, "I am all that has been, that is, and that shall be," was assimilated to Yahweh's declaration to Moses, one of whose multiple interpretations would be "I am who I am," interpreting them both as the divinity's refusal to say its name, that is, to make itself known.[12] Schelling, who understands Yahweh's declaration in the sense of "I will be who I will be," was perhaps influenced by this idea when he posited refusal and negation at the origin of being.[13]

In any case, for the Schelling of the third version of *The Ages of the World*, being deploys itself only by a struggle against itself, and this is what explains the distressing and terrifying character of existence. For him, existence is tragic: "Anguish is the fundamental feeling of every living creature, and all that lives is born and greeted only in the midst of a violent struggle."[14] The foundation of things, for him as for Boehme, as for Schopenhauer, is "sadness," "suffering," "madness," dispositions that must be conquered but are nevertheless inherent in existence.[15]

Schelling makes fun of the philosophers who have long bent everyone's ears with their effusions on the harmony of the cosmos.[16] In fact, in his view, the frightening and the terrible are the true substantial foundation of existence. "The fundamental substance of every living being and of all existence," writes Karl Löwith, "is, for Schelling as for Nietzsche, that which terrifies: a power and a blind force, a barbaric principle that may be transcended but never canceled, and which is the basis of all that is great and beautiful.'"[17] For Schelling, Heraclitus' aphorism "Nature loves to hide" means that Nature originally represents a resistance to evolution, insofar as it is a will to remain within itself. "Nature's modesty" was to become the mystery of being, and this mystery was distressing and terrifying. Goethe and Schelling thus seem to me to be at the origin of a tradition in which there is an impenetrable mystery of existence that provokes anguish. The goal is no longer to vanquish the difficulties and obstacles that Nature opposes to our knowledge but to recognize that it is inherent in nature—or the world, or being-in-the-world, or Being—to be inexplicable, so that one of the essential dimensions of human existence will henceforth be both wonder and anguish, the "sacred shudder," as Goethe and Kant would say, in the face of unfathomable mystery and enigma.

HERACLITUS' APHORISM IN HEIDEGGER

In our contemporary world, people no longer speak of secrets of nature, and Isis has gone off, along with her veil, to the land of dreams. Yet Heraclitus' aphorism is still alive, and still continues to nourish reflection. Heidegger brings Heraclitus' aphorism up to date.[18] He identifies Heraclitus' *phusis* with what he calls Being, and he gives several rather different but convergent translations of it:[19] "Being

304 <a THE VEIL OF ISIS

loves to make itself invisible";[20] "A veiling is an integral part of un-veiling";[21] "Being (appearing when it flourishes) inclines by itself to its self-sealing";[22] "Hiding-itself belongs to the predilection of Being."[23] Again, there are the two formulas cited by Alain Renault: "Being slips away by showing itself in beings as such" and "Being withdraws insofar as it discloses itself in beings."[24] These various translations should be replaced within the context of the evolution, often unexpected, of Heidegger's thought: here the notion of Being, in particular, is subject to perpetual becoming. Such an undertaking would go beyond the framework of this study. Therefore I shall re-tain from these Heideggerian formulas only what relates to the gen-eral perspective of the present work.

To understand the meaning of these translations of Heraclitus' aphorism, we must try to glimpse what the words "Being" and "be-ing" mean for Heidegger. In his view, we are used to paying attention only to determinate objects: a man, a dog, a star, a table. These are what Heidegger calls beings. Beings interest people only by their qualities, their usefulness, or their finality. They are mere things, in relation with other things. The fact that beings *are* does not interest people: "It matters little to the man plunged within everyday exis-tence that things are, or that they are founded by Being. Only beings interest him, but the Being of beings remains foreign to him. 'The weather is bad.' The bad weather is enough for us: this 'is' has no weight . . . All human behavior makes this antinomy burst forth: that man knows beings, but forgets Being."[25]

Here we have a radical opposition between being-with-a-small-*b* (being) and Being-with-a-capital-*B*. The latter is not one thing among others but is actuality or presence. What appears are beings, and what does not appear is the act of appearing itself, that is, Being. What is manifest are the beings that are present; what is hidden is the Presence that makes beings appear; what we completely forget is their surging-forth before us.

This paradox founds the Heideggerian exegesis of Heraclitus' fragment. Heidegger understands the word *phusis* from the perspective of the original meaning it had in Greek: "What does the word *phusis* say? It says that which flourishes from itself . . . , the action of unfolding while opening and, within the act of this unfolding, to make its appearance, to maintain itself within this appearing and to remain there."[26]

He describes this process as an *Aufgehen,* that is, as the action of dawning, growing, or appearing. For Heidegger, the Western idea of nature, in its origins, results from the Greek vision of being as a dawning or an emergence.[27] Heidegger thus understands the three words of Heraclitus' aphorism as meaning that the "dawning," or unveiling, that is, *phusis,* is inseparable from a veiling (Schelling had already said, "Development presupposes an envelopment"):

> Heraclitus means that to restrain oneself, to keep oneself in reserve, is a part of being. By no means does he thereby say that being is nothing other than concealing itself, but rather this: no doubt being unfolds as *phusis,* or unveiling, or as that which is manifest in itself, but its unveiling is inseparable from veiling. Without veiling, how could unveiling still be possible? We now say: being dispenses itself to us, but in such a way that at the same time it conceals from us its essence. Such is the meaning of the words "the history of being."[28]

Yet this theme authorizes many variations. Sometimes, as in the *Principle of Reason,* which has just been cited, we hear of what Heidegger calls "the history of being." This, then, denotes the decline of thought into forgetfulness of Being, which characterizes the history of philosophy. The history of philosophy thus becomes "an approach to the veiling of Being in its forgetfulness."[29]

At other times, we hear of the antinomy, internal to Being, between veiling and unveiling. In an attempt to make understood what Heraclitus' aphorism represents for him, Heidegger says:

What does that mean? It has been thought, and it continues to be thought, that it is: since being is difficult to reach, one must expend a great deal of effort in order to flush it out of its hiding place, and make it lose its taste, if one may say so, for hiding.

It is time—for the need is growing—to think the contrary: to withdraw, to shelter oneself in one's own retreat belongs to the predilection of being, that is, that in which it has consolidated its unfolding. And the unfolding of being is to disclose itself, to blossom into the openness of non-retreat . . . *phusis*. Only that which, following its unfolding, opens and discloses itself, and cannot help but disclose itself, only that can love to close itself once more . . . Only that which is an opening of disclosure can be re-closure. And that is why it is not appropriate to "transcend" the *kruptesthai* of *phusis*, or to extirpate it; much heavier is the task of leaving to *phusis*, in all the purity of its unfolding, *kruptesthai* as an integral part of *phusis*. Being is the openness of disclosure that closes itself.[30]

In Heidegger's view, Heraclitus' aphorism is linked to his own doctrine of *a-lētheia*, according to the Heideggerian etymology of the Greek word that designates truth: *a-lētheia* means non-forgetfulness, or non-veiling. Yet truth, conceived as unveiling, also presupposes a veiling. *Phusis* is also an unveiling that is veiling, or a blossoming that is concealment: to bloom is to veil oneself; to veil oneself is to manifest oneself. This is why Heidegger calls Being the Secret, Enigma, or Mystery *(Geheimnis)*.[31] The movement, sketched from Goethe to Nietzsche, to recognize that Nature or Truth is inseparable from its veils is further accentuated.

It is inherent in mankind to forget Being. In order to live, man must interest himself in beings. Hypnotized by his care for things, which he considers readymade, man cannot pay attention to their blossoming, their surging-forth, or their *phusis*, their nature in the etymological sense of the term. In the words of Jean Wahl: "This act [i.e., the forgetting of Being in favor of beings] constitutes us, in a sense; we always accomplish it; it is our destiny as human beings to accomplish it. We are always the murderers of Being."[32] We can say of Heidegger's Being what Plotinus said of the One: "It is not absent from anything, and yet it is absent from everything, so that although it is present, it is not present, except for those who are capable of receiving it."[33] Its presence is, as it were, a presence/absence. This forgetting of Being explains man's situation: he "wanders." "The agitation that flees mystery to take refuge in current reality and pushes mankind from one day-to-day object to another, making him miss the mystery, is wandering."[34] To borrow the vocabulary used in *Being and Time,* man lives habitually in inauthenticity, but he can, seldom and precariously, accede to authenticity and lucidity by confronting the mystery of Being.

Philosophers and scholars of previous centuries spoke, for the most part, of unveiling Nature and discovering her secrets. Here, Being, which has taken nature's place, is not to be discovered, but it is both what makes things appear and what does not appear. It is "blossoming": that is the absolute enigma. In the study I have mentioned, Alain Renault applies the following formula to this subject: "Here, Being itself is the sphinx."[35]

Was Heidegger right to interpret Heraclitus' aphorism in this way? He was certainly right to understand *phusis* in the sense of "blossoming," or the action of making things appear. He was also right to recognize in this aphorism Heraclitus' method of trying to grasp the identity of contraries. I do not think, however, that Heraclitus could have conceived of Being *(einai)* as blossoming and making-things-appear, that is, that he identified it with *phusis.*

ANGUISH, NAUSEA, WONDERMENT

We also find in Heidegger the feeling of anguish that we have seen appear in German Pre-Romanticism and Romanticism, for instance, in Goethe and Schiller. Heidegger analyzed this feeling above all in *Being and Time.* Alphonse de Waehlens admirably summarized Heidegger's thought in these terms:

> What appalls us in the face of this world . . . to which we are handed over defenseless and without succor is . . . the brute, naked, inexorable, and insurmountable fact of our being-in-the-world. What makes me withdraw in anguish is this externality in which I am plunged in order to make my career as an existent within it, without having willed it, and without being able to stop its progress. Anguish is born from our condition and reveals it. It is the genuine feeling of the original situation.[36]

As in Schelling, terror or anguish is thus produced by pure being-there, that is, by being-in-the-world, perceived in its nudity, and separated from the usual environment of our daily life, in which we take refuge in order to be safe from anguish. Also included in this anguish in the face of being-in-the-world is the awareness of the fact that being-in-the-world is being-for-death, and, more profoundly, that Being is inseparable from Nothingness. Jean Wahl thought that the great difference that exists between Kierkegaardian anguish and Heideggerian anguish consists in the fact that the former is of a psychological and religious order—it is brought about by the consciousness of sin—whereas the latter is "linked to the cosmic fact," or the consciousness of an existence that stands out against a background of nothingness.[37] Alphonse de Waehlens corrects this affirmation by specifying that anguish as Heidegger conceives it is also of a "spiritual" order insofar as this anguish in the face of the world is ultimately "the anguish of mankind in the face of his own solitude."[38]

The feeling of anguish has continued to maintain its place in philosophies since Heidegger. In his novel *Nausea,* Sartre describes his hero's becoming aware of being-in-the-world in the garden of Bouville, in front of a tree stump: here we note that what brings on Sartre's nausea is indeed a natural being. We may wonder if an object fashioned by human beings would have the same effect. What brings about anguish is the inexplicable character of nature's presence. In this experience, all beings lose their diversity, their individuality; they are the pure act of existence: "We had no reason to be there, none of us did." He then discovers the fundamental absurdity of existence: "Nothing—not even a deep, secret delirium of nature—could explain it." For "to exist is *to be there,* simply . . . No necessary being can explain existence . . . All is gratuitous: this garden, this town, and myself. When we happen to realize this, it turns our stomach and everything starts to float . . . That's what nausea is." Sartre's description of becoming aware of existence is almost a caricature: the objects he sees become "monstrous, soft pastes in disorder—frighteningly and obscenely nude." He writes, "We were a bunch of embarrassed existents, embarrassed by ourselves . . . each confused, vaguely worried existent felt superfluous with regard to the others."[39]

In fact, however, becoming aware of the inexplicable and contingent character of our being in the world, by experiencing the pure, brute presence of a given object in the world, does not necessarily give rise to anguish. If a tree stump in the Bouville garden could cause anguish in Sartre at the beginning of the century (1902), an insect in a watering can could just as well bring about the ecstatic wonderment of Hugo von Hofmannsthal:

> The other night I found under a walnut tree a half-full watering can
> that a young gardener had forgotten there, and this watering can,
> with the water in it, hidden by the tree's shadow, with a water bug
> paddling from one shore to the other of that dark water: this combi-
> nation of trivialities exposes me to such a presence of the infinite,
> traversing me from the roots of my hair to the base of my heels, that
> I feel like bursting out in words which I know, if I had found them,
> would have floored those cherubim in whom I do not believe.[40]

As far as I know, the feeling of anguish does not play an important part in the philosophy of Maurice Merleau-Ponty, who preferred to speak of "philosophical astonishment."[41] And yet, he too presents the existence of the world as an inexplicable mystery, at the end of the preface to his book *The Phenomenology of Perception:* "The world and reason do not present a problem; let us say, if you will, that they are mysterious, but this mystery defines them, and there can be no question of dissipating it by some solution. It is beyond solutions. True philosophy is relearning to see the world."[42]

By opposing "problem" to "mystery," Merleau-Ponty was probably alluding to the interesting distinction made by the Christian existentialist Gabriel Marcel. For him, a problem refers to something external to us. We can solve it more or less easily, but it disappears once its solution has been found: "By contrast, mystery is something in which I find myself engaged, and whose essence is, consequently, not to be entirely before me."[43] It cannot therefore be either solved or explained: I am implicated in it and can only experience it.

Merleau-Ponty's declaration definitively eliminates the notion of a secret of nature, conceived as a kind of detective story that it would suffice to unravel for the problem to be solved and curiosity satisfied. It may, however, recall Goethe's attitude with regard to the *Urphänomene,* or originary phenomena, for which there is no explanation and before which we must be silently astonished. For his part, Merleau-Ponty sees in philosophy that which "awakens us to what is problematic in itself about the world's existence, and our own, to the point where we are forever cured of searching, as Bergson used to say, 'in the master's notebook,'"[44] that is, to see in the phenomena of the world the copy of models present in a thought that would be transcendent to the world. For philosophy must not hide the mystery of existence through the intervention of a God or a necessary Being who could explain the world's contingence. The world's existence is not a problem that could be solved by a solution, but it is an inexplicable mystery. All explanations "seem quite prosaic to the philosopher in comparison with this surging-forth of phenomena on all the levels of the world and of that continuous birth that he is busy describing."[45] If we can judge from the pages that follow this passage in his *Praise of Philosophy*, which allude to a new definition of the sacred, I would tend to admit that if all explanations are "prosaic," becoming aware of the inexplicable mystery of the world's surging-forth is "sacred."

At the end of his *Tractatus Logico-Philosophicus* (6.44), Wittgenstein also evokes the existence or being-there of the world: "It is not how [*wie*] the world is that is the mystical, but *the fact that* [*daß*] it is."

"How the world is" is the arrangement of facts internal to the world, that is, the object of science, and thus something that can be the object of language that makes sense, or that is "sayable." "The fact that the world is" corresponds to the world's existence, that is, to something that, for Wittgenstein, is inexpressible and can only be shown. Indeed, this is how Wittgenstein defines "the mystical": "There is something inexpressible; it shows itself, and that is the mystical" (6.5222). In a study written about fifty years ago, I distinguished four types of use of language in Wittgenstein.[46] First, there is the *representative* or sensible use: these are the propositions that have a logical form, that is, a possible meaning, because they are formed from signs, all of which have a signification. Then there is the *tautological* or analytical use, bereft of any content of meaning: these are logical propositions themselves. There is also the use we could call *nonsensical*, which engenders pseudo-propositions. Most philosophical propositions sin against the laws of grammar and logical syntax; they contain signs that have no signification, and they therefore have no logical form or meaning. Finally, there is the use we could call indicative.[47] This use is legitimate for Wittgenstein; the proposition does not represent anything, but it shows us something it cannot express.

Thanks to this indicative use of language, we can speak of an experience of the world's existence. It is indeed an experience, and even an affective experience, for Wittgenstein speaks of a "mystical" feeling with regard to what he calls the "feeling of the world." In his *Lecture on Ethics* (1929–1930), he alludes to an experience that is "his" experience, and that consists in being amazed at the world's existence.[48] It is thus amazement, and not nausea, that Wittgenstein feels in the presence of the world's existence. Yet the world's existence is, for him, totally inexplicable, since it cannot be stated in a representative proposition.

As we have seen, Merleau-Ponty said that with regard to the world, we cannot formulate a problem that would then admit of a solution and could thus be dissipated. Wittgenstein takes his place in the same perspective. The impossibility of answering eliminates the possibility of the question: "With regard to an answer that cannot be formulated, one cannot formulate a question either" (6.5). Merleau-Ponty said that our relation to the world is of the order not of a problem (where we must understand "as is the case in scientific research") but of a mystery. Here, the word Wittgenstein uses is not "problem" but "enigma": "*The Enigma* does not exist" (6.5). Indeed, it could be thought that just as science gradually solves particular problems concerning the facts that constitute the world, so, with regard to the world in its totality, the problem of its existence could be solved; there would thus also be Enigma in itself to solve. Yet since, from the perspective of language use, no solution whatsoever with regard to the world can be expressed, the result is that "with regard to an answer that cannot be formulated, no question can be formulated either," and that, as a consequence, "the Enigma does not exist." For Wittgenstein, as for Merleau-Ponty, metaphysical hypotheses do not contribute any solution: "The soul's temporal immortality, that is, its eternal survival after its death, is not by any means guaranteed, but above all its supposition does not even provide what one would hope to be able to obtain by it. Is any enigma solved because I survive eternally? Isn't this eternal life just as enigmatic as this present life?" (6.432).

As a whole, the world is inexplicable (6.371–372): Wittgenstein reproaches modern science for giving the impression that everything has been explained, whereas this is by no means the case: for we cannot step outside the world in order to treat it as an object of study. We are in the world as we are in language.

For Merleau-Ponty, the world is an unsolvable mystery, and he draws the conclusion that "philosophy is relearning how to see the world." For his part, Wittgenstein, at the end of the *Tractatus*, advises the reader to transcend all the book's propositions, and he will then see the world in a correct way (6.54). We could say—obviously with a great deal of simplification—that for both authors, "to see the world" means to return to the perception of the world as it appears to us: phenomenological and aesthetic perception in Merleau-Ponty, aesthetic perception and ethical attitude in Wittgenstein, since for him, the world and life (in the ethical sense) coincide. We might perhaps discern a certain kinship between the correct vision of the world according to Wittgenstein and the disinterested vision of the world according to Schopenhauer. Speaking of the disinterested contemplation of the world, thus liberated from the principle of reason, Schopenhauer had evoked the Spinozist formula: to conceive of things in the perspective of eternity *(sub specie aeternitatis)*,[49] in order to illustrate the idea that the individual who contemplates in this way transcends his individuality and identifies himself with the eternal subject of consciousness. The author of the *Tractatus* writes in his turn, "To contemplate the world *sub specie aeternitatis* is to contemplate it as a whole—but a limited whole.[50] The feeling of the world as a limited whole constitutes the mystical feeling" (6.45). According to Wittgenstein, eternity must be understood not as indefinite temporal duration but as intemporality: "He lives eternally who lives in the present" (6.4311). The "correct vision of the world" would thus perhaps be disinterested, that is, aesthetic and ethical, perception of the world in the present moment: that is, as if it were perceived for the first and last time, and thus, ultimately, in a kind of intemporality. We thus return to the experience of amazement that Wittgenstein felt in the face of the world, which I discussed earlier.

I have only sketched this comparison between two very different philosophers, Merleau-Ponty and Wittgenstein, in order to allow a glimpse of a specific tendency in twentieth-century philosophy, which consists in renouncing abstract explanations of the world's existence, to open the possibility of an experience of the mystery of existence in the world, and of a lived contact with the inexplicable surging-forth of reality, or *phusis* in the original meaning of the word.

Conclusion

We have now covered nearly twenty-five centuries, and we cannot help being astonished by the extraordinary longevity of the formulas, representations, and images that were invented by ancient Greece. It could be said, for instance, that the thought of Heidegger, writing in the twentieth century, was to a large extent inspired by reflection on the aphorism of which I have spoken throughout this book, which dates from the fifth century BCE. How could we help but think here of what Nietzsche said of the "good maxim": "A good maxim is too hard for the teeth of time, and all the millennia cannot succeed in consuming it, though it always serves as nourishment; it is thereby the great paradox of literature: the imperishable in the midst of all that changes, the food that always remains appreciated, like salt, and, again like salt, never becomes insipid."[1]

A good maxim endlessly nourishes an entire series of generations, but its nutritive substance has undergone many an unexpected mutation over the centuries. Thus, we have seen how Heraclitus' three little words meant successively that all that lives tends to die; that nature is hard to know; that it wraps itself in sensible forms and myths; and that it hides occult virtues within it; but also that Being is originally in a state of contraction and non-unfolding; and finally, with Heidegger, that Being itself unveils as it veils itself. These three little words have served successively to explain the difficulties of the science of nature; to justify the allegorical exegesis of biblical texts, or to

315

defend paganism; to criticize the violence done to nature by technology and mechanization of the world; to explain the anguish that his being-in-the-world inspires in modern man. Thus, throughout the centuries, the same formula has assumed new meanings. To write the history of its reception is to write the history of a series of misunderstandings, but creative misunderstandings, insofar as these three little words have served to express, but also perhaps to cause to appear, ever new perspectives on reality, and also some very diverse attitudes with regard to nature, from admiration to hostility to anguish.

The same holds true for the metaphor of the secrets of nature. It remained alive through the meanderings of the history of the science of nature, both at the time of the mechanistic revolution and during the expansion of Romanticism; yet it implies a whole set of representations, some conceptual, others imaginative, which evolved considerably over the course of the centuries. Originally, it presupposed that the gods jealously keep to themselves the secrets of the fashioning of natural beings. With the personification of nature, which took place beginning in the fourth century of our era, it was imagined that Nature herself refused to unveil her secrets. This metaphorical representation could mean that nature conceals within itself virtualities or hidden seminal reasons, which can manifest themselves or be brought to light under the constraint of magic and mechanics. It can also mean that natural phenomena are hard to know, particularly in their invisible aspects, whether in the case of atoms or the internal parts of the body. This is why, when the microscope opened up the world of the infinitely small to mankind, scientists were able to proclaim that they had discovered the secrets of nature. At that time—that is, in the seventeenth century, at the beginning of the mechanistic revolution—we can detect two levels in the representation of the secrets of nature. On the one hand, there were the natural phenomena that are discovered by observation armed with instruments but also, and above all, the mathematical laws of their workings; and on the other hand, there were the impenetrable divine decisions that brought it about that a given universe was created, among all the possible ones.

Throughout our story we have been able to observe two fundamental attitudes with regard to the secrets of nature: one voluntarist, the other contemplative. I placed the former under the patronage of Prometheus, who, by devoting himself to the service of mankind, steals divine secrets by ruse or by violence. This attitude, moreover, laid claim very early to its legitimacy by affirming mankind's right to dominate nature—conferred on man by the God of Genesis—and to submit it, if necessary, to a judicial procedure and even to torture, in order to make it hand over its secrets: Francis Bacon's famous metaphor would still be used by Kant and by Cuvier. Magic, mechanics, and technology take their place within this tradition, and each, moreover, has as its goal, each in its own way, to defend mankind's vital interests. Metaphorically, Nature's refusal to hand over her secrets is interpreted as a hostile attitude toward mankind. Nature opposes man, and must be conquered and tamed. As far as the other attitude is concerned, I placed it under the patronage of Orpheus. This time, if Nature seeks to hide, it is, in particular, because the discovery of her secrets is dangerous for man. By intervening technologically in natural processes, man risks discovering them and, what is worse, unleashing unforeseeable consequences. From this perspective, it is the philosophical or the aesthetic approach, rational discourse and art, two attitudes that have their end in themselves and presuppose a disinterested approach, that will be the best means of knowing nature. Besides scientific truth, we will thus have to allow for an aesthetic truth, which provides an authentic knowledge of nature.

In themselves, both these attitudes are completely legitimate, even if we can discern serious possible deviations within each of them. However opposed they may be, moreover, they do not mutually exclude each other completely. In particular, modern scientists who, like Jacques Monod, practice a science henceforth linked inseparably with technology, nevertheless proclaim the absolute value of disinterested science, or basic research that has knowledge in itself as its goal.

Yet our story has also been that of the life and death not of nature but of the idea of secrets of nature. Although this idea was still very much alive after the heyday of the mechanistic revolution, it gradually disappeared, under the influence of two factors. On the one hand, the idea of a secret of nature was, whether one likes it or not, associated with a certain personalization of nature, and it implied an opposition between a visible husk and a hidden core, or between an outer and an inner part. The progress of science and rationalism has put an end to these representations. On the other hand, scientific progress has led philosophers to divert their attention from the explanation of physical phenomena, henceforth abandoned to science, to concentrate on the problem of being itself.

Here again we encounter an ancient text that has played a crucial role in the formation of our Western thought. This time the subject is the self-definition of the goddess of Saïs, whom Plutarch assimilates to Isis: "I am all that has been, that is, and that shall be; no mortal has yet raised my veil." Under the influence of the Masonic exegesis of this text, at the end of the eighteenth century, Isis, who until then had been an allegorical personification of Nature, henceforth became the symbol of universal being, infinite and ineffable. The veil of Isis then no longer signifies the secrets of nature but rather the mystery of existence. At the same time, however, the Isis who was seen unveiled, and in a way submissive, on the frontispiece of scientific works of the seventeenth and eighteenth centuries, since she represented nature as the object of observations, experiments, and scientific calculations, now becomes an object of veneration, respect, and even of terror. The warning of the goddess of Saïs was taken seriously: no mortal has lifted my veil. The allegory of the veil of Isis thus provided the Romantics with a literary means for expressing emotions which, to be sure, were not completely new, but which had become more and more intense since the time of Rousseau, Goethe, and Schelling: both amazement and terror before the existence of the world and of mankind within the world. There was henceforth no longer any question of solving particular riddles concerning the workings of natural phenomena, but rather of becoming aware of what is radically problematic and mysterious in the surging-forth of the totality of the real. We can observe the permanence of this tradition down to our own time.

The reader will have noticed, by the way, the themes that seduced me and on which I have tarried perhaps a bit too long: one idea, one experience. An idea: nature is art and art is nature, human art being only a special case of the art of nature, an idea that, I believe, enables us better to understand both what art can be and what nature can be. An experience—that of Rousseau, Goethe, Hölderlin, van Gogh, and many others—an experience that consists in becoming intensely aware of the fact that we are a part of nature, and that in this sense we ourselves are this infinite, ineffable nature that completely surrounds us. Let us recall Hölderlin: "To be but one with all living things, to return, by a radiant self-forgetfulness, to the All of Nature"; and Nietzsche: "To go beyond myself and yourself. To experience things in a cosmic way."

Notes

PREFACE

1. [Essay on the Geography of Plants—Trans.]
2. [Ideas for a Geography of Plants—Trans.]
3. See *Briefe an Goethe,* ed. K.-R. Mandelkow, 4 vols. (Hamburg, 1965–1967), vol. 1, no. 302. In this letter of February 6, 1806, Humboldt announces that he is sending the book to Goethe, accompanied by the illustration alluding to the union of poetry, philosophy, and science that Goethe had realized.
4. Goethe, *Die Metamorphosen der Pflanzen: Andere Freundlichkeiten* (1818–1820), in *Goethes Werke,* ed. Erich Trunz, 14 vols. (Hamburg, 1948–1969), 13:115. [All translations throughout are by Michael Chase unless otherwise noted. English-language editions in brackets are cited only for the convenience of the reader. The translations in the text are not taken from these sources.—Trans.]
5. P. Hadot, "Zur Idee der Naturgeheimnisse: Beim Betrachten des Widmungsblattes in den Humboldtschen 'Ideen zu einer Geographie der Pflanzen,'" *Akademie der Wissenschaften und der Literatur Mainz, Abhandlungen der Geistes- und Sozialwissenschaftlichen Klasse,* no. 8 (1982).
6. B. de Saint-Sernin, "L'ordre physico-chimique," in D. Andler, A. Fagot-Largeau, and B. de Saint-Sernin, *Philosophie des sciences,* vol. 1 (Paris, 2002), p. 420.

PROLOGUE AT EPHESUS

1. Diogenes Laertius, IX, 6 [in English, trans. R. D. Hicks, vol. 2 (Cambridge, Mass., 1925), p. 413—Trans.].
2. Heraclitus in J.-P. Dumont, ed., *Les présocratiques* (Paris, 1988), p. 173,

fragment 123 [in English, Charles H. Kahn, *The Art and Thought of Heraclitus* (Cambridge, 1979), p. 33, fragment 10—Trans.].

3. Aristotle *Rhetoric*, III, 5, 1407b11.

4. Plato, *Protagoras*, 342–343.

1. HERACLITUS' APHORISM

1. Herodotus, *Histories*, II, 27.

2. Democritus in J.-P. Dumont, *Les présocratiques* (Paris, 1988) (hereafter Dumont), p. 891, fragment 123.

3. Heraclitus in Dumont, p. 146, fragment 1 [in English, C. H. Kahn, *The Art and Thought of Heraclitus* (Cambridge, 1979) (hereafter Kahn), p. 29, fragment 1—Trans.].

4. Ibid., p. 167, fragment 93 [Kahn, p. 43, fragment 33—Trans.].

5. This might be implied by a citation of fragment 86 [Kahn, fragment 86—Trans.], which is, however, probably deformed: "To hide" the depths of knowledge is the "correct distrust [of a master with regard to the crowd], for distrust seeks to avoid being known" (see Clement of Alexandria, *Stromata*, V, 13, 88, 5; and see the commentary by A. Le Boulluec in Clément d'Alexandrie, *Stromates*, vol. 2 [Paris, 1981], p. 289). [For an English translation, see http://www.ccel.org/fathers2/ANF-02/anf02–65.htm#P7190_2189438—Trans.]

6. Empedocles in Dumont, p. 376, fragment 8 [in English, B. Inwood, *The Poem of Empedocles: A Text and Translation with an Introduction* (Toronto, 1992), p. 213, fragment 8—Trans.].

7. Heraclitus in Dumont, p. 156, fragment 45 [Kahn, p. 45, fragment 35—Trans.].

8. H. Güntert, *Kalypso* (Halle, 1919), pp. 28–33.

9. Euripides, *Hippolytus*, ll. 245–250.

10. R. B. Onians, *The Origins of European Thought* (Cambridge, 1954), pp. 423, 427.

11. Aristotle, *Politics*, I, 2, 1252b33.

12. Heraclitus in Dumont, p. 160, fragment 62 [Kahn, p. 71, fragment 92—Trans.].

13. Ibid., p. 151, fragment 20 [Kahn, p. 73, fragment 92—Trans.].

14. Ibid., p. 157, fragment 48 [Kahn, p. 65, fragment 79—Trans.].

15. See K. Reinhardt, trans., *Sophocle* (Paris, 1971), p. 49, with the bibliography in the note [in English, Reinhardt, *Sophocles*, trans. H. Harvey and D. Harvey (Oxford, 1979)—Trans.].

16. Sophocles, *Ajax*, ll. 646ff.

17. See Chapter 14.

18. *The Rape of Lucretia*, l. 929, cited by E. Panofsky, *Essais d'iconologie* (Paris, 1967), pp. 118–119 [in English, Panofsky, *Studies in Iconology: Humanistic Themes in the Art of the Renaissance* (New York, 1972)—Trans.], who points to the many quotations on this theme found in B. Stevenson, *Home Book of Citations* (New York, 1934).

19. For example, Reinhardt, *Sophocle*, p. 51.

20. Heraclitus in Dumont, p. 158, fragment 53 [Kahn, p. 71, fragment 94—Trans.].

21. Lucian, *Philosophers for Sale* [*Vitarum auctio*—Trans.], §14, trans. O. Zink (Paris, 1996), p. 45.

22. E. Degani, *Aion: Da Omero ad Aristotele* (Padua, 1961), p. 73.

23. I believe that my interpretation is quite close to that of O. Gigon, *Untersuchungen zu Heraklit* (Leipzig, 1935), p. 101.

24. Marcus Aurelius, *Meditations*, X, 11.

25. R. M. Rilke, *Sonnets to Orpheus*, II, 12.

26. Abbé Mugnier, *Diary* (Paris, 1985), p. 221. [Marthe Lucie Lehovary (1886–1973), Princess Bibesco, French literary figure of Romanian origin. Between the two World Wars, she presided over an influential literary circle in Paris, attended by Proust, Clémenceau, and the Abbé Mugnier, among many others—Trans.]

27. Montaigne, *Essays*, I, 20, in *Œuvres complètes*, ed. A. Thibaudet and M. Rat (Paris, 1962), p. 91 [in English, Montaigne, *The Complete Essays*, ed. and trans. M. A. Screech (London and New York, 2003)—Trans.].

28. C. Bernard, *De la physiologie générale* (Paris, 1872), pp. 327–328, n. 219. In the text published in 1872, one finds the word "good" *(bien)* where one expects "life" *(vie)*. This is probably a typographical error, and I have restored "life."

29. F. Jacob, *La logique du vivant* (Paris, 1970), pp. 330–331 [in English, Jacob, *The Logic of Life: A History of Heredity*, trans. B. E. Spillmann (Princeton, 1993)—Trans.]. See also J. Ruffié, *Le sexe et la mort* (Paris, 1986).

30. "At the Heart of Living Beings: Self-destruction," *Le Monde*, October 16, 1989.

31. F. Ravaisson, *Testament philosophique*, ed. C. Devivaise (Paris, 1938), p. 134.

32. *Les carnets de Léonard de Vinci*, ed. E. Maccurdy and L. Servicen, vol. 1 (Paris, 1942), p. 527 [in English, *The Notebooks of Leonardo da Vinci* (1888), ed. and comp. J. P. Richter, trans. Mrs. R. C. Bell, 2 vols. (New York, 1970)—Trans.].

33. Ibid., pp. 527–528. An entirely parallel passage is cited by E. H. Gombrich in *The Heritage of Apelles* (Oxford, 1976), p. 51 and n. 64, where he gives a bibliography on the subject.

2. From *Phusis* to Nature

1. On this problem, see the important article by D. Bremer, "Von der Physis zur Natur: Eine griechische Konzeption und ihr Schicksal," *Zeitschrift für philosophische Forschung* 43 (1989): 241–264; and the work by G. Naddaf, *L'origine de l'évolution du concept grec de phusis* (Lewiston, N.Y., 1992) [in English, Naddaf, *The Greek Concept of Nature* (Albany, N.Y., 2005)—Trans.]. See also the bibliographies in encyclopedia articles such as "Natur" (by F. P. Hager, T. Gregory, A. Mauerù, G. Stabile, and F. Kaulbach), in *Historisches Wörterbuch der Philosophie*, vol. 6 (Stuttgart and Basel, 1984), pp. 421–478; and "Nature" by P. Aubenque, in *Encyclopaedia universalis*. For a general history of the idea of nature, see R. Lenoble, *Esquisse d'une histoire de l'idée de nature* (Paris, 1969). See also the excellent study by A. Pellicer, *Natura: Étude sémantique et historique du mot latin* (Paris, 1966).

2. Homer, *Odyssey*, X, 303.

3. Empedocles in J.-P. Dumont, *Les présocratiques* (Paris, 1988) (hereafter Dumont), p. 176, fragment 8 [in English, B. Inwood, *The Poem of Empedocles: A Text and Translation with an Introduction* (Toronto, 1992) (hereafter Inwood), p. 213, fragment 8—Trans.].

4. Parmenides in Dumont, p. 266, fragment 10 [in English, A. H. Coxon, *The Fragments of Parmenides* (Assen, 1986), p. 81—Trans.]. The translation proposed here differs from that of Dumont and follows the interpretation of F. Heinemann, *Nomos und Phusis: Herkunft und Bedeutung einer Antithese*

im griechischen Denken des 5. Jahrhunderts (1945), 3rd ed. (Darmstadt, 1978), p. 90.

5. On constitution, see *Illnesses*, II, 3, 55, 3; *Regimen of Acute Illnesses*, 35 and 43, 78, 4; *On Places in Man*, II, 1. On normal state, normal position, see *On Vision*, V, 2; *On Places in Man*, XVII, 1; hence the philosophical concept of *kata phusin*. On the matter of an organ or its constitution: the glands have a spongy "nature," see *Glands*, I, 1. On nature as the organism itself, see *Glands*, IV, 1 and XII, 2. As the result of growth, see *Illnesses*, IV, XXXII, 1: with time, the seed became a *phusis* with a human appearance.

6. *Philebus*, 28a2.

7. Heraclitus in Dumont, p. 146, fragment 1 [in English, C. H. Kahn, *The Art and Thought of Heraclitus* (Cambridge, 1979) (hereafter Kahn), p. 29, fragment 1—Trans.].

8. Hippocrates, *On Ancient Medicine*, ed. and trans. J. Jouanna in Hippocrate, *L'ancienne médecine* (Paris, 1990), intro., p. 89.

9. Hippocrates, *On Ancient Medicine*, XX, 1, ibid., p. 145.

10. Aristotle, *Politics*, I, 2, 1252a24.

11. Cf. Jouanna (Hippocrate, *L'ancienne médecine*, p. 209), who compares Empedocles. See also the translation by A.-J. Festugière, Hippocrate, *L'ancienne médecine* (Paris, 1948), p. 60.

12. See A. Mansion, *Introduction à la physique aristotélicienne* (Paris, 1945), p. 84.

13. Plato, *Sophist*, 265e3.

14. See Chapters 17 and 18.

15. Empedocles in Dumont, pp. 383, 402, 408, and 412, fragments 23 [in English, Inwood, p. 219, fragment 27—Trans.]; 73 [p. 241, fragment 76]; 87 [p. 249, fragment 101]; and 96 [p. 235, fragment 62].

16. L. Brisson, *Le Même et l'Autre dans la structure ontologique du Timée de Platon* (Paris, 1974), pp. 35–50.

17. Aristotle, *Parts of Animals*, II, 9, 654b29.

18. Aristotle, *Generation of Animals*, II, 6, 743b20–25. On *Natura artifex* in the Middle Ages, see M. Moderson, "'Hic loquitur Natura': Natura als Künstlerin. Ein 'Renaissancemotiv' im Spätmittelalter," *Idea: Jahrbuch der Hamburger Kunsthalle* 10 (1991): 91–102.

19. See Chapter 18.

20. Aristotle, *Metaphysics,* XII, 3, 1070a7; *Physics,* II, 1, 192b20.

21. I borrow this formula from V. Jankélévitch (*Bergson* [Paris, 1931], p. 199), who points out the attitude of Schopenhauer and Bergson toward this problem.

22. Marsilio Ficino, *Platonic Theology,* IV, 1, ed. R. Marcel (Paris, 1964–65).

23. Epicharmus in Dumont, p. 199, fragment 4; Hippocrates, *Epidemics,* VI, 5, 1; V, 3, 4; *On Diet,* I, 15.

24. Aristotle, *On the Heavens,* I, 4, 271a33; II, 11, 291b12.

25. Aristotle, *Generation of Animals,* II, 6, 744a35.

26. Aristotle, *Parts of Animals,* II, 16, 659b35; III, 1, 662a18.

27. Ibid., II, 9, 655a23; III, 2, 663a16.

28. Ibid., IV, 5, 681a12.

29. I. Kant, *Critique de la faculté de juger,* intro., §V, trans. A. Philonenko (*Paris, 1968*), p. 30 [in English, Kant, *Critique of Aesthetic Judgment,* trans. J. C. Meredith (Oxford, 1911)—Trans.].

30. See the excellent article by G. Romeyer-Dherby, "Art et nature chez les stoïciens," in M. Augé, C. Castoriadis et al., *La Grèce pour penser l'avenir* (Paris, 2001), pp. 95–104.

31. Diogenes Laertius, VII, 156.

32. Seneca, *On Benefits,* IV, 7.

33. See G. van der Leeuw, *La religion dans son essence et ses manifestations* (Paris, 1970), §17, pp. 142–155 [in English, van der Leeuw, *Religion in Essence and Manifestation,* trans. J. E. Turner (1938; reprint, Princeton, 1986)—Trans.].

34. Pliny the Elder, *Natural History,* XXXVII, 205.

35. See K. Smolak, "Der Hymnus des Mesomedes an die Natur," *Wiener Humanistische Blätter* 29 (1987): 1–14 (Greek text with German translation and commentary).

36. Marcus Aurelius, *Writings for Himself,* IV, 23, 2.

37. Greek text in G. Quandt, *Orphei Hymni* (Berlin, 1955), pp. 10–11. English translation in *Thomas Taylor the Platonist: Selected Writings,* ed. K. Raine and G. M. Harper (Princeton, 1969), pp. 221–223. Greek text, Italian translation, and notes in *Inni Orfici,* ed. G. Ricciardelli (Milan, 2000), pp. 32–35 (with notes pp. 270–279).

38. A. M. Vérilhac, "La déesse Physis dans une épigramme de Salamine de Chypre," *Bulletin de correspondance hellénique* (1972): 427–433.

39. Claudian, *Rape of Persephone*, I, 249. See Ovid, *Metamorphoses*, I, 21: "deus et melior . . . natura."

40. Claudian, *Rape of Persephone*, III, 33.

41. Claudian, *On the Consulship of Stilicho*, II, 424.

42. E. R. Curtius, *Littérature européenne et Moyen Âge latin*, trans. J. Bréjoux (Paris, 1986), chap. 6, §4 [in English, Curtius, *European Literature and the Latin Middle Ages*, trans. W. Trask (Princeton, 1953)—Trans.]. See M. Modersohn, *Natura als Göttin im Mittelalter: Ikonographische Studien zu Darstellungen der personifizierten Natur* (Berlin, 1997).

3. SECRETS OF THE GODS AND SECRETS OF NATURE

1. Alcmeon of Crotona in J.-P. Dumont, *Les présocratiques* (Paris, 1988) (hereafter Dumont), p. 225, fragment 1. For the citation from Homer (*Odyssey*, X, 303).

2. At *Iliad*, XV, 411, Homer speaks of a carpenter who builds while following the advice of Athena. In the *Homeric Hymn to Hermes*, I, 511, Hermes invents the syrinx; and the blacksmithing talents of Hephaestus are well known.

3. That is, Prometheus.

4. Hesiod, *Works and Days*, ll. 42ff.

5. Plato, *Timaeus*, 68d.

6. Seneca, *Natural Questions: On Comets*, IV (VII), 29, 3.

7. See Chapter 11.

8. Cicero, *New Academics*, I, 4, 15.

9. Lucretius, *On Nature*, I, 321.

10. Ibid., III, 29–30.

11. Ibid., I, 71.

12. Ovid, *Metamorphoses*, XV, 63; Silius Italicus, *Punica*, XI, 187.

13. Pliny the Elder, *Natural History*, II, 77.

14. Lucretius, *On Nature*, I, 321.

15. See Celsus, preface to *On Medicine*, 40. See also Chapter 12.

16. Cicero, *Lucullus*, 39, 122.

17. See Chapter 12.

18. Seneca, *Natural Questions*, VII, 30, 4.

19. Seneca, *On Earthquakes*, VI, 3, 1.

20. There is a sketch of this tradition in P. M. Schuhl, "Adèla," *Annales de la faculté des lettres de Toulouse* 1 (1953): 86–94; and in L. Gernet, "Choses visibles et choses invisibles," *Revue philosophique* (1956): 79–87.

21. See P. H. Schrijvers, "Le regard sur l'invisible: Étude sur l'emploi de l'analogie dans l'œuvre de Lucrèce," in *Entretiens sur l'Antiquité classique* 24 (1978): 116–117. For Anaxagoras, see Dumont, p. 680, fragment B21a. For Democritus, see Sextus Empiricus, *Against the Logicians*, I, §140, trans. R. G. Bury (London, 1967), p. 77.

22. H. Diller, "OPSIS ADÉLÔN TA PHAINÓMENA," *Hermes* 67 (1932): 14–42. See also O. Regenbogen, "Eine Forschungsmethode antiker Naturwissenschaft," *Quellen und Studien zur Geschichte der Mathematik* 1, no. 2 (1930): 131ff.; M. Harl, "Note sur les variations d'une formule: Opsis/Pistis tōn Adelōn ta Phainomena," in *Recueil Plassart: Études sur l'Antiquité grecque offerts à André Plassart par ses collègues de la Sorbonne* (Paris, 1976), pp. 105–117.

23. See Aristotle, *On the Soul*, I, 1, 402b20–25. See also I. Düring, *Aristoteles* (Heidelberg, 1966), p. 572.

24. Seneca, *Natural Questions*, VII, 30, 4.

25. W. Eamon, *Science and the Secrets of Nature: Books of Secrets in Medieval and Early Modern Culture* (Princeton, 1994).

26. A.-J. Festugière, *La Révélation d'Hermès Trismégiste*, vol. 1, (1950; reprint, Paris, 1990), p. 196.

27. See Chapter 9.

28. B. Pascal, "Fragment d'un Traité du vide," in *Pensées et opuscules*, ed. L. Brunschvicq (Paris, 1974), p. 78.

29. P. Gassendi, *Syntagma*, I, 68b, cited by W. Detel, *Scientia rerum natura occultarum: Methodologische Studien zur Physik Pierre Gassendis* (Berlin, 1978), p. 65, n. 78. For Cicero, see note 16.

4. HERACLITUS' APHORISM AND ALLEGORICAL EXEGESIS

1. See P. Hadot, *The Inner Citadel: The Meditations of Marcus Aurelius*, trans. M. Chase (Cambridge, Mass., 1998), pp. 141–142, citing Euripides, *Tragoediae*, vol. 3, ed. A. Nauck (Leipzig, 1912), p. 249, fragment 890.

2. In the Greek text, É. des Places rightly adopts the correction

[a]saphestera (instead of *saphestera*) by R. Reitzenstein, *Poimandres* (Leipzig, 1904), p. 164 (accepted by O. Kern, *Orphicorum fragmenta*, 2nd ed. [Berlin, 1963], p. 316, and K. Mras, *Eusebius Werke*, vol. 8, 1 [Berlin, 1954], p. 106), but he translates this as "more clear," whereas the adopted correction should have been translated as "more obscure."

3. This text is most easily found in Eusebius of Caesarea, *Praeparatio evangelica* III, 1, 1, ed. É. des Places, trans. G. Favrelle, Eusèbe de Césarée, *La Préparation évangélique*, vol. 2 (Paris, 1976), p. 141 (translation modified). On this text, see J. Pépin, *Mythe et allégorie* (Paris, 1958), p. 184; O. Casel, *De Philosophorum Graecorum Silentio Mystico* (Giessen, 1919), pp. 88–93; J. G. Griffiths, "Allegory in Greece and Egypt," *Journal of Egyptian Archaeology* 53 (1967): 79–102; F. Wehrli, *Zur Geschichte der allegorischen Deutung Homers im Altertum* (Leipzig, 1927); F. Buffière, *Les mythes d'Homère et la pensée grecque* (Paris, 1956); see also A. Le Boulluec, "L'allégorie chez les stoïciens," *Poétique* 23 (1975): 301–321, a very important article that resituates Stoic allegory within the Stoic theory on language.

4. É. Bréhier, *Chrysippe et l'ancien stoïcisme* (Paris, 1951), p. 201.

5. On this papyrus, see W. Burkert, "La genèse des choses et des mots: Le papyrus de Derveni entre Anaxagore et Cratyle," *Études philosophiques* 25 (1970): 443–455; P. Boyancé, "Remarques sur le papyrus de Derveni," *Revue des études grecques* 87 (1974): 91–110; *Le papyrus de Derveni*, trans. F. Jourdan (Paris, 2003).

6. Xenocrates, fragment 15, trans. R. Heinze in Xenokrates, *Darstellung der Lehre und Sammlung der Fragmente* (Leipzig, 1892); Aristotle, *Movement of Animals*, IV, 699b ff.

7. *Stoicum Veterum Fragmenta*, ed. H. von Arnim, 4 vols. (Leipzig, 1905–1924) (hereafter *SVF*), vol. 2, §910.

8. *SVF*, vol. 2, §1074 (Origen, *Against Celsus*, IV, 48).

9. Cicero, *On the Nature of the Gods*, I, 15, 41.

10. Ibid., III, 24, 63.

11. Diogenes Laertius, VII, 147.

12. Seneca, *Letters to Lucilius*, IX, 16.

13. *SVF*, vol. 1, §538; vol. 2, §§42 and 1008.

14. Strabo, *Geography*, X, 3, 9, trans. F. Lasserre (Paris, 1971), p. 68.

15. Philo, *Legum Allegoriae*, I, §§63–68, on Genesis 2:10–14.

16. R. Goulet, *La philosophie de Moïse: Essai de reconstitution d'un commentaire philosophique préphilonien du Pentateuque* (Paris, 1987).

17. Genesis 18:1–2.

18. Philo, *Quaestiones in Genesim,* IV, 1. Instead of citing this translation, I have preferred to give a version that is closer to the Latin text, which is, by the way, itself only a translation from the Armenian.

19. Philo, *De fuga,* §§178–179.

20. The aphorism is also cited at *De mutatione nominum,* §60.

21. Ibid., §60–76.

22. Philo, *De somniis,* I, §6.

23. Lactantius, *Divine Institutions,* III, 28, 14. For the moderns (Florian, Voltaire), see the article "Puits" in *Le Grand Robert.* See also, for instance, G. de Maupassant, quoted by J. Salem, *Démocrite* (Paris, 1996), p. 161, n. 1.

24. Democritus in J.-P. Dumont, *Les présocratiques* (Paris, 1988), p. 873, fragment 177.

25. An analogous formula can be found in the *Chaldaean Oracles,* ed. É. des Places, fragment 183: "The true [*atrekes*] lies in the deep." See F. W. Cremer, *Die chaldäischen Orakel und Iamblich de mysteriis* (Meisenheim am Glan, 1969), p. 56, n. 2.

26. Cicero, *Lucullus,* X, 32.

27. Seneca, *Natural Questions,* VII, 32, 4. See also *On Benefits,* VII, 1, 5: "Truth is wrapped up and hidden in the abyss." Nature and Truth were already closely linked in Aristotle's *Protreptic;* see I. Düring, "Aristotle on Ultimate Principles from Nature and Reality," in *Aristotle and Plato in the Mid-Fourth Century* (Göteborg, 1960), pp. 35–55.

28. On this question, see Goulet, *La philosophie de Moïse,* pp. 36–37, 544–545.

29. Philo, *De Abrahamo,* §§52, 200.

30. For instance, in Marius Victorinus, *Adversus Arium,* II, 3, 49, trans. P. Hadot, in *Traités théologiques sur la Trinité,* vol. 1 (Paris, 1960), pp. 404–405.

31. Philo, *De Abrahamo,* §236. On the meaning of *pragma* in Philo, see P. Hadot, "Sur divers sens du mot *pragma* dans la tradition philosophique grecque," in *Concepts et catégories dans la pensée antique,* ed. P. Aubenque (Paris, 1980), pp. 309–320, esp. pp. 311–312 (reprinted in P. Hadot, *Études de philosophie ancienne* [Paris, 1998], pp. 61–76, esp. p. 64).

5. "Nature Loves to Wrap Herself Up"

1. This passage from Porphyry's lost commentary on Plato's *Republic* can be reconstituted by comparing Macrobius, *Commentary on Scipio's Dream*, I, 2, 3–21, ed. and trans. M. Armisen-Marchetti (Paris, 2001), and notes to the text; with Proclus, *Commentary on the Republic*, ed. W. Kroll, vol. 2 (1901; reprint, Amsterdam, 1965), pp. 105, 23–107, 14, and the translation by A.-J. Festugière, vol. 3 (Paris, 1970), pp. 47–50, with notes.

2. A.-J. Festugière, *Épicure et ses dieux* (Paris, 1946), pp. 102–103 [in English, Festugière, *Epicurus and His Gods*, trans. C. W. Chilton (Oxford, 1955)—Trans.].

3. This division of myths, which is found in Macrobius, although it is not mentioned by Proclus, seems to me to have been established by Porphyry (in particular because it brings up the Pythagorean symbols and the theogonies of Hesiod and Orpheus). If Macrobius speaks of Petronius and Apuleius, it is because he maintains a certain independence with regard to his source.

4. See Porphyry, *Life of Pythagoras*, §42, trans. É. des Places (Paris, 1982), p. 55.

5. These texts are taken from Macrobius, *Commentary on Scipio's Dream*, I, 2, 3–21 (Armisen-Marchetti); the translation is my own. As I said earlier, this passage from Porphyry's lost commentary on Plato's *Republic* can be reconstituted by comparing Macrobius with Proclus, *Commentary on the Republic*, vol. 2, pp. 105, 23–107, 14 (Kroll); vol. 3, pp. 47–50 (Festugière). When he classifies Plotinus' *Enneads* according to the parts of philosophy, Porphyry (*Life of Plotinus*, §§24ff.) distinguishes ethics (*Enneads*, I); physics, which deals with the world (*Enneads*, II and III); and with souls, that is, the Soul of the world and individual souls (*Enneads*, IV); and finally higher theology, which deals with the Good, the Intellect, and the Soul that has - remained within the intelligible world (*Enneads*, V–VI). According to Macrobius' text, lower theology refers to the Soul of the world and to individual souls; that is, to the ontological level of *Enneads*, IV.

6. See P. Hadot, "Ouranos, Kronos, and Zeus in Plotinus' Treatise against the Gnostics," in *Neoplatonism and Early Christian Thought: Essays in Honour of A. H. Armstrong*, ed. H. J. Blumenthal and R. A. Markus (London, 1981), pp. 124–137.

7. An allusion to Heraclitus' aphorism.

8. Macrobius, *Commentary on Scipio's Dream,* I, 2, 13–17 (see the parallel passage in Proclus, *Commentary on the Republic,* vol. 3, p. 50 (Festugière).

9. Plato, *Timaeus,* 48c.

10. J. Mittelstrass, *Die Rettung der Phänomene* (Berlin, 1962), p. 129.

11. See the definition of Nature in Proclus, *Commentary on the Timaeus,* trans. A.-J. Festugière, vol. 1 (Paris, 1966–1968), pp. 35–40.

12. *Letter to Anebo,* 12, Greek text and Italian trans. in Porfirio, *Lettera ad Anebo,* ed. A. R. Sodano (Naples, 1958), pp. 25, 1–2. See J. Pépin, *Mythe et allégorie* (Paris, 1958), p. 465.

13. On the difference between Stoic and Neoplatonic allegorical methods, see W. Bernard, "Zwei verschiedene Methoden der Allegorese in der Antike," *Wolfenbütteler Forschungen,* vol. 75, *Die Allegorese des antiken Mythos,* ed. H.-J. Horn and H. Walter (Wiesbaden, 1997), pp. 63–83.

6. Calypso, or "Imagination with the Flowing Veil"

1. Macrobius, *Commentary on Scipio's Dream,* I, 2, 20, ed. and trans. M. Armisen-Marchetti (Paris, 2001), p. 9. For the text, see the next chapter.

2. See Plotinus, *Treatise,* 38 (VI, 7), 8–14, trans. P. Hadot in Plotin, *Traité* (Paris, 1988); see also the introduction, pp. 31–36.

3. Porphyry, *Sententiae,* §29, ed. E. Lamberz (Leipzig, 1975), p. 19.

4. I will not go into the details here of the demonstration I have developed elsewhere (P. Hadot, *Porphyre et Victorinus,* vol. 1 [Paris, 1968], pp. 187; 197, n. 7; 332, n. 8), which allows us to reconstitute the theory of the imaginative body in Porphyry. Already in 1913, J. Bidez (*Vie de Porphyre* [Hildesheim, 1964], p. 89, n. 1) had sketched its general outlines. See also I. Hadot, *Le problème du néoplatonisme alexandrin* (Paris, 1984), pp. 100–101. Chapter 29 of Porphyry's *Sententiae* specifies that the ethereal body corresponds to the rational soul and the solar body to the imagination. Synesius, however, inspired by Porphyry, affirms that the imagination is the soul's first body. For our present purposes it suffices to accept that the imagination is defined as the soul's body.

5. Synesius, *Treatise on Dreams*, 5, Greek text and Italian translation by D. Susanetti in Sinesio di Cirene, *I sogni* (Bari, 1992), p. 53.

6. A. Sheppard, "The Mirror of Imagination: The Influence of Timaeus 70e ff.," in *Ancient Approaches to Plato's "Timaeus,"* Bulletin of the Institute of Classical Studies, Supplement 78–2003 (University of London, Institute of Classical Studies), pp. 203–212, shows that this image is based on *Timaeus* 71e.

7. Concerning Proclus, see A. Charles, "L'imagination miroir de l'âme selon Proclus," in *Le néoplatonisme* (Paris, 1971), pp. 241–251.

8. Macrobius, *Commentary on Scipio's Dream*, I, 11, 11–12, 65 (Armisen-Marchetti); in fact, Macrobius is reporting the common opinion of the Platonists, and therefore of Porphyry; see Porphyry, *Sententiae*, §29.

9. See Chapter 1.

10. Greek text in L. G. Westerink, *The Greek Commentaries on Plato's Phaedo*, vol. 1, *Olympiodoros* (Amsterdam, 1976), 6, 2, p. 96. Westerink believes that the formula "imagination of the flowing veil" might come from a Cynic (Crates the Cynic) or from Timon of Phlion. In any event, he points out a possible parallel with Porphyry, *Sententiae*, §40, p. 48, 7 (Lamberz), where imagination and veil *(kalumma)* are linked. On the link between myth and human imagination, see Olympiodorus, *In Gorgiam* (Leipzig, 1970), p. 237, 14; p. 239, 19 (Westerink).

11. See Chapter 2. In fact, in the *Odyssey*, V, 43ff., Hermes or reason does indeed come to the aid of Odysseus, Calypso's prisoner; on this occasion, however, he does not use the plant *molu*, which serves to neutralize Circe's spells.

12. Macrobius, *Commentary on Scipio's Dream*, I, 2, 17, p. 8 (Armisen-Marchetti).

13. R. Klein, "L'imagination comme vêtement de l'âme chez Marsile Ficin et Giordano Bruno," in *La forme et l'intelligible* (Paris, 1970), pp. 65–88.

14. Macrobius, *Commentary on Scipio's Dream*, I, 2, 18–19, p. 9 (Armisen-Marchetti).

15. Iamblichus, *Life of Pythagoras*, 17, §75, intro. and trans. L. Brisson and A.-Ph. Segonds (Paris, 1996), p. 43, alludes to the prohibition against divulging the mysteries of the Eleusinian divinities.

16. The text by William of Conches may be found in P. Dronke, *Fabula:*

Explorations into the Uses of Myth in Medieval Platonism (Leiden and Cologne, 1974), p. 75.

   17. F. J. E. Raby, "*Nuda Natura* and Twelfth-Century Cosmology," *Speculum* 43 (1968): 72–77.

   18. See Chapters 19 and 22.

   19. E. Panofsky, *Essais d'iconologie* (Paris, 1967), pp. 223–233 [in English, Panofsky, *Studies in Iconology: Humanistic Themes in the Art of the Renaissance* (New York, 1972)—Trans.]; E. Wind, *Mystères païens de la Renaissance* (Paris, 1992), pp. 157–166 [in English, Wind, *Pagan Mysteries in the Renaissance* (London, 1958)—Trans.].

   20. E. Panofksy, *La Renaissance et ses avant-couriers dans l'art d'Occident* (Paris, 1976), pp. 194–195 [in English, Panofsky, *Renaissance and Renascences in Western Art* (New York, 1972)—Trans.].

   21. See W. Kemp, "Natura: Ikonographische Studien zur Geschichte und Verbreitung einer Allegorie" (dissertation, University of Tübingen, 1973), p. 19.

   22. Cited by Proclus, *Commentary on the Timaeus*, ed. E. Diehl, vol. 1, p. 395, 10; translation after A.-J. Festugière's in Proclus, *Commentaire sur le Timée*, vol. 2 (Paris, 1966–1968), p. 265.

   23. Plotinus, *Enneads*, III, 8 [30], 2, 3–6.

   24. Porphyry, *On the Animation of the Embryo*, pp. 452, 6ff. (Kalbfleisch), after the trans. by A.-J. Festugière, *La Révélation d'Hermès Trismégiste*, vol. 2, p. 277.

   25. An interesting overview of this tradition may be found in A. Faivre, "L'imagination créatrice (fonction magique et fonction mythique de l'image)," *Revue d'Allemagne* 13 (1981): 355–390.

   26. See Montaigne, "On the Force of Imagination," in *Essays*, bk. 1, chap. 21; on Paracelsus, see A. Koyré, *Mystiques, spirituels et alchimistes du XVIe siècle allemand* (Paris, 1955), p. 58; on Bruno, see Klein, "L'imagination," pp. 74ff.; on Boehme, see A. Koyré, *La philosophie de Jacob Boehme* (Paris, 1929), 2nd ed. (Paris, 1978), p. 263; on Novalis and Baader, see Faivre, "L'imagination créatrice," pp. 375–382; Novalis, *Le brouillon général* (Paris, 2000), p. 215, §826: "The imagination is . . . an extramechanical force."

   27. R. Bacon, *Opus Tertium*, ed. Brewer (London, 1959), pp. 95–96.

   28. See Faivre, "L'imagination créatrice."

29. J. W. von Goethe, *Elective Affinities*, in *Romans* (Paris, 1954), pp. 219, 337.

30. See Chapter 10.

31. See Koyré, *La philosophie de Jacob Boehme*, pp. 214, 218, 481.

7. The Genius of Paganism

1. Macrobius, *Commentary on Scipio's Dream*, I, 2, 20, ed. and trans. M. Armisen-Marchetti (Paris, 2001), p. 9. For Numenius, see Chapter 6.

2. In Proclus, *Commentary on the Republic*, in Kroll, vol. 2, p. 107, 8; trans. A.-J. Festugière, 3 vols. (Paris, 1970), 3:50. Festugière shows that this passage derives from Porphyry (p. 49, n. 3).

3. Iamblichus, *The Mysteries of Egypt*, VI, 7, ed. and trans. É. des Places (Paris, 1966), p. 248, 11ff., according to the marginal numbering (translation modified) [in English, Iamblichus, *De mysteriis*, trans. E. C. Clarke, J. M. Dillon, and J. P. Hershbell (Leiden, 2004)—Trans.]. On the secrets of Abydos, see the commentary by des Places (p. 186, n. 2). According to ancient Egyptian tradition, it was at Abydos, a town in Upper Egypt, that the body of Osiris had been buried.

4. See F. W. Cremer, *Die chaldäischen Orakel und Jamblich De mysteriis* (Meisenheim am Glan, 1969), p. 13, n. 49, who thinks that these conceptions were influenced by the *Chaldaean Oracles*.

5. Porphyry, *On Abstinence from Animal Food*, II, 49, trans. J. Bouffartigue and M. Patillon (Paris, 1979), p. 114 [in English, Porphyry, *On Abstinence from Killing Animals*, trans. G. Clark (London, 2000)—Trans.].

6. A translation of most of the speech may be found in G. Dagron, "L'Empire romain d'Occident au IVe siècle et les traditions politiques de l'hellénisme: Le témoignage de Thémistios," in *Travaux et Mémoires*, vol. 3 (Paris, 1968), pp. 168–172 (p. 170).

7. Themistius, *To Jovian, on the Occasion of His Consulate*, 69b3, ed. W. Dindorf (1832; reprint, Hildesheim, 1961), pp. 82, 10. See also the *Discourse on Religions*, 159b, ibid., p. 194.

8. Homer, *Iliad*, II, 400.

9. A proverbial expression; see Plato, *Sophist*, 226a, who cites the proverb "You won't take it with one hand," meaning that you must use all your strength for the task.

10. Plato, *Timaeus*, 28c.

11. The Latin text may be read in Prudentius, *Psychomachia: Contra Symmachum,* trans. Lavarenne, Prudence, *Psychomachie: Contre Symmaque* (Paris, 1963), p. 110 *(Relatio Symmachi, §10)*.

12. Plotinus, *Enneads,* II, 9 [33], 9, 35.

13. Julian, *Against Heracleios,* 11, 217b–d [in English, *The Works of the Emperor Julian,* trans. W. C. Wright, vol. 2 (London and Cambridge, Mass., 1913)—Trans.].

14. See also Proclus, *Commentary on the Republic,* vol. 1, p. 81, 12 (Kroll); vol. 1, pp. 97–98 (Festugière); and vol. 1, p. 84, 26 (Kroll); vol. 1, p. 101 (Festugière).

15. Julian, *Against Heracleios,* 12, 217c, p. 60.

16. Julian, *Discourse on King Helios,* 28, 148a–b.

17. In Plato, *Phaedrus,* 265b, telestic delirium is related to Dionysos. See I. Hadot, "Die Stellung des neuplatonikers Simplikios zum Verhältnis der Philosophie zu Religion und Theurgie," in *Metaphysik und Religion: Akten des internationalen Kongresses vom 13–17 März 2001 in Würzburg,* ed. Th. Kobusch and M. Erler (Munich and Leipzig, 2002), p. 325, citing Hierocles, *Commentary on the Golden Verses,* XXVI, 26, in *Hieroclis in aureum Pythagoreorum carmen commentarius,* ed. F. G. Köhler (Stuttgart, 1974), p. 118, 10. In the translation by Mario Meunier (Hiéroclès, *Commentaire sur les Vers d'Or des pythagoriciens* [Paris, 1979], p. 330), "telestics" is replaced by "initiatory."

18. See H. Lewy, *Chaldaean Oracles and Theurgy* (Paris, 1978), pp. 252–254.

19. Julian, *Against Heracleios,* 11, 216c, p. 61; cf. Hermias, *Commentary on the Phaedrus,* ed. P. Couvreur (Paris, 1901), p. 87, 6.

20. P. Boyancé, "Théurgie et télestique néoplatoniciennes," *Revue de l'histoire des religions,* no. 147 (1955): 189–209.

See Proclus, *Commentary on the Timaeus,* in *Procli Diadachi in Platonis Timaeum, commentaria,* ed. E. Diehl, 3 vols. (Leipzig, 1903–1906), 1:273, 10; trans. A.-J. Festugière, 5 vols. (Paris, 1966–1968), 2:117. On this subject, see Hadot, "Die Stellung des neuplatonikers Simplikios," p. 327.

21. See C. van Liefferinge, *La théurgie des Oracles Chaldaïques à Proclus* (Liège, 1999), p. 268.

22. Boyancé ("Théurgie et télestique néoplatoniciennes") believes that this is an Orphic tradition.

23. Varro in Augustine, *City of God*, VII, 5; Plotinus, *Enneads*, IV 3 [27], 11.

24. On this subject, see the texts by Hierocles (*Commentary on the Golden Verses*, XXVI, 7, 21 and 24, pp. 113–117), in the translation with commentary by I. Hadot, intro. to Simplicius, *Commentaire sur le Manuel d'Épictète* (Paris, 2001), pp. clii–clvi.

25. Julian, *Against Heracleios*, 12, 217d, p. 61.

26. Proclus, *Commentary on the Republic*, vol. 2, p. 108 (Kroll); vol. 3, p. 51 (Festugière).

27. Ibid., vol. 1, p. 82 (Kroll); vol. 1, p. 98 (Festugière).

28. F. Nietzsche, preface to *Beyond Good and Evil*, in *Œuvres philosophiques complètes*, 14 vols. (Paris, 1974–), 17:18 [in English, Nietzsche, *Beyond Good and Evil*, ed. R. P. Hostmann, trans. J. Norman (Cambridge, 2002)—Trans.].

8. The "Gods of Greece"

1. See Chapters 4–6.

2. J. Seznec, *La survivance des dieux antiques: Essai sur le rôle de la tradition mythologique dans l'humanisme et dans l'art de la Renaissance* (1940; reprint, Paris, 1980) [in English, Seznec, *The Survival of the Pagan Gods: The Mythological Tradition and Its Place in Renaissance Humanism and Art*, trans. B. F. Sessions (1972; reprint, Princeton, 1995)—Trans.]. See the critique by E. Garin, *Moyen Âge et Renaissance* (Paris, 1969), pp. 56–73.

3. M.-D. Chenu, "La notion d'involucrum: Le mythe selon les théologiens médiévaux," *Archives d'histoire doctrinale et littéraire du Moyen Âge* 22 (1955): 75–79. See also P. Dronke, *Fabula: Explorations into the Uses of Myth in Medieval Platonism* (Leiden and Cologne, 1974), p. 56, n. 2.

4. B. Silvestris, *Commentary on Martianus Capella*, in É. Jeauneau, *Lectio Philosophorum: Recherches sur l'école de Chartres* (Amsterdam, 1973), p. 40. See also, in the same work by Jeauneau, the chapter titled "L'usage de la notion d'integumentum à travers les gloses de Guillaume de Conches," pp. 127–192. See also Abelard, *Introductio in Theologiam*, I, 19, *PL* 178, cols. 1021–23.

5. Plato, *Timaeus*, 22c.

6. Jeauneau, "L'usage de la notion d'integumentum," p. 155.

7. Ibid., p. 152.

8. J. Pépin, *La tradition de l'allégorie* (Paris, 1987), p. 278.

9. On these metaphors, see E. R. Curtius, *Littérature européenne et Moyen Âge latin,* trans. J. Bréjoux (Paris, 1986), chap. 16, §7. See also H. Blumenberg, "Gottes Bücher stimmen überein," in *Die Lesbarkeit der Welt* (Frankfurt, 1981), pp. 68–85.

10. Latin text in Dronke, *Fabula,* pp. 74–75.

11. E. Wind, *Mystères païens de la Renaissance* (Paris, 1992), p. 179, n. 51.

12. Ibid., pp. 29–37.

13. P. Hadot, *Histoire des religions,* vol. 2 (1972; reprint, Paris, 2001), p. 96 (see also P. Hadot, *Études de philosophie ancienne* [Paris, 1998], p. 357).

14. See F. Masai, *Pléthon et le platonisme de Mistra* (Paris, 1956). On Pletho and the *Chaldaean Oracles,* see B. Tambrun Krasker, *Oracles chaldaïques: Recension de Gémisthe Pléthon* (Athens, Paris, and Brussels, 1995).

15. A. Chastel, *Marsile Ficin et l'art* (Paris, 1954), pp. 136–156.

16. Garin, *Moyen Âge et Renaissance,* p. 68.

17. Seznec, *La survivance des dieux antiques,* p. 222.

18. On this subject, see C.-H. Lemmi, *The Classical Deities in Bacon: A Study in Mythological Symbolism* (Baltimore, 1933).

19. Translation based on that of R. d'Harcourt, *Schiller: Poèmes philosophiques* (Paris, 1954). See the highly interesting article by W. Theiler, "Der Mythos und die Götter Griechenlands," in *Mélanges W. Wili: Horizonte der Humanitas* (Bern, 1960), pp. 15–36 (reprinted in W. Theiler, *Untersuchungen zur antiken Literatur* [Berlin, 1970], pp. 130–147), who studies Schiller's poem in the perspective of W. Otto's theory of myth.

20. Am[m]athus is a town on the south coast of the island of Cyprus where there was a temple of Venus. Theiler, "Der Mythos und die Götter Griechenlands," p. 34, n. 59, is correct in believing that Schiller found this Venus in Ovid, *Amores,* III, 15, 15: "Culte puer puerique parens Amathusia culti" (Lovable child [i.e., Cupid], and you, goddess of Amantha, mother of this lovable child).

21. A soul was attributed to that which has no soul.

22. In his book *Taille de l'homme* (Paris, 1935), pp. 34–44, C.-F. Ramuz, on the occasion of a mountain excursion, evokes the goddesses and the nymphs of the torrent as if he could see them.

23. The moon.

24. Theiler, "Der Mythos und die Götter Griechenlands," p. 27.

25. A sacred mountain and place of poetry.

26. Firmicus Maternus, *On the Errors of Profane Religions*, III, 2 and VIII, 1, ed. R. Turcan (Paris, 1982), pp. 82–83, 96–97 [in English, Firmicus, *The Error of the Pagan Religions*, trans. C. A. Forbes (New York, 1970)—Trans.].

27. Cited by H. Blumenberg, *Paradigmen zu einer Metaphorologie*, 2nd ed. (Frankfurt, 1999), pp. 104–105.

28. See J. Bernauer, *"Schöne Welt, wo bist du?"*: *Über das Verhältnis von Lyrik und Poetik bei Schiller* (Berlin, 1995), pp. 105–117.

29. Kl. Schneider, *Die schweigenden Götter* (Hildesheim, 1966), esp. pp. 1–12 and 100–103. See also K. Borinski, *Die Antike in Poetik und Kunsttheorie*, vol. 2 (1924; reprint, Darmstadt, 1965), pp. 199–318 ("Antiker Naturidealismus in Deutschland bis Herder"); E. M. Butler, *The Tyranny of Greece over Germany* (London, 1935). I alluded to these problems in my introduction to E. Bertram, *Nietzsche: Essai de mythologie* (Paris, 1990), p. 30.

30. F. Hölderlin, "Bread and Wine," stanza 8 [in English, Hölderlin, *Poems and Fragments*, trans. M. Hamburger (Ann Arbor, 1967)—Trans.].

31. See Chapter 21.

32. F. Hölderlin, *The Death of Empedocles* (1st version).

33. F. Hölderlin, *Hyperion*.

34. See Chapter 21.

9. PROMETHEUS AND ORPHEUS

1. Cicero, *New Academic Books*, I, 4, 15. See also *Tusculans*, V, 4, 10.

2. See Chapters 12 and 22.

3. Cicero, *New Academic Books*, I, 5, 19.

4. Hippocrates, *On Art*, XII, 3, ed. and trans. J. Jouanna (Paris, 1990), p. 240, with the editor's excellent notes; see also Th. Gomperz, *Die Apologie der Heilkunst* (Vienna, 1890), p. 140.

5. See J. Liebig, "Francis Bacon von Verulam und die Geschichte der Naturwissenschaften" (1863), reprinted in J. Liebig, *Reden und Abhandlungen* (Leipzig, 1874), p. 223, quoted in H. Blumenberg, *La légitimité des Temps modernes* (Paris, 1999), p. 439 [in English, Blumenberg, *The Legitimacy of the Modern World*, trans. R. M. Wallace (Cambridge, Mass., 1983)—Trans.].

340 Notes to Pages 93–96

6. F. Bacon, *Novum Organum*, I, §98, trans. M. Malherbe and J.-M. Pousseur (Paris, 1986) [in English, Bacon, *The New Organon*, ed. L. Jardine and M. Silverthorne (Cambridge and New York, 2000)—Trans.].

7. Genesis 1:28.

8. Bacon, *Novum Organum*, I, §129.

9. I. Kant, *Critique of Pure Reason*, trans. A. Tremesaygues and B. Pacaud, 1st ed. (Paris, 1944), p. 17 [in English, *Immanuel Kant's Critique of Pure Reason*, trans. N. K. Smith (New York, 1929)—Trans.].

10. Cited by Blumenberg, *Paradigmen zu einer Metaphorologie*, p. 45, who gives no reference.

11. Bacon, *Novum Organum*, I, §129; E. Garin, *Moyen Âge et Renaissance* (Paris, 1969), p. 145.

12. R. Lenoble, *Histoire de l'idée de nature* (Paris, 1969), p. 121.

13. Aeschylus, *Prometheus Bound*, ll. 445–506; Plato, *Protagoras*, 320–322. On the history of the myth of Prometheus, see O. Raggio, "The Myth of Prometheus: Its Survival and Metamorphoses up to the Eighteenth Century," *Journal of the Warburg and Courtauld Institutes* (1958): 44–62; J. Duchemin, *Prométhée: Le mythe et ses origines* (Paris, 1974); R. Trousson, *Le thème de Prométhée dans la littérature européenne*, 2 vols. (Geneva, 1964), 2nd ed. (1978). Lenoble, *Histoire de l'idée de nature*, p. 120, applies the label "Promethean" to Lucretius' attitude with regard to nature—wrongly, I believe. See Chapter 12.

14. Trousson, *Le thème de Prométhée*, p. 115.

15. Descartes, *Discours de la méthode*, VI, §62, in *Œuvres philosophiques*, ed. F. Alquié, vol. 1 (Paris, 1963), p. 364 [cf. Descartes, *Discours de la méthode: Pour bien conduire sa raison et chercher la verité dans les sciences/Discourse on the Method: Of Conducting One's Reason Well and of Seeking the Truth in the Sciences*, ed. and trans. G. Heffernan (Notre Dame, 1994)—Trans.].

16. Lenoble, *Histoire de l'idée de nature*, p. 323.

17. P. de Ronsard, "Hymne à l'Éternité: À Madame Marguerite, sœur du Roi." The text may be found, for instance, in Ronsard, *Œuvres complètes*, vol. 8, *Les Hymnes* (1555–1556), ed. P. Laumonier (Paris, 1936), p. 246.

18. R. M. Rilke, *Sonnets to Orpheus*, I, 3.

19. See Chapter 14.

20. See F. Graf, *Eleusis und die orphische Dichtung: Athens in vorhellenistischer Zeit* (Berlin, 1974).

21. F. Nietzsche, preface to *Le gai savoir*, 2nd ed., in *Œuvres philosophiques complètes*, 14 vols. (Paris, 1974–), 5:27 [in English, Nietzsche, *The Gay Science*, trans. W. Kaufmann (New York, 1974)—Trans.].

22. C. Ginzburg, "High and Low: The Theme of Forbidden Knowledge in the Sixteenth and Seventeenth Centuries," *Past and Present* 73 (1976): 28–41.

23. See Chapter 14.

24. Ginzburg, "High and Low," p. 40. This motto is taken from Horace, *Epistles*, I, 2, 40.

25. See F. Venturi, "Was ist Aufklärung? Sapere aude!" *Rivista storica italiana* 71 (1959): 119–130; and idem, *Utopia and Reform in the Enlightenment* (Cambridge, 1971), pp. 5–9 (cited in Ginzburg, "High and Low," p. 41, n. 47).

26. This is, moreover, the meaning of Saint Paul's "Noli altum sapere" (Romans 11:20), which is at the origin of the motto "Be not proud."

27. Descartes, *Discourse on Method*, VI, §61, p. 634 (Alquié).

10. MECHANICS AND MAGIC FROM ANTIQUITY TO THE RENAISSANCE

1. Antiphon the Tragedian (late fifth–early fourth century BCE) in B. Snell, *Tragicorum Graecorum Fragmenta*, vol. 1 (Göttingen, 1971), pp. 195–196, fragment 4.

2. To my knowledge, there exists no modern translation of the *Mechanical Problems*. For a critical edition, see the Italian edition by M. E. Bottechia, Aristotele, *Mechanica* (Padua, 1982). See also the text by Pappus of Alexandria, *Mathematical Collection*, VIII, 1–2, cited in translation by G. E. R. Lloyd, *Une histoire de la science grecque* (Paris, 1990), pp. 282–283 [see, in English, Lloyd, *Early Greek Science: Thales to Aristotle* (New York and London, 1970); and idem, *Greek Science after Aristotle* (New York and London, 1973), both in the Ancient Culture and Society series—Trans.].

3. B. Gille, *Les mécaniciens grecs: La naissance de la technologie* (Paris, 1980), p. 222, citing Philo of Byzantium's *Belopoiika* (Throwing-Machines), IV, 77, 15.

4. F. Bacon, *Novum Organum*, I, §129.

5. Simplicius, *Commentary on the Physics*, ed. H. Diels, vol. 1 (Berlin, 1882), p. 4, 8ff.

6. Plutarch, *Life of Marcellus*, XIV, 9.

7. Gille, *Les mécaniciens grecs*, p. 86.

8. See A. Reymond, *Histoire des sciences exactes et naturelles dans l'Antiquité gréco-romaine* (Paris, 1955), p. 98.

9. Gille, *Les méchaniciens grecs*, pp. 54–82; R. Taton, *La science antique et médiévale* (Paris, 1957), pp. 307–311.

10. There is a bibliography in Gille, *Les mécaniciens grecs*, p. 72.

11. Ibid., pp. 170ff.

12. Plutarch, *Marcellus*, XIV, 10–11.

13. See Seneca, *Letters to Lucilius*, 90, 20–25.

14. See E. J. Dijksterhuis, *Die Mechanizierung des Weltbildes*, 2nd ed. (Berlin, Heidelberg, and New York, 1983), p. 556 [for the English version of the Dutch original, see *The Mechanization of the World Picture*, trans. C. Dikshoorn (Oxford, 1961)—Trans.].

15. Leibniz, *Monadology*, §17, ed. É. Boutroux (Paris, 1970).

16. I borrow this metaphor from the excellent work by J. Salem, *L'atomisme antique* (Paris, 1997), pp. 9, 11, 222.

17. On magical practice, see H. D. Betz, *The Greek Magical Papyri in Translation, Including the Demotic Spells* (Chicago, 1986).

18. A. Abt, *Die Apologie des Apuleius von Madaura und die antike Zauberei* (Giessen, 1908).

19. Augustine, *On the Trinity*, III, 7, 12–8, 15.

20. Ibid., III, 9, 16.

21. Augustine, *City of God*, XXII, 24, 2.

22. Augustine, *On the Trinity*, III, 9, 16. The quotation is from *Book of Wisdom*, 11, 21.

23. For instance, in the *Commentary on the Gospel of John*, IV, 4, 11, trans. É. Jeauneau (Paris, 1972, p. 298); see Jeauneau's note *ad locum*, which cites numerous parallels.

24. In the discussion that follows I make use of my article "L'Amour magician," *Revue philosophique* (1982): 283–292, reprinted in M. Ficin, *Commentaire sur le Traité de l'amour ou Le Festin de Platon*, ed. S. Matton (Paris, 2001), pp. 69–81.

25. Plotinus, *Enneads*, IV, 4 [28], 40, 21.

26. Ibid., 40, 4.

27. Ibid., 41, 3–5.

28. Catullus, *Poems*, 62, 54; Ovid, *Amores*, II, 16, 41: "The elm loves the vine, the vine would not leave the elm."

29. Monique Alexandre points out this interesting passage from Achilles Tatius, *Leucippe and Clitophon*, I, 17 (trans. P. Grimal, in *Romans grecs et latins* [Paris, 1958], p. 891): "Plants are in love with one another, and the palm tree in particular is the most subject to fall in love. It is said that there are male and female palm trees. The male palm tree is in love with the female, and if the female palm tree is planted a certain distance away, its lover wastes away. The gardener then understands what is grieving the tree; he goes up to a high place from which one can see the surrounding countryside, and he notes the direction in which the tree is leaning—for it always leans in the direction of its beloved. When he has discovered it, he cures the tree's illness as follows: he takes a branch of the female palm tree and grafts it onto the heart of the male palm tree, and this gives back life to the tree, and its body, which had been dying, rediscovers its vigor, [and] rights itself under the influence of the joy caused by its union with its beloved. It is a wedding of plants."

30. Plotinus, *Enneads*, IV, 4 [28], 42, 24.

31. Ibid., 42, 25–30.

32. Ibid., 43, 16.

33. "Trahit sua quemque uoluptas": Virgil, *Bucolics*, II, 65.

34. Here we find the same idea as in Plotinus: magic consists above all of natural attractions.

35. Marsilio Ficino, *Commentary on Plato's Symposium*, VI, 10, trans. R. Marcel (Paris, 1956), p. 219; trans. P. Laurens (Paris, 2002), pp. 166–168. My translation is based on these two sources.

36. See C. Zinzten, "Die Wertung von Mystik und Magie in der neu-platonischen Philosophie," *Rheinisches Museum für Philologie* 108 (1965): 91ff.

37. E. Garin, *Moyen Âge et Renaissance* (Paris, 1969), pp. 135ff.

38. See P. Zambelli, "Il problema della magia naturalis nel Rinascimento," *Rivista di Storia della Filosofia* 28 (1973): 271–296. See also D. P. Walker, *Spiritual and Demonic Magic from Ficino to Campanella* (London, 1958).

39. *Asclepius*, §6, in *Corpus Hermeticum*, vol. 2, *Traités XIII–XVIII*, in *Asclepius*, ed. A. D. Nock, trans. A.-J. Festugière (Paris, 1945), pp. 301, 18–19;

cf. Garin, *Moyen Âge et Renaissance*, p. 123; and A. Chastel, *Marsile Ficin et l'art* (Paris, 1954), pp. 60–61.

40. Chastel, *Marsile Ficin et l'art*, p. 118.

41. Ibid., p. 74; and Garin, *Moyen Âge et Renaissance*, p. 142.

42. Marsilio Ficino, *Commentary on the Symposium*, VI, 10, 82v, p. 220 (Marcel): "Quemadmodum in agricultura, natura segetes parit, ars preparat." See Chastel, *Marsile Ficin et l'art*, p. 73.

43. A. Prost, *Les sciences et les arts occultes au XVIᵉ siècle: Corneille Agrippa, sa vie et ses œuvres*, 2. vols. (Paris, 1881–1883).

44. Agrippa von Nettesheim, *De occulta philosophia libri tres*, ed. V. Perrone Compagni (Leiden, 1992), p. 414. Cf. C. Nauert, *Agrippa et la pensée de la Renaissance* (Paris, 2002), p. 236.

45. W. Eamon, *Science and the Secrets of Nature: Books of Secrets in Medieval and Early Modern Culture* (Princeton, 1994), p. 211.

46. See Chapter 3.

47. See, in the collective volume titled *Lumière et Cosmos: Cahiers de l'Hermétisme* (Paris, 1981), pp. 191–306, the essays by A. Faivre, "Magia naturalis" and "Ténèbres, éclair et lumière chez Franz von Baader," as well as those by F. C. Oetinger and G. F. Rösler, with Faivre's commentary.

48. R. Bacon, *De mirabili potestate artis et naturae* (Paris, 1542), fol. 37r.

49. Ibid., fols. 42–45.

50. H. Blumenberg, *La légitimité des temps modernes* (Paris, 1999), p. 428; É. Bréhier, *Histoire de la philosophie*, vol. 1 (Paris, 1991), p. 619.

51. R. Bacon, *Opus Maius*, ed. J. H. Bridges, 3 vols. (Oxford, 1897–1900), 2:221. Cf. R. Carton, *La synthèse doctrinale de R. Bacon* (Paris, 1924), p. 94. See also Garin's reflections on Bacon in *Moyen Âge et Renaissance*, pp. 23–25.

52. R. Taton, *La science antique et médiévale* (Paris, 1994), pp. 637–638. On p. 607 of this work, we find a summary of the *Epistola de Magnete* by P. de Maricourt (Petrus Peregrinus), written "in 1269, beneath the walls of Lucera (perhaps he was there as the military engineer of Charles of Anjou)." Taton writes, "For Pierre de Maricourt, the totality of the celestial sphere acts on the totality of a magnetized needle." See P. Radelet de Grave and D. Speiser, "Le *De Magnete* de Pierre de Maricourt," trans. with commentary in *Revue d'histoire des sciences* (1975): 193–234.

53. B. Gille, *Les ingénieurs de la Renaissance* (Paris, 1967), p. 126.

54. Ibid., pp. 126–135.

55. Dijksterhuis, *Die Mechanisierung des Weltbildes*, p. 284.

56. Taton, *La science antique et médiévale*, pp. 595ff.

11. EXPERIMENTAL SCIENCE AND THE MECHANIZATION OF NATURE

1. Hippocrates, *On Art*, XII, 3, trans. J. Jouanna (Paris, 1990), p. 240.

2. See Chapter 9.

3. See G. E. R. Lloyd, *Une histoire de la science grecque* (Paris, 1990), pp. 193–196.

4. On medical experimentation, see M. D. Grmek, *Le chaudron de Médée: L'expérimentation sur le vivant dans l'Antiquité* (Paris, 1997).

5. Lloyd, *Une histoire de la science grecque*, pp. 328–331.

6. Ibid., p. 359.

7. Grmek, *Le chaudron de Médée*, p. 22; N. Tsouyopoulos, "Die induktive Methode und das Induktionsproblem in der griechischen Philosophie," *Zeitschrift für allgemeine Wissenschaftstheorie* 5 (1974): 94–122.

8. F. Bacon, *Novum Organum*, I, §85, trans. M. Malherbe and J.-M. Pousseur (Paris, 1986), p. 147 [in English, Bacon, *The New Organon*, ed. L. Jardine and M. Silverthorne (Cambridge and New York, 2000)—Trans.].

9. F. Bacon, *Du progrès et de la promotion des savoirs*, trans. M. Le Dœff (Paris, 1991), p. 133 [in English, Bacon, *The Advancement of Learning*, ed. M. Kiernan (Oxford and New York, 2000)—Trans.].

10. See Chapter 10.

11. Bacon, *Novum Organum*, I, §109 (translation slightly modified).

12. Ibid., I, §98, p. 159.

13. See Chapter 9.

14. F. Bacon, *The New Atlantis*, trans. M. Le Dœuff, *La Nouvelle Atlantide* (Paris, 1995), p. 119 [in English, Bacon, *"New Atlantis" and "The Great Instauration,"* ed. J. Weinberger (Arlington Heights, Ill., 1989)—Trans.]. W. Eamon has brought out all the historical significance of the Baconian project in chap. 9 of his book *Science and the Secrets of Nature: Books of Secrets in Medieval and Early Modern Culture* (Princeton, 1994).

15. Bacon, *The New Atlantis*, pp. 119–129.

16. C. Merchant, *The Death of Nature: Women, Ecology, and the Scientific Revolution* (1980; reprint, San Francisco, 1990), pp. 182–183.

17. Ibid., pp. 180–186.

18. Letter to Rivet of March 12, 1644, cited by R. Lenoble, *Mersenne ou La naissance du mécanisme* (Paris, 1943), p. 342.

19. R. Lenoble, *Esquisse d'une histoire de l'idée de nature* (Paris, 1969), pp. 310–312.

20. See Chapters 9 and 18.

21. See Chapter 10.

22. La Rochelle (1563), critical ed. K. Cameron (Geneva, 1988).

23. See Chapter 12.

24. See Chapter 14.

25. Descartes, *Discourse on Method*, VI, §77, in *Œuvres philosophiques*, ed. F. Alquié, vol. 1 (Paris, 1973), p. 649.

26. F. Bacon, *Novum Organum*, I, §61, p. 121; Descartes, *Discourse on Method*, I, §3, p. 568. J. Mittelstrass, *Die Rettung der Phänomene* (Berlin, 1962), p. 199, n. 314, alludes to this aspect of the mechanistic revolution.

27. See Chapter 10.

28. Descartes, *Principles of Philosophy*, IV, §203, in Alquié, *Œuvres philosophiques*, vol. 3, p. 520 [in English, *Selections from the "Principles of Philosophy" of Rene Descartes (1596–1650)*, trans. J. Veitch, http://www.classicallibrary.org/descartes/principles/04.htm—Trans.].

29. For instance, J. Kepler, *Mysterium Cosmographicum*, 16C, trans. A. Segonds under the title *Le secret du monde* (Paris, 1984), p. 13: God has measured all things, like a human architect (see Segonds's note); Leibniz, *Monadology*, §87.

30. Voltaire, *Les cabales*, which can be read together with the commentaries of Voltaire himself in Voltaire, *Œuvres complètes*, ed. M. Beuchot, 14 vols., vol. 3, *Poésies* (Paris, 1834), p. 261.

31. Lucretius, *On Nature*, V, 96; Calcidius, *Commentary on the Timaeus*, §§146, 299, Latin text in *Plato Latinus*, vol. 4, *Timaeus a Calcidio translatus commentarioque instructus*, ed. J. M. Waszink (London and Leiden, 1962), pp. 184, 19; 301, 19. For Lactantius in *Divine Institutions*, IV, 6, 1, God is the *machinator mundi*. On the metaphor of the machine, see H. Blumenberg, *Paradigmen zu einer Metaphorologie* (Frankfurt, 1998), pp. 91–96.

32. N. Oresme, *Le livre du ciel et du monde*, II, 2, ed. A. D. Menut and A. J. Denomy, trans. A. D. Menut (Madison, 1968), p. 282, l. 142. On the metaphor

of the clock, see Blumenberg, *Paradigmen zu einer Metaphorologie*, pp. 103–107.

33. H. Monatholius, *Aristotelis Mechanica, Graece emendata, Latine facta* (Paris, 1599), "Epistola Dedicatoria," fol. a III r.

34. Galileo, *L'essayeur*, trans. C. Chauviré (Paris, 1980), p. 141 [in English, Galileo Galilei, Horatio Grassi, Mario Guiducci, and Johann Kepler, *The Controversy on the Comets of 1618*, trans. S. Drake and C. D. O'Malley (Philadelphia, 1960)—Trans.].

35. A. Baillet, *Vie de Descartes*, vol. 2 (Paris, 1691), p. 352.

36. B. Pascal, "Fragment d'un Traité du vide," in *Pensées et opuscules*, ed. L. Brunschvicq (Paris, 1974), p. 78.

37. See Chapter 19.

38. J. Kepler, *De macula in sole observata*, cited by H. Blumenberg, *La légitimité des temps modernes* (Paris, 1999), p. 430, n. 2.

39. A. van Leeuwenhoek, *Arcana Naturae Detecta* (Delphis Batavorum, 1695). See the chapter devoted to Leeuwenhoek in J. Rostand, *Esquisse d'une histoire de la biologie* (Paris, 1945), pp. 9–41.

40. See Eamon, *Science and the Secrets of Nature*, pp. 296–297.

41. Bacon, *Novum Organum*, II, §52, p. 334.

42. Descartes, *Discourse on Method*, VI, §61, p. 634.

43. *Wisdom*, 11:21.

44. Augustine, *City of God*, XII, 19.

45. Plutarch, *Table-Talk*, VIII, 2, 1, 718b–c.

46. For instance, Voltaire spoke of the "eternal geometer" in his notes to the satire *Les cabales*, p. 262: "He whom Plato called the eternal geometer."

47. See Leibniz, *De rerum originatione radicali*, in *Die philosophischen Schriften von Gottfried Wilhelm Leibnitz*, ed. C. I. Gerhard, vol. 7 (Berlin, 1890), p. 304: "In the radical production [*originatione*] of things, divine mathematics operate."

48. Lenoble, *Histoire de l'idée de nature*, p. 323.

49. See the next section, on theological voluntarism.

50. Descartes, *Principles of Philosophy*.

51. Ibid., IV, §204, p. 521.

52. Ibid.

53. See Chapter 13.

54. Descartes, *Principia Philosophiae*, IV, §205, in *Œuvres de Descartes*, ed. C. Adam and P. Tannery, vol. 8 (Paris, 1964), 1:327: "Certa moraliter, hoc est quantum sufficit ad usum vitae, quamvis, si ad absolutam Dei potentiam referantur, sint incerta."

55. As Goulet communicated to me the invaluable indications contained in the then-unpublished manuscript of his edition and translation of the *Monogenes* of Macarios of Magnesia, a Christian work, by means of which we can reconstruct part of Porphyry's anti-Christian arguments [see R. Goulet, *Macarios de Magnésie: Le Monogénès* (Paris, 2003)—Trans.].

56. Galen, *De usu partium*, XI, 1–4, Greek text with Latin translation in Galen, *Opera omnia*, ed. C. G. Kühn, vol. 3 (1821–1833; reprint, Hildesheim, 1964–65), pp. 905–906. V. Boudon, "Galien et le sacré," *Bulletin de l'Association Guillaume Budé* (December 1988): 334, situates this text within the perspective of Galen's attitude toward the sacred.

57. In *Macarios of Magnesia*, IV, 24, 5; and Didymus the Blind, *Commentary on Job*, X, 3 (papyrus of Tura), ed. U. and I. Hagedorn and L. Koenen (Bonn, 1968), p. 280. See fragment 94 of the collection by A. von Harnack, *Porphyrios' Contra Christianos: Abhandlungen der Königlichen Preussischen Akademie der Wissenschaften, Philosophisch-Historische Klasse* (Berlin, 1916). Goulet points out that the same doctrine can already be found in Pliny the Elder, *Natural History*, II, 27: "He cannot prevent two times ten from being twenty."

58. Descartes, *Œuvres philosophiques*, 1:259–260.

59. M. Mersenne, *Questions théologiques* (Paris, 1634), p. 11, cited by Lenoble, *Mersenne ou La naissance du mécanisme*, p. 357. See chapter 20.

60. Descartes, *Principles of Philosophy*, IV, §204.

61. E. J. Dijksterhuis, *Die Mechanisierung des Weltbildes* (Berlin, Heidelberg, and New York, 1983), IV, §330, p. 549 [in English, Dijksterhuis, *The Mechanization of the World Picture*, trans. C. Dikshoorn (Oxford, 1961)—Trans.].

62. Seneca, *Natural Questions: On Comets*, VII, 29, 3.

63. In her article "Secrets of God, Nature, and Life" (*History of the Human Sciences* 3 [1990]: 229–230), Evelyn Fox Keller has shown in a very interesting way that in the sixteenth and seventeenth centuries the secrets of nature and life represented the domain of secrets that were considered feminine, as opposed to divine secrets, which were considered masculine.

64. B. Pascal, *Pensées*, §77, in *Pensées et opuscules*, p. 360.

65. Dijksterhuis, *Die Mechanisierung des Weltbildes*, IV, §330, p. 549.

66. Cited by A. Koyré, *Du monde clos à l'univers infini* (Paris, 1973), p. 336, where one finds an interesting analysis of this evolution [in English, Koyré, *From the Closed World to the Infinite Universe* (Baltimore, 1968)—Trans.].

67. *Correspondance Leibniz-Clarke*, ed. A. Robinet (Paris, 1957), p. 90 [in English, *The Leibniz-Clarke Correspondence*, ed. H. G. Alexander (New York, 1998)—Trans.]. See Blumenberg, *La légitimité des temps modernes*, p. 162.

68. Merchant, *The Death of Nature*.

69. Descartes, *Traité du monde*, chap. 7, in *Œuvres philosophiques*, 1:349 [in English, Descartes, *The World and Other Writings*, ed. and trans. S. Gaukroger (Cambridge and New York, 1998)—Trans.].

70. R. Boyle, *A Free Inquiry into the Vulgarly Received Notion of Nature* (1686), in *The Works of the Honorable Robert Boyle*, ed. T. Bird, 6 vols., 2nd ed. (1772; reprint, Hildesheim, 1966), 5:174ff.

71. See Chapter 18.

72. See Chapter 19.

12. Criticism of the Promethean Attitude

1. See Chapter 9.

2. On the condemnation but also the rehabilitation of curiosity, see H. Blumenberg, *La légitimité des temps modernes* (Paris, 1999), pp. 257–518.

3. See Chapter 9.

4. Seneca, *Letters to Lucilius*, 88, 36.

5. Seneca, *On Benefits*, VII, 1, 5–6.

6. Epicurus, *Capital Maxims*, XI, in *Épicure: Lettres, maximes, sentences*, trans. J.-F. Balaudé (Paris, 1994), p. 201 [in English, *The Epicurus Reader: Selected Writings and Testimonia*, ed. and trans. B. Inwood and L. P. Gerson (Indianapolis and Chicago, 1994), p. 33—Trans.].

7. Philo, *De migratione Abrahami*, §134.

8. Ibid., §136.

9. Augustine, *Confessions*, X, 35, 54. On Augustine's condemnation of curiosity, see Blumenberg, *La légitimité des temps modernes*, pp. 353–371.

10. See Chapter 11.

11. Xenophon, *Memorabilia*, I, 1, 15.

12. Cicero, *Lucullus*, 39, 122. See Chapter 3.

13. According to M. D. Grmek, *Le chaudron de Médée: L'expérimentation sur le vivant dans l'Antiquité* (Paris, 1997), p. 65, Aristotle "was convinced that the realization of artificial conditions places a natural fact in abnormality and distorts events. If we can spy on nature, we cannot extort secrets from it by constraint." Nevertheless, I cannot see on which precise text this interpretation is based.

14. Celsus, *On Medicine*, preface, §40. On the problem of vivisection, see Grmek, *Le chaudron de Médée*, pp. 135–140; and W. Deuse, "Celsus im Prooemium von 'De Medecina': Römische Aneignung griechischer Wissenschaft," in *Aufstieg und Niedergang der römischen Welt*, II, 37, 1 (Berlin and New York, 1993), pp. 819–841, where an abundant bibliography is given.

15. Ovid, *Metamorphoses*, I, 137.

16. Seneca, *Letters to Lucilius*, 100, 10–11. See Seneca, *On Benefits*, VIII, 1, 6: "Nature has hidden nothing of what can make us happy." Cf. Pliny the Elder, *Natural History*, XXIV, 1.

17. Ibid., 90. On Posidonius, see the discussion later in this chapter. On progress, see Chapter 14.

18. Pliny the Elder, *Natural History*, XXXIII, 2–3; see also II, 158. This critique of mining activity was to have an echo in the Renaissance, for instance, in Spenser; see W. M. Kendrick, "'Earth of flesh, flesh of earth': Mother Earth in the *Faerie Queene*," *Renaissance Quarterly* 27 (1974): 548–553. C. Merchant, *The Death of Nature* (San Francisco, 1990), pp. 29–41, analyzes these texts from antiquity from the perspective of her chap. 1, "Nature as Female."

19. Pliny the Elder, *Natural History*, XXXVI, 1–8.

20. Ibid.

21. The Latin text with an English translation may be found in J. W. Duff and A. M. Duff, eds., *Minor Latin Poets* (Cambridge, Mass., 1945), vv. 250ff., pp. 382–383.

22. A. O. Lovejoy and G. Boas, *Primitivism and Related Ideas in Antiquity* (Baltimore, 1935); R. Vischer, *Das einfache Leben* (Göttingen, 1965).

23. Hesiod, *Works and Days*, ll. 109ff.

24. Empedocles in J.-P. Dumont, *Les présocratiques* (Paris, 1988), p. 427, fragment 128 [in English, B. Inwood, *The Poem of Empedocles: A Text and*

Translation with an Introduction (Toronto, 1992), pp. 257–259, fragment 122—Trans.].

25. Ovid, *Metamorphoses*, I, 89. On this theme, see J.-P. Brisson, *Rome et l'âge d'or: De Catulle à Ovide, vie et mort d'un mythe* (Paris, 1992).

26. Lucretius, *On Nature*, II, 1122–74.

27. Seneca, *Natural Questions*, III, 30, 1–7.

28. Seneca, *Letters to Lucilius*, 90. On this letter, see F.-R. Chaumartin, "Sénèque, lecteur de Posidonius," *Revue des études latines* 66 (1988): 21–29.

29. Diogenes Laertius, VI, 44.

30. Dio Chrysostom, *Discourses*, VI, 25, ed. and trans. J. W. Cohoon, vol. 1 (Cambridge, Mass., 1971), pp. 262–263; French trans. L. Paquet, *Les cyniques grecs* (Paris, 1992), p. 283.

31. *Kore Kosmou*, 44–46, in *Corpus Hermeticum*, vol. 4, ed. A. D. Nock, trans. A.-J. Festugière (Paris, 1954), 2nd ed. (1983), p. 15.

32. Mōmos appears as the incarnation of satire, for instance, in Plato, *Republic*, 487a, or in Lucian's *Tragic Jupiter*, where he explains to the gods that they must not be surprised that men doubt their existence, since they allow injustice to reign over the earth.

33. *Kore Kosmou*, 44–46, in *Corpus Hermeticum*, 4:15.

34. For Latin text with French translation, see M. Heidegger, *Être et Temps*, §42, trans. F. Vezin (Paris, 1986) [in English, Heidegger, *On Time and Being*, trans. J. Stambaugh (Chicago, 2002)—Trans.]; and Hygin, *Fables*, ed. J.-Y. Boriaud (Paris, 1997), CCXX, p. 145 [in English, *The Myths of Hyginus*, ed. and trans. M. Grant (Lawrence, Kans., 1960)—Trans.].

35. Agrippa von Nettesheim, *De incertitudine et vanitate omnium scientiarum et artium* (Antwerp, 1530); idem, *De l'incertitude aussi bien que de la vanité des sciences et des arts*, trans. de Gueudeville, 3 vols. (Leiden, 1726). There is a more recent German translation by G. Güpner: *Über die Fragwürdigkeit und Nichtigkeit der Wissenschaften, Künste und Gewerbe* (Berlin, 1993) [in English, Agrippa, *Of the Vanitie and Uncertaintie of Artes and Sciences*, ed. C. M. Dunn (Northridge, Calif., 1974)—Trans.].

36. D. Diderot, *Pensées sur l'interprétation de la Nature*, §VI, in *Œuvres philosophiques*, ed. P. Vernière (Paris, 1964), p. 182 [in English, see Diderot, *Thoughts on the Interpretation of Nature and Other Philosophical Works*, ed. D. Adams (Manchester, 1999)—Trans.].

37. J.-J. Rousseau, *Discours sur les sciences et les arts*, ed. F. Bouchardy (Paris, 1964), p. 39 [in English, Rousseau, *The Social Contract and The First and Second Discourses*, ed. S. Dunn (New Haven, 2002)—Trans.].

38. J.-J. Rousseau, *Du contrat social* (1st version), in *Du contrat social*, ed. R. Derathé (Paris, 1964), p. 105. See A. O. Lovejoy, *Essays on the History of Ideas* (Baltimore, 1948), p. 34, n. 27; Blumenberg, *La légitimité des Temps modernes*, pp. 477–478.

39. Rousseau, *Du contrat social*, p. 110.

40. I. Kant, *Anthropologie*, trans. M. Foucault (Paris, 1994), p. 165 [in English, Kant, *Anthropology from a Pragmatic Point of View*, trans. V. L. Dowdell, rev. and ed. H. H. Rudnick (Carbondale, Ill., 1996)—Trans.].

41. Lucretius, *On Nature*, V, 958.

42. B. Manuwald, *Der Aufbau der lukrezischen Kulturentstehungslehre* (Wiesbaden, 1980). See also P. Boyancé, *Lucrèce et l'épicurisme* (Paris, 1953), pp. 254–261.

43. Lucretius, *On Nature*, V, 1430.

44. Rousseau, *Discours sur les sciences et les arts*, p. 42.

45. J. W. von Goethe, *Faust*, pt. 1, ll. 668–674, in *Théâtre complet* (Paris, 1958), p. 971 [in English, Goethe, *Faust: A Tragedy*, trans. W. Arndt, ed. C. Hamlin (New York, 1976)—Trans.].

46. J. W. von Goethe, *Maximen und Reflexionen*, §498, in *Goethes Werke*, ed. Erich Trunz, 14 vols. (Hamburg, 1948–1969), 12:434. See also §617, p. 449, where we find the image of the torture chamber once again.

47. Ibid., §469, 12:430.

48. Ibid., §664, 12:458.

49. Quoted by E. Cassirer, *La philosophie des Lumières*, trans. P. Quillet (Paris, 1966), p. 332 (German text under the title *Die Freuden* in Goethe, *Gedichte in zeitlicher Folge* [Frankfurt, 1978], p. 67).

50. On this question I refer the reader to the remarkable introduction Catherine Chevalley has written to the French translation of W. Heisenberg, *La nature dans la physique contemporaine* (Paris, 2000), in which she compares Heidegger's attitude to that of Heisenberg.

51. M. Heidegger, *Die Frage nach der Technik*, trans. in *Essais et conférences* (Paris, 1958), cited by Chevalley in *La nature dans la physique contemporaine*, p. 103 [in English, Heidegger, *The Question Concerning Technology and Other Essays*, trans. W. Lovitt (New York, 1977)—Trans.].

52. Heisenberg, *La nature dans la physique contemporaine*, p. 106.

53. See Chapter 17.

54. Heisenberg, *La nature dans la physique contemporaine*, pp. 136–137 [in English, Heisenberg, *Physics and Philosophy: The Revolution in Modern Science*, trans. P. Davies (London, 1989)—Trans.].

13. PHYSICS AS A CONJECTURAL SCIENCE

1. Plato, *Timaeus*, 68d.

2. On this theme, see P. Hadot, "Physique et poésie dans le Timée de Platon," *Revue de théologie et de philosophie* 113 (1983): 113–133 (reprinted in P. Hadot, *Études de philosophie ancienne* [Paris, 1998], pp. 277–305).

3. Plato, *Critias*, 106a.

4. P. Claudel, *Art poétique* (Paris, 1946), p. 62.

5. *Eikōs logos: Timaeus*, 29c, 30b, 38d, 40e, 55d, 56a–b, 57d, 59d, 68b, 90e; *Eikōs muthos: Timaeus*, 29d, 59c, 68d. See B. Witte, "Der *eikōs logos* in Platos *Timaios*: Beitrag zur Wissenschaftsmethode und Erkenntnistheorie bei dem späten Plato," *Archiv für Geschichte der Philosophie* 46 (1964): 1–16; E. Howald, "Eikōs logos," *Hermes* 57 (1922): 63–79; L. Brisson, *Platon: Les mots et les mythes* (Paris, 1982), pp. 161–163 [in English, Brisson, *Plato the Myth Maker*, ed. and trans. G. Naddaf (Chicago, 1998)—Trans.].

6. F. M. Cornford, *Plato's Cosmology* (London, 1937), pp. 30, 29. See, for instance, Xenophanes in J.-P. Dumont, *Les présocratiques* (Paris, 1988), p. 123, fragment 35: "Please consider such conjectures as having some resemblance with the truth."

7. Plato, *Timaeus*, 29c.

8. Ibid., 59c–d.

9. Aristotle, *Poetics*, 8, 1451b.

10. Descartes, *Discourse on Method*, V, §42, in *Œuvres philosophiques*, ed. F. Alquié (Paris, 1973), p. 615.

11. Descartes, *Discourse on Method*, with text and commentary by É. Gilson (Paris, 1939), p. 391.

12. J. Mittelstrass, *Die Rettung der Phänomene* (Berlin, 1962), p. 111.

13. See Chapter 11.

14. Proclus, *Commentary on the Timaeus*, trans. A.-J. Festugière, 5 vols. (Paris, 1966–1968), 2:66–67.

15. Plato, *Timaeus*, 27d.

16. L. Brisson and F. W. Meyerstein, *Inventer l'Univers: Le problème de la connaissance et les modèles cosmologiques* (Paris, 1991).

17. See Chapter 9.

18. See Chapter 11.

19. Simplicius, *Commentary on the Physics*, ed. H. Diels, vol. 9 (Berlin, 1882), pp. 18, 29–34.

20. Proclus, *Commentary on the Timaeus*, 3:160.

21. Cicero, *Lucullus*, 39, 122.

22. Strabo, *Geography*, II, 3, 9.

23. Marcus Aurelius, *Writings for Himself*, V, 10.

24. [Galen], *Introductio sive medicus*, in *Claudii Galeni opera omnia*, ed. C. G. Kühn, vol. 14 (1821–1823; reprint, Hildesheim, 1964–65), p. 684.

25. For instance, Proclus, *Commentary on the Timaeus*, 2:215; the study of the world can be only a probable discourse *(eikotologia)*.

26. Ibid., p. 212.

27. Epicurus, *Letter to Pythocles*, 86–87; *Letter to Herodotus*, 78–80, with explanations by J.-F. Balaudé, *Épicure: Lettres, maximes, sentences*, pp. 102, 107.

28. Lucretius, *On Nature*, translation based on that of A. Ernout, *De la nature* (Paris, 1924).

29. Mittelstrass, *Die Rettung der Phänomene*, p. 16.

30. Pliny the Elder, *Natural History*, II, 77.

31. On this subject, see the highly important text of Simplicius, *Commentary on the Physics*, 1:292, 25ff., of which there is an English translation by B. Fleet in Simplicius, *On Aristotle's Physics*, II, 2 (London, 1997), p. 47.

32. Simplicius, *Commentary on Aristotle's Treatise On the Heavens*, ed. I. L. Heiberg, *In Aristotelis De Caelo Commentaria* (Berlin, 1894), p. 32 (translation based on an unpublished French translation by P. Hoffmann).

33. Osiander (A. Hosemann, 1498–1552), *Ad lectorem, de hypothesibus huius operis*, in Copernicus, *Des révolutions des orbes célestes*, ed. and trans. A. Koyré (Paris, 1934), pp. 28–31. See Mittelstrass, *Die Rettung der Phänomene*, pp. 202–203.

34. See Chapter 11.

35. See H. Blumenberg, *Die Genesis der Kopernikanischen Welt* (Frankfurt, 1975), pp. 347, 350 [in English, Blumenberg, *The Genesis of the Copernican World*, trans. R. M. Wallace (Cambridge, Mass., 1987)—Trans.].

36. Mittelstrass, *Die Rettung der Phänomene*, p. 219.

37. Cf. Blumenberg, *Die Genesis der Kopernikanischen Welt*, p. 350, n. 4, citing letters from Kepler to Heydon in the summer of 1605, and to Fabricius on November 10, 1608.

38. I. Newton, *Philosophiae Naturalis Principia Mathematica*, 3rd ed., book 3 (Cambridge, 1726), scholium generale, p. 530, 12–14 [in English, ed. A. Koyré and I. B. Cohen, vol. 2 (Cambridge, Mass., 1972), p. 764—Trans.]. J. Mittelstrass, *Die Rettung der Phänomene*, p. 262.

14. Truth as the Daughter of Time

1. Seneca, *Natural Questions*, VII, 29, 3.

2. Ibid., VII, 32, 4.

3. Plutarch, *On Curiosity*, 5, 517d.

4. Aratus, *Phenomena*, ed. and trans. J. Martin (Paris, 1998), ll. 766–772, pp. 46–47.

5. Philo, *De specialibus legibus*, IV, §51. On the metaphor of the force of truth, see H. Blumenberg, *Paradigmen zu einer Metaphorologie* (Frankfurt, 1998), pp. 14–22.

6. Philo, *De specialibus legibus*, I, §322.

7. The idea of scientific progress in ancient literature has been studied by B. Meissner, *Die technologische Fachliteratur der Antike: Struktur, Überlieferung und Wirkung technischen Wissens in der Antike (ca. 400 v. Chr.—ca. 500 n. Chr.)* (Berlin, 1999).

8. Xenophanes in J.-P. Dumont, *Les présocratiques* (Paris, 1988), p. 119, fragment B18 [in English, *Xenophanes of Colophon: Fragments*, trans. J. H. Lesher (Toronto, 1992), p. 27—Trans.]. J. Delvaille's *Essai sur l'histoire de l'idée de progrès* (Paris, 1910), is still valuable.

9. Hippocrates, *On Ancient Medicine*, ed. and trans. J. Jouanna (Paris, 1990), notice, p. 40.

10. Aeschylus, *Prometheus*, ll. 445–470; Euripides, *Suppliants*, ll. 202–215.

11. Sophocles, *Antigone*, ll. 332ff.

12. Manilius, *Astronomica*, I, 79ff., Latin text with English translation by G. P. Goold (Cambridge, Mass., 1992); Lucretius, *On Nature*, V, 1448.

13. Aristotle, *Metaphysics*, I, 2, 982b23.

14. See Chapter 12.

15. Diogenes Laertius, VII, 135–136.

16. Seneca, *Natural Questions*, VII, 30, 5.

17. Lactantius, *De ira*, 13 (*Stoicorum Veterum Fragmenta* [hereafter *SVF*], ed. H. von Arnim, vol. 2 [Stuttgart, 1964], §1172).

18. Seneca, *Natural Questions*, VII, 30, 6.

19. Cleanthes, *SVF*, vol. 1, §538, p. 123; Chrysippus in Plutarch, *Contradictions of the Stoics*, 9, 1035a, in *Les stoïciens*, trans. É. Bréhier, ed. P. M. Schuhl (Paris, 1962), p. 96; see K. Reinhardt, *Poseidonios über Ursprung und Entartung* (1921; reprint, Hildesheim and New York, 1976), p. 77; P. Boyancé, "Sur les mystères d'Éleusis," *Revue des études grecques* 75 (1962): 469. See also Plutarch, *On Tranquillity of the Soul*, 20, 477d.

20. Seneca, *Natural Questions*, VII, 30, 1.

21. Ibid., VII, 25, 4.

22. Cicero, *Lucullus*, 5, 15.

23. Seneca, *Natural Questions*, VI, 5, 2–3; VII, 25, 3–5.

24. Pliny the Elder, *Natural History*, II, 62.

25. Seneca, *Letters to Lucilius*, 33, 11.

26. Seneca, *Natural Questions*, VII, 25, 5.

27. Seneca, *Letters to Lucilius*, 45, 4.

28. Seneca, *Natural Questions*, VII, 30, 5; in this quotation the word *mundus* is used in two different senses: first it designates the universe, and then mankind.

29. See Chapters 10–11.

30. R. Bacon, *De Viciis Contractis in Studio Theologie*, in *Opera Hactenus Inedita Rogeri Baconi*, ed. R. Steele, fasc. 1, (Oxford, 1909), p. 5. See Seneca, *Natural Questions*, VII, 25, 4.

31. Cited by W. Eamon, *Science and the Secrets of Nature* (Princeton, 1994), p. 273.

32. F. Bacon, *Novum Organum*, I, §109.

33. Bacon, *De Viciis Contractis*, p. 5.

34. Priscian, *Institutiones, Epist. dedic.*, I, ed. Hertz (Leipzig, 1855), p. 1, 7. See É. Jeauneau, *Lectio Philosophorum: Recherches sur l'École de Chartres* (Amsterdam, 1973), p. 359.

35. G. Bruno, *Supper of Ashes*, in *Œuvres complètes*, trans. Y. Hersant, vol. 2 (Paris, 1994), p. 56.

36. This representation profoundly modifies the theme, very much alive in the Middle Ages, of the dwarfs (the moderns) standing on the shoulders

of giants (the ancients). See É. Jeauneau, "Nains et géants," in *Entretiens sur la Renaissance du XIIe siècle, sous la dir. de M. de Gandillac et d'É. Jeauneau* (Paris, 1968), pp. 21–38; idem, "*Nani gigantium humeris insidentes:* Essai d'interprétation de Bernard de Chartres," *Vivarium* 5 (1967): 79–99 (reprinted in Jeauneau, *Lectio Philosophorum,* pp. 51–72).

37. J. Michelet, *Journal,* vol. 1 (Paris, 1959), March 30, 1842, p. 393.

38. Bacon, *Novum Organum,* I, §84.

39. Ibid.

40. See M. Le Dœff, intro. to F. Bacon, *La Nouvelle Atlantide* (Paris, 1995), p. 59, n. 70.

41. B. Pascal, "Fragment d'un Traité du vide" (Fragment of a treatise on the void) in *Pensées et opuscules,* ed. L. Brunschvicq (Paris, 1974), pp. 76–79.

42. On Truth as the daughter of Time, see H. Blumenberg, "Wahrheit, Tochter der Zeit?" *in Lebenszeit und Weltzeit* (Frankfurt, 1986), pp. 153–172; see also G. Gentile, "Veritas filia temporis," in *Giordano Bruno e il pensiero del Rinascimento,* 2nd ed. (Florence, 1925), pp. 227–248.

43. Hippocrates, *On Ancient Medicine,* II, 1, p. 119, 14.

44. Aristotle, *Nicomachean Ethics,* I, 7, 1098a20–24.

45. F. Dirlmeier, *Aristoteles: Nikomachische Ethik* (Berlin, 1983), pp. 260–281.

46. Plato, *Republic,* 376e.

47. Plato, *Laws,* 768c–770b.

48. Lucretius, *On Nature,* V, 1448. It seems to me that R. Lenoble, *Esquisse d'une histoire de l'idée de nature* (Paris, 1969), pp. 120–123, exaggerates Lucretius' originality. On the subject of Lucretius' theory of the origin of civilization, see B. Manuwald, *Der Aufbau der lukrezischen Kulturentstehungslehre* (Wiesbaden, 1980).

49. Sophocles, *Hipponous,* in A. C. Pearson, *The Fragments of Sophocles,* vol. 1 (1917; reprint, Amsterdam, 1963), p. 217, fragment 301; see also Aulus Gellius, *Attic Nights,* XII, 11, 6.

50. Sophocles, *Ajax,* ll. 646–647. On the illustrations of this motif from the sixteenth to the eighteenth centuries, see F. Saxl, "Veritas filia temporis," in *Philosophy and History: Essays Presented to Ernst Cassirer,* ed. R. Klibansky and H.-J. Paton (New York and London, 1936), pp. 197–222. Most of these illustrations refer to the first interpretation (time unveils secrets and misdeeds). See also E. Panofksy, *Essais d'iconologie* (Paris, 1967), p. 119.

51. For instance, Pindar, *Olympians,* X, 53: "Time, which alone makes known the truth."

52. Seneca, *On Anger,* II, 22, 3.

53. Aulus Gellius, *Attic Nights,* XII, 11, 7.

54. See Chapter 9.

55. On this question, and in general on the notion of progress, see H. Blumenberg, *La légitimité des temps modernes* (Paris, 1999), pp. 94–95.

56. Pascal, "Fragment d'un Traité du vide," p. 80.

57. J.-M. Mandosio, *L'effondrement de la très grande Bibliothèque nationale de France* (Paris, 1999), p. 98, citing P. Lévy, *L'intelligence collective: Pour une anthropologie du "cyberspace"* (Paris, 1994).

58. Goethe to Schiller, February 21 and May 5, 1798, in *Goethes Briefe,* ed. K.-R. Mandelkow, 4 vols. (Hamburg, 1965–1967), 2:333, 343.

59. Pascal, "Fragment d'un Traité du vide," p. 79.

60. Seneca, *Letters to Lucilius,* 102, 21.

61. J. Kepler, *Gesammelte Werke,* vol. 2 (Munich, 1938), pp. 7, 15–18.

62. G. E. Lessing, *Eine Duplik* (1778), in *Werke,* vol. 8 (Munich, 1979), pp. 32–33.

63. Lenoble, *Histoire de l'idée de nature,* pp. 120–123.

64. P.-G. de Gennes, "L'esprit de Primo Levi," *Le Monde,* October 23, 2002, p. 18. Here arises the difficult problem of the notion of provisional truth. On this subject, see the remarkable study by Sandra Laugier, "De la logique de la science aux révolutions scientifiques," in *Les philosophes et la science,* ed. P. Wagner (Paris, 2002), pp. 964–1016.

65. F. Jacob, *La logique du vivant* (Paris, 1970).

15. The Study of Nature as a Spiritual Exercise

1. Plato, *Timaeus,* 59c.

2. See G. Naddaf, *L'origine et l'évolution du concept grec de physis* (Lewiston, N.Y., 1992), pp. 61–90. For a translation of this poem, see R. Labat, *Les religions du Proche-Orient* (Paris, 1970), pp. 36–70.

3. J. Huizinga, *Homo Ludens* (Basel, n.d. pp. 171–191 [in English, Huizinga, *Homo Ludens: A Study of the Play-Element in Culture* (London and Boston, 1949)—Trans.].

4. Plato, *Laws,* 803c.

5. Plato, *Phaedrus*, 265c.

6. Plato, *Timaeus*, 90d.

7. Aristotle, *Parts of Animals*, I, 5, 644b31. For a reflection on this text, see P. Hadot, *What Is Ancient Philosophy?* (Cambridge, Mass., 2002), pp. 83–84.

8. Cicero, *Lucullus*, 39, 122.

9. Ibid., 41, 127.

10. Cicero, *On the Extreme Terms of Goods and Evils*, V, 19, 50–51.

11. Ibid., V, 21, 58.

12. See B. White, "Der *eikōs logos* in Platos *Timaios:* Beitrag zur Wissenschaftsmethode und Erkenntnistheorie bei dem späten Plato," *Archiv für Geschichte der Philosophie* 46 (1964): 13.

13. Philo, *De specialibus legibus*, II, 44–445; Plutarch, *On Peace of Mind*, 20, 477c, reporting Diogenes' remark.

14. Seneca, *Letters to Lucilius*, 65, 17.

15. Plato, *Republic*, 486a.

16. Seneca, *Natural Questions*, III, preface, 18; I, preface, 1–16. See I. Hadot, *Seneca und die griechisch-römische Tradition der Seelenleitung* (Berlin, 1969), p. 115.

17. Simplicius, *Commentary on Aristotle's Physics*, in *Aristotelis Physicorum libros quattuor priores Commentaria*, ed. H. Diels (Berlin, 1882), 1:4, 7ff.

18. Aristotle, *Nicomachean Ethics*, VI, 12, 1144a18; X, 7, 1177b20; *Metaphysics*, I, 2, 982a4ff.

19. Seneca, *Natural Questions*, VI, 4, 2.

20. Hadot, *What Is Ancient Philosophy?* pp. 33ff.

21. J. Monod, *Le hasard et la nécessité* (Paris, 1970), p. 191 [in English, Monod, *Chance and Necessity: An Essay on the Natural Philosophy of Modern Biology*, trans. A. Wainhouse (New York, 1972)—Trans.].

22. See P. Hadot, *Exercices spirituels et philosophie antique*, new ed. (Paris, 2002), pp. 145ff.

23. Monod, *Le hasard et la nécessité*, p. 191 (see also p. 192 on "transcending").

24. Aristotle, *Nicomachean Ethics*, X, 7, 1177b27.

25. Greek text and French translation in *Anthologie grecque: Anthologie palatine*, vol. 8 (bk. 9) (Paris, 1974), §577, p. 98.

26. See Chapter 12.

16. NATURE'S BEHAVIOR

1. F. Jacob, *La statue intérieure* (Paris, 1987), p. 356 [in English, Jacob, *The Statue Within: An Autobiography*, trans. F. Philip (New York, 1988)—Trans.].

2. See Chapter 2.

3. Aristotle, *On the Heavens*, II, 9, 291a24.

4. Aristotle, *Movement of Animals*, 8, 708a10; 12, 711a18; *Parts of Animals*, II, 13, 658a8; II, 1, 661b23; IV, 11, 691b4; IV, 12, 694a15; IV, 13, 695b19; *Generation of Animals*, II, 4, 739b19; II, 5, 741b4; II, 6, 744a36; V, 8, 788b21.

5. R. Boyle, *A Free Inquiry into the Vulgarly Received Notion of Nature* (1686), in *The Works of the Honorable Robert Boyle*, 6 vols., ed. T. Bird, 2nd ed. (London, 1772), 5:174ff.

6. See the note by M. Berthelot on the principle of least action in André Lalande, *Vocabulaire technique et critique de la philosophie*, 10th ed. (Paris, 1968), pp. 1232–34; A. Kneser, *Das Prinzip der kleinsten Wirkung von Leibniz zur Gegenwart* (Leipzig and Berlin, 1928).

7. P. L. Moreau de Maupertuis, *Essai de cosmologie* (1768), ed. F. Azouvi (Paris, 1984), p. 42. On the discussions about this principle, see, in *Pierre Louis Moreau de Maupertuis: Eine Bilanz nach 300 Jahren*, ed. H. Hecht (Berlin, 1999), the studies by H.-H. Borzeszkowski, "Der epistemologische Gehalt des Maupertuischen Wirkungsprinzip," pp. 419–425; and P. Thiele, "Ist die Natur sparsam?" pp. 432–503.

8. Aristotle, *Metaphysics*, XIV, 3, 1090b19: "Nature is not a series of unconnected episodes, like a bad tragedy."

9. Aristotle, *History of Animals*, VIII, 1, 588b4; *Parts of Animals*, IV, 5, 681a12.

10. G. W. Leibniz, preface to *Nouveaux essais sur l'entendement humain* (Paris, 1966), p. 40 [in English, Leibniz, *New Essays on Human Understanding*, ed. and trans. P. Remnant and J. Bennett (Cambridge and New York, 1997)—Trans.].

11. Plato, *Timaeus*, 31b.

12. A. O. Lovejoy, *The Great Chain of Being* (1936; reprint, Cambridge, Mass., 1978).

13. Aristotle, *Parts of Animals*, II, 2, 663a1; III, 2, 664a1.

14. Plotinus, *Enneads*, VI, 7 [38], 9, 40.

15. Plato, *Timaeus*, 29b, 30a, 47.

16. J. W. von Goethe, *Principles of Philosophical Zoology*, in *Goethes Werke*, ed. Erich Trunz, 14 vols. (Hamburg, 1948–1969) (hereafter HA), 13:244, 22–29; idem, *Allgemeine Einleitung in die vergleichende Anatomie*, HA, 13:176, 15–21; idem, *Lepaden*, p. 205, 15–23.

17. See F. Ravaisson, *Testament philosophique* (Paris, 1938), p. 80.

18. On this subject, see the valuable note by P. Vernière in D. Diderot, *Œuvres philosophiques*, ed. Vernière (Paris, 1964), p. 187, n. 1, with essential texts by Buffon, Maupertuis, and Robinet.

19. Cited ibid.

20. F. Jacob, *La logique du vivant* (Paris, 1970), p. 22.

21. M. Cassé, "La mise en ordre du chaos original," *Le Monde*, July 29, 1983.

22. L. Wittgenstein, *Notebooks, 1914–1916*, June 1, 1915.

23. L. Wittgenstein, *Tractatus logico-philosophicus*, 6.34, trans. P. Klossowski (Paris, 1961) [in English, Wittgenstein, *Tractatus Logico-Philosophicus*, trans. C. K. Ogden (London and New York, 1922)—Trans.].

24. Ibid., 6.3211.

25. I. Kant, intro. to *Critique de la faculté de juger*, trans. A. Philonenko (Paris, 1968), p. 30 [in English, Kant, *Critique of Judgment*, trans. W. S. Pluhar (Indianapolis, 1987)—Trans.].

26. D. Diderot, *De l'interprétation de la nature*, XII, in *Œuvres philosophiques*, p. 186 [in English, Diderot, *Thoughts on the Interpretation of Nature and Other Philosophical Works*, ed. D. Adams (Manchester, 1999)—Trans.].

27. Seneca, *Natural Questions*, VII, 27, 5.

28. Chrysippus in Plutarch, *Contradictions of the Stoics*, 21, 1044c. See also Cicero, *On the Extreme Terms of Goods and Evils*, III, 18.

29. On this theme, see the excellent monograph by K. Deichgräber, *Natura varie ludens: Ein Nachtrag zum griechischen Naturbegriff*, Abhandlungen der Akademie der Wissenschafen und der Literatur, Geistes- und sozialwissenschaftliche Klasse (Mainz, 1954), no. 3. See also the texts cited by G. Romeyer-Dherbey, "Art et Nature chez les stoïciens," in *La Grèce pour penser l'avenir*, ed. M. Augé, C. Castoriadis et al. (Paris, 2000), pp. 91–104.

30. Pliny the Elder, *Natural History*, IX, 202; XI, 123; XIV, 115; XXI, 1–2.

31. Ibid., VII, 30; VIII, 33–34.

32. Ibid., XXI, 23.

33. Heraclitus in J.-P. Dumont, *Les présocratiques* (Paris, 1988), p. 158, fragment 52, [in English, C. H. Kahn, *The Art and Thought of Heraclitus* (Cambridge, 1979), p. 71, fragment 94—Trans.].

34. See Chapter 22.

35. See P. Hadot, "L'apport du néoplatonisme à la philosophie de la nature," in *Tradition und Gegenwart: Eranos Jahrbuch, 1968* (Zurich, 1970), pp. 91–99.

36. Goethe to Charlotte von Stein, July 10, 1786, in *Goethes Briefe*, ed. K.-R. Mandelkow, 4 vols. (Hamburg, 1965–1967), 1:514.

37. Goethe, interview with J. F. Falk, June 14, 1809, in *Goethes Gespräche*, ed. F. von Biedermann, vol. 2 (Leipzig, 1909–1911), pp. 37–41.

38. Ibid., p. 37.

39. F. Nietzsche, *The Gay Science*, §349, trans. P. Wotling (Paris, 2000), p. 296; idem, *Beyond Good and Evil*, §§9, 188, in *Œuvres philosophiques complètes*, vols. 1–14 (Paris, 1974–), vol. 7, pp. 27, 101 (translation slightly modified) [in English, Nietzsche, *Beyond Good and Evil . . .* , trans. R. J. Hollingdale (London, 1973)—Trans.].

40. See Chapter 22. On this subject, see the book by E. Fink, *La philosophie de Nietzsche* (Paris, 1965), and especially the conclusion, pp. 240–241 [in English, Fink, *Nietzsche's Philosophy*, trans. G. Richter (London, 2002)—Trans.].

41. H. Bergson, *La pensée et le mouvant* (Paris, 1934), p. 240 [in English, Bergson, *The Creative Mind*, trans. M. L. Andison (New York, 1946)—Trans.].

42. H. Bergson, *L'énergie spirituelle* (Paris, 1930), p. 25 [in English, Bergson, *Mind-Energy Lectures and Essays*, trans. H. W. Carr (New York, 1920)—Trans.].

43. See A. Portmann, *La forme animale* (Paris, 1961) [in English, Portmann, *Animal Forms and Patterns: A Study of the Appearance of Animals*, trans. H. Czech (New York, 1952)—Trans.].

17. THE POETIC MODEL

1. See Chapter 13. On this theme, see P. Hadot, "Physique et poésie dans le *Timée* de Platon," *Revue de théologie et de philosophie* 113 (1983): 113–133 (reprinted in P. Hadot, *Études de philosophie ancienne* [Paris, 1998], pp. 277–305).

2. Philo, *Quod deterius potiori insidiari soleat*, §§124–125.

3. Arrian, *Manuel of Epictetus*, §17, trans. P. Hadot (Paris, 2000), p. 174; Aristotle already compares the universe to a tragedy in *Metaphysics*, XII, 10, 1076a, and XIV, 3, 1090b19; see also Plotinus, *Enneads*, III, 2 [47], 17, 34, and 49.

4. Augustine, *Letters*, 138, 5, ed. A. Goldbacher, p. 130. See also *De musica*, VI, 11, 29.

5. Proclus, *Commentary on the Republic*, ed. G. Kroll, 2 vols. (1899–1901; reprint, Amsterdam, 1965), 1:69, 15; trans. A.-J. Festugière, 5 vols. (Paris, 1970), 1:85.

6. Bonaventure, II *Sentent.*, in *Opera Omnia*, ed. R. P. Bernardini a Portu Rmatino et al., 10 vols. (Quaracchi, 1882–1902), dist. 13, art. 2, quaest. 2, ad 2, p. 316a.

7. A study of this metaphor may be found in E. R. Curtius, *Littérature européenne et Moyen Âge latin* (Paris, 1986), chap. 16, §7 [in English, Curtius, *European Literature and the Latin Middle Ages*, trans. W. R. Trask (Princeton, 1990)—Trans.]; H. M. Nobis, "Buch der Natur," in *Historisches Wörterbuch der Philosophie*, vol. 1 (1971), cols. 957–959; H. Blumenberg, *Die Lesbarkeit der Welt* (Frankfurt, 1981), esp. pp. 211–232.

8. M. Arndt, "Natursprache," in *Historisches Wörterbuch der Philosophie*, vol. 6 (1984), cols. 633–635.

9. See S. Meier-Oser, "Signatur," *Historisches Wörterbuch der Philosophie*, vol. 9 (1995), col. 751.

10. A. Koyré, *La philosophie de Jacob Boehme* (Paris, 1929), p. 460.

11. T. Browne, *Religio medici*, I, 16, ed. W. A. Greenhill (London, 1889), pp. 27–29, cited by Blumenberg, *Die Lesbarkeit der Welt*, pp. 97–98. There is already a kind of relation between hieroglyphs and natural forms in Plotinus, *Enneads*, V, 8 [31], 6.

12. J. G. Hamann, *Letter to Kant*, in *Aesthetica in nuce*, trans. R. Deygout (Paris, 2001), p. 131.

13. I. Kant, *Critique de la faculté de juger*, §42, trans. A. Philonenko (Paris, 1968), p. 133.

14. Goethe, *The Metamorphosis of Plants*, in *Poésie*, trans. R. Ayrault, vol. 2 (Paris, 1982), p. 459 [in English, Goethe, *Selected Poems*, ed. C. Middleton (Princeton, 1994)—Trans.]. See Chapter 19.

15. Goethe, interview with J. F. Falk, June 14, 1809, in *Goethes Gespräche*, ed. F. von Biedermann, vol. 2 (Leipzig, 1909–1911), pp. 40–41.

16. Plotinus, III, 8 [30], 4, 3.

17. Novalis, *Les disciples de Saïs*, in *Petits écrits*, trans. G. Bianquis (Paris, 1947), p. 179 [cf. Novalis, *The Novices of Saïs*, trans. R. Manheim, illus. Paul Klee, pref. Stephen Spender (New York, 1949)—Trans.].

18. F. W. J. von Schelling, *System of Transcendental Idealism*, in *Essais*, trans. S. Jankélévitch (Paris, 1946), p. 175. See also idem, *Philosophie der Kunst*, in *Werke*, vol. 2 (Frankfurt, 1985), p. 459 ("Nature is the first poem of the divine imagination"), and vol. 1, p. 696 ("What we call nature is a poem, which keeps itself hidden in a marvelous coded script") [in English, Schelling, *Philosophy of Art*, ed. and trans. D. W. Stott (Minneapolis, 1989)—Trans.].

19. Cited by A. Béguin, *L'âme romantique et le rêve* (Paris, 1946), p. 71.

20. See Chapter 20.

21. *Homeric Hymn to Hermes*, l. 427 (Benveniste is discussing the translation by J. Humbert [Paris, 1967] p. 133). É. Benveniste, *Le vocabulaire des institutions indo-européennes*, vol. 2 (Paris, 1969), p. 40 [in English, Benveniste, *Indo-European Language and Society*, trans. E. Palmer (London, 1973)—Trans.]. See also M. Detienne, *Les maîtres de vérité dans la Grèce archaïque* (Paris, 1967), p. 54 [in English, Detienne, *The Masters of Truth in Archaic Greece*, trans. J. Lloyd (New York, 1996)—Trans.].

22. R. M. Rilke, *Sonnets to Orpheus*, I, 3.

23. See Chapter 13.

24. Homer, *Iliad*, XVIII, 480ff. See Alain, *Propos de littérature* (Paris, 1934), pp. 77–78; J. Pigeaud, *L'art et le vivant* (Paris, 1995), pp. 21–28; and idem, "Le bouclier d'Achille," *Revue des études grecques* 101 (1988): 54–63.

25. Alain, *Propos de littérature*, p. 77.

26. It was the highly interesting book by G. Lieberg, *Poeta creator: Studien zu einer Figur der antiken Dichtung* (Amsterdam, 1982), pp. 35ff., that drew my attention to this text and its meaning. On the theme of the poet as creator, see also E. N. Tigerstedt, "The Poet as Creator: Origins of a Metaphor," *Comparative Literature Studies* 5 (1968): 455–488; and M. S. Rostvig, "*Ars aeterna*: Renaissance Poetics and Theories of Divine Creation," *Mosaic* 3 (1969–70): 40–61.

27. Virgil, *Bucolics*, VI, 32ff.

28. Lieberg, *Poeta creator*, pp. 22–35.

29. P. Boyancé, *Lucrèce et l'épicurisme* (Paris, 1953), p. 289; P. Friedländer, "Pattern of Sound and Atomistic Theory," *American Journal of Philology* 62 (1941): 6–34.

30. See P. Shorey, "Plato, Lucretius, and Epicurus," *Harvard Studies in Classical Philology* 11 (1901): 201–210.

31. See Chapter 2.

32. See Empedocles in J.-P., Dumont, *Les présocratiques* (Paris, 1988), p. 383, fragment B23 [in English, B. Inwood, *The Poem of Empedocles: A Text and Translation with an Introduction* (Toronto, 1992), pp. 219–221, fragment 27—Trans.].

33. See P. Hadot, "Physique et poésie dans le *Timée* de Platon," *Revue de théologie et de philosophie* 113 (1983): 113–133; L. Brisson, "Le discours comme univers et l'univers comme discourse," in *Le texte et sa représentation: Études de littérature ancienne*, vol. 3 (Paris, 1987).

34. See J. A. Coulter, *The Literary Microcosm: Theories of Interpretation of the Later Neoplatonists* (Leiden, 1976); and A. Sheppard, *Studies on the Fifth and Sixth Essays of Proclus' Commentary on the Republic* (Göttingen, 1980).

35. L. Brisson, *Le Même et l'Autre dans la structure ontologique du* Timée *de Platon* (Paris, 1974), pp. 36ff.

36. See A. Fowler, *Spenser and the Numbers of Time* (London, 1964); S. K. Heninger, *Touches of Sweet Harmony: Pythagorean Cosmology and Renaissance Poetics* (San Marino, Calif., 1974), pp. 287–324.

37. See M. Plath, "Der Goethe-Schellingsche Plan eines philosophischen Naturgedichts: Eine Studie zu Goethes Gott und Welt," *Preussiche Jahrbücher* 106 (1901): 44–71. See also A. G. F. Gode von Aesch, *Natural Science in German Romanticism* (New York, 1941), pp. 262ff.

38. See H. Tuzet, *Le cosmos et l'imagination* (Paris, 1965), pp. 115–120, esp. p. 119: "This masterpiece of divine art causes the birth in the poet of a pure intellectual enjoyment which is not unrelated to that of the young Kant." I take the opportunity to emphasize the importance and interest of the fine book by Hélène Tuzet, an essay on the psychology of the imagination in the tradition of Gaston Bachelard.

39. P. Claudel, *Art poétique* (Paris, 1946), p. 64. See Chapter 18.

18. Aesthetic Perception and the Genesis of Forms

1. See the remark by Cézanne in *Conversations avec Cézanne, Émile Bernard, Joachim Gasquet . . .* , ed. P. M. Doran (Paris, 1978), p. 119 [in English,

Conversations with Cézanne, ed. M. Doran, trans. J. L. Cochran (Berkeley, 2001)—Trans.].

2. M. Merleau-Ponty, *Éloge de la philosophie et autres essais* (Paris, 1960), p. 285; E. Husserl, "L'arché originaire Terre ne se meut pas," *Philosophie* 1 (1984): 4–21.

3. H. Bergson, "La vie et l'œuvre de Ravaisson," in *La pensée et le mouvant* (Paris, 1934), p. 280.

4. Doran, *Conversations avec Cézanne*, p. 157.

5. Bergson, *La pensée et le mouvant*, p. 152. See P. Hadot, "Le sage et le monde," in *Le Temps de la réflexion* (Paris, 1989), pp. 179ff. (reprinted in P. Hadot, *Exercices spirituels et philosophie antique*, new ed. [Paris, 2002], pp. 343–360) [in English, Hadot, *Philosophy as a Way of Life*, trans. M. Chase, ed. A. A. Davidson (Oxford, 1995), pp. 251–263—Trans.].

6. Lucretius, *On Nature*, II, 1023–39.

7. Seneca, *Letters to Lucilius*, 64, 6. See Chapter 21.

8. Seneca, *Natural Questions, On Comets*, VII, 1, 1–4.

9. A. von Humboldt, *Kosmos*, vol. 1 (Stuttgart-Augsburg, 1845–1858), p. 21, trans. H. Faye (Paris, 1847–1851), p. 23 [in English, von Humboldt, *Cosmos: A Sketch of a Physical Description of the Universe*, trans. E. C. Otté, 2 vols. (1858; reprint, Baltimore, 1997)—Trans.].

10. A. G. Baumgarten, *Esthétique*, trans. J.-Y. Prauchère (Paris, 1988), §423, p. 151; §429, p. 154. In his introduction, Prauchère insists on the importance of perception in Baumgarten (p. 20). On A. G. Baumgarten, see E. Cassirer, *La philosophie des Lumières* (Paris, 1966), pp. 327–345 [in English, Cassirer, *The Philosophy of the Enlightenment*, trans. F. C. A. Koelln and J. P. Pettegrove (Princeton, 1951)—Trans.]; J. Ritter, *Paysage* (Paris, 1997), pp. 69–70.

11. I. Kant, *Critique de la faculté de juger*, §29, "General Remark, on the Exposition of Reflective Aesthetic Judgments," trans. A. Philonenko (Paris, 1968), p. 107.

12. Ibid., §42, p. 131.

13. Ibid., pp. 131–132.

14. Cited in T. Gloyna, B.-C. Han, and A. Hügli, "Übung," *Historisches Wörterbuch der Philosophie*, 11 (2001), p. 81.

15. A. Schopenhauer, *Le monde comme volonté et comme représentation*, trans. A. Burdeau, rev. R. Rooz (Paris, 2003), bk. 3, §33–34, pp. 228–234,

esp. p. 231 (quotation from Spinoza, *Ethics*, prop. 31, scholion) [in English, Schopenhauer, *The World as Will and Idea*, 3 vols., trans. R. B. Haldane and J. Kemp (1896; reprint, New York, 1977)—Trans.].

16. I have emphasized these words, which are characteristic of the Goethean conception of nature; see Chapter 20.

17. J. W. von Goethe, *Wilhelm Meister, the Travel Years*, in *Romans* (Paris, 1966), p. 1176 (translation modified) [in English, Goethe, *Wilhelm Meister's Apprenticeship and Travels*, trans. T. Carlyle, 2 vols. (Boston and New York, n.d.)—Trans.].

18. J. W. von Goethe, *Maximen und Reflexionen*, §720, in *Goethes Werke*, ed. Erich Trunz, 14 vols. (Hamburg, 1948–1969) (hereafter HA), 12:467 [in English, Goethe, *Maxims and Reflections*, trans. E. Stopp, ed. P. Hutchinson (London and New York, 1998)—Trans.].

19. See Chapter 20.

20. Goethe, *Wilhelm Meister, the Travel Years*, p. 1184.

21. R. Caillois, *Esthétique généralisée* (Paris, 1969). On philosophy and modern art, one may profitably consult K. Albert, *Philosophie der modernen Kunst* (Sankt Augustin, Germany, 1984).

22. Caillois, *Esthétique généralisée*, p. 14.

23. Ibid., p. 8.

24. On this theme, see R. Caillois, *Méduse et Cie* (Paris, 1960); and A. Portmann, *La forme animale*.

25. Schopenhauer, *Le monde comme volonté et comme représentation*, bk. 3, §39, p. 259.

26. Ibid., citing Augustine, *City of God*, XI, 27.

27. E. Fink, *La philosophie de Nietzsche* (Paris, 1965), p. 32 [in English, Fink, *Nietzsche's Philosophy*, trans. G. Richter (London, 2002)—Trans.].

28. F. Nietzsche, *The Birth of Tragedy*, trans. G. Bianquis (Paris, 1949), §2, p. 27 [in English, Nietzsche, *The Birth of Tragedy and Case of Wagner*, trans. W. Kaufmann (New York, 1967)—Trans.].

29. F. Nietzsche, *Fragments posthumes (Automne 1885–automne 1887)*, 2 [119], in *Œuvres complètes*, 14 vols. (Paris, 1974), 12:125 [in English, Nietzsche, *Writings from the Late Notebooks*, ed. R. Bittner, trans. K. Sturge (Cambridge and New York, 2003)—Trans.].

30. Ibid., 2 [114], p. 124. See J. Granier, *Le problème de la vérité dans la philosophie de Nietzsche* (Paris, 1966), p. 523.

31. P. Klee, *Théorie de l'art moderne* (Basel, n.d.), pp. 43–45 [in English, Klee, *On Modern Art*, trans. P. Findlay (London, 1948)—Trans.].

32. P. Claudel, *Art poétique* (Paris, 1946), p. 52.

33. P. Valéry, "Petite lettre sur les mythes," in *Œuvres*, vol. 1 (Paris, 1957), p. 963.

34. Portmann, *La forme animale*, p. 222.

35. See Chapter 7.

36. On this subject, see R. Ruyer, *La genèse des formes vivantes* (Paris, 1958), p. 255.

37. Letter to Lou Andreas Salomé, August 11, 1903, in Rilke and Salomé, *Correspondance*, ed. E. Pfeiffer, trans. Ph. Jaccottet (Paris, 1985), p. 97.

38. Plotinus, *Enneads*, V, 8 [31], 1, 36. See, for instance, what Cassirer says about Shaftesbury in his book *La philosophie des lumières*, p. 310.

39. J. W. von Goethe, *Voyage en Italie*, January 28, 1787, trans. J. Naujac, vol. 1 (Paris, 1961), pp. 188–189.

40. Shitao, *Les propos sur la peinture de Citrouille-Amère*, trans. P. Ryckmans (Brussels, 1970), citing F. Gilot, *Vivre avec Picasso* (Paris, 1965), p. 69.

41. Klee, *Théorie de l'art moderne*, pp. 28, 30.

42. Caillois, *Esthétique généralisée*, p. 25.

43. Caillois, *Méduse et Cie*, p. 53. For the sake of completeness, let us note the existence of "bionics," the science that studies the processes of nature in order to invent mechanisms that imitate the living world.

44. Kant, *Critique de la faculté de juger*, §42, p. 134.

45. Goethe, *Voyage en Italie*, October 9, 1786, 1:188–189.

46. On this theme, see P. Hadot, "Emblèmes et symboles goethéens: Du caducée d'Hermès à la plante archetype" in *L'art des confins: Mélanges offerts à Maurice de Gandillac*, ed. A. Cazeneueve and F. Lyotard (Paris, 1985), pp. 431–444.

47. J. W. von Goethe, *Polarität*, in *Goethes Werke*, 2nd section, vol. 11 (Weimar, 1887–1919), p. 166.

48. The goddess in question is Isis; see Chapter 19.

49. French trans. H. Lichtenberger, reprinted in H. Carossa, *Les pages immortelles de Goethe*, trans. J. F. Angelloz (Paris, 1942), p. 152. A more recent translation by R. Ayrault may be found in J. W. von Goethe, *Poésies*, vol. 2 (Paris, 1982), p. 459.

50. G. Bianquis, *Études sur Goethe* (Paris, 1951), p. 63. See also the two chapters on "Polarity" and "Metamorphosis" in P. Salm, *The Poem as Plant* (Cleveland and London, 1971), pp. 41–78.

51. See P. O. Runge, *La peinture allemande à l'époque du romantisme*, exhibition catalogue (Paris, 1976), p. 184.

52. See Hadot, "Emblèmes et symboles goethéens."

53. B. Pascal, *Pensées*, ed. L. Brunschvicg (Paris, 1974), §355, p. 492.

54. G. P. Lomazzo, *Trattato dell'arte della pittura, scoltura ed architettura* (Milan, 1585), cited among others in 1753 by W. Hogarth, *L'analyse de la beauté*, trans. O. Brunet (Paris, 1963), p. 140 [in English, Hogarth, *The Analysis of Beauty*, ed. R. Paulson (New Haven, Conn., 1997)—Trans.].

55. See J.-P. Richter, *The Literary Works of Leonardo da Vinci*, vol. 1, no. 48 (London, 1939), p. 29. I owe the identification of this text by Leonardo da Vinci to my friend Louis Frank, whom I thank with all my heart.

56. E. Panofsky, *Essais d'iconologie* (Paris, 1967), pp. 258–259.

57. Hogarth, *L'analyse de la beauté*, p. 182. He had, moreover, been preceded in this path by the French physician and mathematician Antoine Parent (1666–1716); see the introduction by O. Brunet, pp. 49–50; and J. Dobai, "William Hogarth et Antoine Parent," *Journal of the Warburg and Courtauld Institutes* 31 (1968): 336–382.

58. On this question, see M. Podro, "The Drawn Line from Hogarth to Schiller," in *Sind Briten hier? Relations between British and Continental Art, 1680–1880* (Munich, 1961). See also the article by W. Düsing, "Schönheitslinie," *Historisches Wörterbuch der Philosophie*, 8 (1992), pp. 1387–89 (who unfortunately does not discuss Ravaisson, Bergson, and Merleau-Ponty).

59. J. W. von Goethe, *Spiraltendenz der Vegetation*, extracts in HA, 13:130ff.

60. Goethe, *Fossiler Stier*, HA, 13:201.

61. Goethe is more critical with regard to what he calls the "undulists" or the "serpentists," in *Der Sammler und die Seinigen*, HA, 12:92–93, where he charges them with lacking strength.

62. See the highly illuminating pages that D. Janicaud devoted to the theory of the serpentine line in F. Ravaisson, H. Bergson, and M. Merleau-Ponty, *Une généalogie du spiritualisme français: Aux sources du bergsonisme: Ravaisson et la métaphysique* (The Hague, 1969), pp. 11, 53–56. He has the

merit of clearly pointing out the misunderstandings committed by these three philosophers in interpreting the remarks of Leonardo da Vinci.

63. F. Ravaisson, "Dessein," in *Dictionnaire de pédagogie*, ed. F. Buisson (Paris, 1882), p. 673.

64. F. Ravaisson, *Testament philosophique* (Paris, 1938), pp. 83, 133 (notes).

65. Ibid., p. 133 (notes).

66. Bergson, "La vie et l'œuvre de Ravaisson," in *La pensée et le mouvant*, p. 280.

67. Klee, *Théorie de l'art moderne*, p. 45.

68. *Conversations avec Cézanne*, p. 125.

69. On this subject, see the texts collected by N. Vandier-Nicolas under the title *Esthétique et peinture de paysage en Chine: Des origines aux Song* (Paris, 1987).

70. Ibid., p. 113.

71. Ibid., p. 114.

72. By translating in this way, Ryckmans is alluding to the profound pun by Paul Claudel, for whom knowledge *(connaissance)* is being-born-together *(co-naissance);* see Chapter 17.

73. Shitao, *Les propos sur la peinture du moine Citrouille-Amère*, p. 69.

74. Ibid., p. 72.

75. An expression dear to Goethe; see Chapter 20.

76. C. G. Carus, *Neuf lettres sur la peinture de paysage*, ed. M. Brion, in C. G. Carus and C. D. Friedrich, *De la peinture de paysage dans l'Allemagne romantique* (Paris, 1988), p. 103 [in English, Carus, *Nine Letters on Landscape Painting: Written in the Years 1815–1824*, trans. D. Britt (Los Angeles, 2002)—Trans.].

77. Goethe, *Werther*, letter of May 10, in *Romans*, pp. 24–25.

78. Ph. O. Runge, letter of March 9, 1802, in *Briefe und Schriften*, ed. P. Betthausen (Berlin, 1981), p. 72. See A. G. F. Gode von Aesch, *Natural Science in German Romanticism* (New York, 1941), pp. 132–133.

79. V. van Gogh, *Lettres à son frère Théo* (Paris, 1988), p. 418 [in English, van Gogh, *The Letters of Vincent van Gogh to His Brother, 1872–1886* (London, Boston, and New York, 1927)—Trans.].

80. *Conversations avec Cézanne*, p. 110.

81. Ibid., p. 122.

82. Ibid., pp. 124–125.

19. ARTEMIS AND ISIS

1. For the discussion that follows, see two excellent works, one by W. Kemp, "Natura: Ikonographische Studien zur Geschichte und Verbreitung einer Allegorie" (Ph.D. diss., Tübingen, 1973), where all other types of representation of Nature can also be found; the other by A. Goesch, *Diana Ephesia: Ikonographische Studien zur Allegorie der Natur in der Kunst vom 16.–19. Jahrhundert* (Frankfurt, 1996). See also the same author's article "Diana Ephesia" in *Der Neue Pauly: Rezeptions- und Wissenschaftsgeschichte*, vol. 13 (Stuttgart and Weimar, 1999), cols. 836–843. See also the essay by Kl. Parlasca, "Zur Artemis Ephesia als Dea Natura in der klassizistischen Kunst," in *Studien zur Religion und Kultur Kleinasiens: Festschrift für Philip Karl Dörner*, ed. S. Sahin, E. Schertheim, and J. Wagner, vol. 2 (Leiden, 1978), pp. 679–689; H. Thiersch, *Artemis Ephesia: Eine archäologische Untersuchung* (Berlin, 1935).

2. See Kemp, "Natura," p. 18; Goesch, *Diana Ephesia*, p. 24.

3. See, for instance, the Fountain of Regeneration, erected on August 10, 1792, and reproduced in J. Baltrusaitis, *La quête d'Isis* (Paris, 1967), p. 29.

4. H. F. Gravelot and C. N. Cochin, "Nature," in *Iconologie par figures* (Paris, 1791), pl. 1.

5. C. Ripa, "Natura," in *Nova Iconologia* (Rome, 1618).

6. Kemp, "Natura," p. 23, citing Horapollo, *Hieroglyphica*, 1, 11 (Paris, 1574); and P. Valeriano, *Hieroglyphica* (Basel, 1574), p. 131.

7. See Gerardus Blasius, *Anatome Animalium* (Amsterdam, 1681).

8. See G. B. Armenini, *De' veri precetti della pittura* (Ravenna, 1587), p. 196, cited in Kemp, "Natura," p. 28. See also A. Chastel, *Art et humanisme à Florence* (Paris, 1959), p. 335; A. von Salis, *Antike und Renaissance* (Erlenbach and Zurich, 1947), p. 44. See also N. Dacos, *La découverte de la Domus Aurea et la formation des grotesques à la Renaissance* (London, 1969); G.-R. Hocke, *Die Welt als Labyrinth: Manier und Manie in der europäischen Kunst* (Hamburg, 1957), p. 73.

9. Ioannes Sambucus, *Emblemata cum aliquot nummis antiqui operis* (Anvers, 1564), p. 74.

10. Saint Jerome, prologue to *Commentary on the Epistle to the Ephesians*, in *Patrologia Latina*, vol. 26, col. 441.

11. A. Delatte and Ph. Derchain, *Les intailles magiques gréco-égyptiennes* (Paris, 1964), p. 179.

12. See F. Dunand, *Le culte d'Isis dans le bassin oriental de la Méditerranée* (Leiden, 1973), vol. 1, pp. 18, 167, 193–204; vol. 2, pp. 164–165; R. Fleischer, *Artemis von Ephesos und verwandte Kultstatuen aus Anatolien und Syrien* (Leiden, 1973), pp. 74–78, 393–395.

13. Fleischer, *Artemis von Ephesos*, pp. 74–78, 393–395.

14. G. Seiterle, "Artemis, die grosse Göttin von Ephesos," *Antike Welt* 10, no. 3 (1979): 3–16.

15. G. Hölbl, *Zeugnisse ägyptischer Religionsvorstellungen für Ephesos* (Leiden, 1978), pp. 25, 27, 52, 59–61, 64 (nn. 326–327), 69, 72ff., 77–85.

16. On this way of translating *natura rerum*, see A. Pellicer, *Natura: Étude sémantique et historique du mot latin* (Paris, 1966), pp. 228–238.

17. Macrobius, *Saturnalia*, I, 20, 18.

18. Iamblichus, *In Nicomachi Arithmeticam Commentaria*, ed. H. Pistelli (Stuttgart, 1975), pp. 13, 12; [Iamblichus], *Theologoumena Arithmetica*, ed. V. de Falco and U. Klein (Stuttgart, 1975), p. 13, ll. 13, 15. See R. E. Witt, *Isis in the Graeco-Roman World* (London, 1971), pp. 149–150.

19. V. Cartari, *Le imagini con la sposizione de i dei degli antichi* (Venice, 1556), p. 41.

20. Apuleius, *Metamorphoses*, XI, 5.

21. On the confusion between Diana and Isis, see Baltrusaitis, *La quête d'Isis*, pp. 113ff.

22. C. Ménétrier, *Symbolica Dianae Ephesiae Statua a Claudio Manetrio bibliothecae Barbarinae praefecto* (Rome, 1657), 157. See also B. de Montfaucon, *l'Antiquité expliquée*, vol. 1 (Paris, 1719), p. 158.

23. In Dutch, R. de Hooghe, *Hieroglyphica* (Amsterdam, 1735); German trans. (Amsterdam, 1744), p. 159, pl. 75, 3.

24. F. Paknadel, "Shaftesbury's Illustrations of *Characteristics*," *Journal of the Warburg and Courtauld Institutes* 37 (1974): 290–312, pl. 71d.

25. On dressing the divine statue, see Plutarch, *Isis and Osiris*, 77, 382c; see Dunand, *Le culte d'Isis dans le bassin oriental de la Méditerranée*, 1:18, 167, 193, 200–201, 204; 2:164–165.

26. E. Spenser, *The Faerie Queene and Two Cantos of Mutabilities*, canto 7, 5–6, ed. T. E. Roche and C. P. O'Donnell (London, 1987), p. 1041.

27. A. Kirchner, *Œdipus Ægyptiacus*, vol. 1 (Rome, 1652–1654), p. 191.

28. J.-B. Boudard, *Iconologie tirée de divers auteurs*, 1st ed. (Parma, 1759); 2nd ed., vol. 3 (Vienna, 1766), p. 1.

29. H. Lacombe de Prézel, "Nature," in *Dictionnaire iconologique* (Paris, 1779).

30. A. von Humboldt, *Ideen zu einer Geographie der Pflanzen* (Tübingen and Paris, 1807), dedicatory page.

31. Goethe, *Die Metamorphose der Pflanzen*, in *Goethes Werke*, 14 vols. (Hamburg, 1948–1969), 13:115.

32. See note 7.

33. See Goesch, *Diana Ephesia*, p. 224, citing Ripa, "Intelletto," in *Iconologia*.

34. A. van Leeuwenhoek, *Arcana Naturae Detecta* (Delphis Batavorum, 1695).

35. A. van Leeuwenhoek, *Anatomia seu Interiora Rerum* (Lugduni Batavorum, 1687).

36. See Chapter 14.

37. See E. Wind, *Mystères païens de la Renaissance* (Paris, 1992), pp. 136–137.

38. See Thiersch, *Artemis Ephesia*, p. 115.

39. Virgil, *Aeneid*, III, 96.

40. Horace, *Poetic Art*, ll. 48–51.

41. R. Paulson, *Hogarth: His Life, Art, and Times* (New Haven, 1974), p. 116.

42. R. Pomeau, "De la nature: Essai sur la vie littéraire d'une idée," *Revue de l'enseignement supérieur*, no. 1 (January–March 1959): 107–119.

43. Lucretius, *On the Nature of Things*, 3, 1–30. On the iconography of Nature in the revolutionary period, see J. Renouvier, *Histoire de l'art pendant la Révolution* (Paris, 1863), pp. 49, 108, 139, 142, 232, 307, 365, and esp. 406.

20. Isis Has No Veils

1. *Weimars Jubelfest am 3ten September 1825*, sec. 1. (Weimar, 1825).

2. For the poem by W. Gerhardt, see *Goethes goldner Jubeltag, 7 Nov. 1825* (Weimar, 1826), p. 143.

3. *Weimars Jubelfest*, p. 38.

4. In *Goethes Werke* (Weimar, 1887–1919) (hereafter WA), I, 5, pp. 91–92.

5. J. W. von Goethe, "Genius die Büste der Natur enthüllend," in WA, I,

4, p. 127. The German text with French translation can be found in Goethe, *Poésies*, trans. R. Ayrault, vol. 2 (Paris, 1982), p. 733.

6. Georg Friedrich Creuzer (1771–1858) was the author of *Symbolik und Mythologie der alten Völker* (1819–1821).

7. "Symbols explained by history" is my translation of "Die geschichtlichen Symbole," from the perspective of Creuzer's symbolics.

8. Goethe, *Zahme Xenien*, vol. 6, in WA, I, 3, p. 354.

9. Goethe, *Faust*, pt. 1, ll, 668–674, in *Théâtre complet* (Paris, 1958), p. 971 [in English, Goethe, *Faust: A Tragedy*, trans. W. Arndt, ed. C. Tamlin (New York, 1976)—Trans.].

10. Goethe, *Sämtliche Werke nach Epochen seines Schaffens* (Munich, 1992), vol. 13, 1, p. 129, with the commentary p. 701.

11. *Paralipomena zu Faust II*, act 3, in Goethe, *Faust*, ed. Albrecht Schöne (Darmstadt, 1999), p. 694.

12. Goethe, *Faust*, pt. 1, l. 1936, in *Théâtre complet*, p. 998.

13. See Chapter 18.

14. I would like to point out two works on Goethe's scientific method: L. Van Eyde, *La libre raison du phénomène: Essai sur la Naturphilosophie de Goethe* (Paris, 1998); and J. Lacoste, *Goethe: Science et philosophie* (Paris, 1997).

15. A. von Haller, *Die Falschheit menschlicher Tugenden*, in *Versuch schweizerischer Gedichte* (Bern, 1732), p. 78. On this theme, see M. Mersenne, *Questions théologiques* (Paris, 1634).

16. Goethe, "Allerdings: Dem Physiker" (Certainly: To the Physicist), in the group of poems titled *Gott und Welt* (God and the World), WA, I, 3, p. 105; German text with French translation in Goethe, *Poésies*, 2:607.

17. An expression from J. F. Blumenbach taken up by Kant in *Critique de la faculté de juger*, §81, trans. A. Philonenko (Paris, 1968), pp. 235–236; and by Goethe, *Bildungstrieb*, in *Goethes Werke*, 14 vols. (Hamburg, 1948–1969)(hereafter HA), 13:33.

18. Goethe, *Einwirkung der neueren Philosophie*, HA, 13:28.

19. Goethe, *Zur Morphologie: Die Absicht eingeleitet*, HA, 13:56.

20. See C. Gögelin, *Zu Goethes Begriff von Wissenschaft* (Munich, 1972); P. Hadot, "L'apport du néoplatonisme à la philosophie de la nature," in *Tradition und Gegenwart: Eranos Jahrbuch, 1968* (Zurich, 1970), pp. 95–99.

21. Goethe, *Zur Farbenlehre*, §175, HA, 13:368. See the excellent study on the *Urphänomen* in G. Bianquis, *Études sur Goethe* (Paris, 1951), pp. 45–80.

22. Goethe, *Voyage en Italie*, April 17 and May 17, 1787, trans. J. Naujac, vol. 2 (Paris, 1961), pp. 497, 609. See Chapter 18.

23. Goethe, *Zur Farbenlehre, Vorwort*, HA, 13:317, 11.

24. Goethe, *Maximen und Reflexionen*, §488, HA, 12:432.

25. Cited after the translation, modified, by J.-F. Angelloz, in H. Carossa, *Les pages immortelles de Goethe* (Paris, 1942), p. 125.

26. Goethe, *Epirrhema*, WA, I, 3, p. 88; German text with French translation (the last two verses of which have been modified) in Goethe, *Poésies*, 2:605.

27. Goethe, *Tag- und Jahreshefte*, HA, 10:435–436.

28. Goethe, *Xenien*, §155, HA, 1:230.

29. *Goethe's Conversations with Eckermann*, February 18, 1829, trans. J. Chuzeville (Paris, 1988), pp. 277–278 (translation slightly modified) [in English, Goethe, *Conversations with Eckermann, 1823–1832* (1850), trans. J. Oxenford (San Francisco, 1984)—Trans.].

30. Goethe, *Maximen und Reflexionen*, §19, HA, 12:367.

31. Kant, *Critique de la faculté de juger*, §49, p. 146. Kant and Goethe both say that the aesthetic Idea (Kant) or the symbol (Goethe) remain unexpressed and inexpressible, even if they were to be expressed in all languages. On symbols and the aesthetic idea, see M. Marache, *Le symbole dans la pensée et l'œuvre de Goethe* (Paris, 1959), pp. 123–125; T. Todorov, *Théories du symbole* (Paris, 1977), pp. 235–243.

32. Goethe, *Maximen und Reflexionen*, §749, HA, 12:470.

33. Ibid., §752, p. 471.

34. Goethe, *Interview with Falk*, in *Goethes Gespräche*, ed. F. von Biedermann, vol. 2 (Leipzig, 1909–1911), p. 41.

35. Ibid., 2:40. On the word "meaning" here, see Chapter 17.

36. Goethe, *Zur Farbenlehre*, §177, HA, 13:368.

37. Goethe, *Conversations with Eckermann*, December 21, 1831, p. 422.

38. Goethe, intro. to *Versuch einer Witterungslehre*, HA, 13:305.

39. Goethe, *Faust*, pt. 2, l. 4727, in *Théâtre complet*, p. 1076.

40. Goethe, *Pandora*, ll. 955–958, ibid., pp. 932–933.

41. Goethe, *Maximen und Reflexionen*, §290, HA, 12:405.

42. W. Emrich, *Die Symbolik von Faust II* (Frankfurt and Bonn, 1964), pp. 53–54; Goethe, "Aneignung" (Dedication), in *Poésie*, 1:134–135.

43. Goethe, *Tag- und Jahreshefte* (1811), HA, 10:510–511.

44. Letter to Jacobi, May 10, 1812, in *Goethes Briefe*, 4 vols. (Hamburg, 1965–1967), no. 960, 3:190–191.

45. D. Diderot, *Pensées sur l'interprétation de la Nature*, §VI, in Diderot, *Œuvres philosophiques*, ed. P. Vernière, vol. 12 (Paris, 1964), pp. 186–188.

46. Goethe, *Divan oriental-occidental*, trans. H. Lichtenberger, (Paris, n.d.), pp. 228–229.

21. THE SACRED SHUDDER

1. R. Lenoble, *Esquisse d'une histoire de l'idée de nature* (Paris, 1969), p. 317.

2. See Chapter 18.

3. *Letter to Malesherbes*, cited in J.-J. Rousseau, *Les confessions*, vols. 1–6 (Paris, 1998), pp. 407–408, emphasis added [in English, Rousseau, *The Confessions; and Correspondence, Including the Letters to Malesherbes*, ed. C. Kelly, R. D. Masters, and P. G. Stillman, trans. C. Kelly, vol. 5 of *The Collected Writings of Rousseau* (Hanover, N.H., 1995)—Trans.]. See F. Hölderlin "Bread and Wine."

4. J.-J. Rousseau, *Rêveries du promeneur solitaire*, Seventh Promenade (Paris, 1964), pp. 126–129 [in English, Rousseau, *The Reveries of the Solitary Walker, Botanical Writings, and Letter to Franquières*, ed. C. Kelly; trans. C. E. Butterworth, A. Cook, and T. E. Marshall, vol. 8 of *The Collected Writings of Rousseau* (Hanover, N.H., 2000)—Trans.].

5. F. L. Stolberg-Stolberg, "Fülle des Herzens," *Deutsches Museum* (July 1777), cited by A. G. F. Gode von Aesch, *Natural Science in German Romanticism* (New York, 1941), p. 125, n. 11.

6. Plutarch, *Isis and Osiris*, 9, 354c. On the goddess Neith, see R. el-Sayed, *La déesse Neith de Saïs* (Cairo, 1982). On the text by Plutarch, see C. Harrauer, "'Ich bin was da ist . . . ': Die Göttin von Saïs," *Sphairos: Wiener Studien* 1, nos. 107–108 (1994–95): 337–355; Plutarch, *De Iside et Osiride*, ed. J. G. Griffiths (Cardiff, 1970), p. 283; J. Hani, *La religion égyptienne chez Plutarque* (Paris, 1976). See also J. Assmann, *Moïse l'Égyptien* (Paris, 2001), p. 207 [in English, Assmann, *Moses the Egyptian: The Memory of Egypt in*

Western Monotheism (Cambridge, Mass., 1997)—Trans.]. The *peplos* was a piece of cloth that women wound around themselves above their dress. It was thus ultimately a veil, like that of Athena which the women of Athens wove for the Panathenaic procession, and thus would justify us in supposing that Plutarch was probably less "authentic" than Proclus. Harrauer, "'Ich bin was da ist,'" pp. 340–341.

7. Proclus, *Commentary on the Timaeus*, trans. A.-J. Festugière, 5 vols. (Paris, 1966–1968), 1:140; ed. E. Diehl, 3 vols. (1903–1906; reprint, Amsterdam, 1965), 1:98, 19 (cf. the note in Festugière). In Plutarch and in Proclus we find the classic form of self-representation of the divinity in aretalogies: "I am this or that"; see O. Weinreich, "Aion in Eleusis," *Archiv für Religionswissenschaft* 19 (1916–1919): 174–190, esp. p. 179 (reprinted in O. Weinreich, *Ausgewählte Schriften*, ed. G. Wille, vol. 1 [Amsterdam, 1969], pp. 442–461, esp. pp. 448–449).

8. See Plutarch, *De Iside et Osiride*, p. 284, with bibliography. As was pointed out by A.-J. Festugière (Proclus, *Commentaire sur le Timée*, 1:140), the phrase "all that was, is, and shall be" would seem to indicate an assimilation of Isis to Aion, or Eternity. He compares the expression to the one used in a dedication at Eleusis (see W. Dittenberger, *Sylloge Inscriptionum Graecarum*, 4 vols., 3rd ed. [Leipzig, 1915–1924], no. 1125). Yet this dedication merely states that Aion remains what it is, was, and shall be, which is not quite the same thing. See R. T. Rundle Clark, *Myth and Symbol in Ancient Egypt* (London, 1978), p. 157.

9. Plutarch, *Isis and Osiris*, 53, 372e.

10. F. Dunand, *Le culte d'Isis dans le bassin oriental de la Méditerranée*, vol. 1 (Leiden, 1973), p. 85.

11. Herodotus, *Histories*, II, 59. See Chapter 22.

12. K. Preisidanz, *Papyri Graecae Magicae: Die griechischen Zauberpapyri*, 3 vols. (Leipzig and Berlin, 1928–1931), 2nd ed. (1973–1974), 57, 16–17; H. D. Betz, *The Greek Magical Papyri in Translation* (Chicago, 1986), p. 285. See A. D. Nock, *Coniectanea Neotestamentica*, vol. 1 (Lund, 1947), p. 174. Is there a relation between this incantation and the magicians' threats to reveal the mysteries of Isis in Iamblichus, *Mysteries of Egypt*, VI, 5, 245, 16, ed. and trans. É. des Places (Paris, 1966)? See Chapter 7.

13. E. Darwin, *The Temple of Nature, or The Origin of Society: A Poem* (Edinburgh, 1809). See I. Primer, "Erasmus Darwin's *Temple of Nature*: Progress,

Evolution, and the Eleusinian Mysteries," *Journal of the History of Ideas* 25 (1964): 58–76.

14. Primer, "Erasmus Darwin's *Temple of Nature*," p. 70.

15. Assmann, *Moïse l'Égyptien*, pp. 203ff. See also, for the discussion that follows, the very important article by Christine Harrauer, "'Ich bin was da ist.'"

16. On the iconography of Isis in Freemasonry, see J. Baltrusaitis, *La quête d'Isis* (Paris, 1967), pp. 51–70; M. P. Hall, *An Encyclopedic Outline of Masonic, Hermetic, Qabbalistic, and Rosicrucian Symbolic Philosophy* (San Francisco, 1928).

17. Assmann, *Moïse l'Égyptien*, pp. 203–245.

18. K. L. Reinhold, *Die hebräischen Mysterien oder die älteste religiöse Freymaurerey* (Leipzig, 1787). See Assmann, *Moïse l'Égyptien*, pp. 97–199.

19. Reinhold, *Die hebräischen Mysterien oder die älteste religiöse Freymaurerey*, p. 209. See E. Cassirer, *Langage et mythe: À propos des noms des dieux* (Paris, 1973), pp. 96–97 [in English, Cassirer, *Language and Myth*, trans. S. K. Langer (New York, 1953)—Trans.].

20. Assmann, *Moïse l'Égyptien*, p. 210.

21. Ibid., pp. 239–245.

22. Spinoza, *Ethics*, IV, preface. On the sources of Spinoza's phrase, see Assmann, *Moïse l'Égyptien*, p. 364, n. 31.

23. On this term, see ibid., p. 243.

24. See ibid., pp. 219–224.

25. Aristotle, *Fragmenta Selecta*, ed. W. D. Ross (Oxford, 1955), *Peri philosophias*, fragment 15. On this text, compare the study by J. Croissant, *Aristote et les mystères* (Liège and Paris, 1932), with the review of this work by W. Theiler in *Byzantinische Zeitschrift* 34 (1934): 76–78.

26. On this subject, see Baltrusaitis, *La quête d'Isis*, pp. 25–70; W. Kemp, *Natura: Ikonographische Studien zur Geschichte und Verbreitung einer Allegorie* (Tübingen, 1973), pp. 156–176; A. Goesch, *Diana Ephesia: Ikonographische Studien zur Allegorie der Natur in der Kunst vom 16.–19. Jahrhundert* (Frankfurt, 1996), pp. 169–219.

27. See H. Thiersch, *Artemis Ephesia: Eine archäologische Untersuchung* (Berlin, 1935), pp. 117–121, esp. p. 120.

28. In dealing with the subject discussed in this section, I have gained valuable assistance from A. G. F. Gode von Aesch, *Natural Science in Ger-*

man Romanticism (New York, 1941), pp. 93–108; and from Assmann, *Moïse l'Égyptien.*

29. I. Kant, preface to *Critique of Pure Reason*, 2nd ed.

30. See Chapter 19.

31. I. Kant, *Critique de la faculté de juger*, §49, trans. A. Philonenko (Paris, 1968), p. 146.

32. See Chapter 19.

33. F. Schiller, "The Veiled Statue at Saïs," in *Poèmes philosophiques*, trans. R. d'Harcourt (Paris, n.d.), pp. 150–157 [an English translation of Schiller's poems may be found on line at http://www.gutenberg.net].

34. Letter from Herder to Schiller, August 23, 1795, cited in Harrauer, "'Ich bin was da ist,'" p. 351, n. 40.

35. See Chapter 19.

36. F. Schiller, "The Words of Illusion," in *Poèmes philosophiques*, p. 259 (d'Harcourt's translation modified).

37. In *Schillers Werke*, (Weimar, 1983), vol. 2, 1, p. 255; trans. A. Régnier, *Poésies de Schiller*, vol. 1 of *Œuvres de Schiller* (Paris, 1868), p. 286.

38. Schiller, "The Words of Illusion," p. 259.

39. F. Schiller, "The Beginning of a New Century," in *Poèmes philosophiques*, p. 263.

40. F. Schiller, "Moses' Mission," in *Œuvres historiques*, vol. 1, trans. A. Régnier (Paris, 1860), pp. 445–468.

41. See Chapter 8.

42. F. Schlegel, *Ideen*, §1, in *Kritische Neue Ausgabe*, vol. 2 (Paderborn, 1967), p. 256: "Es ist Zeit den Schleier der Isis zu zerrissen und das Geheime zu offenbaren. Wer den Anblick der Göttin nicht ertragen kann, fliehe oder verderbe."

43. Novalis, "The Disciples at Saïs," in *Petits écrits*, trans. G. Bianquis (Paris, 1947), p. 189.

44. Novalis, "Grains of Pollen," §112, ibid., p. 83.

45. Novalis, "The Disciples at Saïs," *Paralipomena*, 2, ibid., p. 257.

46. On the Neoplatonic roots of this idea, see P. Hadot, "L'apport du néoplatonisme à la philosophie de la nature," *Tradition und Gegenwart: Eranos Jahrbuch, 1968* (1970): 91–132.

47. M. Merleau-Ponty in *Annuaire du Collège de France*, 1957, p. 210 (summary of courses).

48. F. W. Schelling, *System of Transcendent Idealism*, trans. S. Jankélévitch (Paris, 1946), p. 175.

49. G. W. F. Hegel, *Vorlesungen über die Philosophie der Religion*, in *Sämtliche Werke*, vol. 15 (Stuttgart, 1965), p. 471 [in English, Hegel, *Lectures on the Philosophy of Religion: The Lectures of 1827*, ed. P. C. Hodgson, trans. R. F. Brown, P. C. Hodgson, and J. M. Stewart (Berkeley, 1988)—Trans.].

50. G. W. F. Hegel, *System der Philosophie: Einleitung in die Naturphilosophie*, ibid., vol. 9 (Stuttgart, 1965), pp. 46–47.

51. G. W. F. Hegel, *Vorlesungen über die Philosophie der Geschichte*, ibid., vol. 11 (Stuttgart, 1961), p. 291.

52. Novalis, "The Disciples at Saïs," pp. 243, 245.

53. Ibid., p. 247.

54. Ibid.

55. C. von Brentano, *Romanzen vom Rosenkranz*, in *Sämtliche Werke*, ed. C. Schüddekopf (Munich, 1909–1917), l. 105, p. 66.

56. This is the opinion of A. G. F. Gode von Aesch, *Natural Science in German Romanticism*, p. 105.

57. P. S. Ballanche, *Orphée: Essai de palingénésie sociale*, vol. 2, in *Œuvres de M. Ballanche*, vol. 4 (Paris and Geneva, 1830), p. 314.

58. On the theme of the sublime, see, among other works, M. Nicholson, *Mountain Gloom and Mountain Glory* (Ithaca, N.Y., 1959).

59. E. Burke, *A Philosophical Enquiry into the Origin of Our Ideas of the Sublime and Beautiful* (London, 1756).

60. E. Cassirer, *La Philosophie des Lumières en France*, trans. P. Quillet (Paris, 1966), p. 320 [in English, Cassirer, *The Philosophy of the Enlightenment*, trans. F. C. A. Koelln and J. P. Pettegrove (Princeton, 1951)—Trans.].

61. Kant, *Critique de la faculté de juger*, §29, Remarks.

62. Ibid.

63. Seneca, *Letters to Lucilius*, 64, 6. On this text, see my article "The Sage and the World," in *Le Temps de la réflexion* (Paris, 1989), pp. 175–188 [in English, Hadot, *Philosophy as a Way of Life* (Oxford, 1995), pp. 251–263—Trans.]. See also Chapter 18.

64. Kant, *Critique de la faculté de juger*, §49.

65. H. Lacombe de Prézel, "Nature," in *Dictionnaire iconologique* (Paris, 1779).

66. F. Schiller, *On the Sublime*, trans. A. Régnier (1859), (reprint, Paris, 1997), p. 67. Cited in Assmann, *Moïse l'Égyptien*, p. 225.

67. A. Schopenhauer, *Le monde comme volonté et comme représentation*, French trans. A. Burdeau (Paris, 2003), bk. 3, §33–34 [in English, Schopenhauer, *The World as Will and Representation*, trans. R. B. Haldane and J. Kemp (London, 1896), bk. 3, §39, p. 264—Trans.].

68. Ibid., p. 265. For reasons different from those of Schopenhauer, Kant also speaks, on the last page of the *Critique of Practical Reason*, of the twofold movement of annihilation and elevation that the contemplation of the starry sky and of the moral conscience produces in us.

69. J. W. von Goethe, *Wilhelm Meister: Les années de voyage*, I, 10, in *Romans* (Paris, 1954), p. 1068 (trans. modified).

70. See Chapter 20.

71. Goethe, *Interviews with Falk*, in *Goethes Gespräche*, ed. F. von Biedermann, vol. 2 (Leipzig, 1909–1911), p. 40.

72. Goethe, *Maximen und Reflexionen*, §16–17, in *Goethes Werke*, ed. Erich Trunz, 14 vols. (Hamburg, 1948–1969) (hereafter HA), 12:367.

73. For instance, ibid., §§16–17, 22, p. 368.

74. See Chapter 20.

75. Goethe, *Faust*, pt. 2, l. 6272, in *Théâtre complet* (Paris, 1958), p. 1127.

76. On this subject, see the excellent discussion by P. Citati, *Goethe* (Paris, 1992), pp. 261–275.

77. Goethe, *Les affinités électives*, II, 5, in *Romans*, p. 287.

78. Goethe, *Werther*, bk. 1, letter of August 18, ibid., pp. 66–67.

79. Review of J. G. Sulzer, *Die schönen Künste* (Leipzig, 1772), HA, 12:17–18. I have followed, with slight modifications, the translation by M. Marche in his book *Le symbole dans l'œuvre et la pensée de Goethe* (Paris, 1960), p. 48.

80. C. G. Carus, *Neuf lettres sur la peinture de paysage*, ed. Marcel Brion, in C. G. Carus, and C. D. Friedrich, *De la peinture de paysage dans l'Allemagne romantique* (Paris, 1988), p. 59.

81. See F. Graf, *Eleusis und die orphische Dichtung Athens in vorhellenistischer Zeit* (Berlin, 1974), p. 131, citing a fragment of Plutarch, the Greek text of which is in Stobaeus, *Anthologium*, vol. 5, ed. O. Hense (Berlin, 1912), p. 1089, 13.

82. Lucretius, *On Nature*, III, 28.

83. Seneca, *Letters to Lucilius*, 64, 6; see note 63.

84. E. Spenser, *The Faerie Queene and Two Cantos of Mutabilities*, canto 7, ll. 5–6, ed. T. E. Roche and C. P. O'Donnell (London, 1987), p. 1041. See Chapter 19.

85. B. Pascal, *Pensées*, §296, trans. L. Brunschvicg (Paris, 1974). See Lenoble, *Histoire de l'idée de nature*, pp. 334–335.

86. Pascal, *Pensées*, §693.

22. NATURE AS SPHINX

1. F. Nietzsche, *Untimely Considerations*, IV, in *Richard Wagner in Bayreuth*, §7, trans. G. Bianquis, vol. 2 (Paris, 1966), p. 237 [in English, Nietzsche, *Untimely Meditations*, trans. R. J. Hollingdale (Cambridge and New York, 1983)—Trans.].

2. The translations of this text are based on the translation of P. Wotling (F. Nietzsche, *The Gay Science* [Paris, 2000]), sometimes slightly modified.

3. The epilogue to *Nietzsche contra Wagner* adds a phrase: "Tout comprendre, c'est tout mépriser" (in French in the text) [To understand everything is to despise everything]. This is an allusion to the saying of Madame de Staël, "To understand everything would be to forgive everything," cited by, among others, Marquis Astolphe de Custine, in *Lettres à Varnhagen* (Geneva, 1979), p. 441. See F. Nietzsche, *Posthumous Fragments (Autumn 1885–Autumn 1887)*, I [42], in *Œuvres philosophiques complètes*, 14 vols. (Paris, 1974–) (hereafter NRF), 12:29.

4. F. Nietzsche, preface to *The Gay Science*, §4, p. 32.

5. Ibid., §121, p. 173.

6. J. Granier, *Le problème de la Vérité dans la philosophie de Nietzsche* (Paris, 1966), p. 512.

7. Nietzsche, *The Gay Science*, §344, p. 287. See K. Jaspers, *Nietzsche* (Paris, 1950) [in English, Jaspers, *Nietzsche: An Introduction to the Understanding of His Philosophical Activity*, trans. C. F. Wallraff and F. J. Schmitz (Lanham, Md., 1985)—Trans.]; Granier, *Le problème de la Vérité*, p. 518.

8. This text may be found in NRF, 5:603.

9. Nietzsche, *The Gay Science*, preface, §4, p. 31.

10. Ibid., §370, p. 332, and preface, §4, p. 31.

11. F. Nietzsche, *Posthumous Fragments (Autumn 1885–Autumn 1887)*, 2 [33], NRF, 12:89.

12. Granier, *Le problème de la vérité*, p. 522.

13. F. Nietzsche, *Posthumous Fragments (Beginning of 1888–Beginning of January 1889)*, 14 [36], NRF, 14:39.

14. Nietzsche, *Beyond Good and Evil*, §59, trans. G. Bianquis (Paris, 1971), p. 83.

15. F. Nietzsche, *The Birth of Tragedy*, §3, trans. G. Bianquis (Paris, 1949), p. 32.

16. See Chapter 21.

17. Nietzsche, *The Gay Science*, §57, p. 111.

18. See Chapter 21.

19. In *Schillers Werke*, vol. 2, 1 (Weimar, 1983), p. 255. See C. Andler, *Nietzsche: Sa vie et sa pensée*, vol. 1, *Les précurseurs de Nietzsche* (Paris, 1958), p. 34. See also Jaspers, *Nietzsche*, pp. 228–232; and above all the highly illuminating discussion in Granier, *Le problème de la Vérité*, pp. 518ff.

20. See Chapter 20.

21. J. W. von Goethe, "Genius die Büste der Natur enthüllend," in *Goethes Werke* (Weimar, 1887–1919), I, 4, p. 127.

22. Not "of the nature of the Sphinx," as in the NRF translation.

23. "The beautiful is the Sphinx's girlish young body." *Posthumous Writings, (1870–1873)*, NRF, 7 [27], p. 186.

24. F. Nietzsche, "The State among the Greeks," in *Posthumous Writings (1870–1873)*, NRF, vol. 1, pt. 2, p. 178.

25. Nietzsche, *The Birth of Tragedy*, §9.

26. Ibid.

27. Nietzsche, *The Gay Science*, preface, §4.

28. Granier, *Le problème de la Vérité*, p. 525.

29. Nietzsche, *The Birth of Tragedy*, §15. 1,

30. Granier, *Le problème de la Vérité*, p. 534.

31. Nietzsche, *The Gay Science*, preface, §4.

32. Nietzsche, *Posthumous Fragments (Beginning of 1888–Beginning of January 1889)*, 20 [48], NRF, 14:303.

33. See Granier, *Le problème de la Vérité*, p. 11, n. 1.

34. M. B. de Launay, "Le traducteur médusé," in *Langue française* 51 (September 1981): 53–62.

35. Nietzsche, *Posthumous Fragments (Beginning of 1888–Beginning of January 1889)*, 20 [73], NRF, 14:307; cf. ibid. (Fall 1887–March 1888), 11 [6],

NRF, 13:214. In both places, we find the same formula, "Man geht zugrunde, wenn man immer zu den Gründen geht," translated in vol. 14 as "By dint of wanting to get to the bottom of things, one falls into a bottomless well," and in vol. 13 as "One sinks by dint of wanting to get to the bottom of things." Both translations correspond well to what Nietzsche means, but I think that the plural *Gründe* needs to be translated as "reasons," as in the numerous passages where it appears in Nietzsche. To make it understood that it is dangerous to try to get to the bottom of things, I have therefore translated *Gründe* by "ultimate reasons," which led me, in order to allude to Nietzsche's play on words, to translate *"zugrunde gehen"* by "goes to his last resting place."

36. J.-J. Rousseau, *Discours sur les sciences et les arts,* ed. F. Bouchardy (Paris, 1964), p. 39.

37. See F. Graf, *Eleusis und die orphische Dichtung Athens in vorhellenischer Zeit* (Berlin, 1974), p. 194; M. Olender, "Aspect de Baubō," *Revue de l'Histoire des Religions* 202 (1985): 3–55; C. Picard, "L'épisode de Baubō dans les mystères d'Éleusis," *Revue de l'Histoire des Religions* 95 (1927): 220–255.

38. Clement of Alexandria, *Protreptic,* II, 20, 3, trans. C. Mondésert (Paris, 1949), p. 76. Eusebius of Caesarea, *Evangelical Preparation,* II, 3, 34, ed. É. des Places (Paris, 1976), p. 95 [English translations of the texts of Clement and Eusebius may be found at http://www.ccel.org].

39. See Chapter 21.

40. On this subject, see M. Broc-Lapeyre, "Pourquoi Baubō a-t-elle fait rire Déméter?" *Recherches sur la philosophie et le langage,* no 5, *Pratiques du langage dans l'Antiquité* (1985): 60.

41. E. Rohde, *Psyché,* trans. A. Reymond (Paris, 1951), p. 608 [in English, Rohde, *Psyche: The Cult of Souls and Belief in Immortality among the Greeks,* trans. W. B. Hillis (New York, 1920)—Trans.].

42. J. W. von Goethe, *Faust,* pt. 1, l. 3962, in *Théâtre complet* (Paris, 1958), p. 1051. On the iconography of Baubo riding a sow, see Broc-Lapeyre, "Pourquoi Baubō a-t-elle fait rire Déméter?"

43. F. Nietzsche, "In the South," in *The Gay Science,* p. 358.

44. Ibid., §377, p. 344.

45. Nietzsche, *Posthumous Fragments (Beginning of 1888–Beginning of January 1889),* 16 [40, 6], NRF, 14:250.

46. See Granier, *Le problème de la Vérité*, p. 530: "Measure is the reconciliation of art and knowledge, the superior balance that is established between two antagonistic instincts whose destiny is to compensate each other mutually, that of illusion and that of knowledge."

47. Ibid., p. 537; E. Fink, *La philosophie de Nietzsche* (Paris, 1965), pp. 239–241.

48. See, for instance, the chapter titled "Eros and Knowledge," in P. Salm, *The Poem as Plant: A Biological View of Goethe's Faust* (Cleveland and London, 1971), pp. 79–103.

49. See Chapter 21. In fact the title of Schiller's poem is "The Veiled Statue at Saïs."

50. On the myth of Actaeon in Giordano Bruno, see N. Ordine, *Le Seuil de l'Ombre: Littérature, philosophie et peinture chez Giordano Bruno* (Paris, 2003), pp. 209–235. Dominique Venner, in *Histoire de la tradition des Européens* (Paris, 2002), p. 228, interprets the punishment of Actaeon, devoured by his dogs because he has seen Diana naked, as the symbol of the danger that humanity incurs if it lets itself be carried away by the inordinate ambition to dominate nature: "The fate of Actaeon reminds us in a timely manner that mankind is not the master of nature."

51. J.-P. Sartre, *L'Être et le Néant* (Paris, 1943), p. 624 [in English, Sartre, *Being and Nothingness: An Essay on Phenomenological Ontology*, trans. H. E. Barnes (London, 1958)—Trans.].

52. See Chapter 20.

53. Montesquieu, *Discours de réception à l'Académie de Bordeaux*, in *Œuvres complètes* (Paris, 1846), p. 559.

54. Nietzsche, *Posthumous Fragments (Autumn 1885–Autumn 1887)*, 2 [119], NRF, 12:125.

55. Ibid., 2 [114], p. 124.

56. See Chapter 23.

57. F. Nietzsche, *Le philosophes préplatoniciens*, trans. N. Ferrand (1994), p. 152.

58. Nietzsche, *Posthumous Fragments (Beginning of 1888–Beginning of January 1889)*, 14 [14], NRF, 14:30.

59. F. Nietzsche, *Twilight of the Idols*, §49, NRF, 8:144.

60. F. Nietzsche, *Posthumous Fragments (Summer 1881–Summer 1882)*, 11 [7], NRF, 5:315.

23. From the Secret of Nature to the Mystery of Being

1. See Chapters 20–22.

2. F. W. Schelling, *Les âges du monde*, trans. S. Jankélévitch (Paris, 1949) [in English, Schelling, *The Ages of the World*, trans. F. Bolman Jr. (New York, 1942)—Trans.]. The other previous versions have been published by Pascal David (F. W. Schelling, *Les âges du monde: Fragments dans les premières éditions de 1811 et 1813*, ed. M. Schröter [Paris, 1991]), together with a post-script titled *La généalogie du temps* [in English, *The Genealogy of Time*. See Schelling, *The Ages of the World: (Fragment) from the Handwritten Remains, Third Version (ca. 1815)*, trans. J. M. Wirth (Albany, 2000)—Trans.].

3. Schelling, *Les âges du monde*, p. 49.

4. A. Koyré, *La philosophie de Jacob Boehme* (Paris, 1929), pp. 186, 383.

5. Schelling, *Les âges du monde*, p. 149.

6. Ibid., p. 65.

7. Ibid.

8. Ibid., p. 66.

9. V. Jankélévitch, *Schelling* (Paris, 1932), p. 111.

10. Ibid.

11. F. W. Schelling, *Aphorismes sur la philosophie de la nature*, §I, in *Œuvres métaphysiques (1805–1821)*, trans. J.-F. Courtine and E. Martineau (Paris, 1980), p. 75.

12. J. Assmann, *Moïse l'Égyptien* (Paris, 2001), pp. 203ff. See also Chapter 21.

13. See J.-F. Courtine, *Extase de la raison: Essais sur Schelling* (Paris, 1990), pp. 200–236.

14. Schelling, *Les âges du monde*, p. 162.

15. See Koyré, *La philosophie de Jacob Boehme*, p. 297.

16. Schelling, *Les âges du monde*, p. 183.

17. K. Löwith, *Nietzsche: Philosophie de l'éternel retour du même* (Paris, 1991), p. 182 [in English, Löwith, *Nietzsche's Philosophy of the Eternal Recurrence of the Same*, trans. J. H. Lomax (Berkeley, 1997)—Trans.]; see M. Merleau-Ponty, *La Nature: Notes. Cours du Collège de France*, ed. D. Séglard (Paris, 1994), pp. 61–62.

18. On this subject, see the excellent article by A. Renault, "La nature

aime à se cacher," *Revue de métaphysique et de morale* 81 (1976): 62–111; and the discussion Marlène Zarader has devoted to this problem in her book *Heidegger et les paroles d'origine* (Paris, 1990), pp. 33–47.

19. See Zarader, *Heidegger et les paroles d'origine*, p. 41.

20. M. Heidegger, *Le principe de raison*, trans. A. Préau, (Paris, 1962), p. 155 [in English, Heidegger, *The Principle of Reason*, trans. R. Lilly (Bloomington, 1991)—Trans.].

21. Ibid., p. 164.

22. M. Heidegger, *Introduction à la métaphysique*, trans. G. Kahn (Paris, 1967), p. 126 [in English, Heidegger, *Introduction to Metaphysics*, trans. G. Fried and R. Polt (New Haven, 2000)—Trans.].

23. M. Heidegger, "What *Phusis* Is and How It Determines Itself," trans. F. Fédier, in *Questions Iet II*, trans. K. Axelos et al. (Paris, 1990), p. 581.

24. Renault, "La nature aime à se cacher," p. 107.

25. Notes taken in Heidegger's logic class (1944) by A. de Waehlens and W. Biernel, cited by them in the introduction to M. Heidegger, *De l'essence de la vérité* (Louvain and Paris, 1948), pp. 19–20.

26. M. Heidegger, *Introduction à la métaphysique*, cited in Zarader, *Heidegger et les paroles de l'origine*, p. 36.

27. Zarader, *Heidegger et les paroles de l'origine*, p. 37.

28. Heidegger, *Le principe de raison*, p. 155.

29. Renault, "La nature aime à se cacher," p. 111.

30. Heidegger "What *Phusis* Is and How It Determines Itself," pp. 581–582.

31. See Zarader, *Heidegger et les paroles de l'origine*, pp. 46–47.

32. J. Wahl, *Sur l'interprétation de l'histoire de la métaphysique d'après Heidegger*, Centre de Documentation Universitaire, Sorbonne, p. 104.

33. Plotinus, *Enneads*, VI 9 [9], 4, 24–26.

34. Heidegger, *De l'essence de la vérité*, p. 96.

35. Renault, "La nature aime à se cacher," p. 109.

36. A. de Waehlens, *La philosophie de Martin Heidegger* (Louvain, 1942), pp. 122–123, summarizing *Being and Time*, §40.

37. J. Wahl, *Études kierkegaardiennes* (Paris, 1938), p. 221, n. 2.

38. De Waehlens, *La philosophie de Martin Heidegger*, p. 127.

39. J.-P. Sartre, *La nausée* (Paris, 1948), pp. 162–167 [in English, Sartre, *Nausea*, trans. L. Alexander (Cambridge, Mass., 1979)—Trans.].

40. Hugo von Hofmansthal, *Letter of Lord Chandos*, trans. J.-C. Schneider

and A. Kohn (Paris, 1992), p. 47 [in English, von Hofmannsthal, *The Lord Chandos Letter and Other Writings*, ed. and trans. J. Rotenberg (New York, 2005)—Trans.].

41. M. Merleau-Ponty, *Éloge de la philosophie* (Paris, 1960), p. 53 [in English, Merleau-Ponty, *In Praise of Philosophy*, trans. J. Wild and J. M. Edie (Evanston, Ill., 1963)—Trans.].

42. M. Merleau-Ponty, *La phénoménologie de la perception* (Paris, 1945), p. xvi [in English, Merleau-Ponty, *Phenomenology of Perception*, trans. C. Smith (London and New York, 2002)—Trans.].

43. G. Marcel, *Être et avoir* (Paris, 1935), p. 145; see also pp. 165, 249 [in English, Marcel, *Being and Having: An Existentialist Diary* (New York, 1965)—Trans.].

44. M. Merleau-Ponty, *Éloge de la philosophie* (Paris, 1960), p. 53.

45. Ibid.

46. P. Hadot, "Réflections sur les limites du langage à propos du *Tractatus logico-philosophicus* de Wittgenstein," *Revue de métaphysique et de morale* 63 (1959): 477.

47. This adjective corresponds to the German verb *zeigen*.

48. L. Wittgenstein, *Leçons et conversations* (Paris, 1992), pp. 148–149.

49. Spinoza, *Ethics*, pt.4, preface.

50. On this translation, see L. Wittgenstein, *Letters to C. K. Ogden* (Oxford, 1983), pp. 36–37.

CONCLUSION

1. F. Nietzsche, *Humain trop humain, suivi de Fragments posthumes (1878–1879)*, §168, in *Œuvres philosophiques complètes*, vol. III, pt. 2 (Paris, 1974–), p. 74 [in English, Nietzsche, *Human, All Too Human: A Book for Free Spirits*, trans. R. J. Hollingdale (Cambridge, 1986)—Trans.].

Index

Maier, Michael, 241–242
Manet, Édouard, 63–64
Marcus Aurelius, 11, 27, 161
Mathematics, 105–106, 155; and models, 159, 163–164
Matter, 136; intelligible, 59
Maupertuis, 192–193, 195; and apologetics, 116; identified with physics, 125; and magic, 119–123; and mathematics, 127; and mechanics, 94, 97, 101–106, 114–117, 125–126, 188; system of, 135
Mechanization, 80, 82, 84–85, 105–106, 122, 127–129, 135, 150, 213, 262–263, 269–270, 272–273; and "delayed-action anguish," 262
Medicine, 20–21, 103, 109, 118, 132
Mentality: difficulty of defining, 123
Merchant, Carolyn, 121–122, 136
Merleau-Ponty, Maurice: on philosophical astonishment, 309–310
Mersenne, Father, 122, 127–128, 130, 133
Mesomedes, 27
Metallurgy, 114, 148
Metaphors, 76, 127, 192, 259; history of, xi
Method: of Goethe, 253–254; hypothetico-deductive, 119; mathematical, 114; scientific, 33, 140, 211
Michelangelo, 223–224
Michelet, Jules, 174–175
Mind, 53, 59
Mines and mining, 141–142, 145
Mirabilia, 35, 114
Mistra, 79
Misunderstanding, creative, 235
Mittelstrass, Jürgen, 158, 163

Model(s), 159, 163–164, 208
Moly, 18, 29, 61
Monod, Jacques, 186–187, 190
Montaigne, Michel Eyquem de, 12, 65
Montesquieu, 297
Moses, 107, 132, 267, 302
Mothers, the, 280
Mysteries, 40, 52, 62, 72–73, 79; Christian versus pagan, 79; and demons, 69; of Eleusis, 96, 170, 268, 282, 295; Hebrew, 267; and initiation, 44, 170; and Orphism, 96
Mysticism, 228; of cosmic unity, 227
Myth and mythology, 40, 44, 49, 50–56, 61–75, 80, 97, 286, 292; as beginning at the level of Soul, 53–54; exegesis of, 62, 78, 251; handbooks of, 79; likely, 156, 182; as poetic physics, 79; revelation of, 74–75; as supplying subjects for art, 76, 80; used to speak of nature, 77–78

Near East, 40; influence of, 183
Neith, 265
Neoplatonism, 44, 49, 52, 55, 58–59, 61, 66, 74–76, 111, 208–209, 218; metaphysics of, 114; and paganism, 79; sacramentalism in, 111
Newton, Isaac, 85, 123, 128, 135, 164, 209, 250; theory of colors, 249
Nietzsche, Friedrich, 75, 91, 96, 197–200, 217, 264, 271, 284–299, 303, 306; on art for artists, 284; on the Dionysian, 298–299; on truth, 295–296
Novalis, 65, 86, 203–205, 273–276, 289
Nudity, 63–64
Numenius, 62, 67, 72